THE OIL AND GAS LEASE IN CANADA
Fourth Edition

John Bishop Ballem is Counsel, Gowling Lafleur Henderson LLP, Calgary, Alberta. Specializing in oil and gas law throughout his career, he has been lead counsel in numerous landmark court cases and hearings before energy tribunals. He has written and lectured extensively on the subject, contributing articles to legal journals, and presenting papers at conferences and symposiums.

Ballem is also well known as a writer of fiction, having published twelve novels, poetry, and many short stories.

JOHN BISHOP BALLEM, Q.C., LL.D.

The Oil and Gas Lease in Canada

Fourth Edition

UNIVERSITY OF TORONTO PRESS
Toronto Buffalo London

© University of Toronto Press Incorporated 2008
Toronto Buffalo London
Fourth Edition 2008
Printed in Canada
www.utppublishing.com

ISBN 978-0-8020-9350-9

Printed on acid-free paper

Library and Archives Canada Cataloguing in Publication

Ballem, John, 1925–
The oil and gas lease in Canada / John Bishop Ballem – 4th ed.

Includes bibliographical references and indexes.
ISBN 978-0-8020-9350-9

1. Oil and gas leases – Canada.   I. Title.

KE1822.B34 2008   346.7104'6823   C2008-901032-9
KF1865.B35.2008

University of Toronto Press acknowledges the financial assistance to its
publishing program of the Canada Council for the Arts.

University of Toronto Press acknowledges the financial support for its
publishing activities of the Government of Canada through the Book
Publishing Industry Development Program (BPIDP).

Dedicated to the memory of my parents
Dr and Mrs J.C. Ballem

Contents

Preface to the Fourth Edition

As always, preparing a new edition of this work has been an enjoyable, if arduous, task. The freehold oil and gas lease has played a central role in the oil industry since the first wells were spudded. This remarkable document and its attendant situations, questions, and issues are the daily fare of many in the industry. It also demands a great deal of time and attention from the courts. In those instances the focus necessarily will be on particular fact patterns and specific clauses. I feel privileged to have occasion to take a step back and survey the lease and its context as a whole.

I am grateful to Melody Williams, who processed a lengthy and complex manuscript with skill and unfailing good humour. Malinda Gelinas, Candace Turner, and Susan Spady were extremely helpful in dealing with a formidable checklist of citations. Susan and Malinda also prepared several of the indexes. My talented daughter, Mercedes Ballem, did a meticulous job of proofreading, and I thank her for that.

I also wish to express my appreciation to Gowling Lafleur Henderson LLP for their encouragement and support of this endeavour.

John Bishop Ballem, Q.C., LL.D.
Calgary

Preface to the Third Edition

Like its predecessors, this edition is meant to be a user-friendly road map through the maze of complexities that surround the Canadian oil and gas lease, and the very substantial body of law that has grown up around it. The oil and gas lease has been evolving for some 125 years and is still evolving. Just when one begins to think that every possible combination of lease terms and facts has been encountered, a new situation is bound to arise. It is this seemingly endless variety of permutations and combinations that makes the oil and gas lease such a challenging and fascinating instrument to work with.

On a personal note, I must say it has been highly gratifying to see how widely this text has been accepted and used by the legal profession and the oil industry, and how extensively it has been cited, quoted, and relied upon by the courts. It is my hope that this edition will be accorded the same generous reception.

As before, this book is essentially a solo effort, arising from years of working with the lease and all its many ramifications. I want, however, to acknowledge the very valuable assistance of Anne Schenkenberger, an associate in the Ballem MacInnes law firm, in researching points of law and checking citations, and Peter Soby's perseverance in the arduous task of preparing indexes.

I also wish to thank Nigel Bankes, Professor of Law at the University of Calgary, for vetting the manuscript and for his valuable comments and suggestions.

John Bishop Ballem, Q.C., LL.D.
Calgary

Preface to the Second Edition

In the twelve years that have elapsed since the first edition of this book, the oil and gas lease has continued to evolve, as has its matrix of case law and legislation. Not surprisingly, the changes in the lease are designed to improve the lot of the lessee and to enhance the security of his tenure, to the disadvantage of the lessor in some instances. This edition provides an update and analysis of the changes that have occurred, and also includes observations and questions arising from the author's ongoing involvement with this fascinating document. When the complexity of the lease is combined with all the things that can happen in the course of exploring for and producing oil and gas, the list of potential problems and questions is almost infinite.

To the non-expert (a category which includes most freehold mineral owners) one printed form of lease looks very much like another, yet their terms can and do vary widely. There is no need for this diversity, whereby the rights of the lessor are determined not so much by equality of bargaining power as by the form of the lease that happens to be used by the oil company he is dealing with. The ground rules required to provide adequately for the exploration for and production of oil and gas are the same regardless of what oil company is the lessee. The oil industry has developed a number of "standard" documents, such as model unit agreements and operating and accounting procedures, through industry associations such as the Canadian Association of Petroleum Landmen. The same approach could be used to develop a "standard" oil and gas lease which would adequately protect the position of the oil company while at the same time treating the mineral owner fairly. The model lease at the end of the book might make a good starting point.

The objective of this edition remains the same: to provide an understanding of a complex and important document that will be useful not only to the legal profession, but also to oil companies and professional landmen who deal with the lease on a daily basis.

This book is essentially a solo effort, arising out of a lifetime of working with the oil and gas lease. I want, however, to acknowledge the valuable assistance of my associate, Terrance Hughes, in drafting the model lease, and to thank Suchitra Varadarajan, currently an articled student with this firm, for her help in looking up citations of cases and authorities. I am also grateful to my secretary, Nora-Lynn Martin, for the efficient and unruffled manner in which she processed and assembled a lengthy and complicated manuscript.

John Bishop Ballem, Q.C.
Calgary

Preface to the First Edition

The oil and gas lease is an intricate legal document designed to establish and regulate the position of lessor and lessee over minerals lurking thousands of feet below the surface, minerals which are migratory in nature and whose very existence is highly problematical. The current form of lease is the product of more than a century of evolution, most of which took place in a foreign country. In the last twenty years the lease has been heavily battered by Canadian courts and has been subjected to much patching and makeshift repairs.

This book is essentially an enquiry into the present state of the oil and gas lease in Canada and how well it discharges the function of governing the relationship between mineral owner and mineral explorer-producer. I have examined every clause that is normally encountered and have attempted to explain the role each is designed to fill and to analyze the suitability of its present wording. I think it will become apparent that the lease: (a) contains hazards to the lessee (the dogged determination of oil companies to continue with the lethal "unless" type of drilling clause is explicable only in terms of a corporate death-wish); (b) has provisions which are undeservedly onerous to the lessor and others which are a source of frustration and irritation to him; and (c) has many variations in wording among the various forms, although every lease has the same purpose, so that documents which appear to the layman as generally similar may yield radically different results. In addition, new techniques and procedures as well as legislation have created areas which are not adequately covered by present forms.

In the light of these conclusions, I feel that we now have had sufficient experience and jurisprudence in Canada to devise a document which would remove the hazards to the lessee, improve the position of the lessor, and generally provide a framework within which the minerals could be developed in a reasonable and equitable fashion. Supported by this belief, I have ventured to prepare a model form of lease which I hope achieves these objectives.

Throughout I have tried to keep in mind not only the requirements of lawyers and law students, but also those of professional landmen who deal with leases every day. The landman's work requires a thorough understanding of the lease. It is hoped that this discussion of the lease and the manner in which the individual clauses operate may prove helpful in reaching this understanding.

As legal documents go, the oil and gas lease is a phenomenon. A substantial body of case law has been constructed around it, to the extent that it may be considered a separate branch of the law. It has forced the re-examination and, in some cases, the redefinition of some basic legal concepts. It still contains unanswered questions and problems that remain to be solved. Add to this the fact that it frequently covers resources of astronomical value and one can see why lawyers who work with the lease regard it as a fascinating and challenging instrument. It is in this spirit that I have approached the lease in the following pages.

PART ONE

Function and Legal Categorization
of the Oil and Gas Lease

1 Introduction

Many years ago I wrote, "The petroleum and natural gas lease is a curious document. It has to be. Any legal instrument that purports to define property rights over minerals inconsiderate enough to move from one place to another, and underground at that, cannot be expected to follow the conventional form."[1]

That statement holds true today. Both the oil and gas lease itself and the body of law that has developed around it continue to evolve and change. This ever-fascinating document is indeed a "living tree." The legal and economic soil in which it grows is rich and well fertilized. Litigation success can be astronomically rewarding; and the lease continues to be challenged and tested in court. In this, the fourth edition, I have attempted to record and analyse this process and keep the reader informed on the state of affairs with this remarkable document.

There will be many references to CAPL leases throughout this work. A joint committee of the Canadian Association of Petroleum Landmen (CAPL) and the Natural Resources Section of the Canadian Bar Association adopted a "standard" lease, which was based largely on a model lease attached as an appendix to the second edition of this book.[2] The original lease form was known as CAPL 88, and in 1991 a revised version was issued as CAPL 91. Another revised version, CAPL 99, was released in 1999.

---

1 Ballem, "The Perilous Life of an Oil and Gas Lease" (1966) 44 Can. Bar Rev. 523.
2 Evans, "The CAPL 88 Petroleum and Natural Gas Lease" Insight – Drafting and Structuring Oil and Gas Agreements, at Tab II.

The CAPL leases enjoy almost universal acceptance in the industry. For our purposes, the term "CAPL lease" will include all three versions, and the individual forms will be identified as "CAPL 88," "CAPL 91," or "CAPL 99" as required. Some companies use their own form, based on the CAPL lease, usually the 1991 version. They can be identified by the lack of the CAPL logo, and extra care must be taken by the lessor and his advisers in examining such forms because, although while they resemble a CAPL lease, they may contain modifications and terms that could be detrimental to a lessor's interest.

I shall also refer to the pre-CAPL forms generally as "conventional" leases, although it must be remembered that there are many variations in the terms of individual leases within this general category.

2 Function and History of the Oil and Gas Lease

An oil and gas lease is a jumbled collection of rights, grants, concessions, and obligations between the owner of minerals and the would-be developer of them. The exploration for these substances is a costly and risky enterprise and one that the average owner of minerals has neither the inclination nor the financial resources to undertake. Unless the landowner happens to be a huge corporation with sufficient resources to run the risk of exploration for oil and gas, he will be happy to delegate the chore to an oil company. This can be achieved by an outright sale of the mineral rights, but such a procedure has little to recommend it from the point of view of either party. The mineral developer could not afford to build up a very substantial land spread if it was forced to pay the fee simple price, while the mineral owner would be ill advised to dispose of all his rights in the minerals and thus lose the chance of participating in the benefits of a discovery.

The lease approach is the one that best meets the requirements of both parties. It grants to the lessee a lesser property right than an outright fee simple conveyance, but in its modern form confers a sufficient grant and term to permit the operator to remove the minerals if discovered. It protects the interest of the mineral owner by imposing certain time limitations within which the operator must explore the lands or lose the lease, and it preserves for the owner a continuing interest in the minerals by reserving a royalty.

There have been many influences at work in the development of the current form of the oil and gas lease. There is the nature of the right itself, which is much more than that granted under the conventional "lease" since the mineral lessee must have the right to remove minerals if the grant is to be effective. The physical characteristics of the substances must also be taken into account. Oil and gas are migratory and are free to move from point to point within the confines of a reservoir. In the earliest American cases, the courts seemed to view these minerals as flowing in underground rivers, and this colourful, if inaccurate, concept clearly affected some of the formative jurisprudence.[1] As late as 1921 a Texas court had this impression of what took place underground: "... they are supposed to percolate restlessly about under the surface of the earth, even as the birds fly from field to field and the beasts roam from forest to forest ..."[2] Oil and gas do not flow of their own volition in underground streams, but they are capable of moving within the pool if the reservoir balance is disturbed. Thus, if a well commences production, the reservoir pressure in the vicinity of the bore will be altered and these fluid and gaseous hydrocarbons will move towards the lowered pressure. Any document that attempts to deal with such substances must reflect their migratory nature.

History of Early Jurisprudence

The lease documents that we use today are the result of nearly a century and a half of evolution and judicial interpretation.

The lessee under a conventional lease has one of the most insecure tenures known to the common law. The slightest misstep may detonate one of many booby traps (all put in place by the lessee), which will terminate the grant. The interpretation of the courts led to further complexities as the lessee attempted to shore up its position. The result is a document "containing language notable for its ambiguity."[3] There is a polite controversy as to whether the first oil well was drilled in Canada or in the United States.[4] The honour seems to belong to a well dug near Petrolia in the province of Ontario in 1858. This preceded by one year the Titusville, Pennsylvania, well, which is generally recognized as having initiated the modern oil industry in North America. Regardless of which well came first, the major development of the industry took place in the United States, and it was in that country that the lease form

---

1 Moses, "The Evolution and Development of the Oil and Gas Lease," *Second Annual Institute on Oil and Gas Law* 1.
2 *Medina Oil Development Co. v Murphy*, 233 S.W. 333 (1921), (Tex. Civ. App.).
3 *Canadian Fina Oil Ltd. v Paschke*, [1956] A.J. No. 12, 19 W.W.R. (N.S.) 184 (Alta. S.C.T.D.); (1957), 21 W.W.R. (N.S.) 260, 7 D.L.R. (2d) 473 (Alta. S.C., App.Div.).
4 *Dusters and Gushers* (Toronto: Pitt, 1968), article by Sproule at 13.

developed its present shape and content. It was the search for salt, that fundamental of life, that led to the establishment of the petroleum industry in America. The need for salt had set in motion the development of techniques and equipment, notably cable drilling rigs, for digging artesian wells to produce salt water. The procedures and equipment were adapted to drilling for oil.

The salt industry had evolved a form of lease since the owners of the land were seldom in a position to test their salt-bearing potential. It was common for the owners to grant to others the right to explore and produce in return for a portion of any salt that might be obtained. This type of document was one that could be readily adapted to drilling for oil. American legal writers usually quote the following document as being the first oil lease agreement ever recorded:

> Agreed, this fourth day of July, 1853, with J.D. Angier, of Cherrytree township, in the county of Venango, Pa., that he shall repair up and keep in order, the old oil spring on land in said Cherrytree township, or dig and make new springs, and the expense to be deducted out of the proceeds of the oil, and the balance if any, to be equally divided, the one half to J.D. Angier and the other half to Brewer, Watson & Co. for the full term of five years from this date. If profitable.
>
> (signed) Brewer, Watson & Co.,
J.D. Angier.[5]

This elementary form of lease included a number of fundamentals of the modern form, namely the requirement of drilling, "dig and make new springs"; the designation of a fixed term; and the recovery of expenses with a sharing of any resulting profits. It differs from the present approach in that it did not provide for a cash payment for the granting of the right and it terminated at the end of the fixed term regardless of whether or not there was production.

Termination of a lease at the expiration of the defined term could work a very substantial hardship on the lessee who had brought the lands into production. The first solution to this problem was the creation of very prolonged primary terms, some indeed containing a grant of the rights and privileges "forever." By 1875 the industry had

---

5 Moses, *supra* n 1 at 6–7; Walker, "Defects and Ambiguities in Oil and Gas Leases" (1950) 28 Tex. L. Rev. 895.

accumulated a fair body of experience and individual operators began to amass large-scale holdings of land. This led to less emphasis on immediate drilling, with the lessor being compensated for the delay by monetary payments and the development of a flexible grant that would return the rights to the owner at the end of a fixed period unless there was production. The typical term or *habendum* clause, developed in the final quarter of the nineteenth century, is virtually identical with that commonly in use today and provides that the lessee shall hold the lands for a specified period and for so long thereafter as oil or gas shall be produced therefrom.

Between 1875 and the close of the century the basic ingredients had been developed and were contained in the common form of lease. These ingredients were: (a) payment of a bonus consideration for granting of the rights; (b) a provision for a fixed period of time after which the lease would terminate unless there was production; (c) the reservation of a royalty to the lessor; and (d) a provision under which the lessee could defer a commitment to drill by a monetary payment to the lessor, with the primary term acting as a time limit beyond which the drilling obligations could no longer be postponed.

Early Canadian Forms

Exploratory operations in Ontario led to the development of some rudimentary forms, which appear to have been based on agricultural leases. The earliest types demised a specified area of land "for the purpose of prospecting for oil" and "for the purpose of digging and boring for oil," with very little else in the way of provisions.[6] There was considerable oil activity in the province of Alberta in the decades following the Dingman well discovery in 1914, but there was no consistency in the type of lease used. Each was an individual contract, some being no more than a few paragraphs that fell far short of delineating the rights between the parties, while other more sophisticated operators used versions of the forms that had developed south of the border. The development of these early Canadian forms is largely irrelevant to the present-day Canadian lease, since a particular type of American lease was imported into this country and quickly gained wide acceptance.

---

6 Lewis, "The Canadian Petroleum and Natural Gas Lease" (1952) 30 Can. Bar Rev. 965 at 968.

The American form was of a type generally described as Producers 88. It is essential to know its background in order to understand the form the conventional lease took in Canada.

Development of Producers 88

More than a hundred years ago a compromise had been worked out between the lessor's desire for immediate drilling and the lessee's wish to have the right to postpone the costly operations. A balance was struck through a clause which provided that, if the lessee did not drill immediately, the lessor would be compensated by the payment of a sum of money. This, in turn, led to a provision whereunder the lessee would either commence drilling within a specified period "or pay the lessor." This would have imposed a liability on the lessee to make periodic payments if he did not drill a well. To avoid this ongoing obligation, the lease granted the lessee the right to surrender.

The Oklahoma Supreme Court interpreted such a clause in *Brown v Wilson*[7] and held that, since the lease was voidable at the option of the lessee by surrender, it must be likewise voidable by the lessor.

Obviously this finding caused great consternation in the oil industry. The view that a right of surrender could not be unilateral was subsequently rejected by later Oklahoma decisions.[8] In the meantime, however, oil attorneys had devised a new form to avoid the *Brown v Wilson* decision, and this form became known as Producers 88. The new form circumvented *Brown v Wilson* by eliminating the surrender clause and by substituting for the "or" clause an "unless" form under which the lessee did not promise to either drill or pay rentals. The new clause resulted in an automatic termination of the lease if the lessee had not drilled by the required time "unless" it elected to make the payment. As is pointed out by Walker, the new type of lease met with popular approval and prior to 1920 had spread throughout Oklahoma, Kansas, and Texas. It was accepted so widely that landowners frequently insisted upon only the Producers 88 being used. It is not surprising that the designation Producers 88, which had originally been nothing more than the printer's means of identifying the form for his own purposes,

---

7 160 P 94 (1915, Okla. S.C.).
8 *Northwestern Oil & Gas Co. v Branine* (1918), 175 P 533; *Rich v Doneghey* 177 P 86 (1918) (Okla.). The details surrounding the drafting of the Producers 88 form are set forth by Walker, *supra* n 5, at 896–7.

began to appear on a great number of leases, some of which bore little or no resemblance to the original document. In subsequent years many revisions were made and the new forms were often described as Producers 88 Revised. The basic Producers 88 document contained an "unless" type of drilling clause, a fixed primary term with provision for continuance in the event of production, and a cash bonus for granting of the lease. It was this form that was imported into Canada.

Leduc

The oil and gas industry may be said to have been carried on in Canada on a sporadic and localized basis ever since 1858, the year of the Petrolia well.[9] But it was the discovery of the Leduc field, near the city of Edmonton, brought in with considerable fanfare by Imperial Oil Limited on 13 February 1947, that gave it the necessary impetus and economic muscle to grow into the giant it is today. The Leduc discovery sparked some highly organized and extensive land plays. The casual approach to mineral leasing, where each lease was typed up on an individual basis, was no longer appropriate. Efficiency demanded a standardized form and one, moreover, that could be completed by the land agent in the field.

---

9 For a fascinating account of the 1914 oil boom that followed the Turner Valley discovery, see Gray, *The Great Canadian Oil Patch* (Toronto: Maclean-Hunter 1970); *Dusters and Gushers, supra* n 4. In the years following 1858, exploration gradually shifted west to the Western Canadian Sedimentary Basin. Natural gas was accidentally discovered in 1883 by railway construction workers drilling for water in the vicinity of Medicine Hat. The first commercial gas field in western Canada was the Medicine Hat field drilled in 1901. Turner Valley, which was discovered in 1913, was the first substantial producer. In the years intervening between Turner Valley and Leduc in 1947 exploration was sporadic, with such discoveries as were made being primarily of gas rather than the sought-after oil. This led to the suspicion that the Western Canadian Sedimentary Basin was gas prone rather than oil bearing. The directors of Imperial were so discouraged by the lack of success in finding oil they decided Leduc No. 1 would be a "last chance" well and there would be no further exploration if it came in dry. Fortunately, it encountered substantial reserves of oil in the Devonian formation, and the rest is truly history.

For a full account of the Leduc discovery, see Kerr, *Leduc* (Calgary: Kerr, 1991). See also, Hunter, *Last Chance Well* (Edmonton: Teddington Lock, 1997) written by the widow of "Dryhole" Hunter, toolpush on Leduc No. 1.

For an extensive and informative history of the oil industry in Alberta, see Breen, *Alberta's Petroleum Industry and the Conservation Board* (Edmonton: University of Alberta Press, 1993).

In June 1947, as a preparatory step in a major land acquisition project, Imperial assembled a group of experts to prepare an acceptable
form of lease. This group included an independent American lease
broker, representatives of an American-affiliated oil company, and
some local lawyers and landmen. The American experts brought with
them a form of the Producers 88 lease.

This form was adapted for Canadian use by adding the appropriate
affidavits of execution, affidavits, or consents and acknowledgment
required under the provincial dower or homestead acts, and was
reworked to the extent that the drilling covenant, for some reason that
remains obscure, was made a proviso to the granting clause rather
than a separate and distinct covenant. The lease was then printed on
both sides of two folded sheets, which made it mechanically easy for
the field landman to slip it into his typewriter and fill in the blanks.
The form was numbered 23620 and provided the basic framework on
which the modern-day conventional lease has been constructed. There
has, however, been an ongoing process of revision as the mineral lessees sought to improve their position and to counteract the strict interpretations placed by the courts on the wording of the various clauses.

The Freehold Lease in Canada

The importance of the oil and gas lease is by no means uniform
throughout Canada. Privately owned minerals are the exception rather
than the rule. Some provinces have vested or revested by legislative
fiat all oil and gas in the Crown.[10] In most other provinces the division
of mineral rights as between private individuals and the Crown

---

10 *Oil and Natural Gas Act*, S.N.B. 1976, c O-2.1, s 3; *Petroleum Resources Act*, R.S.N.S. 1989,
    c 342, s 10; *Petroleum and Natural Gas Act*, R.S.N.L. 1990, c P-10, s 3(2); *Oil and Natural
    Gas Act*, R.S.P.E.I. 1988 c 0-5, s 5. The New Brunswick Act is typical of those of the other
    Maritime provinces and reads as follows: "3. All oil and natural gas are hereby
    declared to be, and to have been at all times prior hereto, property separate from the
    soil and vested in the Crown in the right of the province."
      Newfoundland has also provided for the vesting of petroleum in the Crown; *Petro-
    leum Natural Gas Act*, R.S.N.L. 1990, c P-10, s 3(2), although there are some exceptions:
    sub (3) provided that: "Subsection (2) does not apply to petroleum or a right, title or
    interest in petroleum which, before April 15, 1965, was expressly assured to a person
    other than the Crown by a statute of the province which is not repealed or by a valid
    and subsisting deed, lease, licence or other instrument made under or pursuant to or
    ratified by any statute of the province."

depends on the point of time at which the Crown began to withhold mineral rights in granting patents of the surface. In Quebec, 1880 is the critical year.[11]

There is no statutory cut-off in Ontario and the normal rule of conveyancing applies, so that if the minerals are reserved such reservation is to be found in the original grant. The confusion and uncertainty that had been created by a lack of a uniform practice in dealing with minerals under land grants was removed by legislation.[12]

In what are now the provinces of Manitoba, Saskatchewan, and Alberta, the lands at the time of the major migration of homesteaders were under the control of the federal government. Originally homesteader grants included mines and minerals, but by order-in-council passed in 1887 the government of Canada provided for the reservation to the Crown of all mines and minerals from patents that had not already been made by 31 October of that year. This, however, applied only to lands west of the third meridian, which is at the approximate east-west centre point of what is now the province of Saskatchewan. Mines and minerals in lands lying to the east of the third meridian were reserved from Crown patents after the year 1889. The mineral rights so retained by the federal Crown were ultimately transferred to the individual provinces to place them in a position of equality with the older provinces, which had retained their mineral rights upon entry into Confederation.[13]

When the price of crude oil began its upward spiral in the autumn of 1973, the government of Saskatchewan moved to appropriate unto itself the economic benefits of such increases and passed the *Oil and Gas*

---

11 *Mining Act*, R.S.Q. c M-13.
12 *Public Lands Act*, R.S.O. 1990, c P-43, s 61, which declared void any reservations in letters patent issued before 6 May, 1913, subject to certain prior existing mining rights. Mines and minerals in lands patented after 6 May 1913 are to pass to patentee unless expressly reserved. Section 57 provides that mines and minerals under lands granted for agricultural purposes are reserved after 1 April 1957.
13 *Constitution Act* (1930) 20-21 George V, c 26 (U.K.); *Alberta Natural Resources Act* (1930) (Can.), c 3 (1930) (Alta.), c 21; *Manitoba Natural Resources Act* (1930) (Can.), c 29 (1930) (Man.), c 30; *Saskatchewan Natural Resources Act* (1930) (Can.), c 41 (1930) (Sask.), c 87. See also La Forest, *Natural Resources and Public Property under the Canadian Constitution* (1969), cs 2 & 3. For an account of the negotiations and political manoeuvring leading up to the transfer, see Hogg, "When the West Was Won: A Brief History of Alberta's Natural Resources," which can be found in *History of the Law Society of Alberta*, 2007 and also LASA Accession Number 2006031.

Conservation, Stabilization and Development Act, 1973.[14] Part IV of that Act expropriated as of 1 January 1974 the oil and gas rights of fee simple owners holding more than 1,280 acres. The oil and gas rights so expropriated were those in a producing tract or drainage unit down to and including the producing zone.[15] The Act does not appear to deal with freehold mineral rights acquired subsequent to 1 January 1974, and it does not affect mineral rights in zones below the producing formations.

Those homesteaders who took out land grants from the Hudson's Bay Company received title to mines and minerals until 1908, when the company began to reserve mines and minerals to itself. Similarly, those who acquired land from the Canadian Pacific Railway received title to mines and minerals until 1902.[16]

Since the settlement of western Canada by homesteaders proceeded from east to west, there are more privately held mineral rights in the eastern portions. For example, approximately 75 per cent of the mineral rights in southwestern Manitoba, which is the part of that province where conditions seem most suited to the discovery of oil and gas, is privately owned. Private ownership of minerals in Saskatchewan has been affected by the 1974 legislation, though the exemption of holdings of two sections or less means that not too many individual titles have been expropriated. In Alberta slightly in excess of 80 per cent of the minerals are owned by the Crown, and much of the balance is owned by corporations such as the Hudson's Bay Company and the Canadian Pacific Railway Company and their successors. Nonetheless, there are thousands of privately owned mineral titles in Alberta (it has been estimated there are as many as 26,000),[17] most of which are in active areas for exploration and development. In British Columbia the

---

14 Now the *Oil and Gas Conservation Act*, R.S.S. 1978, c O-2.

15 These provisions are now to be found in the *Crown Minerals Act*, S.S. 1984–85–86, c C-50.2. Section 23 of the Act vests the expropriated rights in the Crown as of 1 January 1974. See also, Lowery, "The Oil and Gas Conservation, Stabilization and Development Act, 1973" (1975) 13 Alta. L. Rev. 100.

16 Generally, see C.E.D. (Western) (3rd ed.), vol. 25, ss 2–5; *Creighton v United Oils Limited*, [1927] 2 W.W.R. 458 (Alta.), 3 D.L.R. 432; [1927] 3 W.W.R. 463, 4 D.L.R. 814 (C.A.); *Starley v New McDougall – Segur Oil Company*, [1927] 2 W.W.R. 379, [1927] 3 D.L.R. 428, (Alta. S.C.T.D.) and the same parties in a separate action at 811 (Alta.); [1927] 3 W.W.R. 464, [1927] 4 D.L.R. 814 (Alta. S.C.T.D.). See also Bennett Jones Verchere and Bankes, *Canadian Oil and Gas*, vol. 1, 2nd ed. (Toronto: Butterworths, 1997) at paras. 1.29–1.39.

17 For example, W. Laurin & L. Campbell, "CBM – Split Title in Alberta," paper delivered at the Canadian Institute seminar, 25 January 2006.

percentage is even smaller, and such privately owned minerals as do exist are in those portions of the province where there have been no substantial discoveries to date.

In the light of the pattern of mineral holdings and the likely occurrence of oil and gas, the lease is of importance in Ontario, Manitoba, Saskatchewan, and Alberta. In the event of future discoveries it could become significant in British Columbia, Quebec, and Newfoundland and Labrador. The freehold lease is not a factor outside the boundaries of the individual provinces since mineral ownership in those areas is clearly vested in government, either federal or provincial.[18] But Canadian lawyers, regardless of where they practise, may still find themselves confronted with the document known as the oil and gas lease, since freehold mineral titles follow their owners wherever they move.

---

18 Minerals in the land areas outside provincial boundaries are the property of the federal government. The ownership and control of offshore minerals has been resolved by a combination of court cases and intergovernmental agreements. In *Re Off-Shore Mineral Rights of British Columbia*, [1967] S.C.R. 792, 62 W.W.R. 21, 65 D.L.R. (2d) 353, [1967] S.C.J. No. 70 (S.C.C.), the Supreme Court held that Canada, and not the littoral province, owned the mineral rights of the seabed and subsoil seaward from the ordinary low-water mark. In 1984 the Supreme Court ruled that British Columbia is the sole owner of the waters and seabed between Vancouver Island and the mainland because they were part of the province ever since 1866 when the British Parliament passed an act uniting the colony of Vancouver Island with the colony of British Columbia: *A.G. Canada v A.G.B.C.*, [1984] 4 W.W.R. 289 (S.C.C.). In *Reference re Seabed and Subsoil of the Continental Shelf Offshore Newfoundland*, [1984] 1 S.C.R. 86, 5 D.L.R. (4th) 385, [1984] S.C.J. No. 7 (S.C.C.), the Supreme Court held that Canada has the right to explore and exploit the continental shelf and has legislative jurisdiction with respect thereto. The federal government and the littoral provinces have reached a political solution; see: *Memorandum of Agreement between the Government of Canada and the Government of Newfoundland on Offshore Petroleum Resource Management*, dated 11 February 1985, and the *Canada-Newfoundland Atlantic Accord Implementation Act*, S.C. 1987, c 3; the *Canada-Nova Scotia Offshore Petroleum Resources Accord* dated 26 August 1986, and the *Canada-Nova Scotia Offshore Petroleum Resources Accord Implementation Act*, S.C. 1988, c 28.

3 Legal Category of the Oil and Gas Lease

One of the more engaging characteristics of the oil and gas lease is that under the common law it is not a lease at all. The conventional property lease contemplates merely the use of property and the return of it to the lessor at the end of the term in a virtually unchanged state, excepting only reasonable wear and tear. The rights granted under an oil and gas lease are of an entirely different order and nature since the lessee, in order to enjoy the grant, must have the right to possess and remove the minerals.

The most commonly quoted judicial definition of a mining lease is that of Lord Cairns in *Gowan v Christie*, as follows:[1] "Not in reality a lease at all in the same sense in which we speak of an agricultural lease ... What we call a mineral lease is really when properly considered a sale out and out of a portion of land. It is a liberty given to a particular individual for a specific length of time to go into and under the land and to get certain things there if he can find them and to take them away just as if he had bought so much of the soil."

Profit à Prendre

The Supreme Court of Canada has characterized the oil and gas lease as a *profit à prendre*, which, simply put, means the right to take something from the soil of another. This judicial definition was arrived at in the case of *Berkheiser v Berkheiser*.[2] In that case the court had to decide whether the grant of a petroleum and natural gas lease amounted to an

---

1 [1873] L.R. 2 Sc. & Div. 273 (H.L.).
2 [1957] S.C.R. 387, 7 D.L.R. (2d) 721, [1957] S.C.J. No. 22 (S.C.C.).

ademption. An ademption occurs whenever a testator, having made a specific devise of land, subsequently conveys or sells it to a third party. This act by the testator deprives the specific devisee of its benefits and diverts the proceeds from the sale or conveyance into the residue of the estate. The principle behind ademption is that the subsequent disposition of the property by the testator acts as a revocation of the will.[3] In *Berkheiser,* the testator in 1947 devised to the appellant a quarter section of land in Saskatchewan. Four years later the testator entered into an oil and gas lease with an oil company. In 1953 she died and sometime subsequent to that event the petroleum and natural gas lease was surrendered by the lessee. The respondents, who were the residuary beneficiaries under the testator's will, argued that the granting by the testator of an oil and gas lease subsequent to the execution of the will amounted to an ademption. The lower courts, the case then being known as *In Re Sykes,*[4] held that the granting of an oil and gas lease was an out and out sale, or agreement for sale, of minerals *in situ,* and therefore an ademption had occurred.

Rand J in the Supreme Court evaluated the terms of the lease as follows:

What as a practical matter is sought by such a lessor is the undertaking of the lessee to explore for discovery and in the event of success to proceed with production to its exhaustion. Neither presence nor absence of the minerals was here known, and initial task was to verify the existence or non-existence of the one or the other. The fugitive nature of each is now well known; a large pool of either, underlying many surface titles, may in large measure be drained off through wells sunk in one of them; tapping the reservoir against such abstraction may, then, become an urgent necessity of the owner.

In that situation the notion of ownership *in situ* is not the likely thing to be suggested to the mind of any person interested because primarily of the difficulty of the factual conception itself. The proprietary interest becomes real only when the substance is under control, when it has been piped, brought to the surface and stored. Any step or operation short of that mastery is still in the stage of capture.[5]

---

3 *In re Dawselt v Meakin,* [1901] 1 Ch. D. 398; *Blake v Blake* (1880), 15 Ch. D. 481.
4 (1955), 16 W.W.R. 172 (Sask.); 16 W.W.R. 459, 5 D.L.R. 183 (Sask. C.A.). I commented on this decision before it reached the Supreme Court of Canada: Ballem, "Pitfalls in the Categorization of Petroleum Leases" (1956) 2 U.B.C. Legal Notes 329.
5 *Supra* n 2, S.C.R. at 391.

Rand J held that an instrument creating such a right was a *profit à prendre* and that under such instruments the title to the substances as part of the land remains in the owner and upon it is imposed the incorporeal right which the termination of the lease extinguishes. The title having remained in the original owner, there could be no ademption.

The judicial designation of the freehold lease as a *profit à prendre* came to the aid of a taxpayer in *NuGas Ltd. v R*.[6] The question before the Federal Court Trial Division was whether or not certain expenses incurred in a drilling program were eligible under a government incentive program. The eligible expense had to be incurred pursuant to a "written agreement," which specifically excluded "a Crown lease or freehold lease." After first remarking that a law adversely affecting a citizen's rights should be interpreted strictly, the court found that the term "freehold lease" did not include a natural gas lease since the courts had consistently held that such instruments were in fact a species of *profit à prendre* or licence. The court further noted that even if the standard oil and gas lease fell within the term "freehold lease," a PanCanadian lease, which was the lease in question, would not. In coming to this conclusion the court relied on the specific terms of the PanCanadian lease, which gave the lessor the right to receive technical data and the right of inspection, provisions that the court found to be more typical of farmout agreements than leases.

Not Void for Uncertainty of Term

One effect of characterizing an oil and gas lease as a *profit à prendre* has been to defeat attacks based on uncertainty of term. It is impossible to predict how long the substances may be taken from lands covered by a lease, and because the lease continues in force until production ceases, it has been argued that a lease is void for uncertainty of term. This issue was raised in *Crommie v California Standard Company*.[7] The court applied the *Berkheiser ratio* that the grant conferred by an oil and gas lease was really a *profit à prendre* and not that of the usual tenancy of freehold created in a lease. Accordingly, such a lease cannot be struck down because its term is uncertain.

---

6 (1992), 58 F.T.R. 54, [1992] F.C.J. No. 1015 (F.C.T.D.).
7 (1962), 38 W.W.R. 447, [1961] A.J. No. 28 (Alta. S.C.T.D.).

Contract for Sale of Property and Real Estate

The judicial categorization of a lease as a *profit à prendre* does not prevent it from fitting into other legal pigeon-holes under different circumstances. In the Supreme Court of Canada decision of *McColl-Frontenac v Hamilton*,[8] decided prior to *Berkheiser*, an oil and gas lease was held to be "a contract for the sale of property" sufficient to bring it within the provisions of the former section 9(1) of the Alberta *Dower Act*. In the *McColl* case there was a defect in the dower affidavit in that the wife had not executed it apart from her husband as required by the statute. Section 9(1) was a curative provision to the effect that when any woman has executed a contract for the sale of property and the consideration has been totally or partly performed by the purchaser and in the absence of fraud, she shall be deemed to have consented to the sale. The Supreme Court applied the definition of Lord Cairns in *Gowan v Christie*[9] wherein the mineral lease was treated as being a sale out and out of a portion of land to find that the instrument came within the definition in the *Dower Act*. It is clear from the judgment of Estey J that he regarded even a *profit à prendre* as being a sale of property within the meaning of the Act, so that a *profit à prendre* can also be "a contract for the sale of property."

A lease, although legally a *profit à prendre*, and therefore not a "lease" that the personal representative could have entered into with the approval of the court under the *Devolution of Real Property Act*, has nonetheless been held by the Saskatchewan Court of Appeal to be a "disposition" within the meaning of section 9 of the *Infants Act*. Thus, the court could order the leasing of minerals in which an infant had an interest. The lease is a disposition of at least a part of the contingent interest of the infant.[10]

Mines and minerals comprise part of a testator's real estate, and a lease of those minerals is an incorporeal hereditament that runs with the land. The rental payable under such a lease is to be dealt with pursuant

---

8 [1953] 1 S.C.R. 127, [1953] 1 D.L.R. 721 (S.C.C.).

9 *Supra* n 1.

10 *Re Thomas Estate* (1958), 24 W.W.R. 125, 12 D.L.R. (2d) 135 (Sask. C.A.). This case ante-dated a 1960 statutory amendment, which specifically provided that a "lease" under the *Devolution of Real Property Act* includes a petroleum and natural gas lease. Thus, an application in Saskatchewan under the *Devolution of Real Property Act* would now be effective.

to a testamentary direction relating to "the proceeds realized from any sale of any real estate."[11]

An oil and gas lease is a sufficient interest in land to entitle the lessee to redeem a mortgage on the land. Because it creates only a *profit à prendre*, however, the granting of such a lease does not offend against a covenant in an agreement for sale that prohibited any assignment by the purchaser of his interest unless it was approved in writing by the vendor.[12] A lease is a trade in real estate within the meaning of the Alberta *Real Estate Agents Licensing Act*, which prohibits the bringing of an action for commission or remuneration for services in connection with a trade in real estate unless the person bringing the action was licensed as an agent under the Act. Accordingly, a lease "broker" not licensed as a real estate agent could not bring an action for commission resulting from a transaction in oil and gas leases.[13] Subsequent legislation exempts a person dealing in mineral rights from the requirement of being licensed as a real estate agent. This is discussed *infra* in Chapter 4.

A lease, however, is not an "agreement for the sale of land" within the meaning of the Alberta enactment restricting foreclosure-style remedies. *Sharon Co. Ltd. v British American Oil Company Ltd.*[14] involved an ingenious defence against an action to enforce an agreement to purchase two petroleum and natural gas leases. The purchaser who had elected not to complete the transaction relied, *inter alia*, upon a provision of the *Judicature Act*,[15] which reads: "34.(17) In an action brought upon a mortgage of land, whether legal or equitable, or upon an agreement for the sale of land, the right of the mortgagee or vendor

---

11 *Re Cleveland Estate* (1963), 41 W.W.R. 193 [1962] S.J. No. 101 (Sask. Q.B.).

12 *Gallagher v Gallagher and Freeholders Oil Company, Ltd.* (1962), 40 W.W.R. 35, 35 D.L.R. (2d) 770 (Sask. C.A.); *Andrusiak v Sitko* (1953), 62 Man. R. 117, 8 W.W.R. (N.S.) 449, [1953] 2 D.L.R. 800 (Man. Q.B.).

13 *Arkansas Fuel & Minerals Ltd. v Dome Petroleum Ltd. and Provo Gas Producers Ltd.* (1966), 54 W.W.R. (N.S.) 494, 54 D.L.R. (2d) 574 (Alta. C.A.). Where the services rendered were primarily those of a geological expert, the prohibition in the Act will not bar the action: *Western Oil Consultants v Great Northern Oils Ltd.* (1981), 15 Alta. L.R. (2d) 165, 121 D.L.R. (3d) 724 (Alta. Q.B.); *Russ Burns Petroleum Consultants Ltd. v Union Oil of Canada* (1978), 5 Alta. L.R. (2d) 39, [1977] A.J. No. 463 (Alta. S.C.T.D.).

14 (1963), 45 W.W.R. (N.S.) 191 (Alta. S.C.T.D.); affirmed (1964), 48 W.W.R. (N.S.) 347, 45 D.L.R. (2d) 66 (Alta. S.C., App.Div.).

15 R.S.A. 1955, c 1-64. This provision is now in the *Law of Property Act*, R.S.A. 2000, c L-7, s 40.

thereunder is restricted to the land to which the mortgage or agreement relates and foreclosure of the mortgage or cancellation of the agreement for sale as the case may be, ... " If the phrase "an agreement for the sale of land" as it appears in this provision could apply to an agreement to sell the petroleum and natural gas leases, then the vendor would be without remedy other than cancellation of the transaction. The *Judicature Act* did not contain a definition of "land," but the purchaser argued that the definition of "land" as contained in the *Land Titles Act* should be adopted since the two pieces of legislation were *in pari materia* – that is, they dealt with the same subject matter.[16] The definition of "land" in the latter Act specifically included "mines, minerals and quarries thereon or thereunder lying or being." The Alberta Court of Appeal held that the two Acts were not *in pari materia* because the scope and purpose of the Acts were not similar since the particular section of the *Judicature Act* was really to protect debtors and had been enacted in times of economic depression. The case should be interpreted as holding that an agreement for the sale of an oil and gas lease is not subject to the debtor-protection legislation that applies to agreements for the sale of surface rights.

It has been held that an action to terminate a sublease of an oil and gas lease is not a proceeding to recover possession of land within the meaning of a Rule of Court that permits such a proceeding to be commenced by originating notice.[17] On the other hand, the Supreme Court of Canada in later cases appears to have been prepared to accept the proposition that in appropriate circumstances an action to recover possession of petroleum and gas rights *in situ* may be considered an action to recover land within section 18 of the Alberta *Limitation of Actions Act*.[18]

---

16 Maxwell on *Interpretation of Statutes*, 11th ed. (1962), at 34, 35. See also R. Sullivan, ed., *Driedger on the Construction of Statutes*, 3rd ed. (Toronto: Butterworths, 1994) at 285–8.

17 *Stockford and Jackson v Willow Creek Holding Co. Ltd.*, [1938] 3 W.W.R. 260, [1938] 4 D.L.R. 792 (Alta. S.C.T.D.). Although this case concerned a sublease of Crown lands, the reasoning ("the lease is not one of land but of petroleum and natural gas rights in an area") would appear to apply to a freehold lease.

18 R.S.A. 1980, c L-15. A similar provision is now to be found in R.S.A. 2000, c L-12, s 3(4). *Turta v C.P.R.* (1954), 12 W.W.R. (N.S.) 97, 4 D.L.R. 87 at 119 (per Rand J) and 131–2 (per Estey J); *Kaup v Imperial Oil Ltd.* (1962), S.C.R. 170, 37 W.W.R. (N.S.) 193, 32 D.L.R. (2d) 112, S.C.J. No. 2 at 208. Neither of these cases concerned oil and gas leases.

Sometimes a Lease

A *profit à prendre* can also be a lease. This paradox involves two cases and one legislative enactment. In *Re Heier Estate*[19] the Saskatchewan Court of Appeal was faced with an application for approval of a petroleum and natural gas lease granted by the executors of the estate. The application was made under section 15 of the *Devolution of Real Property Act*,[20] which then read as follows: "15.(1) The personal representative may, from time to time, subject to the provisions of any will affecting the property: (a) lease the real property or any part thereof for any term not exceeding one year; (b) lease the real property or any part thereof with the approval of the court, for a longer term." The court held that it could not approve the instrument under the above section since "the so called lease here under review is a sale of a portion of the land in the form of petroleum and natural gas with liberty to enter upon the lands mentioned in the instrument for the purpose of searching for and severing and carrying away the petroleum and natural gas within, upon or under the said lands. The application is made under Section 15 of the *Devolution of Real Property Act* for the approval of a lease and as the instrument is not a lease the application must be dismissed."

In 1956 Alberta enacted the *Land Titles Clarification Act*, which provides:

> It is hereby declared that the term "lease" as used in the *Land Titles Act* and any Act for which the *Land Titles Act* was substituted includes, and shall be deemed to have included, an agreement whereby an owner of any estate or interest in any minerals within, upon or under any land for which a certificate of title has been granted under the *Land Titles Act* or any Act for which the *Land Titles Act* was substituted, demises or grants or purports to demise or grant to another person a right to take or remove any such minerals for a term certain or for a term certain coupled with a right thereafter to remove any such minerals so long as the same are being produced from the land within, upon or under which such minerals are situate.[21]

---

19 (1952), 7 W.W.R. (N.S.) 385, [1953] 1 D.L.R. 792 (Sask. C.A.).
20 R.S.S. 1940, c 108.
21 This provision is now found in the *Law of Property Act*, R.S.A. 2000, c L-12, s 79.

Professor Thompson writes that it is generally believed that the section was passed so that oil and gas leases could be caveated under the *Land Titles Act*. Financial institutions lending money on the security of leases desired a means whereby their interest could appear on the register.[22]

The issue in the second case, a decision of the Supreme Court of Canada, was identical with that in the *Heier* case, but in *Hayes v Mayhood*[23] an Alberta executrix was involved and the *Land Titles Clarification Act* had been passed. In the *Hayes* case the testator died in 1938, and his executrix granted an oil lease to an oil company in 1957 with the approval of the court made pursuant to that section in the Alberta *Devolution of Real Property Act* that corresponds to section 15 of the Saskatchewan Act quoted above. The lease was challenged on the ground that court approval could not be obtained since an oil and gas lease was not a lease within the meaning of the *Devolution of Real Property Act*. The appellant relied upon the *Berkheiser* characterization of a mineral lease as a *profit à prendre* and also referred to the decision of the Saskatchewan Court of Appeal in the *Heier* estate. The Supreme Court of Canada, however, found that the *Land Titles Clarification Act* had the effect of bringing a mineral lease within the applicable section of the Alberta *Devolution of Real Property Act*. This result was achieved despite the fact that the *Land Titles Clarification Act* referred only to the term "lease" as used in the *Land Titles Act*.

Martland J imported the statutory interpretation into the *Devolution of Real Property Act*, noting that, while the word "lease" was not defined in the Act, it must have been intended to include in its application leases of real property under the *Land Titles Act*. The learned judge also observed, as a sort of second ground for his finding, that, if the meaning of the word "lease" in the *Devolution of Real Property Act* was ambiguous, then under the rules of statutory interpretation the definition in the subsequent Act, the *Land Titles Clarification Act*, could be looked at to see the proper construction applicable to the earlier statute. This rule applies where both statutes are *in pari materia*. Martland J held the two statutes to be *in pari materia* since both had provisions relating to real property in the province of Alberta. Hence, the subsequent definition of the word "lease" in the *Land Titles Clarification Act* could be applied to the *Devolution of Real Property Act*.

---

22 Thompson, "The Nature of the Oil and Gas Lease – A Statutory Definition" (1960) 1 Alta. L. Rev. 463.

23 [1959] S.C.R. 568, 18 D.L.R. (2d) 497, [1959] S.C.J. No. 36 (S.C.C.).

Insofar as Alberta is concerned, the decision in *Hayes v Mayhood* could have far-reaching implications. It would seem that it is a sufficient ground to hold the word "lease" to be ambiguous (a necessary condition for the application of the *pari materia* rule) if there is no definition of it in the particular statute. Accordingly, any Alberta statute that deals with leases and does not contain a definition of "lease" may apply to the oil and gas lease. This means that Alberta statute law covering ordinary leases of property may be considered as applying to oil and gas leases. Without attempting to catalogue all such statutes, Professor Thompson lists the *Landlord's Rights on Bankruptcy Act*,[24] the *Limitation of Actions Act*,[25] the *Seizures Act*,[26] the *Judicature Act*,[27] and those English statutes of pre-1870 origin dealing with real property law that are deemed to have been imported into the province.

That the Alberta Legislature was alive to this hazard is shown in the *Landlord and Tenant Act*.[28] This Act was passed in 1964, well after *Hayes v Mayhood*. Section 2 of the Act provided as follows: "This Act does not apply to minerals held separately from the surface of land or any dealings in minerals."

In the absence of any legislation such as the *Land Titles Clarification Act*, both the *Berkheiser* and *In Re Heier* decisions remain undisturbed by *Hayes v Mayhood*. In those provinces that do not have the equivalent of the *Land Titles Clarification Act* it would seem impossible for an executor of an estate to grant an oil and gas lease unless so empowered by specific legislation. In Saskatchewan the problem has been overcome by the enactment of an amendment to the *Devolution of Real Property Act*,[29] which includes a new subsection authorizing the executor, with the approval of the court, "to lease, grant a *profit à prendre* in respect of or otherwise deal with or dispose of mines and minerals or sand and gravel forming part of the real property." This permits the granting of a lease without the side effects of *Hayes v Mayhood*.

Manitoba has followed the example of Saskatchewan and has amended the *Devolution & Estates Act* by including a specific authorization to

---

24 R.S.A. 2000, c L-5.

25 R.S.A. 2000, c L-12.

26 Since repealed and replaced by the *Civil Enforcement Act*, R.S.A. 2000, c C-15.

27 R.S.A. 2000, c J-2.

28 Now the *Residential Tenancies Act*, S.A. 2004, c R-17.1. Section 2(1) of this Act achieves the same result by providing that it applies to a "person who was a tenant of premises whose tenancy has expired or has been terminated and who has vacated the property."

29 S.S. 1960, c 8, now the *Devolution of Real Property Act*, R.S.S. 1978, c D-27, s 15.

the personal representative to grant mineral leases subject to the approval of the court under certain circumstances: "23(1) Subject to subsection (2), a personal representative in whom the mines and minerals in, on or under land are vested under this Act may grant, or join in, or consent to, grants of, rights and licences to search for, mine for, drill for, take, win or gain in remove, the minerals or any specified mineral by instrument commonly called a 'lease' or otherwise."[30]

Application of Landlord and Tenant Law

The extent to which the ordinary law of landlord and tenant applies to an oil and gas lease, if at all, remains unclear. In a 1947 decision of the Saskatchewan King's Bench, *Kendall v Smith and Northern Royalties Ltd.*,[31] the court expressed the view that it was doubtful whether the statutory or common law of landlord and tenant should be applied to a contract such as an oil and gas lease, but nonetheless applied such law on the basis that the courts of Alberta, where the documents were most common, have for some years been applying the law of landlord and tenant in establishing the rights of the parties to such contract.[32] The application of the law was further justified by the assumption of the parties that it did apply to their contract. In this instance the lessor had proceeded under the Saskatchewan *Landlord and Tenant Act* by serving notices to quit, there being no provision for re-entry in the unusual form of lease involved. The court was prepared to assume that such procedures apply to an oil and gas lease, but went on, for other reasons, to hold that the contract had not terminated.

A decade later, the Manitoba Court of Appeal held, again on the basis of *Berkheiser,* that an oil and gas lease, being a *profit à prendre*, did not create the relation of landlord and tenant and that the common law rights and liabilities arising out of such relationships could not apply, at least insofar as the right of re-entry for breach of condition or covenant is concerned.[33] This latter view appears to be more in line with the present-day approach.

---

30 Now the *Intestate Succession and Consequential Amendments Act*, C.C.S.M., c 185, s 17.8(1).
31 [1947] 2 W.W.R. 609 (Sask. K.B.).
32 The learned trial judge did not cite any authorities for this proposition.
33 *Langlois v Canadian Superior Oil* (1957), 23 W.W.R. 401, 12 D.L.R. (2d) 53 (Man. C.A.). It is noteworthy that the trial judge, whose decision was upheld without written reasons, was Williams, CJQB, the original author of *Canadian Law of Landlord and Tenant*.

The legal categorization of the lease does not alter the fact that it is essentially a contract embodying detailed terms and provisions. Its status as a *profit à prendre*, an interest in land, is of vital importance in determining the applicability of certain statutes and rules of the common law. The fact that in some of its aspects it partakes of a landlord-tenant relationship may allow the importation of some concepts and techniques from that area of the law, such as the use of a notice to quit, the apportionment of a royalty as rent,[34] or possibly the right to distrain for payments due under the lease. Nonetheless, the express terms of the document itself must play the decisive role in ascertaining the rights and obligations of the parties to each other.

---

34 *Re Dawson* and *Bell*, [1945] O.R. 825, [1946] 1 D.L.R. 327, [1945] O.J. No. 563 (Ont. C.A.). For a detailed discussion of this case, and the characterization of royalty as "rent," see that portion of the text dealing with royalties in Chapter 8, *infra*.

PART TWO

Entering into the Lease

4 Negotiations for and Capacity to Grant a Lease

The typical acquisition procedure begins with a decision by an oil company to move into a particular area. Land titles in the land registry office are searched to ascertain the registered owner of the mineral rights. The owner, as disclosed by the register, is then contacted by an employee of the company or by an independent leasing agent acting on its behalf. (The independent agent is often referred to by the apt, if not altogether flattering, sobriquet "lease hound.") Although such agents deal in mineral rights which are interests in land, provincial legislation exempts them from being licensed under the various provincial real estate agents licensing acts.[1]

In Saskatchewan the agents are required to be licensed under the *Securities Act*,[2] which includes oil and natural gas leases in the definition of a "security." In Manitoba they must be registered as Mineral Interest Brokers.[3]

---

1 *Real Estate Act*, R.S.B.C. 2004, c 42 s 2; Saskatchewan *Real Estate Act*, S.S. 1995, c R-1.3, s 3(1). It was not until 1984 that Alberta enacted the *Real Estate Agents Licensing Amendment Act*, S.A. 1984, c 36, to remove the hazard posed by *Arkansas Fuel & Minerals Ltd. v Dome Petroleum Ltd. and Provo Gas Producers Limited*, (1966) 54 W.W.R. (N.S.) 494, 54 D.L.R. (2d) 574 (Alta. C.A.), which held that no action could be brought for a commission or remuneration in connection with a trade in mineral leases where the agent was not licensed under the *Real Estate Agents Licensing Act*. The Real Estate Agents Licensing Amendment Agreement is now included in *Real Estate Act*, R.S.A. 2000, c R-5 s 2(2).

2 *Securities Act*, S.S. 1988, c S-42-2.

3 *Securities Regulation*, Man. Reg. 491/88 R, s 2(1).

The employee or agent usually will have qualified as a commissioner for oaths so that he may take the required affidavits or acknowledgments where permitted by statute.[4] He will have with him the form of lease currently used by the oil company. The lease will, almost invariably, be in printed form covering both sides of two legal-size folded sheets.

Execution

The federal *Lord's Day Act*[5] formerly prohibited entering into a contract for the sale of land on a Sunday. While the Act was in force the Supreme Court of Canada had held that contracts involving the sale and transfer of lands made on a Sunday in violation of the Act are illegal and unenforceable.[6] In 1985 the Supreme Court of Canada found the *Lord's Day Act* to be unconstitutional because it infringed on the right to freedom of conscience and religion guaranteed in the *Charter of Rights and Freedoms*.[7] The Act was subsequently repealed.

Alberta had legislation on the books, section 58 of the *Law of Property Act*,[8] which provided that all contracts or agreements for sale or purchase of real property made on Sunday are void. However, section 58 was repealed by the *Charter Omnibus Act*.[9] Thus, leases executed on a Sunday, whether in Alberta or elsewhere in Canada, are no longer void.

In the eyes of the prospective lessor the bonus consideration to be paid for the granting of the lease undoubtedly will loom as the single

---

4 The Saskatchewan *Homesteads Act* specifically disqualifies a person from taking an acknowledgment of a wife when such person, his employer, partner, or clerk has prepared the document in question or is otherwise interested in the transaction involved. This language would appear to be sufficiently broad to disqualify a land agent who negotiates the lease and would certainly disqualify him if he filled in any of the blanks: *Homesteads Act, 1989*, S.S. 1989–90, c H-5.1.

5 R.S.C. 1970, c L-13 (repealed by the *Municipal Government Amendment Act, 1985*, S.A. 1985, c 43, s 42).

6 *Neider v Carda of Peace River District Ltd.*, [1972] S.C.R. 678, 4 W.W.R. 513, 25 D.L.R. (3d) 363, [1972] S.C.J. No. 55 (S.C.C.).

7 *R v Big M Drug Mart*, 28 Alta. L.R. (2d) 289, [1984] 1 W.W.R. 625, 5 D.L.R. (4th) 121, [1983] A.J. No. 766 (Alta. C.A.); affirmed [1985] 3 W.W.R. 481, S.C.R. 295, [1985] S.C.J. No. 17 (S.C.C.).

8 R.S.A. 1980, c L-8.

9 *Charter Omnibus Act*, S.A. 1985, c 15, s 19. The *Municipal Government Amendment Act, 1985*, S.A. 1985, c 43, s 42 repealed the *Alberta Lord's Day Act*.

most important factor. Once the dollar figure has been agreed upon, whether at the first or at subsequent meetings, the other terms of the lease will be discussed. In an attempt to head off later attacks on the lease, it is the universal practice of all professional landmen to review each clause with the lessor. Any remaining blanks, such as the depository for payments under the lease, are completed and the lessor then executes the lease. This is done by signing the document in front of a witness who may be, and frequently is, the land agent himself, and such witness, then or later, swears the affidavit of execution. There will, or should be, a wafer seal affixed opposite the signature of the lessor and its significance should be explained to the lessor. The dower or homestead formalities are completed, whether by way of consent and acknowledgment of the spouse, or by affidavit of the lessor.

On rare occasions, if the person acquiring the lease also happens to be a principal of the lessee company, the lease may be executed by it at the same time. Usually, however, the agent takes with him the lease for subsequent execution by the lessee, leaving an extra copy with the lessor. Frequently the lease will be taken in the name of the leasing agent's company, which will subsequently assign its interest to the client company.

Payment

At this stage of the proceedings the lessee probably would not have made an exhaustive investigation of the lessor's title and any charges or prior claims that might be registered against it. Nor would the lessee have been able to protect its position by registration of the new lease or a caveat. Consequently, the lessor will be advised that the lease is subject to title and to registration of the lessee's interest. Payment of the bonus consideration is postponed until this has been accomplished, with sometimes a definite understanding as to the time period within which payment must be made. More frequently, however, the undertaking as to time within which payment must be made is left quite indefinite. Most land agents now appear to have adopted the practice of leaving at least a token cash payment, presumably to avoid a total failure of consideration. Alternatively, the agent may give the lessor a bank draft or cheque for the full amount conditional upon title approval.

CAPL 88 and 91 recite " ... in consideration of $10.00 paid to the Lessor by the Lessee, the receipt of which is hereby acknowledged by the

Lessor, and of an additional consideration of ... Dollars ($ ...) to be paid within ... days of the date hereof ... " Query, what is the situation where the $10.00 has been duly paid, but the additional consideration (which will be a substantial sum and is the real monetary consideration for granting the lease) has not been paid within the specified period. Has there been a failure of consideration? See discussion in Chapter 5, *infra*.

CAPL 99 provides an unequivocal answer to this question. The payment clause in CAPL 99 is a radical departure from any previous forms. It provides that if payment is not made on or before the specified date the lease shall terminate.

The period of time within which payment must be made is usually 60 or 90 days. Sometimes 120 days will be specified, but this seems excessive and should not be accepted by the lessor in the absence of special circumstances.

CAPL 99 also does away with delay rental payments on the basis that the majority of leases are now likely to have very short primary terms, such as one or two years, so there is no practical need for rental payments.

A further departure is that, despite the lease having been terminated, the lessee remains liable to make the lease payment. The only exception is where the lessee finds deficiencies in the lessor's title and has given the lessor written notice of such deficiencies on or before the specified date.

If a lessor who has received a notice of title deficiency disputes the existence of such deficiency, he could, of course, challenge the notice in the courts so as to require payment of the specified sum.

Query, what is the situation when the lessee not only fails to make the payment, but does not execute the lease? This is an extremely unlikely occurrence, but it is possible to visualize a scenario where an unscrupulous lessee becomes disenchanted with the potential of the property for some reason, such as dry holes in the vicinity, or discouraging seismic, and decides not to complete the transaction.

The *Statute of Frauds* will not be a problem, but the absence of the lessee's seal could make the lease unenforceable, per se.

While the unsigned lease may be unenforceable, the mineral owner may have a reasonable chance of success in an action of specific performance. As can be gleaned from the case discussed in Chapter 5 under the heading "Sufficiency of Terms," everything will depend on the extent to which the parties have agreed on the material terms and conditions.

Negotiations for a lease will generally follow this path: an oil company, or, more likely, a land agent acting on its behalf, will contact the mineral owner, initially by phone, sometimes by letter or e-mail, to discuss the possibility of leasing the mineral rights; this will be followed by a written offer, usually by fax or e-mail; the offer may be accepted, again either by phone or some form of written communication, or there may be further negotiations, which often will be verbal, resulting in an agreement. The basic terms, i.e., the bonus consideration, royalty rate, the length of the primary term, will be spelled out, but many others will not. The lessor's case will be strengthened if there is a reference in the negotiations to a specific form of lease, usually one of the CAPL versions. Failing that, the lessor will attempt to rely on the lease he has signed. This will contain all of the terms and would more than meet the "sufficiency" test. Since it was not signed by the lessee, however, the court may refuse to consider it.

In the normal course of events, the lessor would appear to have the grounds for an action for specific performance. He would, however, be faced with the discouraging fact that, in the event of success, the award may not cover the cost of litigation.

Capacity

The fact that an oil and gas lease involves an interest in land, which means that there is an aspect of title as well as contract, complicates the question as to when and how a lease comes into existence and who may grant it. The ideal mineral lessor would: (a) be the registered owner of the mineral rights free of any lien or encumbrance, (b) have attained his full age of majority, (c) be single, and (d) be of sound mind. Such a paragon has full capacity to enter into a lease. Any variation from this model, however, brings its own subset of problems.

Registered Owner

A lease taken in good faith from a registered owner of the mineral title remains valid even if the title of that registered owner is subsequently upset. The new owner takes subject to the lease.[10] The personal represen-

---

10 *Henderson v Montreal Trust Company* (1954), 11 W.W.R. (N.S.) 289, [1954] A.J. No. 7 (Alta. S.C.T.D.); affirmed although this specific point not dealt with, 14 W.W.R. (N.S.) 210, [1955] 2 D.L.R. 528 (C.A.).

tative of a deceased owner can, if so authorized by the will or by statute, grant a lease without becoming the registered owner of the land.[11]

Majority

Under the common law a person does not become fully responsible for his deeds and actions and fully able to bind himself by contract until he has attained the age of twenty-one years. This age limit has been reduced in most of the jurisdictions with which we are concerned.[12] British Columbia has selected nineteen years as the legislative majority, while Alberta, Saskatchewan, Manitoba, and Ontario have reduced it to eighteen. Upon attaining his majority, whether it be twenty-one or less, the mineral owner may dispose of his rights. While he remains an infant, however, he does not have this power. Provincial legislation offers a way in which an infant's mineral rights can be dealt with, provided certain safeguards are observed.[13] The Alberta legislation is a typical example of the procedure which must be followed; section 2 sets forth the tests that are to be applied and the authority that is to be obtained:

> 2(l) The Court, on application, may order, authorize or direct a sale, lease or other disposition of or action respecting property of a minor if in the Court's opinion it is in the minor's best interest to do so, except that the Court shall not authorize a disposition or action prohibited by an instrument that created the minor's interest in the property.

> (2) An order under subsection (1) may give any direction as to the method of carrying out a sale, lease, disposition or action authorized by the order and may impose any restriction or condition that the Court considers appropriate.

The above section refers to "disposition," which has been held sufficiently wide to include a petroleum and natural gas lease.[14] Most

---

11 *Kissinger Petroleums Ltd v Nelson Estate*, (1984), 33 Alta. L.R. (2d) 1, [1984] 5 W.W.R. 673, 13 D.L.R. (4th) 542, [1984] A.J. No. 2587 (Alta. C.A.); affirming 26 Alta. L.R. (2d) 378, 14 E.T.R. 207, 45 A.R. 393, [1983] A.J. No. 814 (Alta. Q.B.) (leave to appeal to the Supreme Court denied).

12 *Age of Majority Act*, R.S.A. 2000, c A-6; *Age of Majority Act*, R.S.S. 1978, c A-6; *Age of Majority Act*, C.C.S.M., c A7; *Age of Majority Act*, R.S.B.C. 1996, c 7.

13 *Minors Property Act*, R.S.A. 2000, c M-18; *Children's Law Act, 1997*, S.S. 1997, c C-8.2; *Children's Law Reform Act*, R.S.O. 1990, c C-12; *Infant's Act*, R.S.B.C. 1996, c 223; *Child and Family Services Act*, C.C.S.M., c C80.

14 *Re Thomas Estate* (1958), 24 W.W.R. (N.S.) 125, 12 D.L.R. (2d) 135. See *ante*, c 3.

provincial legislation contains a reference to "disposition," so it would appear that a lease may be validly granted where the minerals are owned by an infant if the required procedure is followed.[15]

The grounds on which a lease may be approved by the court are cast in very wide and generalized terms. The test is what "is necessary or proper for his maintenance or education, or his interest requires or will be substantially promoted" by the granting of the lease. In the case of *In Re Bonner Estate*[16] the application was brought by the administratrix of the estate holding the lands as trustee for four minors. The official guardian had consented to the lease, and those of the four infants who were over the age of fourteen years[17] had also consented. The court reviewed the terms of the lease, noting that the bonus seemed reasonable since there was no production of petroleum or natural gas in the immediate area, that the delay rental was at the usual annual rate of $1.00 per acre, and that the royalty of 12½ per cent was also standard. The court, holding that the interest of the infants would be substantially promoted by the proposed disposition of the substances, approved the application and directed the administratrix to complete the lease.

The same judge refused approval in a subsequent application, *In Re Crumley Estate*.[18] Section 11 of the then *Saskatchewan Infants Act* provided that the application for the order approving the disposition shall be made in the name of the infant by his next friend or guardian. In the *Crumley* case the lease had actually been signed by the executor some two years before the application was brought. The application was not made by the guardian or next friend but by the oil company lessee. The infant had never consented to the granting of the lease and was seventeen years of age at the time of the application. The official guardian also opposed the application. In the interval between the time the executor signed the lease and the making of the application there had been an intensive search for oil and gas in the general area of the lands. The bonus and delay rentals payable under the lease as signed were considerably less than the sums

---

15 British Columbia does not refer to a "disposition," but in the *Infant's Act*, R.S.B.C. 1996, c 223, s 36 the Supreme Court is authorized to direct the leasing of land owned by the infant for various purposes including "the working of mines." This could be interpreted as including the right to make mineral leases, which, in turn, could be extended to include oil and gas leases.

16 (1953), 8 W.W.R. (N.S.) 140 (Sask. Q.B.).

17 The *Children's Law Act, 1997*, S.S. 1997, c C-82, s 31(2) now provides that the threshold age is twelve years. The consent of a reluctant minor may be dispensed with by order of the court.

18 (1953), 10 W.W.R. (N.S.) 284 (Sask. Q.B.).

that were being offered at the time of the application. It was contended by the applicant that the court must consider the circumstances in the light of the conditions at the time that the lease was made. The court dismissed the application, seemingly on a number of grounds, including that it was not brought by the proper party, the official guardian opposed the application, and there was no evidence that the disposition was in the interest of the infant. In fact, the court looked at the circumstances existing at the time of the application – this being the appropriate time as the transaction could not be complete or binding until the approval of the court was obtained – and held that the proposed disposition was definitely not in the interest of the infant.

Saskatchewan, but not the other provinces, dispenses with the approval of the court if the official guardian consents to the disposition of the property and, (a) the value does not exceed $10,000.00 or (b) where one or more infants own not more than an undivided one-third share in a parcel of land and the owners of the remaining shares desire to sell or otherwise dispose of the land. In view of the fluctuations in the value of mineral rights it would seem that one would rely on the exemption under (a) at one's peril. Under proper circumstances, however, the second exception is workable.

Personal Representatives

The effect of provincial legislation concerning the real property of deceased persons is to vest such property in the personal representative of the deceased. The personal representative holds the property as trustee for the persons by law beneficially entitled thereto and ultimately is required to convey the real property to such persons. If the will expressly empowers the executor to lease the minerals, he can do so. A general power to "lease" property might not be sufficient authority, however, having regard to the way in which the courts differentiate between a conventional lease of real property and a *profit à prendre.*

In the absence of express authority in the will, the personal representative of the estate can lease the minerals only if he is given the power by statute. In those provinces in which freehold leases are most common, there is legislation that provides a means of obtaining a lease from the personal representative.[19] The Ontario *Estates Administration*

---

19 The *Devolution of Real Property Act*, R.S.S. 1978, c D-27; *The Intestate Succession Act*, C.C.S.M., c I85; Alberta has accomplished the same result by a combination of the *Law of Property Act*, R.S.A. 2000, c L-7, and *Hayes v Mayhood*, [1959] S.C.R. 568, 18 D.L.R. (2d) 497, [1959] S.C.J. No. 36 (S.C.C.). See discussion of *Hayes v Mayhood, ante,* Chapter 3.

Act[20] gives the personal representative the power to "lease" real property with the approval of the majority of persons beneficially interested. It is doubtful if this provision is sufficient to authorize a personal representative to grant an oil and gas lease that creates a greater interest in land than the conventional real estate lease. So it would seem that no lease could be entered into during the interval between the death of the original mineral owner and the registration of a new title in the name of the heirs.

Saskatchewan and Manitoba specifically provide that the personal representative may lease the minerals with either the approval of the court or the concurrence of the beneficiaries. The Alberta Act, however, provides that the personal representative may lease (which, in Alberta, includes the grant of a *profit à prendre* under *Hayes v Mayhood*) for a term longer than one year with the approval of the court. Unlike that of its sister provinces, the Alberta legislation does not mention the concurrence of the beneficiaries as an alternative to court approval. In *Kissinger Petroleums Ltd. v Nelson Estate*, the Alberta Court of Appeal held that, where all the beneficiaries had signed written consents to the lease, it was unnecessary to obtain court approval.[21]

Incapacitated Persons

There are two problem areas in dealing with persons whose ability to contract is affected by mental infirmity. First, there is the question of how to obtain a lease where the mineral owner has been officially certified as mentally incapacitated, and secondly, the possibility that a lease granted by an owner not officially certified might be upset subsequently on the grounds that he lacked contracting capacity because of mental infirmity.

Once a person has been declared incapacitated, provincial legislation provides that the affairs of such person are to be administered by a

---

20 *Estates Administration Act*, R.S.O. 1990, c E-22, s 22.
21 (1984), 33 Alta. L.R. (2d) 1, [1984] 5 W.W.R. 673, 13 D.L.R. (4th) 542, [1984] A.J. No. 2587 (Alta. C.A.); affirming 26 Alta. L.R. (2d) 378, 14 E.T.R. 207, 45 A.R. 393, [1983] A.J. No. 814 (Alta. Q.B.) (leave to appeal to the Supreme Court denied). The trial judge had found that court approval was necessary, *supra*, n 11, and was reversed on this point by the Court of Appeal. The Court of Appeal decision also effectively overruled *Dooley and Caldwell v McLean Construction Ltd.* (1982), 19 Alta. L.R. (2d) 297, [1982] A.J. No. 724 (Q.B.), *In re R Estate*, [1948] 1 W.W.R. 695 (Alta. S.C.T.D.), and *dicta* in *Panchot v Hutton (Administrator of Hutton Estate)* (1952), 8 Alta. L.R. 87, 7 W.W.R. (N.S.) 97, 20, D.L.R. 100, [1952] A.J. No. 3 (Alta. S.C.T.D.).

committee. The legislation also grants the committee certain powers to deal with the property of such person.[22] In some instances, notably in Saskatchewan and Ontario, the question of mineral leases is specifically dealt with and the committee with the requisite order from the court is empowered to grant leases of minerals. In British Columbia the same result would appear to be achieved by section 17, which grants to the committee all the rights, privileges, and powers with regard to the mental patient's estate as he himself would have had. In Alberta there is no express authorization for a trustee to grant mineral leases, but he is authorized to "do any other thing approved by the Court." The result must be that a trustee can grant an oil and gas lease provided that the approval of the court is obtained.

The legislative procedures, where they exist, offer a clear-cut route by which a mineral lease may be validly obtained from a person who has been declared to be mentally incapacitated. Dealing with a mineral owner who, while not subject to a judicial determination of incompetency, nonetheless betrays signs of imbalance can be both hazardous and unpredictable. The capacity of the lessor may be attacked and, if the attack is successful, the lease will be treated as voidable.

The principles that govern in a situation of this type were laid down in *Fyckes v Chisholm*[23] as follows: "The contract of a lunatic or person mentally incapable of managing his affairs is not *per se* void, but only voidable on its being shown that the other party had knowledge, actual or constructive, of such lunacy or mental incapacity, failing which such contract, if fair and bona fide, is binding." Not only must the signing party be established as being incapacitated, but there must be knowledge on the part of the other party to the contract. The knowledge may be either actual or constructive; a party may not avoid knowledge by mere failure to make proper enquiries. The existence of such knowledge is always a question of fact, but there are certain guidelines, which were well summarized in *Jones v Gordon*:[24] "My Lords, the law upon the subject is clear, and in full accordance with sound policy and common sense. It is thus stated in a work of very high authority: 'A wilful and fraudulent absence of inquiry into the circumstances, when they are known to be such as to invite inquiry, will (if a jury think that the abstinence from inquiry arose

---

22 *Dependent Adults Act*, R.S.A. 2000, c D-11; *Public Trustee Act*, S.S. 1983, c P-43.1; *Patients Property Act*, R.S.B.C. 1996, c 349; *Mental Incompetency Act*, R.S.O. 1990, c M-9; *Mental Health Act*, C.C.S.M., c M110.

23 (1911), 19 O.W.R. 977, 3 O.W.N. 21, [1911] O.J. No. 697 (Ont. H.C.).

24 (1877), 2 A.C. 616 (H.L.).

from a suspicion or belief that inquiry would disclose a vice in the bills) amount to general or implied notice.'"[25] In *Hunt v Texaco Exploration Company*[26] the lessee had been negotiating sporadically for about six years with the lessor in an attempt to obtain a lease, always without success. There was evidence that the lessor, who was eighty years old, suffered from cerebral sclerosis and that his mental condition had deteriorated progressively over a period of years. Two other agents who had attempted to negotiate an oil and gas lease with the lessor testified that they considered him to be mentally incapacitated and so abandoned their efforts to close a transaction with him. Prior to the signing of the lease, there had been an adjudication under which the lessor was found incapable of handling his own affairs, but because of the difficulty of raising the required bond, the committee was not appointed until after the execution of the lease. The action to have the lease set aside on the ground of incapacity of the lessor was brought by the committee.

The trial judge analysed the evidence, including the testimony of the two land agents and the fact that the lessee had known the lessor for several years, during which time the lessor had consistently refused to make any deals with him. This analysis led to the finding that the lessee must have been aware of the incapacity of the man with whom he was dealing. The lease was therefore set aside.

In *Hill Estate v Chevron Standard Ltd.*[27] a mentally incapacitated man signed his "X" to a general power of attorney in favour of his wife. She knew he was mentally incapacitated. Using the power of attorney, she executed a lease of her husband's minerals to Chevron. The court found the power of attorney was void, not voidable as a contract would have been, and everything done under it, including the lease, was also void.

Dower and Curtesy

Under the English common law the wife had a right on her husband's death to have a life estate on one-third of the lands he owned at death or had owned since marriage. The right only vested upon the husband's death, but a wife nevertheless had an inchoate interest in the husband's

---

25 Passage quoted is from Byles on *Bills of Exchange*, 25th ed. (London: Sweet & Maxwell, 1983), at 206.

26 (1955), 14 W.W.R. 449, [1955] 3 D.L.R. 555 (Alta. S.C.T.D.). This point is discussed further under the heading "Unconscionable Transaction," *infra*.

27 85 Man. R. (2d) 67, [1993] 2 W.W.R. 545, M.J. No. 665 (Man. C.A.). For a full discussion of this case see Chapter 17, "Accounting for Past Production."

real property during his lifetime. That interest could not be alienated or interfered with by the husband without the wife's consent.[28] Similarly, a husband had a life estate on certain property owned by the wife at the time of her death. This estate was known as curtesy and was subject to his having issue by her born alive and capable of inheriting the property.[29] In the course of years there were many refinements as to what type of property and estate was subject to dower or curtesy and as to the requirements that must be fulfilled before the estates vested. Fortunately, we need not concern ourselves with these fine distinctions since our only enquiry is the restriction or limitation that these ancient rights place upon the granting of an oil and gas lease by a mineral owner.

Dower and curtesy, being part of the existing law of England, were imported by operation of law into the provinces and territories of Canada, except Quebec.

The Western Provinces

Both these common law marital estates have been eliminated in western Canada. In what is now Alberta and Saskatchewan, the Territories *Real Property Act*, passed in 1886, established a Torrens system of land title registration and did away with these two survivors of feudalism. They were abolished in Manitoba in 1885, while British Columbia did not remove them until 1925.[30]

The total disappearance of dower rights created hardships for the wife, and there was pressure to protect her interest. These were well described in a passage from *Overland v Himelford*:

> Previous to the year 1915, the people of this province had experienced a land boom, particularly in the cities and towns, with all its attendant speculation. The wives in Alberta said, in effect, to the Legislature, where this speculation affects our homes we want it stopped. We have a home in the morning but it is sold or mortgaged at night. Our husbands may deal

---

28 *Freedman v Mason*, [1956] O.R. 849, 4 D.L.R. (2d) 576, [1956] O.J. No. 566 (Ont. H.C.); La Forest, *Anger and Honsberger Law of Real Property*, 3rd ed., vol. 1 (Toronto: Canada Law Book, 2006) at 15–17.

29 Ibid. at 15–17.

30 See Bowker, "Reform of the Law of Dower in Alberta" (1955–61) 1 Alta. L. Rev. 501; the present-day form of the legislation abolishing these estates is to be found in *Estate Administration Act*, R.S.B.C. 1996, c 122: *Law of Property Act*, R.S.A. 2000, c L-7; *Law of Property Act*, C.C.S.M., c L90; *Devolution of Real Property Act*, R.S.S. 1978, c D-27; *Intestate Succession Act, 1996*, S.S. 1996, c I-13.1.

with their lands as they please subject only to their duty of providing us with a home which shall be placed beyond the risk of their speculation. These representations resulted in legislation in 1915 called the *Married Woman's Home Protection Act*, c 4. The name of this Act is very suggestive, although it created no right of property in the wife. It gave her only a right of filing a caveat which forthwith clouded the title, and prevented the husband from dealing with the land, in so far as registration was required, from the moment the caveat was lodged.[31]

The three prairie provinces, Alberta and Saskatchewan in 1915, and Manitoba in 1918, responded to this pressure by enacting legislation protecting the family's right to the homestead. In British Columbia the absence of dower persisted from 1925 until homestead protection legislation was passed in 1948.

While these provincial enactments are referred to interchangeably as relating to dower or homestead rights, they are really homestead acts and are based upon the homestead laws that were developed in many state jurisdictions in the United States. These laws protected the family homestead by restricting the right of the owner to dispose or encumber it, granting the wife or family a life estate in it after the owner's death and making it exempt from seizure or sale under execution.[32]

There is a general similarity in purpose and structure among the western legislation dealing with dower and homestead rights, but there is also a considerable variation as to the procedures and forms that are to be followed. Consequently, when dealing with leases in each province, it is essential to scrutinize the appropriate legislation to determine that the precise requirements have been met. The main areas of concern, if not the details of compliance, are common to all the legislation.

Application of Dower or Homestead to Oil and Gas Leases

The various provincial acts, in effect, prohibit a disposition of the homestead without the consent of the spouse. The language used in describing what is prohibited, whether it be a "disposition" or "transfer any interest in land," is certainly broad enough to include the granting of an oil and gas lease, which is both an interest in land and a

---

31 (1920), 15 Alta. L.R. 332, [1920] 2 W.W.R. 481, 52 D.L.R. 429 at 490 (Alta. S.C., App.Div.).

32 This latter feature is achieved in western Canada by separate enactments; see, for example, *Homesteads Act*, R.S.B.C. 1996, c 197; *Civil Enforcement Act*, R.S.A. 2000, c C-15.

disposition. The Alberta legislation expressly applies dower to mines and minerals contained in a homestead,[33] but this specific reference does not appear necessary. In *Champagne v Aljean Construction Ltd.*[34] it was held that a sand and gravel lease on homestead lands was a disposition within the meaning of the Alberta *Dower Act* and was void without the consent of the spouse. British Columbia, as will be noted later, requires the added element of registration before the homestead law applies.

If, however, title to the minerals is held under a separate certificate of title, dower will not attach. A "homestead" cannot exist on a mineral title that does not include the surface; hence the Acts have no application. Alberta expressly provides in its *Dower Act* that the spouse of a married person has no dower interest in mines and minerals contained in a certificate of title other than the certificate of title to the homestead and that no consent or acknowledgment is required.

Definition of Homestead

The three prairie provinces impose an area limitation on the homestead. In a city, town, or village, the limitation will be the parcel of land on which the dwelling place is located up to a certain number of lots. In rural areas, much more relevant to oil and gas leases, the limitation is based on acreage. In Alberta and Saskatchewan the limitation is 160 acres, while in Manitoba it is 320 acres.

If lands are involved in addition to the homestead, i.e., if an oil and gas lease covered 320 acres in Alberta or Saskatchewan, the transaction could not be enforced as against the homestead portion, nor could damages be recovered from the owner for failure to perform an agreement to sell the homestead. The Supreme Court of Canada reasoned that if damages were assessed against the husband because of his wife's refusal to consent to a disposition of the homestead, then, since the fortunes of husband and wife are intertwined, there would be an element of compulsion on the part of the wife to so consent.[35] With respect to the remaining portion of the lands, the court has jurisdiction to either grant specific performance of the transaction, or damages in lieu thereto.[36]

---

33 *Dower Act*, R.S.A. 2000, c D-15-24.

34 (1980), 11 Alta. L.R. (2d) 1, 106 D.L.R. (3d) 61, [1979] A.J. No. 583 (Alta. Q.B.).

35 *McKenzie v Hiscock*, [1967] S.C.R. 781, 61 W.W.R. 453, 65 D.L.R. (2d) 123, [1967] S.C.J. No. 69 (S.C.C.).

36 Ibid. But see *Harris v Morsky*, [1998] 8 W.W.R. 340, [1998] S.J. No. 199, 168 Sask. R. 27 (Sask. C.A.), where the Saskatchewan Court of Appeal refused to grant specific performance in the sale of a farm that included lands in addition to the homestead.

Applying this to an oil and gas situation, it is likely that the lessee could obtain specific performance of the lease against that portion of the lands not included in the homestead.

Whether a given parcel of land does or does not constitute the homestead usually is self-evident from the facts. Occasionally, however, there may arise a situation where the circumstances of the transaction or of the parties themselves may create doubt as to the applicability of the Act. In *Anderson v Reid*[37] the land originally had been acquired by the plaintiff and his wife from the Soldier Settlement Board, but his agreement for sale was subsequently cancelled owing to default. He continued in possession under yearly leases until the lands were put up for sale by public tender. The board assured him that he would be given prior consideration when the tenders were reviewed. In order to submit a bid he raised money from the defendant, and the arrangement between them was that the money would be advanced not by way of loan, but solely on the condition that the defendant would obtain absolute title. The plaintiff would be allowed to continue living on the land until it was required by the defendant. The plaintiff's bid was accepted and the defendant advanced the purchase price. In order to complete the transaction the plaintiff executed a transfer of the land to the defendant, but the plaintiff's wife did not consent to it. The two transfers, from the board to the plaintiff and from the plaintiff to the defendant, were registered only one minute apart. The court held that the *Homesteads Act* did not apply because the transfer given by the plaintiff husband did not convey or transfer any equitable interest in the land but was necessary merely for the completion of the proposed transaction.

The Manitoba Court of Appeal dealt with homestead and a single person in *Langan v Ducharme*.[38] Langan, a widower, owned and occupied a house. He then married the plaintiff, who was a widow, and moved into her home. The plaintiff wife did not on any occasion reside at the home owned by her husband. Some months after the marriage, Langan transferred his own house to the defendant and himself as joint tenants. The plaintiff wife did not give a consent under the *Dower Act*, and Langan's affidavit on the transfer stated that no part of the land was or ever had been his homestead within the meaning of the Act. Langan then left the plaintiff and moved back to his former home at a time which the court found to be subsequent to the execution of the

---

37 (1957), 21 W.W.R. (N.S.) 186, 7 D.L.R. (2d) 523 (Sask. C.A.).
38 (1957), 65 Man. R. 268, 22 W.W.R. 126, 8 D.L.R. (2d) 749 (Man. C.A.).

transfer. The court held that at the time of the marriage Langan's home was not a "homestead" within the purpose and object of the Act and that in fact the homestead of the marriage was the plaintiff's residence. It also adopted the words of Kilgour J in *National Trust Co. v Greengard*: "Although in some contexts a man may be said to have several homes, in my opinion, the essential scheme of the statute under consideration excludes the possibility of more than one home at a time."[39]

In Alberta, however, the *Dower Act* expressly recognizes that there may be multiple homesteads. A homestead is defined as a parcel of land on which the dwelling house occupied by the owner of the land as his residence is situated. Section 3 provides that when land becomes the homestead of a married person it continues to be his homestead notwithstanding the acquisition of another homestead or a change of residence of a married person. The land ceases to be the homestead when a transfer of the land is registered in the Land Titles Office, or when a release of dower rights is registered in the Land Titles Office.

In *Langan*, the court expressly refrained from dealing with some other points that were raised but were not necessary for the disposition of the appeal. The questions that remained open were:

> Whether if a *married* owner occupies a dwelling house as his or her home, the other spouse never living in the house, it is a "homestead" within the meaning of the *Dower Act*; whether if the spouses each own a dwelling house and both houses are during the marriage occupied by the owner as the home (with or without the other spouse) there could be two "homesteads" within the meaning of the act, with each spouse having dower rights in the "homestead" of the other; whether a house owned by one spouse can be the "homestead" of both spouses or whether it can be the "homestead" only of the owner, the other spouse having rights therein as provided by the *Dower Act*?[40]

Right of the Husband in Homestead

The four western provinces wiped the slate clean of dower and curtesy and replaced it with specific legislation. In addition to the traditional rights of the wife, Manitoba,[41] Saskatchewan,[42] Alberta,[43] and British

---

39   [1929] 3 W.W.R. 363, [1930] 1 D.L.R. 58 (Man. K.B.).
40   *Supra* n 38 at 130.
41   *Homesteads Act*, C.C.S.M., c H80.
42   *Homesteads Act, 1989*, S.S. 1989–90, c H-5.1.
43   *Dower Act*, R.S.A. 2000, c D-15.

Columbia[44] granted the husband a claim against the homestead of the wife. The various dower and homestead acts use words such as "married person" and "spouse," which are applicable equally to both husband and wife.

Effect of Lease Where Consent of Spouse Not Obtained

Dower and homestead rights are an anomaly in the Torrens land registry system. This system, which prevails in Alberta, Saskatchewan, British Columbia, and in Manitoba and Ontario with some admixture of the old registry system, is based upon the indefeasibility of the register. The main feature of the Torrens system has been described as follows: "The object is to save persons dealing with registered proprietors from the trouble and expense of going behind the register, in order to investigate the history of their author's title, and to satisfy themselves of its validity. That end is accomplished by providing that everyone who purchases, in *bona fide* and for value, from a registered proprietor, and enters his deed of transfer on the register, shall thereby acquire an indefeasible right, notwithstanding the infirmity of his author's title."[45] With the exception of British Columbia, dower rights are invisible. They do not appear on the register and there is nothing against the title to show whether the lands in question are subject to any such claim. British Columbia has circumvented this aspect by structuring its legislation so that the existence of dower rights depends on an entry made on the register. If the register does not disclose this entry, then the right to dower is defeated. While this undoubtedly contributes to the certainty of a registered title, it has some obvious drawbacks in that the spouse may not know of the requirement to file or may be reluctant to do so since such action may introduce an undesirable arm's-length aspect into the marriage relationship. In the other provinces, the purchaser must always seek out and deal with dower rights.

The conflict between dower and the Torrens system has led to some uncertainty as to the precise status of a disposition of the homestead where the consent of the wife has not been obtained. The British Columbia legislation makes such a disposition "void for all purposes," and Manitoba provides that such a disposition shall be "invalid and ineffective." This language would seem to establish that in those provinces, at

---

44 *Land (Spouse Protection) Act*, R.S.B.C. 1996, c 246.
45 *Gibbs v Messer*, [1891] A.C. 248 (P.C.) at 254.

least, such a disposition would be totally unenforceable and would give rise to no rights against the homestead.

Alberta and Saskatchewan follow a somewhat different route in protecting the homestead rights. Saskatchewan requires that every disposition or encumbrance of the homestead shall be signed by the spouse. Alberta prohibits a married person from disposing of the homestead unless the spouse consents in writing and makes a married person who so disposes guilty of a summary conviction offence. The Alberta legislation also provides that where a married person makes a disposition without the consent of the spouse that results in a registration of title in the name of another person, that title is valid and the spouse's rights are for damages equivalent to one-half of the money paid for the property. This does not apply to oil and gas leases which do not result in a new title.[46] Apart from this, neither province specifies the legal status of a disposition without the required consent. Two decisions of the Supreme Court of Canada appear to hold that a defective disposition is totally unenforceable in these provinces.

Meduk v Soya[47] involved the Alberta *Dower Act* and an agreement for sale of a house in Edmonton that was owned by the wife and was the homestead of the couple. (Remember that in Alberta the husband also has dower rights.) Her husband did not consent to the agreement. He was asked by the real estate agent in the presence of the prospective purchasers whether he would sign the agreement, but declined on the ground that the property belonged to his wife and she could do what she wanted with it. It was obvious from the evidence that both the vendors and the purchasers were unaware that the provisions of the *Dower Act* applied to the transaction. The purchasers moved into possession of the premises, and there was evidence that the husband assisted in turning over possession to them and even suggested that the deal be postponed until the listing with the real estate agency had expired so as to avoid payment of commission. Since it was an agreement for sale only, no new title had been created under the Torrens system. Some two

---

46 For a full discussion of the various versions of Alberta legislation and the development of the present act, see Bowker, *supra* n 30 at 502–8.

47 [1958] S.C.R. 167, 12 D.L.R. (2d) 289, [1958] S.C.J. No. 8 (S.C.C.); consent of the spouse must be obtained even when the agreement is only a preliminary agreement. In *Rose v Dever*, [1972] 2 W.W.R. 431 (Man. C.A.); affirmed, [1973] S.C.J. No. 49 (S.C.C.), the Manitoba Court of Appeal held that where a married man signed a standard real estate form of offer to purchase, which did not contain the consent of the wife, the document was unenforceable.

months after the purchasers had moved in, the vendor wife commenced proceedings to obtain possession on the grounds that the spouse had not consented to the disposition. Cartwright J said "the making of the agreement by her without the consent in writing of her spouse was expressly forbidden by section 3(l) of the Act and unless John Meduk did consent in writing, *her acceptance was ineffective to form a contract"* (italics mine).

The Saskatchewan *Homesteads Act* was subsequently reviewed by the Supreme Court on the same point. In *McKenzie v Hiscock*[48] the court interpreted *Meduk v Soja* as establishing that without the required consent there could be no enforceable contract. While the latter case dealt with the Alberta legislation, which differs in some respects from that of Saskatchewan, it was clear that the court applied the same principles and also considered a previous decision of the Saskatchewan courts, which, dealing with an earlier form of the *Homesteads Act*, held that the assent of the husband alone to an agreement of sale respecting the homestead is "an ineffectual assent."[49]

Despite the fact that the Alberta and Saskatchewan legislation do not expressly make such a disposition null and void, the current weight of judicial opinion is that a defective disposition, not creating a new registered title, will be so considered.

Requirements of Dower

A proper compliance with the requirements of dower will have three elements: (a) consent, (b) form of consent, and (c) acknowledgment by spouse. As will be seen, the courts place the greatest emphasis on consent and, if that element is present, the disposition will likely be upheld, even though the other two are defective or absent. Nevertheless, the lessee should ensure that the requirements of all three elements are scrupulously compiled with. Only in this way will the lease be free from attack and possible upset.

All of the provincial acts require the written consent of the spouse to a disposition of the homestead. Manitoba provides that the consent may be embodied in or endorsed upon the actual disposition or may be by a separate document. British Columbia provides that the consent may be embodied in or endorsed upon the instrument and also that the execution by the spouse of any disposition by itself constitutes the necessary

---

48 *Supra*, n 35.
49 *Halldorson v Holizki*, [1919] 1 W.W.R. 472 (Sask. K.B.); affirmed (1919), 12 Sask. L.R. 498, [1919] 3 W.W.R. 86, 47 D.L.R. 613 (Sask. C.A).

consent. Alberta and Saskatchewan are more particular as to the affixing of the consent and require that the disposition shall contain, or have annexed to, or endorsed, or written thereon, a declaration by the spouse that it has been executed for the purpose of relinquishing rights in the homestead. If the form of declaration is contained in the instrument, the signature of the spouse to the instrument will also be a sufficient signature to the consent. In Saskatchewan, although not in Alberta, this has led to the practice of inserting the declaration in the body of the lease, immediately preceding the space provided for execution by the lessee, and lessor. Saskatchewan also requires the express acceptance of the lease by the lessee, and this provision will also be contained in the body of the lease. If, however, the consent is annexed to the instrument, the spouse must sign both the consent and the instrument.

The distinction between "contained in" and "annexed to" caused much judicial soul searching in *Reynolds v Ackerman*.[50] The lease in this case did not follow the normal printed form, but consisted of two pages of typewriting, with both the consent and certificate of acknowledgment appearing on another page attached to the lease. Both the form of consent and the certificate of acknowledgment were properly completed by the wife, but she had not signed the lease itself.

The neat point at issue was whether the consent should be considered as "annexed to the instrument" or "contained in the instrument." If the latter, then the signature of the spouse to the consent form would be sufficient. It would be otherwise, however, if the consent was merely annexed to the instrument, since under those conditions both documents required the signature of the spouse. The judge concluded that, because the consent was on a separate sheet, it must be considered as having been annexed to the instrument rather than forming part of it. This conclusion was reached with reluctance, the court rather wistfully declaring that if the consent had been placed on the front of page one, or somewhere on page two, or even on the back of page two, it would have been considered as having been contained in the instrument. In the result, the lease was declared invalid.

Certificate of Acknowledgment

Provincial dower legislation provides for a consenting spouse to acknowledge that she (or he, where applicable) is aware of the nature of

---

50 (1953), 32 W.W.R. (N.S.) 289 (Alta. S.C.T.D.).

the disposition and of the protection offered by the homestead legislation and that the consent was given free of compulsion. To fortify the latter requirement, the legislation uniformly requires that this acknowledgment be taken separate and apart from the disposing spouse. Each province has its own form of acknowledgment, which must be strictly complied with, but the foregoing represents the purpose of such a precaution. The legislation also lists the officials who are authorized to take the certificate. British Columbia and Alberta include any person so authorized under the respective Land Titles or Land Registry Acts. These are judges, court and land registry registrars, notaries public, magistrates, justices of the peace, down to and including commissioners for the taking of affidavits. The other two provinces are more selective. Manitoba requires that where the disposition is with respect to a mineral interest, the acknowledgment must be made before a barrister-at-law or a notary public. Saskatchewan does not include commissioners in its list of acceptable officials and excludes any person from taking an acknowledgment of the wife when that person, his employer, partner, or a clerk has prepared the document in question or is otherwise interested in the transaction involved.

In some early cases, the courts were prepared to set aside transactions where there had not been a perfect compliance with the requirements of the acknowledgment. In *Brown v Prairie Leaseholds Ltd.*[51] the wife signed the acknowledgment in a room where the husband was in and out dressing the children in snowsuits to attend a Christmas party. The court held that this irregularity made the document "invalid and ineffective." In an early Alberta case, *Reddick v Pearson,*[52] the defendant wife signed at the foot of the petroleum and natural gas lease but signed the acknowledgment in a room where her husband was also present. The court held that the fact that the wife had concurred in the granting of the lease did not estop either her or her husband from invoking the Act to nullify the lease.[53]

In *Friess v Imperial Oil Limited*[54] the male plaintiff lived on a half-section of land as purchaser under an agreement for sale; one quarter-section of

---

51 (1953), 9 W.W.R. (N.S.) 577 (Man.); affirmed without written reasons (1954), 12 W.W.R. (N.S.) 464 (C.A.).

52 [1948] 2 W.W.R. 1144, [1948] A.J. No. 24 (Alta. S.C.T.D.).

53 Bowker suggests that this case may have been overruled by *McColl-Frontenac Oil Co. v Hamilton*, [1953] 1 S.C.R. 127, [1953] 1 D.L.R. 721 (S.C.C.). The latter case applied a curative provision to cure a defect in the acknowledgment, and presumably the same route was available to the court in the *Reddick* case. In the absence of any observation on the curative provision from the court in the *Reddick* decision this must remain conjecture. In any event, since the curative clause no longer exists in Alberta, the point is academic.

54 (1954), 12 W.W.R. (N.S.) 151, [1954] 4 D.L.R. 100 (Sask. C.A.).

the land was the homestead. An agent of the defendant company met with the plaintiff and negotiated an oil and gas lease. At this time the plaintiff's wife was ill and the declaration and acknowledgment were not taken, nor was the lease discussed with her apart from her husband. At the request of the agent, the fourteen-year-old daughter of the plaintiffs signed her mother's name to the declaration, and a justice of the peace completed the required certificate. For a number of years the delay rental payments were made and accepted; then an action was brought to set aside the lease on the grounds of non-compliance with the *Homesteads Act*. There was no evidence to warrant the conclusion that the wife would have signed the lease had she been in good health. As she was considered a non-consenting wife, the lease was held to be null and void with respect to the homestead, although still binding with respect to the other quarter-section.

While non-consent of a spouse is fatal to the validity of the document, it would seem that consent by itself is sufficient to sustain the document even if the required acknowledgment has not been taken. In *Senstad v Makus*[55] the Supreme Court of Canada considered the Alberta *Dower Act* in connection with an agreement of purchase and sale of lands that included the homestead. The spouse executed the consent in the proper form but did not acknowledge her consent as provided in the Act. The court pointed out that the 1942 version of the *Dower Act*, which had been considered in *Reddick v Pearson*, specifically provided that any disposition made by a husband (a husband did not have dower until the 1948 Act) without the wife's consent was absolutely null and void. The 1948 Act that replaced the 1942 Act did not contain the provisions making it null and void without written consent, but, rather, prohibited a married person from disposing of the premises without the written consent of the spouse. Unlike the earlier Act, the 1948 version spelled out the nature and form of the written consent. The court pointed out that the Act does not provide that a written consent is not a consent unless acknowledged. The Act imposes an obligation on the spouse of a married person who executes a consent to acknowledge that consent, but it is a consent nonetheless, even if it has not been acknowledged. The Supreme Court went on to characterize the purpose of the acknowledgment as being to prevent the spouse from challenging the validity of his or her consent. Without an acknowledgment the validity of the consent would still be open to

---

55 [1977] 2 S.C.R. 44, [1977] 5 W.W.R. 731, 79 D.L.R. (3d) 321, [1977] S.C.J. No. 112 (S.C.C.).

attack on the ground that the spouse was not aware of the nature of the transaction, was not aware of the dower rights conferred by the Act, did not appreciate the effect of the consent, or did not give a free and voluntary consent without compulsion. An acknowledgment is evidence that the consent was properly given[56] and is required to enable the registrar to register a transfer. Even without the acknowledgment, however, a written consent will remain valid, unless successfully attacked by the evidence on one or more of the above grounds, and specific performance can be ordered.

The sufficiency of the spouse's written consent, without more, has also been upheld in Saskatchewan. In *Suppes v Wellings*[57] the defendant wife had willingly signed a purchase of sale agreement and the court found that she was aware of her rights under the *Homesteads Act* but the Act's requirements were not complied with. The defendants subsequently decided not to complete the sale. The transaction was upheld on the grounds that a transfer of interest in a homestead is valid and enforceable when the wife, being aware of her rights under the *Homesteads Act*, freely and without compulsion from her husband consents to such a transfer. In this case the acreage had a "peculiar and special value" to the plaintiffs and specific performance was awarded rather than damages. This line of reasoning would seem to apply to oil and gas leases so that the remedy of specific performance would be available to the lessee. In *McClenaghan v Haley*[58] the husband and wife signed an offer to sell the property, but the provisions of the *Homesteads Act* were not complied with. The agreed statement of facts did not specifically state that she was aware of her rights under the Act, nor did it state that she was not aware. The court found that the fact that there was an existing mortgage on the premises led to the inference that the wife was aware of her rights. Damages in lieu of specific performance were awarded.

---

56 This observation by the Supreme Court on the effect of the acknowledgment appears to give it the same evidentiary effect as conferred by the Saskatchewan and Manitoba Acts, which provide that no person acquiring an interest under the instrument shall be bound to make inquiry as to the truthfulness of the facts alleged in the affidavit or in the certificate of acknowledgment and, upon delivery, the instrument will become valid and binding except for fraud. See discussion under "Curative Provisions and Presumptions," *infra*.

57 [1982] 4 W.W.R. 106, [1982] S.J. No. 392 (Sask. Q.B.).

58 [1983] 5 W.W.R. 586, [1983] S.J. No. 507 (Sask. C.A.).

It can thus be said with considerable confidence that if a spouse has consented in writing and is aware of the rights granted by the homesteads or dower acts, the transaction will be upheld, and in the case of oil and gas leases, specific performance will likely be given. There is still a question as to whether the spouse has to be aware of his or her statutory rights, although the courts seem prepared to infer this knowledge from the flimsiest of evidence.

In Alberta at least there may also be some remaining question as to whether the signature of a spouse by itself is sufficient. In *McColm v Belter*[59] both husband and wife had signed a memorandum in writing under which they agreed to sell their farm. The Court of Appeal relied on the fact that there was no consent in the prescribed form. It was the view of the Court of Appeal that the consent must contain certain prescribed matters and must be formally acknowledged. Mere signature by a spouse that complies with neither the form of consent prescribed by the Act nor with the section requiring an acknowledgment does not constitute a consent as envisaged under the *Dower Act*. This decision was briefly referred to in the Supreme Court of Canada decision in the *Senstad* case and the court pointed out that the facts differed from the *Senstad* situation since in *McColm* there had been no consent as required by section 5 of the Act. Because of the *Senstad* decision, we now know that the absence of an acknowledgment is not sufficient to set aside a document. Since the *McColm* decision was not expressly overruled, there may still be a possibility in Alberta that the form of the consent as specified in the *Dower Act* must be complied with. In an Alberta Queen's Bench decision[60] it was held that where the landowner's husband had signed an agreement granting a charge to a bank but did not execute a consent or acknowledgment in accordance with the requirements of the *Dower Act*, the bank was nonetheless entitled to maintain the priority of its caveat. All that was necessary was that the consent of the husband could be proved in some manner. The husband's execution of the agreement was sufficient proof of his consent. The court does not appear to have considered whether the decision of the Court of Appeal in *McColm* has some residual effect despite *Senstad*, so there is still an element of doubt about the requirement that the consent must take the form specified in the *Dower Act*.

---

59 [1975] 1 W.W.R. 364, 50 D.L.R. (3d) 133 (Alta. C.A.).
60 *Gibraltar Mortgage Corporation Ltd. v Korner* (1983), 27 Alta. L.R. 31, [1983] A.J. No. 799 (Alta. Q.B.).

Dispensing with Consent

Each provincial act contains machinery whereby the requirement of consent may be dispensed with. The approval or direction of the court is required in each instance, and there is some variation among the provinces as to the grounds on which such an order may be obtained. British Columbia provides that it may be obtained where the husband and wife are living apart or where the wife has not lived within the province since the marriage, or her whereabouts are unknown, or she is mentally incompetent, or the consent has been unreasonably withheld. The grounds in Manitoba obtain when the parties have been living apart for six months or more or the spouse is mentally incompetent. Alberta allows the dispensation when the parties are living apart, where the spouse has not lived within the province since the marriage, where the whereabouts of the spouse are unknown, where there are two or more homesteads, or where the spouse is a mentally incompetent person.

The dispensing power in an earlier form of the Manitoba *Dower Act* was reviewed by the Court of Appeal in *Monchamp v Monchamp*.[61] At that time the requirement was that the wife had been living apart from the husband for two years or more. The period has now been shortened to six months, but the wording "living apart" has been retained. In the *Monchamp* situation the husband had previously obtained an order to dispense with the consent of the wife since the parties had been living apart for more than the required period of time. The order provided that one-third of the purchase price was to be held in trust pending the disposition of a then existing divorce action. The husband subsequently obtained a divorce and applied to have the monies paid out to him. There was evidence that the wife had separated from her husband because of his cruelty. The court held that, where a separation had been caused by the cruelty of the husband, the wife should not be deprived of her dower rights. The same approach was applied in *Hall v Neff*,[62] the court interpreting another provision of the Manitoba Act, which disentitled the wife from any right under the Act where she had left her husband, "with the intention of living separate and apart from him." In this case the widow had been living separate and apart from

---

61 (1953), 60 Man. R. 412, 8 W.W.R. (N.S.) 366, [1953] 2 D.L.R. 246 (Man. C.A.).
62 (1953), 8 W.W.R. (N.S.) 380 (Man. Q.B).

her husband under a separation agreement, and upon his death she claimed an interest in a dwelling house that her husband had purchased some six years after the parties had separated. The court held that the section which deprived a widow of her dower rights where she had left her husband with the intention of living separate and apart could not apply where the parties had separated by agreement. Under those conditions the wife could not be said to have left or abandoned him. Both cases quoted with approval an earlier decision of the Manitoba Court of Appeal:

> What the legislature had in view in enacting this section was that if the wife, on her own initiative, elects to abandon or desert her husband, she shall then be taken to have forfeited her rights in his property, but if she lives apart from her husband under an agreement between them she surely cannot be said to have left or abandoned him within the meaning of the section. What might be regarded as a proper penalty for the wife's desertion of her husband would, where the husband agrees and consents to her leaving and living apart from him, be a manifest act of injustice, which the legislature never intended, and, where the wife is compelled by the acts and conducts of the husband to leave, and live apart from him, the injustice would still be more glaring. I am of the opinion, therefore, that this case does not come within sec. 20 and the widow is, consequently, entitled to her share in her late husband's estate under the provisions of the *Dower Act*.[63]

Release of Dower Rights

The Alberta Act provides that a spouse may execute a release of dower rights that, when registered in the Land Titles Office, puts an end to any dower rights of the spouse. The spouse can cancel the release at any time by filing a caveat, but any revived dower rights will be subject to the rights acquired by a third party in good faith and for valuable consideration before the filing of the caveat. Manitoba and British Columbia also provide that dower may be released by a document in writing.[64]

---

63 *In re Lenius*, 4 Alta. L.R. 35, [1923] 1 W.W.R. 272 (Man. C.A.).

64 *Homesteads Act*, C.C.S.M., c H80, s 11(1); *Land (Spouse Protection) Act*, R.S.B.C. 1996, c 246, s 10.

Affidavits

All of the jurisdictions, save British Columbia, provide an alternative to the consent of the spouse if certain conditions are met. The owner may make an affidavit that he is not married or that the land in question is not his homestead.[65] This procedure has no place under the British Columbia scheme, which depends upon actual registration of the homestead before it becomes operative.

Joint Ownership

The Alberta Act contains a specific exception to dower where the married person is a joint tenant, tenant-in-common, or owner of a partial interest in the land with a person or persons other than the spouse. Under these conditions the Act does not apply. In a sense this clause may be regarded as an extension of the common law dower position which held that dower could not apply to a joint tenancy, but the wife was entitled to her dower rights where the land was held as a tenant-in-common since there was a separate and divided title in the latter instance. The other western provinces do not contain this exception, and it would seem that the particular requirements of the relevant acts must be complied with, although one would not expect to encounter many instances where a homestead would be owned jointly with a third party.

Curative Provisions and Presumptions

At one time the Alberta *Dower Act* contained a curative provision, which was considered by the Supreme Court of Canada in *McColl-Frontenac Oil Company v Hamilton*,[66] a case that involved an oil and gas lease. The defect was that the acknowledgment of the wife's consent was made in the presence of her husband. The lessee relied upon the curative provision then present in the Alberta Act: "9.(1) When any woman has executed a contract for the sale of property, or joined in

---

65 Once again there is some variation in the precise form and wording of this affidavit among the various provinces, but the effect is the same. Manitoba requires an additional affidavit by the grantee that, when the wife consents, the consenting woman is in fact his wife.

66 [1953] 1 S.C.R. 127, [1953] 1 D.L.R. 721 (S.C.C.). See also *supra* n 53.

execution thereof with her husband, or given her consent in writing to the execution thereof, and the consideration under the contract has been totally or partly performed by the purchaser, she shall, in the absence of fraud on the part of the purchaser, be deemed to have consented to the sale, in accordance with the provisions of this Act." The court held that the granting of an oil and gas lease came within "sale of property" and applied the clause to uphold the lease.

This provision was removed from the Alberta Act in 1948,[67] but the British Columbia Act contains a similar clause, although the reference to "sale of property" has been changed to "sale of the homestead." Bowker queries whether this language would cover an oil lease. The point is a nice one and in the absence of any authority must remain open.

While Saskatchewan and Manitoba do not have curative provisions in the strict sense of the word, they do provide that no person acquiring an interest under the instrument shall be bound to make enquiry as to the truthfulness of the facts alleged in the affidavit or in the certificate of acknowledgment, and upon delivery of such instrument it will become valid and binding, except for fraud.[68] The acts also define what constitutes fraud as knowledge on the part of the person taking under the instrument that the land is in fact the homestead and that the person making the disposition has a wife who is not a party to the document. If fraud is present, the wife can have the new certificate of title cancelled. The curative provisions in both Saskatchewan and Manitoba undoubtedly will cover most instances and protect the purchaser. They cover both affidavits by the grantor that the land was not the homestead and acknowledgments by a consenting spouse.

A false affidavit was involved in *Prudential Trust Co. Ltd. and Canadian Williston Minerals Ltd. v Olson*[69] wherein the grantor swore that the lands were not his homestead, although in fact they were. There were two subsequent assignments of the lease; Canadian Williston was the lessee at the time the action was brought. The Supreme Court of Canada held that the non-enquiry provision applied to protect a *bona fide* purchaser for value and there was no evidence that Canadian Williston had any knowledge of the fact that the lands had included the grantor's homestead; nor was there any evidence that the original agent who took the lease had any such knowledge.

---

67 *Dower Act*, S.A. 1948, c 7. See *Land (Spouse Protection) Act*, R.S.B.C. 1996, c 246.
68 The *Senstad* decision seems to have achieved the same result in Alberta.
69 [1960] S.C.R. 227, 21 D.L.R. (2d) 603, [1959] S.C.J. No. 85 (S.C.C.).

In *Farmers Mutual Petroleum v Jackson*[70] the farmer transferred his mineral rights. The document was obtained by an agent of the plaintiff company at the farmhouse. The farmer completed an affidavit that the land was not his homestead, although in fact it was. Apparently the grantor felt that the reference to homestead in the affidavit meant taken and "homesteaded" under the *Dominion Lands Act*. The trial judge found that the agent knew, or should have known, that the land was the defendant's homestead and therefore the agent's principal could not rely on the protection of the non-enquiry section.

In *Lavoie v Marchildon*[71] the action was brought for specific performance of an agreement for sale. The defence relied upon the fact that the person who took the wife's acknowledgment had also typed in a clause that was inserted into the agreement and thus was disqualified. The Saskatchewan trial court found that both the plaintiff and his wife fully understood the nature of the transaction, but that subsequent developments had made them unwilling to proceed with the sale. Offended by such a use of the Act, the court declared that to permit the defendant to escape his obligations by setting up his wife's rights under the *Homesteads Act* would be unconscionable and would be using the Act as an instrument to further unconscionable dealing since the acknowledgment was complete and proper on its face; the statutory presumption was applied to make the agreement "valid and binding."

The same provision came to the rescue of an assignee of the original lessee in *Bonkowski v Rose and Cordillera Petroleum Ltd.*[72] At the time of granting the lease the wife was willing to join, and she signed the prescribed forms. On the evidence, however, she not only signed the certificate in the presence of her husband, but also never appeared before the justice of the peace who signed the form. The document appeared perfectly regular. The lessee's interest in the lease was subsequently assigned to the defendant Cordillera, whose agent testified that, following his normal practice, he would have examined the form of consent and acknowledgment and, on the basis of such examination, concluded that the requirements of the Act had been met. The lease was upheld on the basis that it was the intent of the curative provision to protect a purchaser who relies on facts stated in the certificate. This decision is significant in that there can be no doubt that the agent who

---

70 (1956), 19 W.W.R. 625, 5 D.L.R (2d) 246 (Sask. C.A.).
71 (1953), 9 W.W.R. (N.S.) 263 (Sask. Q.B.).
72 (1955), 16 W.W.R. (N.S.) 481, [1955] 5 D.L.R. 229 (Sask. C.A.).

originally took the lease had knowledge of the deficiency; nonetheless, a *bona fide* subsequent purchaser can rely on a certificate that has no patent defect.

The *Bonkowski* decision was applied in *Kuball v Prudential Trust Company and Canadian Williston Minerals Ltd.*,[73] where the same defect occurred in that the wife had not appeared before the justice of the peace who completed the certificate. The Supreme Court of Canada expressly approved the *Bonkowski ratio* in *Prudential Trust Co. Ltd. v Forseth*.[74] The document in the *Forseth* situation was actually a transfer of an undivided one-half interest in the mineral rights, but was referred to as a lease in both the form of consent and certificate of acknowledgment. Martland J held that the essential requirements of the *Homesteads Act* are "that the wife shall sign the instrument; that, on separate examination by a proper officer, she shall acknowledge that she understands her rights to the homestead and signs the instrument of her own free will and consent, without compulsion by her husband, and that she has executed it for the purpose of relinquishing her rights in the homestead." It was the view of the court that the inaccuracy of the description of the documents in the true form was not material to the circumstances of the case. It would appear from the foregoing passage that such a misdescription would not have been fatal even as between the original parties. The *Bonkowski* case was referred to and its finding that the object of the curative section is to give a transferee in good faith protection where there has been a *prima facie* compliance with the act was approved.

Ontario

Dower as such no longer applies in Ontario, having been abolished by section 70 of the *Family Law Reform Act*.[75] In place of the old dower rights, the Act provides that no spouse shall dispose of or encumber any interest in the matrimonial home unless the rights of the other spouse are protected as provided in the Act.

---

73 (1957), 21 W.W.R. 273 (Sask. Q.B.).
74 [1960] S.C.R. 210, 30 W.W.R. 241, 21 D.L.R. (2d) 507, [1959] S.C.J. No. 84 (S.C.C.).
75 R.S.O. 1980, c 152, now the *Family Law Act*, R.S.O. 1990, c F-3. See also *Royal Bank of Canada v Nicholson* (1981), 29 O.R. (2d) 141, 112 D.L.R. (3d) 364, [1980] O.J. No. 3644 (Ont. H.C.J.).

Ontario oil and gas leases provide for spousal consent or, in the alternative, an affidavit of the lessor that he or she was not a spouse at the time of disposition or that the property has never been occupied as a matrimonial home or that the other spouse has released all rights by a separation agreement.

It may be that obtaining a consent of the spouse or an affidavit in lieu thereof represents an abundance of caution on the part of the lessee since it is difficult to see how mineral rights would fit within the definition of a matrimonial home. The Act defines the matrimonial home as the residence only and such property as reasonably necessary to the enjoyment of the residence. Oil and gas rights would not appear to fit within this definition. Nonetheless, the practice when taking an oil and gas lease is to comply with the *Family Law Reform Act*.

Estoppel

The doctrine of estoppel[76] has on occasion been advanced in an attempt to cure a dower defect that lies outside the scope of the curative provisions. In light of the cases decided to date the chances of success appear remote. The Supreme Court has expressly stated that the possibility of avoiding a statutory requirement by estoppel is at least questionable.[77]

Martens v Burden[78] contains a thorough review of the cases that dealt with the possible application of estoppel to overcome a failure to comply with the requirements of the *Dower Act*. At the end of his analysis of the authorities, Shannon J had this to say: "I have concluded that the doctrine of estoppel can rarely and perhaps never be used to avoid the consequences of non-compliance with the *Dower Act*."[79]

See also *Warne v Sweet*,[80] which followed the authority of *Martens v Burden* in refusing to apply estoppel.

---

76 For a full discussion on the elements of estoppel and when it may be invoked, see Part 5, "Involuntary Termination," *infra*.

77 *B.A. Oil Company v Kos*, [1964] S.C.R. 167, 46 W.W.R. (N.S.) 141, 42 D.L.R. (2d) 426, [1963] S.C.J. No. 80 (S.C.C.).

78 [1974] 3 W.W.R. 522, 45 D.L.R. (3d) 123 (Alta. S.C.T.D.).

79 Ibid., at 543.

80 (1980), 12 Alta. L.R. (2d) 104, 13 R.P.R. 180, [1980] A.J. No. 593 (Alta. Prov. Ct.).

5 Formation of the Lease

Even if the lessee is blessed with a lessor having full capacity to contract, and successfully navigates the shoals of dower and homestead, the lease may yet founder. The negotiations and resulting documentation still must add up to a binding, enforceable agreement between the parties. In addition to its other attributes, the lease is an agreement and must pass all the tests that determine the existence of a valid contract.

Contract

There are as many definitions of contract as there are text writers. All, however, agree that a valid contract must have the following elements: (a) an intention to be bound – the parties must intend that their obligations each to the other are enforceable and that any failure to perform will involve legal consequences – there must be a binding offer, properly accepted; (b) a consideration or price to be paid for the promises or undertakings; (c) an understanding between the parties as to the subject matter of the contract.[1]

In the case of a lease it is not enough, however, that the arrangement between the parties includes all the foregoing ingredients. Because a lease is an interest in land, due respect also must be paid to the ancient canons of real property law.

---

1 See Beale, ed., *Chitty on Contracts*, 29th ed., vol. 1 (London: Sweet & Maxwell, 2004).

Statute of Frauds

In 1677 the Imperial Parliament passed an act "for prevention of many fraudulent practices commonly endeavored to be upheld by perjury and subornation of perjury." The *Statute of Frauds* sought to achieve this objective by providing that, with respect to certain classes of contracts, no action could be brought unless the agreement, or some memorandum or note thereof, was in writing. The *Statute of Frauds* contains four sections that relate to contracts involving land. Section 1 requires that where a contract makes or creates an interest of freehold or leasehold it must be in writing and signed by the parties or it will have the effect of a lease or estate at will. Section 4 provides that a contract or sale of land must be in writing and signed by the party to be charged.

An oil and gas lease would clearly fall under section 4 and thus require a note or memorandum to be signed by the party to be charged. It would also seem that an oil and gas lease could fall within section 1, which requires that the contract be signed by the parties, i.e., both the lessor and the lessee.

Despite its great age and several centuries of severe criticism, the Statute is alive and well in Canada. Some provinces have passed their own legislative version of it,[2] while in others it flourishes through the migration of English common and statutory law to the colonies.[3] The Statute does not purport to affect the validity of those contracts that are subject to it. It does, however, make them unavailable as grounds for an action unless they are in writing or there is some written memorandum of their terms. In the eyes of a litigant with an unenforceable contract, this may well appear to be a distinction without a difference.

Gordon v Connors[4] established that the Statute applies to oil and gas leases: "There is an additional reason, in my opinion, for refusing to regard the landmen's lease as part of the option. The contract is one that

---

2 *Statute of Frauds*, R.S.B.C. 1979, c 393; repealed by the *Law Reform Amendment Act, 1985*, S.B.C. 1985, c 10, s 8, and replaced by *Law and Equity Act*, R.S.B.C. 1996, c 253, s 54; *Statute of Frauds*, R.S.O. 1990, c S-19.

3 See Côté, "The Introduction of English Law into Alberta" (1962–64) 2–3 Alta. L. Rev. 262; "The Reception of English Law" (1977) 15 Alta. L. Rev. 29.

4 (1953), 8 W.W.R. (N.S.) 145, [1953] 2 D.L.R. 137 (Alta. C.A.); affirmed [1953] 2 S.C.R. 127, [1953] 4 D.L.R. 513. (The Supreme Court of Canada did not deal with the issue of the applicability of the *Statute of Frauds*.)

must be in writing under the *Statute of Frauds*."[5] In view of the express inclusion of interest in lands in the Statute, together with the judicial categorization of the lease, it is hard to conceive of any other result.

The courts have been generous in defining what comprises a note or memorandum, and undoubtedly this has avoided many hardships that otherwise would have been created by operation of the Statute. The memorandum will be enforced if it contains the essential particulars, namely, a description of the parties, the property, and the price.[6] The memorandum must, however, contain all the essential features; thus, where verbal evidence of a contract established that payment of a portion of the purchase price was to be deferred for a year, a written receipt that did not contain that term could not meet the statutory requirements.[7]

Canadian Williston Minerals Ltd. v Forseth and Imperial Oil Ltd.[8] is an example of how far the courts will reach, when so motivated by the equities, to find a memorandum that will satisfy the requirements of the Statute. This case was a follow-up to *Prudential Trust Co. v Forseth*,[9] where Forseth unsuccessfully attacked an agreement under which he was required to assign one-half of his mineral rights. Despite the judicial determination, he subsequently refused to assign the minerals or to account for the one-half share of the royalties accruing under the Imperial lease. The assignee sued for specific performance and the owner defended on the basis of the *Statute of Frauds*. There had been some earlier litigation in which Forseth sued one Benson, who had negotiated the assignment as agent of Prudential. The statement of claim in that action recited that an offer of $100.00 had been made to Forseth by Benson for an option to take a petroleum and natural gas lease, and that the offer had been accepted and the assignment completed. Additionally, in the action where the assignment was upheld by the Supreme Court, the statement of claim issued by Forseth embodied the full text of the assignment, together with the offer of $100.00 pursuant to which it was made. These pleadings were filed as

---

5 Ibid., Alta. C.A. at 153.

6 *Petroleum Engineering Company Limited v Clark and Elliott* (1952), 5 W.W.R. (N.S.) 119 (Sask. C.A.).

7 *Lesiuk v Schneider*, [1917] 2 W.W.R. 747, 36 D.L.R. 598 (Alta. S.C.T.D.).

8 (1962), 33 D.L.R. (2d) 72 (Sask. C.A.).

9 17 D.L.R. (2d) 341 (Sask. C.A.); affirmed, [1960] S.C.R. 210, 30 W.W.R. 241, 21 D.L.R. (2d) 507 S.C.J. No. 84: see discussion, *infra*.

exhibits and made part of the record in the subsequent case. Both the trial judge and the Saskatchewan Court of Appeal held that the pleadings provided a sufficient memorandum to meet the statutory requirements. The earlier statement of claim was "not to be viewed as a pleading but as a memorandum."

The judicial disposition to find that almost any sort of written note, receipt, or memorandum will satisfy the Statute can only go so far. There has to be at least something in writing and it must contain the essential terms. It is well known that a lease embodies numerous terms and involves many complicated points and issues that require agreement between the parties. Hence, the *Statute of Frauds* when applied to an oil and gas lease will prove difficult to satisfy with anything short of a fully detailed document signed by the lessor. In other words, the only note or memorandum that one can say with confidence will satisfy the Statute is an oil and gas lease itself.

Seal

Williams CJ, Manitoba Q.B., in *Langlois v Canadian Superior Oil*[10] in a passage that was clearly *obiter*, had this to say about the necessity of an oil and gas lease being executed under seal: "This decision [the *Berkheiser* case], and the decisions referred to therein, and the other cases I have read, justify me in saying that the document I have to construe – and I am here confining my remarks to a document in such terms – is not a lease but is a grant of a *profit à prendre* which is itself an interest in land and an incorporeal hereditament. As an incorporeal hereditament it can be created only by grant, that is by a document under seal" (parenthetical words added). This passage is *obiter* because the lease in question had in fact been executed under seal. *Obiter* or not, the statement is correct, and an oil and gas lease must be executed under seal. An oil and gas lease, being a *profit à prendre*, is an incorporeal hereditament, which under the common law requires a seal.[11] In addition to the common law there may also be a statutory requirement for a lease to be under seal. The *English Real Property Act*,[12] if in force in the applicable province, would also require that oil and gas rights be

---

10 (1957), 23 W.W.R. 401, 12 D.L.R. (2d) 53 (Man. C.A.).

11 Megarry, *A Manual of the Law of Real Property*, 8th ed. by Dakley (Toronto: Carswell, 2002), 399; *Mason v Clarke*, [1955] A.C. 778.

12 1845 (U.K.) c 106.

granted by a deed, i.e., a document under seal. There is some debate about whether or not the *English Real Property Act* was imported into the British North American colonies, although it was in existence prior to the reception dates of 1858 in the case of British Columbia and 1870 for the three prairie provinces.[13] In any event, the common law requirement is sufficient by itself to justify the statement that an oil and gas lease must be under seal.

Where a seal (corporate in this instance) is properly affixed to an agreement, no evidence of consideration is required.[14]

All may not be lost, however, for the lessee who finds himself with a lease that is not under seal. If there is no intervening equity, he may be in a position to obtain an order of specific performance requiring the lessor to affix a seal. A document not under seal cannot create a legal easement or profit, although if it is made for value, it may create a valid equitable profit. If an agreement for value is evidenced by either a written memorandum or by an act of part performance, the party may invoke the doctrine of equity that the grantor must be regarded as having already done what he ought to have done.[15] Despite the possibility of being able to force a lessor to subsequently affix his seal, the prudent lessee should always ensure that a seal is affixed to the document by the lessor.

Another avenue that may be open to a lessee who finds himself with a lease not under seal is to treat it as an option given for valuable

---

13 See *Horse and Carriage Inn Limited v Baron* (1975), 53 D.L.R. (3d) 426 (B.C.S.C.) where the court took the position that the proper date for determining whether a law was received is the present rather than 1858. The decision appears to turn on the fact that the B.C. *English Law Act* was worded in the present tense and that the *Interpretation Act* of B.C. requires an enactment to be construed as always speaking. The same argument is advanced by Côté in his two articles, *supra* n 3. However, the court in the *Horse and Carriage* case overlooked the fact that the English *Real Property Act* was printed with the Revised Statutes of B.C. 1897 and thus must have been adopted into that province. It is submitted that the more logical view is that the English Act was imported into the British North American colonies at the relevant dates and remains in force unless displaced by some subsequent inconsistent provincial legislation or judicial determination.

14 *Northwestern Utilities Limited v Peyto Oils Ltd.*, 49 A.R. 1, [1983] A.J. No. 987 (Alta. Q.B.); *Royal Bank v Miller*, [1979] 5 W.W.R. 220 (Alta. T.D.) It has also been held that the seal itself is the consideration: *Alberta (Director of Employment Standards) v Sanche* (1992), 2 Alta. L.R. (3d) 14, [1992] A.J. No. 206 (Alta. Q.B.).

15 *Frogley v Earl of Lovelace* (1859), Johns. 33, 70 E.R. 450; *Hubbs v Black* (1919), 46 D.L.R. 583, [1918] O.J. No. 48 (Ont. S.C., App.Div.); *Campbell, Wilson & Horne Co. Ltd. v Great West Saddlery Co. Ltd.* (1921), 16 Alta. L.R. 465, [1921] 2 W.W.R. 63, 59 D.L.R. 322 (Alta. S.C., App.Div.); Burn, ed. *Cheshire and Burn's Modern Law of Real Property*, 16th ed. (Markham, Ont.: Butterworths, 2000) at 583.

consideration. Such an option is irrevocable within the time specified for its acceptance. In *Vipond (D.M.) Co. Ltd. v Rustum Petroleums Ltd.*,[16] although the lease was stated to be under seal, no seal was attached to the document. The court found that there was valuable consideration in the form of a promise to pay the bonus consideration within twenty-five days. In order to become an enforceable contract the lessor's irrevocable offer would have to have been accepted by the lessee within the specified time. Unfortunately for the lessee, he did not make the payment within the twenty-five-day period and the lessor was entitled to treat the offer as having lapsed. While the court held there was no lease, it is clear that it would have found a valid lease if the bonus consideration had been timely made. But there still would have been no seal on the lease. Maybe the doctrine described in the preceding paragraph could be invoked or, more likely, the fact that the lease was stated to be under seal would have been held, as we shall see later, to have been sufficient to constitute a seal.

Time of Affixing Seal

The usual practice is to have a red wafer seal affixed to the lease prior to its execution by the lessor. The existence or significance of the seal may or may not be pointed out to the lessor by the agent. However, the mere fact that the seal was affixed prior to execution is sufficient under the test laid down in *Stromdale & Ball v Burdon*:[17] "If a party signs a document bearing wax or wafer or other indication of a seal, with the intention of executing the document as a deed, that is sufficient adoption or recognition of the seal to amount to due execution as a deed." A lessor certainly intends the lease to be a deed since it will invariably contain the phrase "SIGNED, SEALED AND DELIVERED" above the space where the lessor signs.

It sometimes happens, however, that the agent may not affix the seal until his return to his office. This is a very dangerous practice and may lead to the lease being declared invalid. In *Petro Canada Exploration Inc. v Tormac Transport Ltd., Torgerson and McConnell*[18] the document in question was not an oil and gas lease but a personal guarantee of a company's indebtedness. An employee of the plaintiff affixed red wafer seals beside the defendants' names after they had signed the

---

16 49 Alta. L.R. (2d) 135, [1987] 2 W.W.R. 57, [1986] A.J. No. 1145 (Alta. Q.B.).
17 [1951] 2 T.L.R. 1192.
18 [1983] 4 W.W.R. 205, 44 B.C.L.R. 220, [1983] B.C.J. No. 37 (B.C.S.C.).

document and without their authorization. The court held that this was an unauthorized alteration of the document that varied its legal force or effect as originally expressed and forever debarred the party responsible from enforcing any covenant contained in it. In the *Petro Canada* case the form of guarantee contained the words IF INDIVID- UAL DO NOT SEAL, which meant that the document was intended *not* to be under seal. The court applied the principle that the law will not assist a party who has placed the other party in jeopardy, to enforce a bargain, by unilateral alteration of the instrument by which the bar- gain was made.[19]

Since an oil and gas lease is clearly intended to be executed under seal, the principle of the *Petro Canada* case may not apply and a court might hold that the legal effect of the instrument as originally expressed, i.e., to be under seal, has not been unilaterally varied. While this argument may be open to the lessee, it is clearly imprudent for him to affix a seal opposite the lessor's name after the document has been executed and without authorization to do so.

What Constitutes a Seal

The requirement of a seal is a legal anachronism whose *raison d'être* has long since disappeared. Nevertheless, the requirement persists. The courts have responded by constantly whittling away at the formalities of the seal itself, a process that seems to be accelerating in recent years. The act of sealing a document is an ancient one dating back to the period before the ability to write became a common accomplishment. Originally a seal had to be of wax impressed on the document and bearing an impression sufficient to identify the owner. Now, however, no wax, wafer, or other adhesive substance is required; anything attached to the document, or a physical impression or perforation, may be a valid seal if the executing party intended to adopt it as such.[20]

---

19 *Johnson v Trobak*, [1977] 6 W.W.R. 289, 79 D.L.R. (3d) 684 (B.C.C.A.).
20 *Re Bell & Black* (1882), 1 O.R. 125, [1882] O.J. No. 105 (Ch.D); *Halsbury's Laws of England* 4th ed., vol. 12, para. 1325. See also review of authorities in *Sawyer & Massey Ltd. v Bouchard* (1910), 13 W.L.R. 394 (Alta. T.D.). See also *Re/Max Garden City Realty Inc. v 828294 Ontario Inc.* (1992), 8 O.R. (3d) 787, [1997] O.J. No. 1080 (Ont. Gen. Div.), where it was held that a black circle resembling a seal, and labelled "seal" was sufficient to be deemed a seal.

In *Bell & Black*[21] it was held that a circle made by a pen with the word "seal" written inside was sufficient. An impression upon a paper without wax or any other extraneous substance can be a seal.[22] The real test is whether the impression was made for the purpose of sealing and the essential requirement is that the party adopt whatever impression there may be as his seal. There is an indication in *Wulff v Oliver*[23] that the court might have been prepared to accept the signor placing his finger on the document if it could have been proved that he was aware of the significance of so doing.

The court also speculated that the testimonium clause, in the absence of evidence to the contrary, could be sufficient to presume the sealing of a contract. In other words, it creates a rebuttable presumption that the seal was affixed. This is of great significance in the case of oil and gas leases since, almost invariably, they will contain the words SIGNED, SEALED AND DELIVERED in bold, block letters above the place where the lessor signs.[24]

The trial judge in *Vipond (D.M.) Co. Ltd. v Rustum Petroleums Ltd.*[25] noted that the lease was not under seal, but did not expressly strike down the lease on that ground, although the lease was invalidated on other grounds.

While the absence of an incontestably valid seal may not be the "kiss of death" it once might have been, there is no doubt that the prudent course for the lessee is to make sure that a proper wafer seal is affixed to the lease before the lessor signs and that it is pointed out to him.

---

21 *Supra* n 20.

22 *Foster v Geddes* (1856), 14 U.C.Q.B. 239.

23 (1967), 61 W.W.R. 632, 65 D.L.R. (2d) 155 (B.C.S.C.).

24 In *Canadian Imperial Bank of Commerce v Dene Mat Construction Ltd.*, [1988] N.W.T.R. 174, [1988] 4 W.W.R. 344, [1988] N.W.T.J. No. 25 (N.W.T.S.C.) the court found that the words "Given Under Seal" were sufficient, because the court found that the parties had the requisite intention to execute the document under seal and the words were intended to be the seal.

In *Canadian Imperial Bank of Commerce v Kean* (1985), 55 Nfld. & P.E.I.R. 88, [1985] N.J. No. 210 (Nfld. S.C.T.D.), the document was expressed to be under seal and there was a testimonium that the document was under seal. The court found on this basis that the word "seal" was sufficient as there was no doubt that the parties intended the document to be a sealed instrument.

Both these cases go beyond the rebuttable presumption approach and hold that if the testimonium is there, the document will be treated as having been sealed.

25 *Supra* n 16.

This not only puts the status of the lease as a deed under seal beyond all question, but also makes the lessor's offer to lease irrevocable within the specified time.

It is of course possible that a court when faced with an oil and gas lease will prefer to apply the more conservative rebuttable presumption approach of *Wulff v Oliver*.[26] This may be because the practice of having oil and gas leases executed under seal is so well established and universal.

If the lease does not bear a seal opposite the lessor's signature, there are two possibilities: (a) the lease was never sealed, or (b) the seal has become detached from the document in the interval since its execution. Under these circumstances, what weight is to be given to the statement in the testimonium clause that the document was sealed? If the lessor testifies that there was no seal or impression when he signed, the presumption will be rebutted. Challenges to the validity of oil and gas leases frequently occur many years after the document was signed, and it may be impossible for the parties to recollect whether or not a seal was affixed at the critical time. If a court is faced with this evidentiary uncertainty, the presumption could be of great assistance to the lessee in maintaining the lease. Also relevant would be any evidence the lease agent might be able to give as to his standard practice in affixing seals.

Virtually all of the conventional leases, and all of the CAPL leases, have "seal" printed opposite the line where the lessor will sign. This is meant to indicate where the actual seal is to be placed. However, in the light of the *Re/Max* decision,[27] and the testimonium clause, this word alone would probably stand up in court. But affixing a wafer seal at or before the time the lessor signs puts the matter beyond doubt.

Delivery

Another ancient, but still surviving, formality is the requirement of delivery: "A conveyance, though signed and sealed, does not take effect until it is delivered."[28] Once again, the requirements have been whittled away, and today any act or words of the party which show

---

26 *Supra* n 23.

27 *Supra* n 20.

28 La Forest, *Anger and Honsberger Law of Real Property*, 3rd ed., vol. 2 (Toronto: Canada Law Book, 2006) at 25–50; *Styles v Wardle* (1825), 107 E.R. 1297 (K.B.); *Dillabaugh v McLeod* (1910), 16 W.L.R. 149 (Sask. T.D.).

that he intended to deliver the deed as an instrument binding on him is sufficient, even though he may not part with actual possession. The act of delivery should be relatively easy to establish under the circumstances of most oil and gas transactions since the lease is usually handed over by the lessor to the other party for execution. In addition, there is a recital in the testimonium clause that it has been delivered, and this should be sufficient even if the lessor retained the document in his own possession. Even oral communication of the execution of a document by counterpart could constitute delivery.[29]

Completion of the Contract

The precise legal status of the parties in the interregnum between execution by the lessor and receipt by him of a copy signed by the lessee is an intriguing question. There are several possibilities: (a) Is there a completed contract subject only to the deficiency that the lessor could not sue on it by reason of the *Statute of Frauds*? (b) Is the execution and delivery by the lessor merely an offer that must be accepted by the lessee before it becomes effective? (c) Does it, in effect, create an option that can be withdrawn by the lessor prior to acceptance?

One thing at least seems clear. Like any other contract, an oil and gas lease must include the element of an offer duly accepted. Sometimes there may be a question as to whether the offer emanates from the lessor when he signs the lease, or whether from the lessee when it offers to lease the rights for a specified consideration. Assuming for the moment that the offer is created when the lessor signs the lease and gives it to the lessee or its agent, then the normal rules of offer and acceptance apply. An offer, unless it is stated to be open for only a limited period, can be accepted at any time prior to revocation. There must be some overt act on the part of the offeree to indicate his acceptance; it is not enough that he has made up his mind to accept the offer; he has to do something that the law will treat as a communication for the acceptance to the other party. Sometimes the precise manner of communication is prescribed, but more often the parties are silent as to this point. The law has long ago decided, arbitrarily, but also on a balance of convenience, that, if the parties can be said to have contemplated the use of the mails

---

29 *Paddon Hughes Development Co. Ltd. v Pancontinental Oil Ltd.* (1992), 2 Alta. L.R. (3d) 343, [1992] 5 W.W.R. 106, [1992] A.J. No. 488 (Alta. Q.B.).

as a means of communication of the acceptance, then the acceptance is effective the moment it is mailed.[30] Such acceptance is effective even if the letter or other communication is delayed or lost and never received by the offeror.[31]

There remains the question as to whether the parties contemplated the use of the mails for communication of acceptance. If the offer itself had been mailed, there could be no question that they so intended. When it comes to a lease, however, it is quite common for it to be handed personally from the lessor to the lessee or its agent. Even under these circumstances, mailing of an executed copy of the lease by the lessee should be good communication of acceptance since, according to ordinary commercial usage, the lessee could reasonably be expected to return an executed copy through the mails.[32]

On the other hand, the offeror who wishes to withdraw his offer cannot rely on the mere act of mailing. The revocation must be actually communicated to the offeree before it becomes effective. If acceptance of the offer has been mailed by the offeree, a completed copy of the lease mailed by the lessee prior to actual receipt of the withdrawal, the contract is complete and the cancellation is ineffective.[33] Withdrawal of an offer by a lessor is further complicated by the fact that he will have signed the lease under seal, which may create an offer irrevocable for a reasonable time, although under the circumstances of the oil industry a reasonable time could be very brief.

The courts have, on several occasions, pondered the status of parties to a lease signed by the lessor but not yet signed by the lessee. The

---

30 *Adams v Lindsell* (1818), 1 B. & Ald. 681, 106 E.R. 250 (K.B.). See Waddams, *The Law of Contracts*, 5th ed. (Toronto: Canada Law Book, 2005) at paras. 98–111 for a discussion of some of the complications arising from this "post box" rule.

31 *Household Fire Insurance Co. v Grant* (1879), 4 Ex. D. 216.

32 *Henthorn v Frazer*, [1892] 1 Ch. 27. There may be some instances where the facts indicate that the parties did not intend the mails to be used; see *Public Trustee of Alberta v Bottoms*, (1960), 33 W.W.R. 427 (Alta. S.C.) where the court found on a construction of the option that the parties intended that the acceptance of an offer was to be delivered, and see also the discussion of *Paddon Hughes Development Co. v Pancontinental Oil Ltd.*, 33 Alta. L.R. (3d) 7, [1995] 10 W.W.R. 656, [1995] A.J. No. 811 (Alta. Q.B.); affirmed 67 Alta. L.R. (3d) 104, [1999] 5 W.W.R. 726, 223 A.R. 180, [1998] A.J. No. 1120 (Alta. C.A.); [1998] S.C.C.A. No. 600 (leave to appeal dismissed), in the section dealing with delay rentals, *infra*. Both the trial and appellate courts found that the parties contemplated the use of mails.

33 Furmston, *Cheshire, Fifoot & Furmston's Law of Contract*, 14th ed. (Toronto: Butterworths, 2001) at 63; *Cochrane v McKay* (1921), 54 N.S.R. 514, 61 D.L.R. 338 (N.S.S.C).

results undoubtedly depend to a very great extent on the individual fact patterns; nonetheless, there are some useful guidelines to be found.

Option

The ordinary circumstances of a typical lease acquisition do not lend themselves to the concept of an option. It sometimes happens, however, that for one reason or another the lessee desires to tie up the lands for a period of time without committing itself to the expenditure of a substantial bonus consideration. If the documentation properly reflects this position, then the relationship will be treated as one of optionor and optionee. On the other hand, the negotiations may be such that they may alter the nature of a document that on its face purports to be an option.

In *Canadian General Associates Ltd. v Fedor*[34] the documentation consisted of a typewritten portion with a printed form of lease attached to it. Originally the typewritten part was entitled "Option to Lease," but the word "Option" was struck out because the lessor stated he wanted a deal, not an option. The court paid careful attention to all of the circumstances surrounding the actual negotiations. The document was signed by the lessor after a discussion of about one and a half hours at which the president of the lessee company was present, as well as other witnesses who also testified. Despite the deletion of the reference to "Option," there remained language in the instrument that was consistent only with an option. For example, the operative words were: "Do hereby offer to lease," and there were two other clauses that were cast in terms of an option. They related to the manner in which the offer could be accepted and the period for which it remained open, together with a right of extension.

> $1,900.00 cash upon completion and return of papers from Calgary, $2,000.00 cash if and when No. 3 Imperial well is declared a producer, $10,000.00 cash upon the first producing well obtained on the above lease, 8 per cent royalty on each well thereafter drilled on the NE ¼ Section 19, Township 51, Range 25, W.4th and continuous drilling until such time as the property is drilled out. I, J. F. Anderson, to return from Calgary not later than Monday, May 12th, 1947.

---

34 [1948] A.J. No. 10, [1948] 2 W.W.R. 287 (Alta. S.C.T.D.).

The lessor contended that the document was an option only and that the limit of time fixed for payment of the $1,900.00 was 12 May 1947, when Anderson, the president of the lessee company, would return from Calgary. Since the required payment of $1,900.00 was not made by that date, he argued that the option had lapsed.

The evidence as to the meeting revealed that the document was discussed clause by clause, with both parties agreeing on each clause as they proceeded. The sum of $100.00 was given to the lessor as a deposit at the time the agreement was signed, and the $1,900.00 referred to in the above clause represented the remaining balance of the initial $2,000.00 payment. It had been agreed between the parties that the lessor, who was purchasing the land under an agreement for sale, would produce a copy of it for inspection by the lessee's solicitors and that the $1,900.00 would be paid upon approval of this document. The lessor, who obviously repented of his bargain, refused to produce a copy of the agreement and the court found this refusal to be deliberate.

When it became apparent to the lessee company that the lessor would not cooperate in producing the document, it left two cheques, one for $1,900.00 and a further one in the sum of $2,000.00 payable because the Imperial well was a producer, with the lessor's agent. This was done on 6 June, long after the expiration of the 12 May date referred to in the typewritten portion. Under all these conditions, the court found:

> I am unable to construe the document as granting an option only to lease the oil and gas rights on this land for the consideration of $100.00. The lessee did not merely purchase the right to obtain a lease. It undertook, if my interpretation of the meaning of the words quoted is sound, to pay definite sums of money for the lease, the terms of which are set out therein. In my opinion, it was intended to be a lease operative from its date, with the initial cash payment of $2,000.00, divided into $100.00 deposit, and the balance of $1,900.00 deferred for such time as was considered sufficient for the title of the defendant Fedor to be inquired into and passed upon by the solicitor for the plaintiff at Calgary. [Wording rearranged to correct obvious printing error in original report.]

It should be noted that both parties had signed the document. The sole issue was whether the document amounted to a mere option or a valid and binding lease. The court held it was the latter and that it was not defeated by any delay in making the required payments since this was occasioned by the deliberate act of the lessor.

The fact that both parties had signed the document was also the deciding factor in *Paddon-Hughes Development Co. v Pancontinental Oil Ltd*.[35] The oil company lessee had an option to acquire a lease that expired on 17 August 1984. The lessee purported to exercise the option on 20 August and sent a letter to the lessors stating that the acceptance would be retroactive to 17 August and enclosing the specified consideration. The lessors accepted the exercise of the option by signing the letter agreement on 28 August 1984 and accepting the consideration.

Rooke J held that there was a valid lease effective 17 August 1984. He based this on the fact that the lessors had accepted the exercise of the option by signing the letter agreement and accepting the consideration. It was immaterial whether the transaction was characterized as a delayed exercise of an option or a bilateral agreement creating a new lease. It should be noted that there were no intervening third party interests.[36]

Offer

A lease signed by a lessor, but not the lessee, has been characterized by the Saskatchewan Court of Appeal as an offer under seal. The facts in *McAlester Canadian Oil Company v Petroleum Engineering Company Ltd*.[37] were quite typical of the oil industry. During January 1956 a landman employed by the lessee company contacted a representative of the company that owned the minerals. The lessee had its offices in the United States and its landman was not authorized to make binding commitments on its behalf. The negotiations between the agent and the representative of the lessor company led to a lease being signed by the lessor company under seal. It was dated 11 January 1956, and together with a certificate of title and a certified copy of a caveat filed on the property, was delivered to solicitors for the lessee. These documents were immediately forwarded to the head office of the lessee in the United States where it was signed by the lessee on 2 February 1956, but was retained

---

35 *Supra* n 29. This was the second of three cases involving the same parties and the same spacing unit. This case also involved a pooling issue and will be discussed under that heading as well.

36 In this connection see *Pan American Petroleum Corporation v Potapchuk and Scurry-Rainbow Oils Limited* (1964), 46 W.W.R. 237 (Alta. Q.B.); affirmed, 51 W.W.R. 700, [1964] A.J. No. 11 (C.A.); affirmed 51 W.W.R. 767 (S.C.C.), which will be discussed under the heading "Top Lease" (Chapter 13).

37 (1958), 25 W.W.R. 26, 13 D.L.R. (2d) 724 (Sask. C.A.).

in its possession. On 8 February 1956, the lessor's solicitors withdrew the offer to "sell" the mineral rights and asked for return of the documents. At this point there had been no indication from the lessee that the offer had been accepted. On the next day the completed lease was received by the lessee's solicitors in Regina, who prepared and filed a caveat against the land. On 21 February they wrote the lessor's solicitors stating that the title had been approved and they had requisitioned a cheque to cover the bonus payment. This cheque was duly tendered on 29 February but was refused by the lessor.

There are two things that should be noted in this case: (a) the landman had no power to bind his employer; (b) the fact that the lessee had executed the lease was not "communicated" to the lessor, by mailing or otherwise, before the offer was withdrawn. The lessee contended that, since the document had been sealed, it could not be revoked. This contention was defeated by the Supreme Court of Canada decision in *Davidson v Norstrant*,[38] in which Idington J said:

> I agree that a unilateral offer of an option without consideration can be revoked at any time, unless under seal as this contract was.

> I am of the opinion that if the offer is made under seal and not accepted it may be withdrawn within a reasonable time and that the measure of such time might under certain circumstances be very brief indeed.

> I am further of opinion that, if there is no other consideration than mutual promises, an agreement for an option without seal may be enforceable.

On the question of what was a reasonable time, the court in *McAlester* cited *Barrick v Clark*,[39] which held that an offer to sell farmland, not containing a definite time limit, dated 15 November had expired prior to a purported acceptance made on 10 December. The Saskatchewan Court of Appeal emphasized that the value of oil and gas rights fluctuates very rapidly, "at any rate, far more rapidly than farmlands which were offered for sale in the *Clark* case."[40] An offer, even under seal, can be withdrawn after it has been in force for a reasonable time, before acceptance by the lessee.

---

38 (1921), 61 S.C.R. 493, [1921] 1 W.W.R. 993, 57 D.L.R. 377 (S.C.C.).
39 [1951] S.C.R. 177, [1950] 4 D.L.R. 529 (S.C.C.).
40 *Supra* n 37, at 30.

The power, or lack of it, of the agent to bind the lessee can be of decisive importance. In *Sial Explorations Ltd. v Leask*[41] the Alberta Appellate
Division indicated in the course of argument that the signing of a lease
by the lessor may be the acceptance of an offer made by the lessee. In
this case there had been considerable negotiation as to the price per
acre to be paid prior to the meeting that resulted in the execution of the
lease by the lessor. The land agent had been expressly authorized to
make a binding commitment in this regard. Under these circumstances
the court was inclined to treat the lease as having been completed
when signed by the lessor subject only to the fact that the lessor could
not have sued upon it since it did not comply with the *Statute of Frauds.*

In the event, however, the court held that the lease had not come into
force because the lessee had not paid the bonus consideration within
the stipulated forty-five days.

The *Sial* case was followed in *Vipond (D.M.) Co. Ltd. v Rustum Petroleums Ltd.*[42] This was another case involving the status of a lease signed
by the lessor but not accepted and paid for by the lessee within the
stipulated time.

The mineral owner, Wieloch, signed a petroleum and natural gas lease
in favour of Vipond on 25 November 1983. (The mineral owner could not
write in English, which led the defendant who was attacking the lease to
argue *non est factum.* Virtue J held that the mineral owner had sufficient
knowledge of the language and sufficient dealings previously with oil
and gas leases so that she understood what it was that she was signing.
The onus was on the defendant to establish *non est factum* by showing
that the document signed was of a different class or character than that
which she thought she was signing. The court held that the mineral
owner knew she was signing an oil and gas lease and that she was aware
of its essential terms, and dismissed the claim of *non est factum.*)

When the mineral owner signed the Vipond lease on 25 November
1983, the landman left with her an unusual document in the form of a
promissory note for $602.25, but which was unsigned. In the place pro-
vided for signature, the words "payable within 25 days" were inserted.
The court concluded that this document was the plaintiff's promise to
pay the bonus consideration within 25 days of 25 November 1983.
Although the lease was stated to be under seal, no seal was affixed to
the document.

---

41 [1971] 4 W.W.R. 654 (Alta. S.C., App.Div.).
42 49 Alta. L.R. (2d) 135, [1987] 2 W.W.R. 570, [1986] A.J. No. 1145 (Alta. Q.B.).

Nothing further happened until 28 December 1983 when the plaintiff Vipond received from the lessor the document described as a promissory note which she sent to the plaintiff for payment. The plaintiff, however, did not pay the lessor nor send her an executed copy of the lease. On 27 March 1984, Vipond received a letter written on 15 March for the mineral owner by her daughter in which she advised that she had not received the payment of the lease she signed a few months ago and that she had submitted the promissory note in January and requested "Please advise."

Vipond did nothing about this letter until 26 April 1984, when it mailed to the depository bank specified in the lease a copy of the lease signed by Vipond and a cheque for $602.25 as bonus consideration. The plaintiff did not take any steps to notify Wieloch of what it had done.

On 19 April 1984, five days before the plaintiff mailed its cheque to the depository bank, Wieloch, the mineral owner, signed a petroleum and natural gas lease for the same property in favour of the defendant, Rustum.

The trial judge held that the petroleum and natural gas lease signed by the mineral owner on 25 November 1983 constituted nothing more than an offer to lease on the terms contained in the document. Had the lease been under seal it would have been an irrevocable offer within the time specified for payment. Despite the absence of the seal, Vipond's promise to pay a bonus for signing constituted consideration and thus the offer was irrevocable within the time limited for acceptance. Payment not having been made within that time, the mineral owner was entitled to treat the offer as having lapsed. The act of the plaintiff in mailing its bonus cheque and a signed copy of the lease to the depository bank on 26 April 1984 was not, in the eyes of the court, a valid acceptance of the offer. That would have been the end of the matter except for the 15 March 1984 letter from the mineral owner, which was received by Vipond on 27 March 1984. Virtue J held that this letter constituted a renewal of the original offer and pointed out that there was no new consideration for that new offer and it was a simple offer to lease, revocable by the defendant Wieloch at any time before acceptance and open for acceptance by the plaintiff, if not revoked, for a reasonable length of time. The finding that the new offer was open for acceptance, but only for a reasonable length of time, was crucial to the decision since the mineral owner did not specifically revoke the offer.

Having heard nothing from Vipond in response to her letter of 15 March 1984, Wieloch concluded that the plaintiff had no further interest in her property when she was approached to lease her petroleum and natural gas rights by the defendant Rustum, on 19 April 1984.

The court concluded that not having heard from the plaintiff, despite the passage of over four weeks from the date of the letter, she was entitled to deal with Rustum because her renewal offer had lapsed.

Death of Lessor Prior to Acceptance

What is the contractual state of affairs if the lessor, having signed a lease, dies before it is accepted by the lessee? Death by itself would not act as a revocation of the offer since the contract is not personal, such as a contract to appear at a concert or write a book where, for obvious reasons, the death of the offeror automatically terminates the matter.[43] Moreover, the granting of a lease can be satisfied out of the lessor's estate. It would appear, therefore, that the lessee can validly accept a lease after the death of the lessor, at least until he has knowledge that it has occurred.

Formal notice by the lessor's representative acts as a revocation and the lessee cannot unilaterally accept the lease after being so notified.[44] The situation where the lessee may have knowledge of the death but may not have been officially notified of it appears to be an open question.[45] There are a number of factors that would seem to favour the view that knowledge, informally acquired, should not act as a revocation. Actual knowledge, or the lack thereof, might be very difficult to prove; the offer to grant a lease is not personal in nature, and readily can be satisfied out of the estate. The fact that a lease may have been sealed does not appear to change the situation; the *McAlester* decision[46] makes it clear that an oil and gas lease signed and sealed by the lessor can be withdrawn on short notice.

Consideration and Payment as a Condition Precedent

A lease may be executed and delivered subject to certain conditions that do not appear on its face but are embodied in a collateral instrument or by verbal understanding. These conditions most often refer to the mode of payment, but they may deal with other matters such as the verification of title.

---

43 *Supra* Waddams n 30 at para. 116.
44 Ibid.
45 *Halsbury's Laws of England,* 4th ed., vol. 9, para. 243.
46 *Supra* n 37.

In *California Standard Co. v McBride*[47] the lease had been executed by both parties and contemporaneously they had also signed a receipt. The lease specified a bonus consideration of $16,000.00, while the receipt acknowledged payment of $5.00 and an agreement that the balance was to be paid upon the company's solicitors being satisfied as to title. It turned out that there was a defect in the lessor's title, which required some curative documentation from both the Crown and an intervening transferor. The lessee, faced with this defect, and a demand by the lessor for the balance of the bonus monies, deposited $15,995.00 with the depository bank pending correction of the title. The lessor did not cure the defect until nearly two years after the lease had been executed. In the meantime he served notice upon the lessee requiring it to either remove the caveat or commence proceedings. As soon as the lessee was advised by its solicitors that the lessor's title was in order, it notified the bank to release the bonus consideration, but the lessor refused to accept it. The lessor argued against the validity of the lease on the basis that the proper payment of the bonus money was a condition precedent. The receipt, however, was admitted to prove that payment within any given period of time was not meant to be a condition precedent to the lease, but had been expressly postponed until the title was examined and the lessee's solicitors were satisfied with it. Since the receipt would be fatal to the lessor's position, it was attacked on a variety of grounds, including one that its language was so vague and uncertain as to be meaningless and ineffective. It required the solicitors to be satisfied with title and, since this was a purely subjective test, they could grant or withhold their satisfaction capriciously. The court rejected this and declared that once the lessor had produced a good and valid title the lessee could have been compelled to pay the balance of the purchase price. A claim that its solicitors were not yet satisfied would not have been a valid defence for payment. This statement can have a wide application since many deals in the oil industry are made subject to title approval. Clearly, the court is prepared to substitute its judgment as to title for that of a solicitor where the latter may attempt to withhold approval on unjustifiable grounds. As the court pointed out, the lessor was not in a very good position to complain about the lessee's delay in making payment since it had been occasioned by the former's lackadaisical approach to perfecting his title.

---

47 (1963), 38 D.L.R. (2d) 606 (Alta. S.C., App.Div.).

When a lessor signs the lease it will contain a typewritten insert of the amount of the bonus consideration, followed by a printed parenthetical phrase, "the receipt whereof is hereby acknowledged." Only under the most unusual circumstances will the lessor have actually received payment at the time he signed and delivered the lease. At most, he might have received a token sum as a deposit or down payment. The payment of the real consideration is almost invariably postponed until both title approval and registration of the lease or a caveat. The mode of payment will be covered in a very informal manner and very seldom reduced to writing. There are primarily two situations: (a) the parties may agree that payment will be made in any event by a certain date, or (b) the payment may be postponed until title approval and registration, with no definite time limit.

The recital in the lease that payment has been received is not a bar to the admission of evidence to establish that in fact no payment has been made.[48] The courts are also disposed to treat payment of the purchase price, or bonus consideration, as a condition precedent, which means that, unless the condition is performed, the agreement has no force and effect. If it is determined that the parties have agreed upon a definite time period within which payment is to be made, as described in (a) above, failure of a timely payment appears to be fatal. If the court construes the agreement as requiring payment by a certain date, then no enforceable agreement is created in the absence of such payment. Nor would there seem to be any requirement on the part of the lessor to formally demand payment; he is entitled to treat the agreement as having come to an end.[49]

If the lease contains the usual acknowledgment of receipt and no payment has in fact been made, the lessor, in the absence of any collateral agreement, can immediately terminate the lease on the ground that the condition precedent has not been fulfilled. The recital of receipt has the effect of making payment a condition precedent: "The parties do not, it is true, in formal terms provide that the payment of that sum is to be a condition; but the intention that it should be so is manifested by the frame of the agreement as a whole, the stipulations of which pre-suppose that this payment has already been made and

---

48 *Cushing v Knight* (1912), 46 S.C.R. 555, 2 W.W.R. 704, 6 D.L.R. 820 (S.C.C.).
49 *Sial v Leask, supra* n 41.

shew unmistakably that it is upon the basis of this assumed state of facts that the parties are contracting."[50] The lessor may be required to demand payment and give the lessee an opportunity to pay before he is entitled to terminate the lease. In *Cushing v Knight*, which involved an agreement for the sale of land, the vendor gave the respondents four days within which to make payment. One of the Supreme Court judges notes that fact in his judgment but seems to treat it as merely adding weight to the termination of the contract, the main thrust of the case being that developed in the above passage, namely, that the contract required payment of the specified sum before it became enforceable.

The position of a lessee where there has been some agreement or understanding that payment would be postponed until title approval and registration was illustrated in *Davidson v Norstrant*.[51] This case, which culminated in a fragmented decision in the Supreme Court, involved an option to acquire an undivided half-interest in certain lands. The option agreement was under seal and recited a consideration of $100.00 "now paid." In fact, the $100.00 was neither paid nor demanded. The evidence, which was purely oral, established that both parties agreed the option was not to become operative unless and until the optionee, who was the agent for the owners, had disclosed his position to them and obtained their consent to his becoming a part purchaser. This led the court to conclude that the signed option was merely tentative, depending for its coming into effect upon the agent obtaining the consent of his principals. The court treated the non-payment of the $100.00 as not being fatal to the agreement. The transaction was not "closed" unless the necessary consent was obtained and, when it was obtained, there was no unreasonable delay on the optionee's part in tendering the money.

The element of demand and refusal was introduced by Idington J, who took the view that an option could not be revoked unless and until the offeror has demanded payment and been refused. None of the other members of the court dealt with this point. The *Davidson* case contains elements that do not appear in the lease situation, mainly that

---

50 *Supra* n 48, S.C.R. at 561, Duff J.
51 *Supra* n 38.

the $100.00 consideration was purely nominal when compared to the purchase price of the property whereas the initial bonus consideration normally will be the entire purchase price of the oil and gas lease. This feature, plus the fact that all five judges who sat on the case wrote individual judgments – including two dissents – encompassing a wide variety of points, undermines the effectiveness of the *Davidson* decision as an authority. It may, however, be held to apply where payment of the bonus consideration has been verbally agreed to be postponed pending title approval, and it does appear to reinforce the element of demand and refusal as a necessary ingredient prior to termination.

Both the circumstances of the industry, where the courts are prepared to take judicial notice of the rapid fluctuations in value, and the wording of the lease that expressly acknowledges receipt of the bonus consideration make it virtually certain that payment of the purchase price will be treated as a condition precedent.[52]

The parol, or extrinsic, evidence rule continues to be a troubling possibility in this area. The rule deals with the admissibility of evidence and may be paraphrased: if a transaction has been put in writing, extrinsic evidence is, in general, inadmissible to *contradict, vary, add to, or subtract from* the written terms. The rationale underlying the rule is that, when the parties have deliberately put their agreement into writing, it should be conclusively presumed between themselves that they intended the writing to form a full and final statement of their intentions.[53] Although the evidence excluded by the rule is usually of the

---

52 If it were to be treated otherwise and regarded merely as a condition subsequent, there is no doubt that a lessor wishing to terminate the lease would be required to give notice to the lessee allowing a period of time within which to make payment. In *Sim v Jenkins* (1951), 4 W.W.R. (N.S.) 352, [1951] A.J. No. 6 (Alta. S.C., App.Div.) the agreement involved the purchase of royalty "points" for a stated sum, a small down payment being made at the time the agreement was entered into. The agreement did not specify any fixed date for the payment of the balance. Time was not expressed to be of the essence and the court held that there was nothing in the circumstances surrounding the transaction that would make it so. It is clear that in the view of the court there would have to be notice from the vendor making time of the essence, i.e., specifying a time within which payment must be made, before he could terminate the agreement for failure to pay. The purchaser in fact tendered the balance within two weeks following the execution of the agreement and prior to any notice of any alleged default in payment.

53 See Howard, Crane, & Hochberg, eds., *Phipson on Evidence*, 16th ed. (London: Sweet & Maxwell, 2005) at para. 42-01.

parol or oral type, even written materials will be excluded if they are found to be extraneous to the document under review. There are several exceptions to the exclusionary rule. Parol evidence is admissible to contradict the purported receipt of money.[54] It now appears established that oral evidence may also be admissible to explain the circumstances under which payment is to be made.[55]

The practice surrounding the determination of the lessee's obligation to pay the bonus consideration under a lease is notoriously loose. The document speaks as though the payment had actually been made, which can be contradicted by extrinsic evidence, and there is seldom any firm agreement on the time within which the payment must be made. The entire area of bonus payment is uncertain and confusing. Commonly employed procedures are subject to the vagaries of the parol evidence rule, reliance on evidence, which is generally vague and inconclusive, the uncertainties of what the court may consider to be a reasonable time, and whether or not prior notice is required before the lessor is free to treat the lease as at an end.

The CAPL 88 and 91 leases provide for payment of $10.00, the receipt of which is acknowledged by the lessor, at the time of the lessor executing the lease and of an additional consideration of ... dollars to be paid within ... days of the date hereof. The additional consideration will be much greater than the trifling sum of $10.00 and constitutes the "real" consideration for granting the lease. What is the situation where the $10.00 has been paid to and accepted by the lessor but the additional consideration is not paid within the specified time?

The answer would seem to be that the courts would treat the timely payment of the additional consideration as a condition precedent to the lease coming into effect. In the context of an oil and gas lease, it is not likely that the initial $10.00 payment would satisfy the condition. It could be argued that the courts will not look into the adequacy of

---

54 Parol evidence has always been permitted to contradict a receipt, and there are numerous authorities to this effect; see, for example, those quoted in Phipson. For our purposes it is not necessary to go beyond *Cushing v Knight, supra* n 48, wherein evidence was admitted to show that the payment had not in fact been made although the agreement said, "the receipt of which is hereby acknowledged."

55 *Davidson v Norstrant, supra* n 38. See also *Long v Smith*, 23 O.L.R. 121, [1911] O.J. No. 111 (Ont. Div. Ct.) where oral evidence as to a condition precedent of the contract was admitted.

consideration,[56] and thus the $10.00 payment should be sufficient. However, the parties to the lease clearly contemplated the payment of the entire consideration to be a condition of the lease, which would influence the courts to treat such payment as a condition precedent.

Since the condition precedent had not been met, the lease would not have come into effect, and the delinquent lessee could not rely on its provisions, notably the default clause with its period of grace, to assist him.

The effect of the $10.00 payment would bind the lessor not to deal further with the lands until the deadline for the payment of the additional consideration has passed. The same result would be achieved if the lessor had signed the lease under seal.

CAPL 99 provides for a payment of $10.00 but also contains a separate clause dealing with the payment of the "real" consideration. It specifically provides that if payment is not made by the specified date, the lease will terminate. Furthermore, unless there is a deficiency in the lessor's title, the lessee remains liable to make the payment despite the termination of the lease. Operations under the lease cannot be commenced until the payment has been made. This clause is treated in somewhat more detail in Chapter 4.

Title

The lessor's title to the minerals is the other condition precedent commonly encountered in lease negotiations. It is normally imposed by the lessee, who makes the entire deal contingent upon title. In *California Standard Company v Chiswell*,[57] however, it was the lessor who insisted on it. The defendants were the registered owners of both surface and

---

56 Fridman, *The Law of Contract in Canada*, 5th ed. (Toronto: Carswell, 2006) at 91: "The courts do not inquire as to the adequacy or inadequacy of the consideration; they leave the parties to form their own judgment as to this and to make their own bargain. This is one, and a very important aspect of the common law doctrine of freedom of contract ... There may be a general equitable jurisdiction to upset a contract for inadequate consideration, but such inadequacy will not vitiate a contract unless it is such that it indicates a strongly unconscientious transaction or one involving fraud." See also *Chitty on Contracts*, 29th ed. (London: Sweet & Maxwell, 2004) at para. 3-014: "Courts generally will not judge adequacy. Under the doctrine of consideration, a promise has no contractual force unless *some* value has been given for it. But as a general rule the courts do not concern themselves with the question whether 'adequate' value has been given, or whether the agreement is harsh or one-sided."

57 (1955), 14 W.W.R. (N.S.) 456, [1955] 5 D.L.R. 119 (Alta. S.C.T.D.).

minerals of a certain tract of land, which they had sold under an agreement for sale. The purchaser had not troubled to register a caveat to protect his position and the payments were in arrears. The defendants had begun an action for foreclosure, which resulted in an arrangement between themselves and the purchaser under which he had made some additional payments but not enough to put them on a current basis. The defendants executed an oil and gas lease covering the lands, and at their request the lessee's agent prepared another document that was signed at the same time. This referred to the lease and postponed the payment of the bonus consideration until the successful completion of the foreclosure proceedings. It also contained a statement that the lessee recognized that the lessors were granting only such interest as they themselves had. At about the same time the purchaser granted a lease to another oil company. The cash bonus was substantial enough to pay off the entire amount remaining under the agreement for sale, and it was to be held in trust until the purchaser obtained title by paying his obligations.

When the purchaser became aware of the prior lease, his solicitor made enquiries of the defendant's solicitors and was assured that he was protected in this regard because of the collateral document. The lessee under the first lease attempted to exclude this collateral agreement on both the parol evidence rule and a clause in the lease itself to the effect that the lease constituted the whole of the agreement between the parties. The court held that neither the exclusionary clause nor the parol evidence rule could operate to prevent the collateral agreement being admitted as evidence. Since it was clear that the lease was to come into effect only if and when the condition was satisfied, namely, the successful completion of the foreclosure proceedings, the exclusionary clause could not have any vitality. It was in a state of suspended animation until the agreement became effective. Similarly, extrinsic evidence that indicated the lease was a conditional one could not be excluded under the operation of the parol evidence rule because the prohibition against contradicting a written document can apply only to one that is fully effective.

CAPL 88 and 91 eliminate this uncertainty by providing a specified time within which the payment must be made. Not unexpectedly, the lessee will often insert a lengthy period, frequently 120 days, within which he can make payment. While this may be to the advantage of the lessee, it can unnecessarily delay the lessor's receipt of the bonus money. The purpose of delaying the payment of the bonus is to allow the lessee time to execute the lease, check the lessor's title, and register his interest. Normally this can be accomplished in a reasonably short time, say thirty to forty-five days, and the lessor should be entitled to the benefit of such shorter period. Only when there is a known defect in the lessor's title requiring remedial work should the period be longer.

CAPL 88 and 91 do not expressly make the lessor's mineral title a condition precedent to the lease. The same result is achieved by delaying the time within which the bonus consideration must be paid, thereby allowing the lessee time to check the title before paying out serious money.

The payment of the consideration clause in CAPL 99 has been substantially changed. It was fully described in preceding pages.

Sufficiency of Terms

It is not enough for the parties to properly complete all the formalities of a contract; there must also be a clear understanding of what are the terms of the contract. The minds of the parties must not only meet, but they must do so with sufficient precision to constitute an enforceable agreement.

In the Alberta case of *Falcon Exploration Limited v Gunderson*[58] negotiations between the parties resulted in an exchange of telegrams, which commenced with an offer from the plaintiff oil company as follows: "Reyurlet May thirty first fifty six we hereby offer twelve thousand dollars consideration for a standard ten year lease offer open until midnight June fifth nineteen fifty six please confirm by wire." In reply the defendant lessor wired on 5 June: "Retel June first 56 I accept offer of twelve thousand dollars for standard ten year petroleum and natural gas lease of Section eight Township nineteen Range 29 West of the Fourth Meridian subject to reservation to McIrvine and reduction of acreage as described in Certificate of Title 102R65 with twelve and one half per cent gross royalty reserved and annual rental of six hundred and forty dollars." After this the plaintiff wrote a letter on 7 June to the defendant in which were enclosed partially completed forms for execution and which stated: "This is our approved standard lease form and you will note that the terms are as agreed upon, namely: The sum of twelve thousand ($12,000.00) dollars, as consideration, the sum of

---

58 (1958), 25 W.W.R. (N.S.) 416, [1958] A.J. No. 12 (Alta. S.C.T.D.).

six hundred and forty ($640.00) dollars as annual delay rental, and twelve and one-half per cent (12½%) gross royalty reserved to the lessors," and added: "It will be necessary for the beneficiaries of the estate to give their consent to the lease and there are several forms included for execution on their behalf." The letter also enclosed 10 per cent of the consideration, although there had been no previous mention of a deposit.

The two telegrams amounted to an offer and acceptance in the clearest possible terms. Nonetheless, the oil company was unsuccessful in its attempt to have the documentation declared a binding lease. One of the grounds relied upon by the court in holding that there was not an enforceable agreement was that there were not sufficient terms agreed upon to constitute an agreement for a lease.

The telegrams and the plaintiff's letter covered a good many features of the proposed arrangement, namely, the initial consideration to be paid, and that it was a "standard ten year lease" embodying a 12½ per cent gross royalty and an annual rental of $640.00. The defendant introduced expert testimony at the trial to establish that there were many other important matters that must form part of the lease agreement, such as a pooling clause, a drilling commitment, and an offset drilling provision. The expert also testified that the industry did not have something that would represent "a standard petroleum and natural gas lease."

The trial judge found, "because of these features, that there had not been sufficient essential terms agreed upon between the parties, even if there had been agreement upon some of the terms usually found in leases, to constitute a binding agreement to grant a lease."

The law concerning sufficiency of terms has been summarized for conventional real estate leases as follows: "To be valid, an agreement for a lease must show (1) the parties, (2) a description of the premises to be demised, (3) the commencement and (4) duration of the term, (5) the rent, if any, and (6) all the material terms of the contract not being matters incident to the relation of the landlord and tenant, including any covenants or conditions, exceptions or reservations."[59] Despite this summary of the necessary ingredients, it is difficult to predict just when any particular court will be satisfied that documentation, which falls short of a properly executed and completed lease, should be treated as constituting a lease.

---

59 Bentley, McNair, & Butkus, eds. *William and Rhodes, Canadian Law of Landlord and Tenant*, 6th ed. (Toronto: Carswell, 1988) at §3:2.

In the early Ontario case of *Acme Oil v Campbell*[60] there was a claim for specific performance of a document under which the mineral owner agreed to lease to Acme "at such time as the company shall move a drilling rig into this immediate district preparatory to drilling for oil." It was specified that the royalty would be one barrel in every ten, that the lessor would have gas to heat his house, and that an annual rental would be paid if the well was not completed. The agreement further provided that the lease would be null and void if a well was not started in the district within sixty days from the date on which the drilling rig was moved into the area. The agreement was found lacking in two essential conditions: the time from which the term was to commence, because there was no indication as to when, if ever, the company would move a drilling rig into the general area, and there was no provision as to the duration of the term. Accordingly, the court refused to grant specific performance.

Welland County Lime Works Co. v Shurr[61] illustrated a different approach by the Ontario judiciary when it enforced an undertaking by a mineral owner to give "the usual oil leases." He was required to "execute a lease to the plaintiffs in the form in which gas and oil leases were framed in 1903," that being the year in which the undertaking was given.

When this decision, where an undertaking to give the usual "oil leases" was implemented, is compared with *Falcon*, which refused to uphold the arrangement embodied in the telegrams and correspondence, it must remain a matter of conjecture as to what will or will not be accepted as a binding agreement.

Kopf v Superior Oils Ltd.[62] does not illuminate this area to any great extent since the preliminary documentation was remarkably detailed. The company sought to implement a document that was in reality a checklist of terms to be later inserted into a surface lease. The checklist contained such detail that it would have been remarkable had it not been enforced:

Owner: (Mrs.) Aurelia Kopf
Wife or Husband: Widow
Company: Superior Oils Ltd.

---

60 (1906), 8 O.W.R. 627 (Ont. T.D.).
61 (1912), 8 D.L.R. 720, 4 O.W.N. 336 (Ont. C.A.).
62 (1951), 4 W.W.R. (N.S.) 682, [1952] 2 D.L.R. 572 (Alta. S.C.T.D.).

Commencement date: When road conditions permit.
Lands: (Legal Description) LSD 8 SE 1/4-Sec. 14-50-22-W.4th

Note: Plans of wellsites, roadways, etc. to be made up by Company and forwarded to owner for lands required for Company's operations. Areas used to be reduced as operations may permit. Term: For as long as petroleum and natural gas produced or until company surrenders lease. Rental per acre per year: $80.00

Owner agrees:
(a) To pay taxes;
(b) That he has good title;
(c) To accept surrender of lease when lands not required by the Company;
(d) Wife and husband each consent hereto and release each other in respect of dower, and agree to execute formal consent under Dower Act.

Company agrees:
(a) To pay taxes resulting from its operation;
(b) To pay the annual rental per acre, annually in advance;
(c) To fence wellsite and roadways;
(d) To comply with provincial regulations;
(e) To pay compensation for damage to fences, buildings or growing crops;
(f) To bury pipe lines below plow depth;
(g) To forfeit prepaid rental on surrender of lease.

Dated April 20-1959.   Signed: (Mrs.) Aurelia Kopf (Owner)
At New Sarepta   Signed: N.A.
                                  (Wife or husband of Owner)
                                  Company: Superior Oils Ltd.
                                  Per: A.C. Jensen

Note: Lease to be drawn containing above terms, at Company's expense, and forwarded for execution.

The landowner subsequently refused to execute the formal lease as prepared by the oil company. The outline or checklist by itself was held to be a valid and enforceable agreement.

Setting Aside the Transaction

Even if all the formalities have been completed and the terms of the agreement have been delineated with sufficient precision, there may still be circumstances under which the contract, although it may appear perfect and complete on its face, may still be set aside if there is a failure of the parties to understand and agree upon the subject matter. The circumstances under which a lease may be attacked because of this failure are frequently pleaded together and to some degree are interwoven.

Non Est Factum

This plea, which means literally that it was not done, is directed not to the contents of the document, but to the mind of the executing party. In order for this defence to succeed, the party executing the document must show that he was mistaken not merely with respect to what the document contained, but also as to the essential nature of the contract itself.[63] The only cases in which the defendant has been successful are those in which, by the fraud of another party, the promisor has been mistaken as to the nature of the contract into which he is entering.

Although the doctrine originated for the protection of blind or illiterate persons, there now would appear to be no doubt that it also extends to those not labouring under these disabilities so long as they can discharge the onus of establishing that they were so misled or ignorant of the nature of the document that, notwithstanding the execution, it was not their deed or act in contemplation of law. It was once thought that the omission of a literate person to read a document tendered to him would be a fatal bar to the defence, but it now appears that failure to read the contents of the document is not necessarily negligence of a type that will deprive a party of the defence. If he can show that he relied upon the fraudulent misrepresentation of the other party as to the nature and character of the instrument, he still may escape liability. On the other hand, if a party reads a document before executing it, he cannot rely on the doctrine. "A literate person who signs a document

---

63 Beatson, *Anson's Law of Contract*, 28th ed. (Oxford and New York: Oxford University Press, 2002) at 333.

after reading it through, or hearing it fully read, must, I think, be presumed to know the nature of the document which he is signing."[64]

As previously noted in the *Vipond*[65] case, the fact that the mineral owner could not write English did not establish *non est factum* when she had had previous dealings with oil and gas leases and understood what it was that she was signing.

Once *non est factum* has been established, the instrument is deemed to have been void *ab initio* on the basis that the deed or contract never came into existence, since the mind of the party did not follow his pen. The consequences of this is that subsequent purchasers or assignees for value are not afforded any protection, their title deriving from a document which by operation of law is deemed never to have come into existence.

The boundaries of the doctrine were outlined in two early English cases. In *Howatson v Webb*[66] the defendant, formerly the managing clerk to a solicitor, acted as the nominee for the solicitor in a building speculation. Shortly after leaving the solicitor's employment he was requested to execute certain deeds and, on asking what they were, was informed that they were transfers of the property in question, and he then signed them. One of the deeds was in fact a mortgage between the defendant as mortgagor and a third party and contained the usual covenant for payment of principal and interest. In an action by the transferee of the mortgage for payment of the principal the defendant pleaded *non est factum*. It was held that the representation was only as to the contents of a deed and that the defendant knew that the deed dealt with the property. Therefore, the plea of *non est factum* failed. In the view of the court the fact that the defendant was told the deeds related to property was sufficient.

> His mind was therefore applied to the question of dealing with that property. The deeds did deal with that property. The misrepresentation was as to the contents of the deed, and not as to the character and class of the deed. He knew he was dealing with the class of deed with which in fact he was dealing, but did not ascertain its content. The deed contained a covenant to pay. Under those circumstances I cannot say that the deed is absolutely void. It purported to be a transfer of the property, and it was a

---

64 *Prudential Trust Co. Ltd. v Forseth, supra* n 9 (S.C.R.) at 220.
65 *Supra* n 16.
66 [1907] 1 Ch. 537.

transfer of the property. If the plea of *non est factum* is to succeed, the deed must be wholly, and not partly, void. If that plea is an answer in this case, I must hold it to be an answer in every case of misrepresentation. In my opinion the law does not go as far as that.

A wider concept was entertained in *Carlisle and Cumberland Banking Company v Bragg*,[67] where the defendant pleaded *non est factum* with respect to a document that he had signed without reading, having been induced by the fraud of another to believe that it dealt with insurance. The document turned out to be a continuing guarantee of the indebtedness of the fraudulent party to the plaintiff, the banking company. The deliberate act of misleading the signing party as to the nature of the document led the court to uphold the defence of *non est factum*.

> The true way of ascertaining whether a deed is a man's deed is, I conceive, to see whether he attached his signature with the intention that that which preceded his signature should be taken to be his act and deed. It is not necessarily essential that he should know what the document contains: he may have been content to make it his act and deed, whatever it contained; he may have relied on the person who brought it to him, as in a case where a man's solicitor brings him a document, saying, "this is a conveyance of your property," or "this is your lease," and he does not inquire what covenants it contains, or what the rent reserved is, or what other material provisions in it are, but signs it as his act and deed, intending to execute that instrument, careless of its contents, in the sense that he is content to be bound by them whatsoever they are. If, on the other hand, he is materially misled as to the contents of the document, then his mind does not go with his pen. In that case it is not his deed. As to what amounts to materially misleading there is of course a question. *Howatson v Webb* was a case in which the erroneous or insufficient information was not enough for the purpose.[68]

The doctrine was extensively ventilated in litigation arising from certain mineral transactions that took place in Saskatchewan during the early 1950s. The pattern was substantially as follows: A land agent, acting on behalf of an undisclosed principal (Prudential Trust figured

---

67 [1911] 1 K.B. 489.
68 Ibid., at 495.

prominently as a trustee for the beneficial owner) would approach a farmer who had already leased his mineral rights. In consideration of a cash payment, usually quite insignificant, the farmer would grant an option to take a lease in the event of the expiry of the then existing lease. The usual period for the exercise of the option was ninety-nine years. In addition, the transaction involved an assignment of one-half of the owner's interest in the mines and minerals and one-half of any royalties that might become payable under the existing lease if the land became productive.

It was the assignment of the minerals and the royalties that gave rise to the litigation, the mineral owners claiming that, while they realized they were granting an option to lease, they were not aware that they had disposed of one-half of their ownership in the minerals and royalties. The only cases in which the owners were successful in having the transaction set aside were those in which the evidence established a definite act of misrepresentation.[69] In *Prudential Trust Co. Ltd. and Canuck Freehold Royalties v Cugnet*[70] the court was persuaded the landowner had relied on the misrepresentation of the agent that the documents were nothing more than an option. It is noteworthy that the agent himself was not called as a witness since his whereabouts were unknown. Nolan J observed, "The learned trial judge further found that the respondent Edmond Cugnet was mistaken as to the nature and character of the assignment and transfer and that this mistake was induced by the fraudulent misrepresentation of Hunter, the agent of the

---

69 These transactions ultimately led to some extraordinary legislation: the *Mineral Contracts Re-negotiation Act, 1959*, S.S. 1959, c 102, which set up a board to which an aggrieved mineral owner could apply. If the board found that the contract constituted an unconscionable bargain, or that the owner was induced to enter into the contract through misrepresentation, it would attempt to renegotiate the contract. If its efforts at renegotiation proved unavailing, the board could call a public hearing. If the hearing failed to produce a renegotiation and the board found the mineral owner entitled to relief, it would extend financial aid so he could seek relief in the courts. Some of these transactions surfaced in litigation before the courts many years after the events that gave rise to them. See *Bell v Guaranty Trust Company* (1982), 30 Sask. R. 256, [1982] 5 W.W.R. 52, [1982] S.J. No. 375 (Sask. Q.B.), where the *Statute of Limitations* was held not to apply to the assignee under a "Prudential" type assignment. The court held that the assignee was in the position of a *cestui que trust* and was entitled to have a certificate of title issued in its favour despite the years that had elapsed since 1951 when the transaction was entered into.

70 [1956] S.C.R. 914, 5 D.L.R. (2d) 1, [1956] S.C.J. No. 67 (S.C.C.); see also *Brown v Prairie*, *infra* n 77.

appellant Prudential."[71] Thus, the necessary ingredient was established and the plea of *non est factum* prevailed. Nolan J also extensively reviewed the authorities on *non est factum* and preferred the approach of *Carlisle v Bragg*, as opposed to that of *Howatson v Webb*. In dealing with the latter he noted that the defendant was a solicitor and he should have realized that he was signing a mortgage and not a transfer. Furthermore, when the defendant asked what the deeds were, he was told that they were just deeds transferring the property. In fact, one deed was a mortgage, but as the court pointed out, in England a mortgage is an actual transfer of property by way of a mortgage. Thus, the court could treat the documents signed by the defendant as not being of a character "wholly different" from that which was represented to him. In the *Cugnet* case, however, while the defendant knew he was dealing with his petroleum and natural gas rights, the representation made to him was as to the nature and character of the document, not merely as to its content. The agent led him to believe it was merely an option to grant a petroleum and natural gas lease when it was really an assignment to Prudential of an undivided one-half interest in the mineral rights. Accordingly, the mind of the defendant Cugnet did not go with his hand.

One of the plaintiffs, Canuck Freehold Royalties Limited, was a subsequent transferee for value without notice, and it contended that the transaction could not be set aside as far as it was concerned. This argument was met by the fact that a transaction set aside on the ground of *non est factum* is void and not merely voidable. Hence, a plea of *bona fide* purchaser for value could not assist the plaintiff since there is no way to breathe life into a transaction that never existed.

The Alberta trial decision in *Falcon Exploration Ltd. v Gunderson*,[72] which struck down a contract for an oil and gas lease on the basis of *non est factum*, is difficult to reconcile with the main stream of authority on the doctrine. The facts of this case were set out in detail under the section "Sufficiency of Terms." Cairns J held, as the first ground for not enforcing the agreement, that the minds of the parties had not met in such a way as to constitute a contract. He reached this result on the basis that, while the oil company was at all times thinking of its standard form of lease, which by judicial definition was in fact a *profit à prendre*, the defendant, who was not familiar with the oil and gas

---

71 *Supra* n 70 at 918, 919 (S.C.R.).
72 *Supra* n 58.

industry, thought that he was required to give a lease. This distinction is not altogether convincing. There can be no doubt that both parties knew they were dealing with an oil and gas lease; the fact that such a document fits within the legal category of interest in land known as a *profit à prendre* would not appear to warrant the finding that the parties were not addressing their minds to the same thing. "Lease" is a term generally used in the industry to mean that very document which constitutes a *profit à prendre*, and since both telegrams specifically referred to a lease, the defendant's telegram being even more particular as it referred to a "petroleum and natural gas lease," there would not appear to be any misunderstanding as to what was to be granted.

Unconscionable Transaction

The oil and gas lease is so heavily weighted in favour of the lessee that it is not surprising counsel for mineral lessors are sometimes tempted to allege it is an unconscionable transaction. In order to succeed on such a plea, however, the lessor must establish both a dominant and overreaching position on the part of the lessee and gross inadequacies of consideration.

In *Crommie v California Standard Company*,[73] the court noted that the lessor appeared to be an intelligent man who carried on a successful farming operation and had a complete understanding of the English language and could read and write with facility. The court found that such a lessor could not be said to be in any way subservient to the defendant oil company or its agent. Thus, it would appear that the average lessor would not be able to establish the first criterion of an unconscionable contract. A senile patient in a nursing home or a foreigner with no command of the English language and not assisted by independent advice are examples of the type of lessor that a court might regard as being in a subservient position. The concept is not unlike that of a mentally incapacitated person, although the grounds for such incapacity are not necessarily confined to mental illness.

---

73 (1962), 38 W.W.R. 447, [1961] A.J. No. 28 (Alta. S.C.T.D.). The reported decision does not include Milvain J's (as he then was) finding on the unconscionable argument, but that portion of the judgment may be found in Bennett Jones Verchere and Bankes, *Canadian Oil and Gas*, vol. 1, 2nd ed. (Toronto: Butterworths, 1997) at Dig. 338.

Even if the lessor were found to be in a subservient position to an overreaching lessee, the consideration must also be found to be totally inadequate before the transaction will be set aside as unconscionable. Again, this would be impossible to establish under the normal circumstances of an oil and gas lease. The terms may be onerous insofar as the lessor is concerned, but they are more or less uniform among all lessors, whether incapacitated or not. Nor would some individual variations meet the test of unconscionability; for example, royalties have increased from the once traditional 12½ per cent to something in the order of 18 per cent. The fact that a lease might specify a royalty of 12½ per cent would not persuade the court to set aside the transaction. It might be otherwise, however, if the royalty were to be set at 5 per cent or less and the lessor also suffered from some weakness or incapacity that would make him vulnerable to the unconscionable conduct of the lessee or its agent.

Misrepresentation

A completed contract or lease may be set aside if it can be established that one of the parties entered into it by reason of a fraud or misrepresentation on the part of the other. This attack differs from *non est factum* in that the misrepresentation can be as to the contents or legal effect of the document, as well as its nature. Furthermore, it is not essential that the fraud or misrepresentation go to the root of the contract itself so long as it relates to a material point and affected the mind of the party executing the document. Also, unlike the doctrine of *non est factum*, a contract vitiated by misrepresentation is not void *ab initio*, but merely voidable. Thus, it cannot be a good defence against a party who subsequently acquired rights under the document *bona fide* and for value.

The ingredients that must be established for the defence of misrepresentation have been laid down by the Supreme Court of Canada in *Robert v Montreal Trust Company*:

> In order to maintain a plea that he was induced by false representation to make the contract sued upon, a defendant must establish (1) that the representations complained of were made; (2) that they were false in fact; (3) that the person making them either knew that they were false or made them recklessly without knowing whether they were false or true; (4) that the defendant was thereby induced to enter into the contract; and (5) that

immediately on, or at least within a reasonable time after, his discovery of
the fraud which had been practised upon him he elected to avoid the contract and accordingly repudiated it.[74]

It is to be noted that the court refers to fraud and false statements made
knowingly or recklessly. Mere innocent representation is not sufficient to
set aside a completed contract. The party who seeks to upset a contract
on the basis of misrepresentation faces an uphill struggle. The main
problem is a matter of evidence; the misrepresentation must be established at the trial, and the trial judge's finding in this regard is not likely
to be overturned. In *Bakker v Winkler*,[75] the Supreme Court of Canada
restored a finding by the trial judge that there had been a fraudulent
misrepresentation and that the contract was induced by such misrepresentation. The issue revolved around a sublease under which the plaintiff granted rights pursuant to an existing lease. The head lease
contained obligations on the part of the plaintiff to drill wells by certain
specified dates. The plaintiff had failed to meet the prescribed commencement date but had managed to obtain an extension of the time. At
this point the defendants entered the picture and negotiations led to the
execution of a written agreement, which simply provided that upon
payment of certain cash considerations a sublease would be granted.
There was also a verbal agreement, which was admitted on the grounds
that it showed the true consideration for the granting of the sublease
under which the defendants agreed to drill the first well and commence
operations thereon as required by the terms of the head lease. The plaintiff sued to set aside the agreement and to be freed from the obligation to
grant a sublease to the defendant on the basis that he had been induced
to enter into the agreement because of verbal assurances given him as to
the financial ability of the defendants to carry out their drilling commitments. The trial judge pointed out that it was of vital importance to the
plaintiff that the well should be commenced on the required date
because it was on this that all his rights under the head lease depended.
Apparently, the plaintiff did not extend his investigations beyond
enquiring of the defendants themselves and relied on their assurances.
As matters turned out, the defendants did not have the financial ability
to drill the well. The trial judge held that the verbal assurances of the

---

74 (1918), 56 S.C.R. 342, 41 D.L.R. 173 at 183 (S.C.C.).
75 [1931] S.C.R. 233, [1930] 4 D.L.R. 266 (S.C.C.).

defendants as to their financial condition amounted to a fraudulent mis-representation, which had the effect of inducing the plaintiff to sign the agreement,[76] and the Supreme Court reinstated this finding after it had been upset by the Appellate Division.

Misrepresentation upset an "assignment" type of transaction in *Brown v Prairie Leaseholds Ltd.*[77] The facts are fully set forth in Chapter 4, *ante*. It was one of those situations where the agent visited the farm-house and ended up with both an option to take a lease on the expira-tion of the existing lease and an assignment of one-half of the mineral rights including royalties. In *Brown* there were two parcels of land, only one of which was subject to a prior lease. The Browns granted a lease on the other parcel, and its validity was not challenged. The les-sor and his wife (she for dower only) also signed an assignment and transfer of a one-half interest in the mines and minerals in the other portion of land, together with an assignment of one-half of the royalty interest under the existing lease. There was a direct conflict of evidence between the testimony of the lessor and his wife and that of the agent. The trial judge accepted the evidence of the former and concluded that the parties had discussed only the granting of an option to take a lease upon the expiry of the existing lease and not an assignment of one-half of the interest in mines, minerals, and royalty. The mineral owners did not read the documents when they signed them, nor did they give more than a cursory glance at the completed documents when they were returned by the defendant. The two cheques that accompanied the completed documents were cashed by the landowner. It was not until some conversation with neighbours had alerted his suspicions that Brown realized the documents might have done more than he had bargained for. The court put aside the entire transaction, noting "mere negligence and unwise reliance upon a stranger will not make a man a party to a contract he does not intend."

---

76 (1929), 4 D.L.R. 107 (Alta. S.C.T.D.); reversed (1929), 24 Alta. L.R. 258, [1929] 3 W.W.R. 465, [1930] 1 D.L.R. 557 (App.Div.).

77 (1953), 9 W.W.R. (N.S.) 577 (Man. Q.B.); affirmed (1954), 12 W.W.R. (N.S.) 464 (Man. C.A.). A similar transaction in Saskatchewan was challenged in *Taylor v Scurry-Rainbow Oil (Sask.) Ltd.*, 170 Sask. R. 222, [1999] 5 W.W.R. 424, [1998] S.J. No. 589 (Sask. Q.B.); reversed, 207 Sask. R. 266, [2001] 11 W.W.R. 25, 203 D.L.R. (4th) 38, [2001] S.J. No. 479 (Sask. C.A.). This case is discussed *infra* under the sections dealing with "Confidentiality," "Perpetuities," and "Top Lease."

Under the plea of misrepresentation everything turns on the findings as to the facts and credibility. In *Prudential Trust Co. v Forseth*[78] the trial judge believed the evidence of the agent and preferred it to that of the landowner and his wife. He held that there was no fraudulent misrepresentation and that the owners were not misled as to the real nature and character of the documents. The Court of Appeal reversed these findings, but they were restored by the Supreme Court of Canada on the fundamental principle that the findings of fact by the trial judge who had the benefit of observing the witnesses in the stand should only be reversed or upset under the most exceptional circumstances.

In *Prudential Trust Co. Ltd. and Canadian Williston Minerals Ltd. v Olson*[79] there was a direct conflict of evidence. The mineral owner asserted the agent had led him to believe that he was granting only an option. He had not troubled to read the assignment document before signing it. The agent testified he had worked on and off for four or five months during 1951 making similar deals; that he interviewed about one hundred farmers in all and was successful in obtaining agreements in about two dozen instances. He did not remember Olson or the transaction in question but declared that he followed the same procedure in all cases. He would introduce himself, explain that he was representing Prudential and was interested in acquiring one-half of the mineral rights. If the existing lease expired or was cancelled, Prudential would have the option of leasing the mineral rights. After hearing the evidence, the trial judge stated that he did not believe Olson's story that the agent had been guilty of misrepresentation and found that when Olson signed the documents he was fully aware of their contents. He specifically stated that in the event of any conflict he preferred the evidence of the agent to that of the owner. The Court of Appeal, however, reversed the judgment on the basis that the landowner's evidence was uncontradicted because the agent stated he did not recognize Olson and did not have any recollection of the particular transaction. Martland J, speaking for the Supreme Court of Canada, commented on this:

I do not think that such a conclusion must follow because of that evidence, since Fesser (the agent) went on to say that he had followed the same pattern in his dealings with Olson as that which he followed in his

---

78 17 D.L.R. (2d) 341 (Sask. C.A.); affirmed [1960] S.C.R. 210, 30 W.W.R. 241, 21 D.L.R. (2d) 507, [1959] S.C.J. No. 84 (S.C.C.).

79 (1958), 17 D.L.R. (2d) 341 (Sask. C.A.); reversed, [1960] S.C.R. 227, 21 D.L.R. (2d) 603, [1959] S.C.J. No. 85 (S.C.C.).

interviews with other persons who had executed similar documents, which pattern he described ... [I]t seems to me that a person can properly deny fraudulent representation attributed to him on a specific occasion, even though he may not remember the exact occasion or the person who alleges that such representations were made, if he is able to say that he followed the same pattern as in other cases and describes what that pattern was. Having made such a denial of fraud, I do not think that it can properly be said that the allegations were uncontradicted.[80]

Confidentiality

It may be that the circumstances under which a lessee learns of a possible defect in an existing lease prior to taking out his own lease from the same mineral owner may create a breach of confidentially that may invalidate, or at least impair, the validity of his lease. In *Taylor v Scurry-Rainbow Oil (Sask.) Ltd.*,[81] Maxx Petroleum Ltd., in the course of its attempt to negotiate a farmout with Scurry-Rainbow, was provided with a copy of the lease held by Scurry-Rainbow. This lease was one of those taken pursuant to an arrangement whereunder it became effective upon the termination of an existing lease. Armed with knowledge of this potential defect, Maxx had a land agent take out a new lease from the mineral owner.

The Scurry-Rainbow lease was struck down on the grounds that it offended the rule against perpetuities; however, the trial judge went on to find that the information provided to Maxx was confidential and was communicated in confidence. The parties were attempting to finalize a commercial arrangement, and the judge found that they both recognized the document and that the information therein was provided for the sole purpose of due diligence. Having found a breach of confidence, the court imposed a trust in favour of the defendant upon the interest held by Maxx, e.g., the lease.

On appeal,[82] a majority found that top leases did not offend the rule against perpetuities, and since the rule was a judge-made law, the court could make exceptions when warranted. Since the top lease was

---

80 Ibid. S.C.R. at 231.

81 *Supra* n 77. The case is indexed as *Taylor v Scurry-Rainbow*, Taylor being the mineral owner, but the real plaintiff was Maxx Petroleum Ltd., which company was the lessee under the second lease.

82 207 Sask. R. 266, [2001] 11 W.W.R. 25, 203 D.L.R. (4th) 38, [2001] S.J. No. 479 (Sask. C.A.).

upheld, the majority did not deal with the issue of breach of confidentiality. In his dissenting opinion Jackson JA did deal with the issue of confidentiality and agreed with the trial judge that it had been breached. In the circumstances, a constructive trust was not appropriate but an account of profits would be.

The issue of confidentiality in connection with an oil and gas lease arose in *Cinabar Enterprises Ltd. v Richland Petroleum Corp.*,[83] where a plaintiff had shown the defendant several documents and plats in connection with a possible purchase of the property by the defendant. The material showed that the well on the land had been abandoned. There was no reference to confidentiality on either side. The defendant acquired a new lease because he believed that the existing lease had expired. The trial judge found that the circumstances under which the information was imparted to the defendant did not have the necessary quality of confidentiality. More telling was the fact that, before the meeting with Cinabar, Richland had obtained a township plat from Petroleum Information Canada Ltd. that showed the relevant well to be abandoned, thus placing the information in the public domain.

The matter of confidentiality can be a very difficult one in dealing with oil and gas leases. In many transactions such as a proposed purchase of properties, or share acquisition or other business arrangement, it is usual and customary to enter into confidentiality agreements. In the case of oil and gas leases, however, this would not appear to be practical as the party carrying out due diligence would not want to be foreclosed from dealing in the areas in which he was interested. Furthermore, as shown by *Cinabar*, much of the information will be in the public domain, or readily obtainable. But, when it comes to attacking an oil and gas lease, no hold seems to be barred.

Procedure for Taking a Lease

The hazards discussed in this and the preceding chapter all arise from the circumstances that lead up to and surround the execution of the lease. They are a mixture of form and substance and combine both the status and conduct of the parties. A lessee can do much to improve the chances of its lease being sustained by following proper procedures. The lessee (or agent) should:

---

83 (1998), 225 A.R. 161, [1998] A.J. No. 891 (Alta. Q.B.).

1 Keep a full record, by memos to file, of all that transpired in each meeting or contact with the lessor.
2 Enquire into the homestead status of the lessor and the property, and ensure that the statutory requirements of the particular province are strictly complied with (the most common defect occurs in the "separate and apart" feature of the spouse's acknowledgment).
3 Inform the lessor of the exact nature of the instrument itself; in normal circumstances where the documentation is limited to an oil and gas lease, this may almost be taken for granted, but any variation such as an option or assignment of minerals must be clearly indicated.
4 Complete the lease form, filling in all blanks prior to execution by the lessor.
5 Review the contents of the lease clause by clause with the lessor.
6 Affix a proper seal (the common wafer form will do) opposite the lessor's signature prior to execution.
7 Pay some portion of the bonus consideration, however nominal, at the time of execution.
8 Reach a firm understanding as to the terms on which the balance is to be paid and have them reduced to writing signed by the lessor. The time period should be sufficient to permit the proper investigation of title, curative title work, and registration of either a caveat or the lease itself. Under most circumstances a time period of thirty to forty-five days should be sufficient (the lessor cannot take advantage of any title defect by neglecting to cure same).
9 Pay the full bonus consideration prior to the expiration of the specified time.
10 Mail or deliver a copy of the lease duly executed by the lessee to the lessor prior to the expiration of the time set for payment.

PART THREE

The Lease

6 What the Lease Grants

Standard Form of Lease

Until CAPL, there was no such thing as a "standard" oil and gas lease in Canada. Manitoba came the closest to this by requiring that the form of lease used by an oil company in the province be filed with and accepted by the Securities Commission. This does not mean that there is a "standard" lease as such in Manitoba but only that the form must be approved before it is used. Any subsequent amendments must also be approved. The practical result of this requirement was that relatively few forms of lease are in use in Manitoba and most of these forms remained virtually unchanged for a long period of time. Today, all new leases in Manitoba use the CAPL form.

Although until 1988 a "standard" oil and gas lease did not exist in Canada, it is nonetheless true that every lease must deal with the same issues, i.e., what rights are granted, the obligation to drill, royalties, the length of the primary term, and numerous other points that must be spelled out between the lessor and the lessee. Individual leases will deal with these matters in different ways and with markedly different results. For example, one form of lease may permit the lessee to pay shut-in well royalties and so preserve his lease when the well is shut in because of "a lack of or an intermittent market, or any cause whatsoever beyond the lessee's reasonable control." This means the lessee must establish that the well is shut in because of market conditions or some other cause beyond his control before he can take advantage of the clause. Another form of lease simply states that if a well is shut in, the lessee shall make the payment and the well shall be deemed to be producing, thereby continuing the lease in force. In other words, the lessee does not have to establish a cause, such as market conditions, for the well being shut in; it is enough that the well be shut in. Clearly, the lessee is in a much more advantageous position vis-à-vis the lessor in the second situation.

The insidious part is that conventional leases all look the same – they are printed forms that to the uninitiated appear to be identical. Not surprisingly, oil company lessees sought to improve their position from time to time by altering the language, with the result that there are some conventional leases that are unreasonably onerous insofar as the lessor is concerned, yet he will be bound by their terms if he signs them.

While the CAPL lease is by far the one most commonly encountered today, there are other forms preferred by individual oil companies, and numerous leases dating back to the 1950s and 1960s remain in force.

Because of the difference in the terms of the various conventional leases, it is impossible to generalize, and in each instance it is essential that the wording of the individual lease be examined before any conclusions are drawn. Nevertheless, the majority of the leases do contain clauses that either are identical or are identical in effect. Thus, it is both possible and useful to analyse the provisions, and one can be assured that the analyses will have a wide, if not universal, application. It is also possible to identify the variations that are commonly found and determine how they differ from the standard.

American Authorities

Since the Canadian lease is derived directly from the United States, it would seem reasonable to suppose that the body of case law and authority that has grown up around its American counterpart would be of particular assistance to Canadian courts. By and large, however, this has not been the case. Where the case is one of first impression and the facts are novel, however, American authorities can be influential.

At the Supreme Court of Canada level the only reference to American authorities in oil and gas lease cases has been a passing bow where the court acknowledged that some American authorities took a different view of the *habendum* clause than the one it entertained. The brief discussion was followed by this statement: "[T]he essential task in the present case is to construe the terms of the lease which is in question."[1]

---

1 *Canada-Cities Service Petroleum Corporation v Kininmonth*, [1964] S.C.R. 439, 47 W.W.R. (N.S.) 437, 45 D.L.R. (2d) 36, [1964] S.C.J. No. 24 (S.C.C.).

In the early days of Canadian jurisprudence on the oil and gas lease the Alberta Appellate Division in *East Crest Oil Company Ltd. v Strohschein*[2] applied the California case of *Richfield Oil Corporation v Bloomfield*[3] to hold that an "unless" form terminates automatically if drilling has not commenced, or the delay rental payment was not made within specified time. The Alberta Court of Appeal in *Telstar Resources Ltd. v Coseka Resources Ltd.*,[4] a case involving an overriding royalty agreement rather than a lease, stated: "Canadian courts have consistently accepted help in the use and interpretation of terms in the oil and gas business from the courts in the United States because of their much wider experience in problems arising from the development of oil and gas fields and the production of these substances."

In *Prism Petroleum Ltd. v Omega Hydrocarbons Ltd.*[5] Stratton JA, after having reached his decision by following the Canadian precedent of *Borys v Canadian Pacific Railway and Imperial Oil Ltd.*,[6] commented: "It is also worthy of note that American case law is in accord with the inclusion of solution gas with 'oil' or 'petroleum,' whichever term is used."

A formidable obstacle to the use of American case law is the diversity of opinion among the various oil and gas producing states on basic principles and theories, so much so that if a plaintiff introduces the theory of ownership of minerals espoused by Texas courts, the defendant can counter with a totally different judicial approach taken by the courts in other states. More importantly, there is now a very substantial body of Canadian law on the oil and gas lease so that there are very few areas where there is not an existing Canadian precedent.

An example of where American case law might have been of some assistance was in *Anderson v Amoco Canada Oil and Gas*[7] which dealt with the ownership of solution gas that evolved out of the oil leg as production decreased reservoir pressure. In the course of her judgment, which held that ownership of the evolved gas remained with the owners of the

---

2 (1951), 4 W.W.R. (N.S.) 70, [1951] A.J. No. 2 (Alta. S.C.T.D.); affirmed [1952] 2 D.L.R. 432, 4 W.W.R. (N.S.) 553 (Alta. S.C., App.Div.).

3 229 P. (2d) 838 (1951, California).

4 (1980), 12 Alta. L.R. 187, [1980] A.J. No. 623 (Alta. C.A.).

5 18 Alta. L.R. (3d) 225, [1994] 6 W.W.R. 585, [1994] A.J. No. 225 (Alta. C.A.).

6 [1953] 2 D.L.R. 65; [1953] A.C. 217, 7 W.W.R. (N.S.) 546 (J.C.P.C.).

7 (1998), 63 Alta. L.R. 3d 1, [1999] 3 W.W.R. 255, [1998] A.J. No. 805 (Alta. Q.B.); varied (2002), 5 Alta. L.R. (4th) 54, [2003] 1 W.W.R. 174, 214 D.L.R. (4th) 272, [2002] A.J. No. 829 (Alta. C.A.); affirmed [2004] 3 S.C.R. 3, [2004] 11 W.W.R. 1, 241 D.L.R. (4th) 193, [2004] S.C.J. No. 47 (S.C.C.).

petroleum, the trial judge, Fruman J, considered a number of American cases dealing with ownership of casinghead gas ("white oil") and coal-bed methane gas. While the learned trial judge relied on two Canadian cases, *Borys v Canadian Pacific Railway and Imperial Oil Limited*[8] and *Prism Petroleum Ltd. v Omega Hydrocarbons Ltd.*,[9] to form her opinion, Fruman J did take note of Texas white oil case law.

As mentioned, American case law can be influential, indeed dispositive, where there is no existing Canadian law on the point. Such a case was *White Resource Management Ltd. v Durish*,[10] an action on a counter-claim by Durish in a chain of litigation that has extended over many years. The point at issue was whether Durish could maintain a lease where he had not paid any delay rentals, based on a well drilled by another party under a different and competing lease which it held. In dealing with this point, Mason J cited eight American cases that a well drilled by a rival lessee could not satisfy the drilling clause under a different lease. It is the lessee that must drill the well or cause it to be drilled by arrangement with another party.

Although it does not appear to have been cited in the *Durish* case, there is a Canadian precedent to much the same effect. In *Young v Mesa Petroleum (N.A.) Co.*[11] the lessee attempted to rely upon two shut-in wells on the lands that had been drilled a number of years before he took out a lease on the lands. Subsequent to taking out the lease, cheques were duly sent to the lessor in the amount of the delay rental specified in the lease. After the expiry of the primary term the lessee tried to argue that the payments were shut-in royalties. The court held that the lessee could not, in order to justify the payment of shut-in royalties, rely on two gas wells that were capped before the lease was even entered into.

In the third *Paddon Hughes v Pancontinental* case,[12] O'Leary JA stated that American oil and gas cases are persuasive when not in conflict with authoritative Canadian decisions.

---

8 *Supra* n 6.

9 *Supra* n 5.

10 54 Alta. L.R. (3d) 207, [1998] 3 W.W.R. 204, (1997), 154 D.L.R. (4th) 158, [1997] A.J. No. 1092 (Alta. Q.B.).

11 [1989] O.J. No. 1043, 16 A.C.W.S. (3d) 198 (Ont. S.C.).

12 *Paddon Hughes Development Co. v Pancontinental Oil Ltd.*, 33 Alta. L.R. (3d) 7, [1995] 10 W.W.R. 656, [1995] A.J. No. 811 (Alta. Q.B.); affirmed, 67 Alta. L.R. (3d) 104, [1999] 5 W.W.R. 726, 223 A.R. 180, [1998] A.J. No. 1120 (Alta. C.A.); [1998] S.C.C.A. No. 600 (leave to appeal dismissed).

Canadian Jurisprudential Approach

The lack of enthusiasm for American authorities provides a useful clue to the approach of the Canadian Supreme Court to the oil and gas lease. The American cases, in addition to suffering from a considerable divergence of results arising from the differing views of individual state courts, introduce other elements such as equitable considerations, relief against forfeiture, intention of the parties, and implied covenants. The Canadian approach, on the other hand, has been to look only to the actual words of the lease and to exclude any outside influences or considerations.

This has led on occasion to interpretations so much at variance with what the draftsmen undoubtedly intended that it prompted Locke J to remark, "I am by no means satisfied that the result accords with the intention of the parties to the instrument,"[13] and has dismayed writers and commentators.[14] Some writers have suggested that the approach may have been caused by judicial sympathy for the plight of the lessor under a document drafted by the other party and heavily weighted in favour of the lessee.[15]

The actual decisions of the court itself, however, do not reveal any particular bias for or against either party. The common theme that runs throughout all the judgments is that of strict attention to the actual wording of the particular lease itself, and a determinedly literalistic application of that language. The literalistic approach is subject to one further refinement in that if the language creates an ambiguity it should be construed against the party who prepared and tendered the document.[16] The lessee, almost invariably, will be the party who proffers the document, so that if there is any ambiguity it will be resolved in favour of the lessor.

The court has very seldom been forced to rely upon the maxim since the wording of the individual clauses has usually been found to be clear and free from ambiguity. This is so despite the fact that the court's

---

13 *Shell Oil Co. v Gibbard*, [1961] S.C.R. 725, 36 W.W.R. (N.S.) 529, 30 D.L.R. (2d) 386.

14 Bennett Jones Verchere and Bankes, *Canadian Oil and Gas*, vol. 1, 2nd ed. (Toronto: Butterworths, 1997) at para. 4.30.

15 Angus, "Voluntary Pooling in Canadian Oil and Gas Law" (1955–61) 1 Alta. L. Rev. 481.

16 This maxim is one of those that, regrettably, is still most frequently expressed in Latin. In that language it takes the following formidable form: *verba chartarum fortius accipiuntur contra proferentem*, usually and mercifully shortened to the *contra proferentem* rule.

view of the "clear meaning" has frequently astounded those who originally prepared the document and has caused a good deal of frantic
redrafting to reverse the interpretation of the courts. Virtually every
lease now contains language that has been revised in an attempt to
repair the judicial ravages. As might be expected, the lease is drafted
so as to adequately protect the position of the lessee.

At the time when the judicial approach was being formulated by the
Supreme Court of Canada, access to that court was virtually as of right.
Now that the right of appeal to the Supreme Court has been severely
restricted and leave to appeal must be applied for, the chances of a civil
case involving a private document, such as an oil and gas lease, being
granted leave are slim indeed. The success rate for such applications is
less than 10 per cent.[17] The Supreme Court no longer considers itself to
be a court of error and does not grant leave merely because it perceives
the decision in the court below to be incorrect. Denying leave to
appeal, therefore, does not mean that the Supreme Court thinks the
decision is correct in law, but rather that it does not view the issue
raised by the case as being of "national importance." The result is that
in most instances the provincial courts of appeal, especially Alberta's,
are now the court of last resort for oil and gas cases.

It should be noted that the line of Supreme Court cases that evolved
the strict and literalistic approach to the lease upheld, rather than overturned, decisions of the Alberta courts. In other words, the strict
approach of the Supreme Court was not imposed on the Alberta Appellate Division but was consistent with its own judgments. Accordingly,
Alberta courts would only be following their own example if they continue to interpret the lease strictly. Moreover, the imprimatur of the
Supreme Court has already been placed on the interpretation of many of
the most important provisions of the lease.

It has been pointed out, correctly, that when it comes to property law
the courts may be inclined to adopt an approach more in keeping with
the "realities" of the oil and gas industry.[18] Perhaps the most striking
example is *Taylor v Scurry-Rainbow (Sask.) Ltd.*[19] where the court

---

17 Crane, *Supreme Court of Canada Practice 2005* (Toronto: Thomson Carswell, 2004) at
    18–30.
18 Quesnel, "Modernizing the Property Laws That Bind Us" (2003–4) 41 Alta. L. Rev. 159.
19 203 D.L.R. (4th) 38 (Sask. C.A.), reversing [1999] 5 W.W.R. 424 (Sask. Q.B.). This case
    is discussed *infra* in the sections dealing with "Confidentiality," "Perpetuities," and
    "Top Lease."

refused to apply the common law rule against perpetuities. The trial judge noted that while the Saskatchewan legislature had debated the matter, it had not passed legislation, such as Alberta's "Wait and See" presumption of validity;[20] therefore, it was not open to the court to make an exception to the rule. On appeal, the court held that a top lease did not offend the policy behind the rule and should be treated as an exception. Top leases were an "accepted business practice in the oil and gas industry," and the application of the rule would not reflect "modern realities."

Bank of Montreal v Dynex Petroleum Ltd.[21] is another example of how the appellate levels are prepared to change, or not follow, common law principles when these principles are not compatible with the oil industry and its practices. The issue in *Dynex* was whether or not an overriding royalty was an interest in land. Dynex had acquired oil and gas interests in Alberta, which were subject to overriding royalty interests. The Bank held registered security for its loans to Dynex in excess of $60 million. Dynex became bankrupt, and its oil and gas interests were sold to recover the indebtedness. The holders of the overriding royalty interests claimed they held a property interest in the lands. The trial judge applied existing law to hold that overriding royalties could not be an interest in land since they were derived from a lease which is itself an interest in land granted by the mineral owner. There "cannot be an interest in land downstream from a *profit à prendre*."[22] On appeal, both the Court of Appeal and the Supreme Court of Canada held that the real issue was whether or not the parties intended the overriding royalty to be an interest in land, and was that intention evidenced by the language of the document and any admissible relevant evidence?

That in turn led to a trial of the issue as to whether the parties intended to create an interest in land by the agreements. Hawco J held that they did not.[23] The agreements did not expressly grant an interest in land, nor did they grant any rights that could be construed as being consistent with such an interest.

---

20 R.S.A. 2000, c P-5.
21 [2002] 1 S.C.R. 146, 208 D.L.R. (4th) 155, [2001] S.C.J. No. 70 (S.C.C.); affirming (1999), 74 Alta. L.R. (3d) 219, 182 D.L.R. (4th) 640, [1999] A.J. No. 1463 (C.A.); reversing 39 Alta. L.R. 66, [1996] 6 W.W.R. 461, [1995] A.J. No. 1279 (Alta. Q.B.)
22 Ibid, 39 Alta. L. Rev. at 71.
23 I.C.B.R. (5th) 188; [2003] A.J. No. 349.

While these cases indicate a judicial willingness to depart from the principles of the common law under appropriate circumstances, it must be kept in mind that they did not deal with the oil and gas lease itself, but only with the matrix of common law in which the lease functions. In *Kissinger Petroleums Ltd. v Nelson Estate*[24] the Alberta Court of Appeal, while finding that the language of the relevant clauses (which dealt with the continuation of the lease by a shut-in well) was not as precise as it might be, held the clauses were not ambiguous, and so did not apply the *contra proferentem* rule. That was the end of the matter, but McDermid JA did go on to look at the result of accepting the interpretation urged by those challenging the validity of the lease: "No lessee would enter into such a lease and no reasonable lessor would expect a lessee to consent to such a term. If the language clearly provided for such a result, so be it; but where there is any other reasonable construction, such should be adopted. A court should adopt a construction which results in a *reasonable result* rather than one which gives an unreasonable result" (emphasis added).[25]

One of the early instalments in the *Durish v White Resource Management Ltd.*[26] saga was decided in the same time frame as *Kissinger*. In *Durish*, the principal issue was whether or not the default clause could apply to maintain the lease where there had been a defective shut-in payment. In reaching the conclusion that the payment of the shut-in amount was an option, not an obligation, on the part of the lessee, Bracco J relied upon both the wording of the shut-in well clause and existing judicial precedents:

In the subject leases the primary terms are 5 years during which the Lessee White can drill, pay delay rental or do neither. The leases do not oblige White to drill or pay delay rental. Thus White had the option of doing neither but by doing neither during the primary term, White ran

24 (1984), 33 Alta. L.R. (2d) 1, [1984] 5 W.W.R. 673, 13 D.L.R. (4th) 542, [1984] A.J. No. 2587 (Alta. C.A.); affirming 26 Alta. L.R. (2d) 378, 14 E.T.R. 207, 45 A.R. 393, [1983] A.J. No. 814 (Alta. Q.B.) (leave to appeal to S.C.C. denied).
25 Ibid. W.W.R. at 690.
26 (1988), 55 Alta. L.R. (2d) 47, [1987] A.J. No. 804 (Alta. Q.B.); the lease provided for payment "at" the anniversary date. The trial judge found the word "at" to be imprecise and stated that the shut-in payment may be paid on the anniversary date or "within a reasonable time either before or after." Alta. L.R. at 54, 55. In the context of the case, this statement was *obiter* and was not raised, nor dealt with on appeal. The standard "on or before" would remove the uncertainty.

the risk of having the leases terminate. In Krysa *v* Opalinski 32 W.W.R. 346 Milvain, J. at p. 353 stated that the lessees had the right but no obligation to continue the lease. He then expressly adopted the interpretation of a similar clause by Frank Ford, J.A. in East Crest Oil Co. Ltd. *v* Strohscheim (1951) 4 W.W.R. (N.S.) 553 that the lease contains no covenant on the part of the lessee to either drill or pay but may do either if he so chooses, and that (at p. 558), "the lease carries within its own phraseology an automatic termination which becomes effective when the lessee fails to commence drilling operations within the time specified and also fails to exercise his privilege of paying delay rental ... ". Martland, J. in Canadian Superior Oil of California Ltd. *v* Kanstrup[27] decided that the lessee could not extend the term of the lease by continuing his drilling operation beyond the end of that primary term; at p. 105 he said:

> ... This lease contained within itself a provision which operated automatically to terminate it upon the expiration of the primary term. Thereafter there were no steps required to be taken by Kanstrup in order to bring it to an end. There was no election for him to make. There was no obligation on the part of the appellant to make any royalty payment in respect of the capped well, even assuming that cl. 3(b) was applicable to it. There was no default on the part of the appellant in not paying that money before the primary term had expired. There was, therefore, no forfeiture to relieve against.

In connection with this aspect of the case, I agree with the view expressed by Frank Ford J.A. in East Crest Oil Co. *v* Strohschein.

The default clause applied only to obligations and so could not come to the aid of the lessee to maintain the lease.

The decision of the trial judge was upheld on appeal.[28] In an oral judgment, Kerans JA noted that the lease granted the lessee an option to extend the term of the lease after the cessation of production but did not oblige him to do so. Therefore, the default clause could not apply.

In a wide-ranging judgment in *Kensington Energy Ltd. v B & G Energy Ltd.*,[29] LoVecchio J would have interpreted the word "shall" as being obligatory. It was one of the issues put forward by the plaintiff in an attempt to maintain a lease. As will be discussed in the section dealing with the shut-in well clause, the lease was held to have expired

---

27 [1965] S.C.R. 92. *East Crest Oil Co. v Strohschein* is cited in the quote from *Durish*, n 26.
28 (1989) 63 Alta. L.R. (2d) 265, [1988] A.J. No. 1162.
29 [2005] A.J. No. 1672.

because there was no "well" within the meaning of the clause. Thus, the learned judge's comments on "shall" are *obiter*. He arrived at his opinion that "shall" ... "was intended to impose an obligation" by looking at the lessor's position when "'all' the wells on his land were not producing for a cause beyond the Lessee's reasonable control or for any cause which is in accordance with good oilfield practice. If these conditions are met, the time of such interruption or suspension, shall not be counted against the Lessee."

Under these circumstances, where the lessor's right to have the lease terminated is in limbo and the lessor was not receiving any royalty, "It is only fair that the Lessor receive something in the 'all' scenario and this provision fills the void." This result led the judge to treat "shall" as imposing an obligation on the lessee to make a shut-in payment when "all" the wells were not producing for a cause that met the requirements of the third proviso.

That it was the concept of fairness to the lessor that influenced the judge to treat the shut-in clause as obligatory is shown by his observation that there is not a similar rationale "when the cessation of production is partial," i.e., not "all" the wells are shut-in, since the lessor will continue to receive some royalty payments.

Since there was no qualifying well on the lands and the lease expired on its own terms, these observations are clearly *obiter*. LoVecchio J mentioned that he was aware that the interpretation of the shut-in wells clause could potentially give rise to a default for non-payment which may not be on all fours with some of the language in the *Durish* case. He reiterated this in a footnote where he said that this view might differ from the context given the word "shall" by Bracco J in *Durish*. With respect, it differed not only from Bracco J's interpretation, but from that of the Court of Appeal and earlier authorities.

Both the default clause and the judicial approach to the lease were front and centre in *Freyberg v Fletcher Challenge Oil & Gas Inc.*[30] This case will be considered in greater detail in Part 5, "Involuntary Termination," but for our present purpose it is sufficient to note that the default clause was one of the grounds relied on by the lessee to maintain a lease on which a prolific gas well had been drilled but not placed

---

30 323 A.R. 45, [2002] A.J. No. 1173 (Alta. Q.B.); reversed, 42 Alta. L.R. (4th) 41, [2005] 10 W.W.R. 87, 363 A.R. 35, [2005] A.J. No. 108 (Alta. C.A.). Leave to appeal to S.C.C. refused, [2005] S.C.C.A. No. 167. I commented on *Freyberg* in Ballem, "The Further Adventures and Strange Afterlife of the Oil and Gas Lease" (2006) 44 Alta. Law Rev. 429.

on production for twenty years. The default clause provides that if there is a well capable of producing the leased substances (as there was in this case) the lease will not terminate because of the lessee's breach of any covenant, proviso, condition, restriction, or stipulation, and the lessor's remedy for any default shall be for damages only. Since the default clause refers only to obligations and has been so interpreted by a long line of judicial decisions, it would be necessary to find some kind of obligation to produce if the defence were to succeed. The trial judge attempted to do this by finding an implied term requiring the lessee to produce from the lands in the secondary term (the secondary term being that which follows the expiration of the primary term).

The Court of Appeal rejected the implied term, noting that it circumvents case law "which states that failure to produce, when economical and profitable to do so, results in termination of the lease."[31] Ritter JA referred to a number of leading precedents: *Canadian Superior Oil of California Ltd. v Kanstrup*,[32] which held that failure to produce when economical to do so results in termination of the lease; *East Crest Oil Company v Strohschein*,[33] that there cannot be a default in neglecting to do something that one is not obligated to do; and, significantly, *Canada-Cities Service Petroleum Corp. v Kininmonth*,[34] where Martland J stated, "the essential task ... is to construe the terms of the lease which is in question."[35]

Ritter J also observed that the entire agreement clause in the lease precluded "terms like the one implied by the trial judge."[36]

On occasion, a court, having arrived at its interpretation of the language used in the lease, will go on to point out that the result is reasonable, or, as McDermid JA did in *Kissinger*,[37] that the arguments advanced by the unsuccessful party would lead to an unreasonable result. But these are after the fact, "make weight" arguments, not meant to affect the interpretation of the relevant terms of the lease.

---

31 Ibid. A.R. at 48.
32 [1965] S.C.R. 92, 49 W.W.R. (N.S.) 257, 47 D.L.R. (2d) 1, [1964] S.C.J. No. 54 (S.C.C.).
33 (1952) 4 W.W.R. (N.S.) 70, [1951] A.J. No. 2 (Alta. S.C.T.D.); affirmed [1952] 2 D.L.R. 432, 4 W.W.R. (N.S.) 553 (Alta. S.C., App.Div.).
34 [1964] S.C.R. 439, 47 W.W.R. (N.S.) 437, 45 D.L.R. (2d) 36, [1964] S.C.J. No. 24 (S.C.C.).
35 Ibid., at 448.
36 *Supra*, n 30 A.R. at 49.
37 *Supra*, n 24 W.W.R. at 690.

Against this background let us now examine the clauses in the conventional lease together with judicial interpretations of their effect. A number of the provisions acquired their present form as a result of drafting changes to avoid the interpretation placed by the courts on their predecessors. Hence, they can best be understood when seen against this background. Wherever applicable, we will trace such clauses through their earlier versions and judicial fates. A number of the decisions resulted in the abrupt and involuntary termination of the leases. This has become such an important feature of Canadian law that the cases are given full and exhaustive treatment in Part 5, "Involuntary Termination." Here they are discussed only in enough detail to indicate the development of the present form of certain clauses in the lease.

The Parties and Leased Lands

The lease begins by identifying the date on which it was made, usually the date on which it was signed by the lessor. This is to the advantage of the lessor since it starts the clock ticking on the time periods that are prescribed in the lease, such as the length of the primary term, and the payment of delay rentals. The lease then describes the parties, that of the lessee frequently being printed as part of the form while the name and description of the lessor is typed in as occasion serves. The lessor is further described as the owner of the leased substances "within, upon or under" lands, which are set forth in their full legal description, including the Certificate of Title number, if one exists. Usually all the lands that may be owned by a lessor in a given locality are included in one lease; for example, if he has title to a full section rather than the more customary quarter section, all 640 acres will be leased. Some very important consequences flow from this practice, and they may not be fully appreciated by the average lessor. Since the covenants and undertakings of the lessee relate to all the lands covered by the lease, certain operations conducted by the lessee anywhere on the lands will keep the lease in force. If one lease embraces a number of sections, even though they may not be adjacent or contiguous, they will all be lumped together under the definition of "said lands," with the result that the drilling of one well on the lands will satisfy the drilling requirement. Similarly, production from only a portion of the entire area serves to prolong the lease with respect to the entire leased area. It is very much to the benefit of the lessee to embody all the lands owned by a single lessor under one lease and, conversely, it is to the advantage of the lessor to enter into a separate lease for each parcel. The same holds true in the case of the CAPL lease.

Consideration

The description of the lands covered by the lease is immediately followed by the bonus consideration, which is typed in after the negotiated figure has been agreed upon. The dollar figure is followed by the phrase "paid to the Lessor by the Lessee, (the receipt whereof is hereby acknowledged), and in consideration of the covenants of the Lessee hereinafter contained." In view of the practice followed by most lessees in paying the initial bonus consideration, the clause has several drawbacks. It recites that the full consideration has been paid, which usually is not the case until after the lessor's title has been checked and the lessee's interest has been registered. It also contains the phrase "the receipt whereof is hereby acknowledged." This can be contradicted by evidence that the payment has not, in fact, been made; furthermore, the wording has the effect of making payment a condition precedent to the agreement itself. It ignores the fact that the usual practice is to agree upon some time period within which full payment must be made. There is no provision for a deposit or payment of a portion of the bonus consideration as a down payment. The courts will likely treat the express acknowledgment of receipt as making payment of the full sum a condition precedent, and it is unlikely that embodiment of the "covenants of the Lessee hereinafter contained" as part of the consideration would be very useful to counteract the requirement of immediate and full payment, or, alternatively, a collateral agreement as to when a postponed payment must be made. Moreover, since payment of the bonus consideration is a condition precedent, failure to pay it in a timely manner would mean that the lease and the covenants it contained would not come into force. Hence, the lessee's covenants, being unenforceable, could not constitute a valid consideration.

CAPL 88 and 91 provide for an initial payment of $10.00 and payment of the additional consideration within a specified time. CAPL 99 makes the $10.00 payment and the covenants of the lessee the consideration for the lease, with payment of the remaining amount of the bonus being one of the covenants. The payment clauses in the CAPL leases, including the radically different one in CAPL 99, have been discussed and analysed extensively in Chapter 5.

The bonus consideration also has tax consequences for both the lessee and the lessor. Under the *Income Tax Act*,[38] various expense pools are available as deductions from income. The lessee can include bonus payments in calculating its Canadian Oil and Gas Property Expense (COGPE) pool, which can be deducted from income at the rate of 10 per cent per year under section 66.4(2)(b) of the *Income Tax Act*.

The lessor does not have to bring the payment directly into income. Instead, this amount will reduce the lessor's COGPE pool. When the COGPE pool becomes negative, the *Income Tax Act* provides that the Canadian Development Expense (CDE) pool will be reduced by the negative COGPE amount. Upon the CDE pool becoming negative, the negative amount must be brought back into income. The lessor must only include these proceeds in income when there are no further expenses against which these amounts can be set off. If, as is usually the case, the lessor does not have COGPE expenses against which the payments can be set off, the amounts must be included in income and taxed accordingly.

The Grant

The operative words of an oil and gas lease are those which grant or lease the substances. There is a remarkable degree of unanimity in conventional leases insofar as the wording is concerned:

DOTH HEREBY GRANT AND LEASE unto the Lessee all the petroleum, natural gas and related hydrocarbons (except coal and valuable stone), all other gases, and all minerals and substances (whether liquid or solid and whether hydrocarbons or not) produced in association with any of the foregoing or found in any water contained in any reservoir (all hereinafter referred to as "the leased substances"), subject to the royalties hereinafter reserved, within, upon or under the lands hereinbefore described and all the right, title, estate and interest, if any, of the Lessor in and to the leased substances or any of them within, upon or under any lands excepted from, or roadways, lanes, or rights-of-way adjoining, the lands aforesaid, together with the exclusive right and privilege to explore, drill for, win, take, remove, store and dispose of the leased substances and for the said purposes to drill wells, lay pipelines and build and install such tanks, stations, structures and roadways as may be necessary.

---

38 *Income Tax Act*, R.S.C. 1985, c 1 (5th Supp.), as amended.

The clause is an outright grant of the substances. It is not enough to merely lease the minerals since they are to be produced into the possession of the lessee. A conventional property lease covering, say, a commercial building, envisages the eventual return of the premises in an unchanged condition, normal wear and tear excepted. Under an oil and gas lease, however, the parties recognize that the minerals are to be depleted prior to the termination of the lease.

The granting clause also confers upon the lessee certain exclusive rights. The words of grant and lease are probably the most unambiguous ones in the entire document. Possibly for this reason the granting portion of the clause has been free from litigation. As we have seen in Chapter 3, the rights granted by the clause amount to a *profit à prendre*. A right of this nature is not necessarily exclusive, although it is hard to conceive that a right to remove minerals would not be so considered. In any event, the standard clause removes all doubt by expressly providing that the specific rights and privileges are, in fact, exclusive.

Some leases insert the exclusive feature as an integral part of the lease and grant itself: "DOES HEREBY LEASE AND GRANT exclusively." This would seem to be the better practice. This is the approach taken in the CAPL lease.

The granting clause in the CAPL lease includes the express right to inject substances into the lands, the pooled lands, or the unitized lands, for the purpose of obtaining, maintaining, or increasing production and to store and recover any such substances injected into the said lands. This additional language makes it clear that the lessee has the right to inject substances into the lands for the purpose of maintaining or improving the production and also has the right to recover such substances. This is certainly a worthwhile precaution, although the right to inject substances for the purposes of production has never been challenged under the conventional lease. The CAPL lease also eliminates any reference to surface use such as laying pipelines and installing tanks, etc., since those rights can only be obtained under a separate agreement with the owner of the surface, whether or not he also owns the minerals. See the discussion *infra* under "Surface Rights."

Rule of Capture

Despite the unrestricted language of the grant, the lessee only receives those substances that are ultimately reduced into its possession regardless of what quantities originally may have underlain the leased lands.

The "rule of capture" – as succinctly phrased by Hardwicke, "[T]he owner of a tract of land acquires title to the oil and gas which he produces from wells thereon, though it may be proved that part of such oil and gas migrated from adjoining lands"[39] – is firmly entrenched in Canadian law. In *Borys v Canadian Pacific Railway and Imperial Oil Limited*, the Privy Council said:

> The substances are fugacious and are not stable within the container although they cannot escape from it. If any of the three substances is withdrawn from a portion of the property which does not belong to the appellant, but lies within the same container and oil or gas situated in his property thereby filters from it to the surrounding lands, admittedly he has no remedy. So, also, if any substance is withdrawn from his property, thereby causing any fugacious matter to enter his land, the surrounding owners have no remedy against him. The only safeguard is to be the first to get to work, in which case those who make the recovery become owners of the material which they withdraw from any well which is situated on their property or from which they have authority to draw.[40]

The rule of capture has been modified and amended by conservation legislation that regulates well density, production, and oilfield practice. In *Lickacz v Magna Petroleums Ltd.*[41] the plaintiff was the owner of a quarter section of land and had leased his mineral rights to an oil company in 1948, reserving a 12½ per cent gross royalty on production. The same oil company entered into an oil and gas lease with three other owners of one-quarter sections in the same section of land. Subsequently, the oil company drilled an oil well in the plaintiff's one-quarter section, which continued the 1948 lease in force.

Years later, drilling in the area alerted the lessee to the fact that the lands had potential for natural gas, and it applied for a compulsory pooling order in order to drill a gas well, which application was denied by the Conservation Board on the ground that the oil company had the entire section under lease. In 1981 the oil company drilled a gas well on the plaintiff's quarter section.

---

39 "The Rule of Capture and Its Implications as Applied to Oil and Gas" (1935) 13 Tex. L. Rev. 391 at 393.
40 *Supra* n 6, W.W.R. at 550.
41 160 A.R. 193, [1993] A.J. No. 1056 (Alta. Q.B.).

In 1952 the *Oil & Gas Conservation Act* had been amended to establish a spacing unit of one section, or 640 acres, per gas well.

The plaintiff sought to obtain an accounting of royalties under the 1948 lease, claiming that since the well was on his quarter section he was entitled to a full 12½ per cent of royalties on the gas produced through that well, arguing that the *Oil & Gas Conservation Act* amendments were not retroactive and that the rule of capture therefore applied.

Miller J held that the amendments to the *Oil & Gas Conservation Act* were retroactive and superseded the rule of capture and that the plaintiff was entitled only to that portion of the royalties attributable to his quarter section, being 25 per cent of the spacing unit.[42]

The Court of Appeal upheld the trial decision,[43] holding that the amendments to the Act were retroactive, and observed that if the amendments had not been retroactive, the lessor would still have had to share the royalty under the equitable doctrine of unjust enrichment. The Court of Appeal was obviously not prepared to accept the trial judge's notion of equitable pooling, noting that it may have been overtaken by legislation.

In *Anderson v Amoco*[44] Fruman J (as she then was) held that the rule of capture is narrow and deals with the migration of substances between two tracts of land. It does not apply to a change in phase condition of substances within a single tract of land, i.e., solution gas that evolves out of the oil in a reservoir.

Fruman J's decision was upheld by the Court of Appeal[45] with respect to the important point that ownership was to be determined at the time of the initial grant at which time the hydrocarbons were in initial reservoir conditions. Therefore, solution gas belongs to the petroleum owners and solution gas that emerged or evolved from the liquid hydrocarbons in the reservoir at the bottom of the wellbore, at the surface, or anywhere else between, also belongs to the petroleum owners. This means that the rule does not apply to changes in phase conditions within one tract of land.

---

42 Miller J's judgment also referred to other grounds for holding as he did, such as unjust enrichment and equitable pooling. The latter concept was not accepted by the Court of Appeal and will be discussed in the section dealing with pooling.

43 162 A.R. 180 (Alta. C.A.).

44 *Supra* n 7.

45 (2003), 5 Alta. L.R. (4th) 54, [2003] 1 W.W.R. 174, 214 D.L.R. (4th) 272, [2002] A.J. No. 829 (Alta. C.A.).

The appellate court, however, did not agree with the trial judge that gas which emerges from connate water belongs to the petroleum owner. Nor did the court determine who owned the hydrocarbons from connate water, observing that the grant reserved only petroleum, not water. Connate water is saline water that has been present since the formation of the reservoir. It is a film of water around grains of sand in reservoir rock and is held in place by capillary action. Very little connate water is produced in oil or gas wells[46] and, to date, gas from this source has not been of commercial value. Ownership of hydrocarbons from connate water was not an issue on appeal to the Supreme Court.[47] The parties were content with the disposition made by the Court of Appeal. The Supreme Court did note that it appears that water in Alberta is owned by the province as a result of the *Water Act*.[48]

In summary, the Supreme Court upheld the decision of the Court of Appeal that the petroleum owner is entitled to all hydrocarbons that were in liquid phase at initial reservoir conditions, regardless of the phase they are in when recovered. The non-petroleum owner is entitled to all hydrocarbons that were in gas phase at initial reservoir conditions, regardless of the phase they are in at the time of recovery.

The Substances That Are Granted

The granting clause in the conventional lease uses an all-embracing definition of the minerals covered by it. The wording is the result of experience and knowledge of the difficulty in defining the various substances, hydrocarbons or otherwise, that might be produced from a well. Earlier leases had definitions that were much more limited, typically: (1) petroleum and natural gas; (2) petroleum, natural gas, and all related hydrocarbons (except coal and valuable stone); (3) oil, gas, casing head gas, casing head gasoline, and related hydrocarbons.

These narrower definitions are often found in leases negotiated during the early 1950s, many of which remain in force by reason of continued production. Some substances produced from a well are not

---

46 B.M. Kramer & Patrick H. Martin, *Williams & Meyers Manual of Oil and Gas Terms*, 12th ed. (New York: Matthew Bender & Company, 2003), at 210.

47 [2004] 3 S.C.R. 3, [2004] 11 W.W.R. 1, 241 D.L.R. (4th) 193, [2004] S.C.J. No. 47 (S.C.C.). In delivering the court's decision, Major J traced the historic events that led to the split title situation.

48 R.S.A. 2000, c W-3.

hydrocarbons, but do have a commercial value. The most significant example is sulphur, which is produced in vast quantities from "sour" gas and is the basis of a substantial industry by itself. There are other materials, such as helium and carbon dioxide, which, while not as common or important, have, or could have, a commercial value. Are they included in a grant of "petroleum, natural gas and related hydrocarbons"? The issue is further confused by the changing physical nature of the hydrocarbon substances themselves. They may be in liquid form at reservoir pressure, but may evolve out of the oil into the gas cap as the pressure is reduced by production. Are they petroleum or natural gas?

The judicial starting point for considerations of this sort must be the decision of the Privy Council in *Borys v Canadian Pacific Railway and Imperial Oil Limited*.[49] The issue here did not involve a lease, but rather the reservation in a transfer of land; the proper interpretation of the word "petroleum," however, was in question. Borys was the owner of an estate in fee simple in a section of land that had been acquired from the Canadian Pacific Railway Company through a conveyance that reserved "all coal, petroleum, and valuable stone." In 1949 the CPR leased to Imperial Oil Limited all petroleum under the lands together with the exclusive right to work and carry away the same.

Imperial commenced drilling pursuant to its lease, but before the well had reached the productive formation Borys obtained an interim injunction prohibiting Imperial from drilling into the formation. Simultaneously he brought an action for a declaration that he was the owner of the natural gas within the land and for a permanent injunction restraining Imperial from interfering with or disposing of his natural gas.

The trial court granted a declaration that Borys was, in fact, the owner of all gas, whether it was free or in solution. The Appellate Division of Alberta held that the gas in solution under reservoir conditions was petroleum, not gas, and that Imperial was entitled to extract all of the substances belonging to them, i.e., the petroleum, even if this caused interference with and wastage of the gas belonging to Borys, so long as modern methods were used.

Borys appealed to the Privy Council, claiming that he was the owner not only of the gas contained in the cap situated on top of the petroleum, but also any gas in solution with the petroleum. The other parties

---

49 *Supra* n 6.

claimed that the reservation of petroleum included all gas whether it was in the cap or in solution. In dealing with this question the Judicial Committee agreed that the vernacular meaning should be applied, if one could be ascertained. The court referred to a statement in *Glasgow v Farie*[50] with respect to mines and minerals: "'Mines' and 'minerals' are not definite terms; they are susceptible of limitation or expansion, according to the intention with which they are used." Similarly, the court felt that the meaning of petroleum could vary according to the circumstances in which it was used. After examining all the evidence, expert and otherwise, the Privy Council concluded it was impossible to find any clear indication as to what the uninstructed mind would define as petroleum, at the time of the original grant or, indeed, at any time. Receiving no help from a non-existent vernacular meaning, the court was driven to consider, purely as a matter of construction, the meaning that the word "petroleum" bears when the substance referred to is *in situ* in a container below ground. Their Lordships agreed with the observations of the Appellate Division that the test as to what was included in petroleum was the state of affairs in the natural condition of the reservoir, since what had been reserved to the railway company was petroleum in the earth and not a substance when it reached the surface. The fact that a change in pressure and temperature releases gas at the surface should not affect the original ownership.

More than forty years after *Borys*, the Alberta Court of Appeal in *Prism Petroleums Ltd. v Omega Hydrocarbons Ltd.*[51] referred to "the strong precedential value of the *Borys* decision."

In the *Prism* case the question as to who owned the gas in solution in the reservoir revolved around the wording of "Unitized Substances" in a gas unit, which definition excluded crude oil and all other hydrocarbons, regardless of gravity, that are or can be recovered in liquid form from the Viking Member of the Colorado Formation through a well by ordinary crude oil production methods. Omega, which had leased the substances excluded from the gas unit, drilled two oil wells within the unit boundary, which wells produced natural gas along with oil. The gas was solution gas that had separated into free gas by the time it reached the surface. By agreement, the gas unit processed the gas for Omega and it was sold by Omega to a pipeline company. Early on,

---

50 (1888), 13 App. Cas. 657, 58 L.J.P.C. 33 (U.K.H.L.).
51 *Supra* n 5, Alta. L.R. at 235.

doubts began to surface as to whether or not Omega was the owner of the natural gas, and a lawsuit was launched to determine the issue.

The trial judge focused on the word "recovered" and used that to distinguish *Borys*. Egbert J found that the intention of the parties to the agreement when they used "recovered" was that the word was related to surface and not reservoir conditions. This meant that the determination was to be made at the surface where the gas had come out of solution and not in the reservoir, and thus the gas belonged to the owners of the natural gas unit and not Omega. The trial judge termed his decision a "Pyrrhic victory" for the natural gas owners since in order to avoid unjust enrichment he held them liable to reimburse Omega for the cost of producing the gas with the result that the natural gas owners had to pay Omega the sum of $835,641.54.

Reciting that it was common ground that solution gas emerges at the wellhead as a vapour but is in liquid form in the reservoir, the Court of Appeal found that the issue was reduced to whether the plain words of the definition relate to surface or reservoir conditions. While not disagreeing with the trial judge that circumstances of the two cases were different, Stratton JA quoted passages from Lord Porter's judgment in *Borys* as clearly indicating it was the reservoir that would govern. Stratton JA highlighted the following words from the Privy Council judgment: "What was reserved to the railway company was petroleum in the earth and not a substance when it reached the surface ... In my opinion, all the petroleum reserved, including all hydrocarbons in solution or contained in the liquid in the ground, is the property of the [petroleum owners] who are entitled to do as they like with it." Thus, Omega as the owner of the oil, which the courts agreed was the same as "petroleum," was the owner of the solution natural gas produced along with the oil. Presumably, losing the appeal came as a relief to the unit owners.

Ownership of evolved gas was also the issue in *Anderson v Amoco et al.*[52] except that, as in *Borys*, the word in question was "petroleum" under the CPR reservation. The plaintiff, owners of the natural gas, argued that ownership should be determined from time to time by the phase of the hydrocarbons at the point they enter the bottom of the wellbore. They claimed ownership of all solution gas that emerged from liquid hydrocarbons in the pool, brought about by changes in

---

52 *Supra* n 7.

pressure. The petroleum owners argued that ownership should be determined at initial reservoir conditions, prior to human intervention, and claimed ownership of all solution gas, including evolved gas, as it is liquid at initial reservoir conditions.

The trial judge applied *Borys*, as confirmed by *Prism*, to find that hydrocarbon entitlement is determined under initial reservoir conditions; therefore, solution gas belongs to the petroleum owners. Her decision was upheld by the Court of Appeal. Changes in phase condition, whether they occur in the pool, in the wellbore, or at the surface, do not affect ownership.

Insofar as the word "petroleum" is concerned, therefore, we may safely say that under the circumstances of the normal lease it includes all hydrocarbons in a liquid state under initial reservoir conditions. While the Privy Council has informed us what substances are included in or excluded from the word "petroleum," the problem becomes more complicated when additional words are included, and substances other than hydrocarbons are produced.

The meaning of such terminology came before the Saskatchewan courts in a rather backhanded way in *Amoco Canada Resources Ltd. v Potash Corp. of Saskatchewan Inc.*[53] The potash company became the owner of all mines and minerals with respect to certain lands, and its titles were subject to this exception: " ... all coal, petroleum, natural gas and all other hydrocarbons, all other gases whether hydrocarbon or not and all minerals and substances, occurring in association with any of the foregoing in a fluid state." Amoco had leases on the same lands that granted "all the petroleum and natural gas related hydrocarbons except coal and valuable stone." Amoco registered caveats against Potash's titles and Potash filed notices to lapse the caveats on the basis that the substances held by Amoco under lease were specifically excepted from Potash's mineral title. Not content with this, Amoco responded by applying to continue the caveats protecting its leases. Potash argued that the language of the exception was clear and that *any* hydrocarbon was excepted. The chambers judge agreed with this contention and ordered that Amoco's caveats be lapsed.

The wording in two other leases held by Amoco was cast in wider terms: "all minerals and substances (whether liquid or solid and

---

53 (1990), 85 Sask. R. 87, [1990] 5 W.W.R. 641, [1990] S.J. No. 312 (Sask. Q.B.); reversed, (1991), 93 Sask. R. 300, [1992] 2 W.W.R. 313, (1991), 86 D.L.R. (4th) 700, [1991] S.J. No. 613 (Sask. C.A.).

whether hydrocarbons or not), produced in association with any of the foregoing or found in any water contained in an oil or gas reservoir." Potash conceded that this definition might include solid minerals or substances in any water and that these would fall outside the title exception. The chambers judge concluded, however, that, since there was no information with respect to whether or not solid minerals could exist in any water and the point was not argued by either counsel, and that counsel conceded solid minerals or substances cannot exist in water found in an oil or gas reservoir, there was no interest to support a caveat.

On appeal, the Court of Appeal was highly critical of the lower court judge dealing with the matter on the basis of a chambers application, rather than referring the issue to be determined by trial. The court noted the importance of the issue, stressing that the definition of "leased substances" contained in Amoco's leases is to be found, in the same or similar terms, in thousands of such instruments and titles to mines and minerals. The court asked the rhetorical question: "Should the meaning of these titles be made to depend upon a case such as this, summary in form, lacking in evidence, and featuring a concession of doubtful validity?" The Court of Appeal, however, did not expressly disagree with the chambers judge's understanding of the exception. Instead, it ordered that the caveat be continued for ninety days to permit an action to be commenced. Subject to the commencement of an action, the caveat would be continued until the matter was decided. If no action was commenced within the ninety-day period, the caveat would lapse. This is in fact what happened.[54]

The Saskatchewan Court of Appeal in an earlier case, *Block v Sceptre Resources Ltd.*,[55] which involved the question of whether or not a petroleum and natural gas lease had been effectively granted so as to be binding on the mineral owner, also determined that the matter should not be decided in a summary application, but rather should be disposed of at trial.

The potential ambiguity of "petroleum, natural gas and related hydrocarbons" may be shown by asking whether or not sulphur

---

54 The Court of Appeal also demolished other findings of the chambers judge, namely, that an interest in the nature of a *profit à prendre* is capable of arising in relation only to fugacious subject matter, and that Amoco's lease granted an interest in minerals and substances "produced," and if no production occurs, no interest exists. The Court of Appeal overturned both these findings.

55 (1988), 73 Sask. R. 68, [1988] S.J. No. 721 (Sask. C.A.).

would be included in the grant. Over the years the courts have evolved certain rules as guides to aid in the interpretation of documents.[56] The rules are easy to describe, even though some have been graced with Latin tags, but are not always so easy to apply.

1 If the phrase has a plain and unambiguous meaning, then that meaning must be implemented. To apply this to our example, if the word "sulphur" occurred in the grant there would be no need for further enquiry.
2 The vernacular meaning, if there is one, will control, and it will be the meaning existing at the time the document was drafted. Since sulphur is not a hydrocarbon, if it is to be found anywhere in the above phrase, it can only be in "natural gas." Sulphur under reservoir conditions is normally encountered as a gas known as hydrogen sulphide, so one would think it might well be included in "natural gas." Is there, however, a popular meaning to the words "natural gas" that restricts them to hydrocarbon substances? Certainly some evidence could be led to establish that the average person, when he speaks of "natural gas," has in mind the fuel that is used for space heating and which consists only of hydrocarbons. Despite this, it is doubtful that a court could be persuaded that there was a popular meaning sufficiently precise to exclude all non-hydrocarbons.
3 *Expressio unius est exclusio alterius*, which may be translated to mean that the inclusion of one person or thing implies the exclusion of other persons or things of the same class but which are not mentioned. The rule is usually illustrated by this example: "Suppose one man says to another: 'we are looking forward to seeing you on Tuesday, bring the family with you; my wife wants to meet your mother.' Does 'the family' include everybody living in the other man's house or only his wife and children with the expressed addition of his mother? Is his father or his sister-in-law not invited?"[57] This principle, if held to be applicable, would favour the exclusion of sulphur, because since the words "natural gas" are preceded by "petroleum" and followed by "and related hydrocarbons," so they would include only hydrocarbons.

---

56 See generally, Dworkin, ed., *Odger's Construction of Deeds and Statutes*, 5th ed. (London: Sweet & Maxwell, 1967).
57 Ibid. at 94. *Odger's* warns that this maxim must be applied with great caution, as it is capable of being stretched beyond its proper limits.

4 The document as a whole should be looked at to interpret a particular provision. This might be of assistance if, for example, the lease contained in its royalty provision a specific reference to sulphur. There might then be an implication that the parties must have intended to include sulphur in the grant.
5 The *ejusdem generis* rule is to the effect that if there is a particular description of property sufficient to identify what the parties intend, accompanied by some general description, the latter will be confined to objects of the same class or kind as those particularly described. The rule is sometimes paraphrased: a word is known by the company it keeps. If this maxim were applied, it could lead to the exclusion of sulphur since the references to both "petroleum" and "related hydrocarbons" are clearly specific as to hydrocarbons, thus limiting the general phrase "natural gas."

In the absence of any judicial decisions, the question as to whether sulphur in its gaseous form is included in the grant of "petroleum, natural gas and related hydrocarbons" remains open. It seems abundantly clear that, if sulphur were encountered in solid or crystal form in the reservoir, then it would not be included in the grant. On balance, one must incline to the view that the words "natural gas" are sufficiently wide to include any constituents that are found in a gaseous state. This is lent some support by American decisions, notably *Lonestar Gas Co. v Stine*,[58] which concerned the right of the gas owner to liquid hydrocarbons separated from the gas at the surface. Since the substances in dispute were all hydrocarbons, the issue as to natural gas being limited to hydrocarbons did not arise. The judge examined the term "natural gas": "The term 'all natural gas' would include all the substances that come from the well as gas, and that regardless of whether such gas be wet or dry. It is undisputed in the evidence that the term 'natural gas' includes numerous elements or component parts, but the very language of the conveyance is such as to include therein all those component parts which were in gaseous form when they came from the wells."

The American courts edged somewhat closer to the problem in *Navajo Tribe of Indians v The United States*,[59] where the lease was a grant of "all the oil and gas deposits." The question was whether such a

---

58 (1931), 41 S.W. (2d), 48 (Tex. Com. of App.).
59 (1967), 25 O. & G. Rep. 858 (U.S. Ct. of Claims).

grant included helium. The plaintiff asserted that the term "gas deposits" referred solely to gaseous hydrocarbons because of the presence of the word "oil." The court had this to say:

> The position asserted by plaintiff appears to overlook the fact that gases existing in nature do not fall into neat, mutually exclusive categories such as hydrocarbon and non-hydrocarbon. The various elements are co-mingled. With respect to the Rattlesnake gas, the hydrocarbon content could not be produced separately from the other components and, even under plaintiff's view, the lessee would have the right to produce the hydrocarbon gases. Perhaps, plaintiff would impose upon the lessee an obligation to produce the gas, extract the helium, and deliver the refined helium to the lessor. Of course, it would have been possible for the parties to create such an arrangement ... However, the lease in question contains no such provision, and there is no basis for holding that such an understanding arose by implication.
>
> We consider defendant's approach to be the proper one. Although the parties to the lease may have been thinking mainly of fuel-type gases, it is still more realistic to presume that the grant included not only hydrocarbons but the other gaseous elements as well. It follows that, whether its percentage was high or low, the helium component was part of the gas deposit which passed to the lessee.

Popular dictionaries display the same lack of certainty as to whether "natural gas" is confined to hydrocarbon substances. *Webster* defines natural gas as "a mixture of gaseous hydrocarbons, chiefly methane, occurring naturally in the earth in certain places." The *Random House* dictionary, while acknowledging the predominance of hydrocarbons, also admits the possibility of other substances forming part of natural gas. It defines "natural gas" as "combustible gas formed naturally in the earth, as in regions yielding petroleum, consisting usually of over 80 per cent of methane together with minor amounts of ethane, propane, butane, nitrogen, and sometimes, helium: used as a fuel and to make carbon black and acetylene." The reference to nitrogen and helium indicates that natural gas is not necessarily confined to hydrocarbons, and the definition also emphasizes the naturally occurring feature of gas.

The natural origin aspect appears in scientific definitions, which also make it clear that natural gas may contain substances other than hydrocarbons, although such may be considered to be impurities.

Natural gas is defined as any gas of natural origin as produced from or existing in oil or gas wells and consisting primarily of the light hydrocarbons methane and ethane.

Deposits of natural gas occur in rock of sedimentary origin wherein layers of rock are folded upward to form anticlines or dome-shaped structures with oil and gas being trapped under non-porous layers of rock which cover the structure, thus forming a structural trap.

Natural gas may contain undesirable impurities such as carbon dioxide, nitrogen, water vapor, hydrogen sulphide and thiols or other organic sulphur compounds.

Hydrogen sulphide is one of the more important impurities present in natural gas.

In some instances, the presence of appreciable concentrations of impurities has been turned to economic advantage. Natural gas containing high concentrations of hydrogen sulphide ... are processed for recovery of hydrogen sulphide, which in turn is reduced to elemental sulphur, a valuable, basic, chemical raw material. As a result of the Laq installations, France has become one of the world's major suppliers of sulphur. Numerous sulphur recovery plants are also in operation in the U.S. and Canada. The recovery of sulphur from natural gas is an important economic factor to the sulphur industry as well as segments of the natural gas industry.

Helium is present in a few natural gases, but should be regarded as a valuable component rather than an impurity if present in concentrations sufficiently large for economical recovery (about 0.3–0.7% or higher).[60]

On the basis of the above, therefore, it seems at least probable that a Canadian court, faced with the question of whether or not substances such as hydrogen sulphide, nitrogen, helium, and carbon dioxide that form part of the natural gas in a reservoir are included in a grant of

---

60 The above definitions are found in Kirk and Othmar, *Encyclopedia of Chemical Technology*, 2nd ed. (1966), vol. 10 at 443, 441, and 449. The fourth edition of the *Encyclopedia*, vol. 12 (Toronto: John Wiley & Sons, 1994), does not include these definitions, but that does not diminish their usefulness.

"petroleum, natural gas and related hydrocarbons," would hold that they were so included.[61]

The result might be otherwise under another description of the minerals that is occasionally encountered: "oil, gas, casinghead gas, casinghead gasoline, and related hydrocarbons." The non-hydrocarbon substances, if included at all, could only be found within the word "gas." All the other words used in the grant relate specifically to hydrocarbons: oil, casinghead gas, casinghead gasoline, and related hydrocarbons, although it is possible that "casinghead gas" could also include impurities and other substances in a natural state. One might speculate that in view of the number of references to hydrocarbon substances, "gas" might be limited through association to hydrocarbons.

Coalbed Methane

The courts have adjudicated with finality on the ownership of petroleum and natural gas. The issue of ownership is also of vital and pressing importance in the matter of coalbed methane.

Coalbed methane (CBM) is a mineral of ever increasing importance from both an economic and energy supply point of view. An analysis of the legal ownership of CBM must commence with an understanding of what CBM is.

Methane is created by the decay of organic matter during the peat stage of coal deposition and was expelled as the coal deposits were formed under increasing depths and pressures over geological time. It is chemically similar to conventional natural gas. The methane is stored in coal as an adsorbed component on or within the coal matrix, and as free gas in the micropore structure or cleats (small fractures) in the coalbed.

CBM can exist in three states: (1) free gas; (2) gas dissolved in water and coal; and (3) gas "adsorbed" on the surface of the coal.

Coal is formed by the transformation of plant material into carbon by the same forces of depth and pressure as created methane. Its major components are carbon, hydrogen, and oxygen.

The dispute will be between the owners of coal and the owners of natural gas. As of the date of writing, there have been no cases in which Canadian courts have dealt with the issue.

---

61 The opposite view is expressed by Holland, "Is Helium Covered by Oil and Gas Leases?" (1963) 41 Tex. L. Rev. 408. See also Bennett Jones Verchere and Bankes, *supra* n 14, at para. 4.39, where the authors suggest that the mere fact that helium is intermingled with "natural gas" may not be enough to treat it as being included.

Three provinces have enacted legislation dealing with the ownership of CBM:

Alberta

The *Mines and Minerals Act*[62] provides as follows:

> 67(1) A coal lease grants the right to the coal that is the property of the Crown in the location in accordance with the terms and conditions of the lease, but, subject to subsection (2), does not grant any rights to any natural gas, including coalbed methane.

> (2) The Minister, on the recommendation of the Alberta Energy and Utilities Board that it is necessary to do so for safety or conservation reasons, may authorize the lessee of a coal lease to recover natural gas, including coalbed methane, contained in a coal seam in the location of the coal lease.

The Alberta legislation applies only to mineral rights owned by the province and has no application to freehold mineral rights. While approximately 80 per cent of minerals in Alberta are owned by the provincial Crown, the Crown owns less than 50 per cent in south and central Alberta where the most productive and potential areas of CBM occur.

British Columbia

The British Columbia legislation is not confined to provincially owned minerals but applies generally. The *Coalbed Gas Act*[63] provides a definition of coal, which states coal does not include "coalbed gas" and also states that the natural gas tenure includes coalbed gas.

Nova Scotia

The *Petroleum Resources Act*[64] includes "coal gas" within the definition of "petroleum" and further states that all petroleum is vested in the province.

---

62 R.S.A. 2000, c M-17 s 67.
63 S.B.C. 2003, c 18.
64 R.S.N.S. 1989, c 12.

Thus, in British Columbia, by executive fiat, CBM belongs to the natural gas owner, in Nova Scotia it is a component of petroleum, and in Alberta, insofar as Crown lands are concerned, it is not included in a coal lease unless the minister finds it necessary for safety or conservation reasons. The Alberta legislation applies only to Crown lands and does not affect freehold minerals. Therefore, in Alberta and the other provinces, save British Columbia and Nova Scotia where the matter has been resolved by legislation, the ownership of CBM in freehold lands remains within the jurisdiction of the courts. Alberta is the "hot spot" in Canada for CBM activity. Those who argue in favour of the natural gas owner will no doubt cite the legislation in support of their position, but the courts can be counted on to follow their own line of reasoning in arriving at their decision.

Nor is it likely that Canadian courts will attach much, if any, weight to American case law. This reluctance will be based in part on the fact that opposite results have been reached in different states, resulting in widespread inconsistencies in the coalbed methane case law of the United States. Further, none of the American decisions are from the state courts of Texas, whose decisions on oil and gas law Canadian courts have sometimes considered. There is also the fact that a number of the decided cases arose in states where the economies rely heavily on the coal industry. This means that the commercial context in which the cases were decided will be different from the context of Canadian disputes, particularly in Alberta. In any event, Canadian courts in the many years they have been dealing with oil and gas matters have shown little inclination to rely on American authorities. On occasion, they have cited American authorities as a "make weight" argument in support of a position they have already decided on.

Since there are no Canadian precedents directly on point, it seems reasonable to suggest that the matter will eventually be decided by the physical and chemical composition of the relevant substances. This would seem to follow from the split title decisions involving petroleum and natural gas. We now know that in split title cases, entitlement is determined by examining the reservoir conditions at the time the reservation was made. In the *Borys* and *Anderson* cases, this meant reservoir conditions as they existed prior to human disturbance. We also know that any phase change that takes place within the reservoir after the date of the reservation does not alter the ownership of these substances.

"Natural gas" is a separate substance from "petroleum." If natural gas and petroleum are separate substances, CBM and coal are much more so. Natural gas is a hydrocarbon; coal is not. CBM has the same chemical composition as natural gas. In the case of CBM, coal can be likened to a reservoir rock similar to the sandstone or other porous rock in a conventional oil and gas reservoir.

CBM is sometimes found in open spaces or "gobs" in the coal seam. This would seem to be comparable to gas-cap gas found in the conventional reservoir and which clearly belongs to the owner of the natural gas. The same could be said for gas adsorbed (adhering to the surface) of the coal.

As of this writing, some litigation has been initiated, but is still in the pleadings stage. Although the arguments in favour of coal gas methane being classified as natural gas are very persuasive, nothing in litigation is final until it's final. Appeals are inevitable and, if the *Anderson* case is any guide, it could be up to ten years before the final answer is known. Faced with a lengthy period of uncertainty, and anxious to get on with their CBM projects, some owners of substantial coal and natural gas properties have, and are, entering into sharing arrangements that combine both interests and provide for a split of the economic benefits regardless of how the ownership may finally be determined.

The Alberta Energy and Utilities Board Decision

The Alberta Energy and Utilities Board (as it was then constituted) had to deal with entitlement to coalbed methane in a hearing to determine which party had the right to drill and produce CBM. In its decision[65] the board concluded that "CBM is a form of gas that should be considered to be gaseous at initial (undisturbed) in situ conditions and should not be considered to be part of the coal. Further, the Board views those conclusions to be consistent with the existing statutory definition of gas found in the OGCA."[66]

Not surprisingly, there was some dispute concerning the board's jurisdiction to determine entitlement or ownership of CBM. The board held that it had jurisdiction to determine whether an applicant "for a well licence under Section 16 of the OGCA 'is entitled to the right to produce the oil, gas, or crude bitumen from the well ...' for the purpose of granting a licence notwithstanding that there is *bona fide*

---

65 EUB decision 2007 – 024.
66 Ibid. at 9. OGCA is the *Oil and Gas Conservation Act*, R.S.A. 2000, c O-6.

ownership, proprietary, or other legal dispute over an applicant's entitlement. Even where it is unlikely that a Board decision on ownership of other proprietary rights under Section 16 of the OGCA will constitute a final and binding determination between parties for all purposes, the Board finds that it must take ownership or other proprietary rights into account when deciding whether to issue a well licence."[67]

Thus, the board acknowledged that its finding on the matter of CBM ownership may not be the final and binding determination, but held that it must take the matter of ownership or other proprietary rights into account when deciding whether to issue a well licence. The decision has been appealed by two major coal interests.

CBM in Connate Water

Ownership of CBM found in connate water may be a special case. It will be recalled that this was one of the issues placed before the courts in *Anderson*, but was not definitively decided. The Court of Appeal in *Anderson* did not determine who owned gas located in connate water, and at the Supreme Court of Canada level, by agreement of the parties, the issue was no longer in dispute. Major J commented that "it appears that in Alberta this water is owned by the province as a result of the *Water Act*."[68] This could have a bearing with regard to CBM found in connate water within a coalbed. It would not confer ownership on the owners of the coal rights, but it could remove CBM from ownership by the holders of natural gas rights.

Specific Reference to Coalbed Methane in Lease

Out of what may be an abundance of caution, some lessees specifically provide that coalbed methane is included in the substances that are granted. This is achieved by including coalbed methane in the definition of "leased substances." A typical example would be:

> "leased substances" means all petroleum, natural gas and related hydrocarbons (except coal but including coalbed gas), and all materials and substances.

---

67 Ibid. at 10.
68 *Supra*, n 34.

There will also be a definition of coalbed gas as follows:

"coalbed gas" means natural gas including without limitation coalbed methane, coal gas, coalbed gas, coal seam gas and all other related hydro-carbons derived from, found in or producible from coal seams, coalbeds or carbonaceous shales.

If coalbed methane is eventually found by the courts to be natural gas, the specific provisions would not appear to be necessary. Similarly, if the courts eventually rule that coalbed methane is not a natural gas, the provisions would be of no avail. In the meantime, however, the specific reference should put the matter to rest as between the individual lessor and lessee. On the other hand, the lessor may wish to exclude coalbed methane from the grant under the lease, in which case the definition of leased substances should specifically exclude coalbed gas and there should be a definition of coalbed gas along the above lines.

Another practical consideration that should be considered when a lease includes coalbed methane is the physical fact that CBM wells frequently produce at comparatively low rates. Accordingly, the lessee may want to include a provision that adjusts the percentage royalty rate and the taxes payable by the lessee in an ascending scale depending on the volume of production. An example of such a provision is as follows:

1)   A gas production royalty rate schedule as detailed below:

GAS PRODUCTION RATE Averaged on a Monthly basis	ROYALTY RATE (Clause ( )	TAXES PAYABLE BY THE LESSEE (Clause ( )
Greater than 0 and less than 100 mcf/day	8.00%	92.00%
Equal to or greater than 100 and less than 250 mcf/day	16.00%	92.00%
Equal to or greater than 250 mcf/day	18.00%	92.00%

2)   On leased substances, exclusive of gas but including condensate (such leased substances hereinafter referred to as "petroleum" or "crude"), a royalty of 18% as defined in clause ( ) with taxes payable by the Lessee at 82% as defined under the conditions of clause ( ).

Minerals under the Standard Clause

The most prevalent granting clause in the conventional lease is cast in very wide terms: "All the petroleum, natural gas and related hydrocarbons (except coal and valuable stone), all other gases, and all minerals and substances (whether liquid or solid and whether hydrocarbons or not) produced in association with any of the foregoing or found in any water contained in any reservoir." There is a specific reference to "all other gases," which makes it abundantly clear that substances found in gaseous form, although not hydrocarbons, are meant to be included. The reference to all "minerals and substances" is wide-ranging, although qualified by the words "produced in association with any of the foregoing or found in any water contained in any reservoir." Certainly this phraseology would be broad enough to capture substances such as hydrogen sulphide, nitrogen, carbon dioxide, and helium, since those substances are produced in association with natural gas. The wording, although broad, does not include, nor is it meant to include, any solid or "hard" minerals, since "minerals" are limited to those produced in association with the other substances, which are only those substances normally produced from an oil or gas well in a liquid or gaseous state. The reference to "found in any water contained in any reservoir" is clearly meant to reflect the fact that formation water is very often produced with the petroleum substances and the grant makes it clear that any substances found in such formation water also belong to the lessee.[69]

---

69 For a discussion of what is included in the reservation from land transfers of "All Mines and Minerals," see Stewart, "The Reservation or Exception of Mines and Minerals" (1962) 40 Can. Bar Rev. 329. This, of course, is a different matter from the grant under an oil and gas lease where the reference to minerals is referable back to petroleum, gas, and hydrocarbons. See also the *Law of Property Act*, R.S.A. 2000, c L-7, s 58, which makes it clear that, regardless of any reservations that may have occurred in the transfer, the owner of the surface of land is deemed to be also the owner of sand and gravel obtained by stripping off the overburden, excavating from the surface, or otherwise recovered by surface operations. See also *Earl of Lonsdale v Attorney General*, [1982] 3 All E.R. 579 (Ch.D.), where it was held that "mines and minerals" was not a definite term that had a literal meaning and, although the term might in the appropriate context mean every substance that could be obtained under the earth's surface for profit, the actual meaning depended, unless the meaning was clear from the instrument itself, on the factual matrix of the grant and the vernacular meaning at the time of the grant. The case also contains a useful review of the authorities.

When it comes to connate water, however, it must be kept in mind that the Alberta Court of Appeal in *Anderson v Amoco*[70] cast doubt on the ownership of hydrocarbons in connate water. The question was not raised in the Supreme Court,[71] but Major J observed that water in Alberta is owned by the province pursuant to the *Water Act*.[72]

In many leases, including the CAPL lease, the word "materials" is substituted for "minerals." "Materials" would seem to cast a somewhat wider net.

Until CAPL 99, it was the invariable practice, where the lessor had only natural gas, to enter into a natural gas lease. The lease would describe the "leased substances" as all natural gas and related hydrocarbons (except coal) and all materials and substances (except valuable stone), whether liquid, solid, or gaseous and whether hydrocarbons or not, produced in association with natural gas or related hydrocarbons or found in any water contained in any reservoir.

CAPL 99 is designed to apply whether the lessor owns both the petroleum and natural gas or just the natural gas. It achieves this purpose by using a definition of leased substances that includes all petroleum, natural gas, and all other hydrocarbons, but by describing the lands as being those described in the certificate of title. The certificate of title will specify whether the lessor has title to petroleum and natural gas or just natural gas, which in turn will limit the leased substances that are granted.

Mother Hubbard Clause

After describing the substances, the standard clause continues: "and all the right, title, estate and interest, if any, of the lessor in and to the leased substances or any of them within, upon or under any lands excepted from, or roadways, lanes, or rights-of-way adjoining the lands aforesaid." It sometimes happens that a person's title will be subject to certain exceptions; portions of his land are carved out of his title because of utility easements, roadways, and similar public uses. Ownership of the minerals under any excepted portion is often a complex legal question. The provision, usually known as the Mother Hubbard

---

70 (2002), 5 Alta. L.R. (4th) 54, [2003] 1 W.W.R. 174, 214 D.L.R. (4th) 272, [2002] A.J. No. 829 (Alta. C.A.).

71 [2004] 3 S.C.R. 3, [2004] 11 W.W.R. 1, 241 D.L.R. (4th) 193, [2004] S.C.J. No. 47 (S.C.C.).

72 R.S.A. 2000, c W-3.

clause, simply ensures that if the lessor, in fact, owns minerals under these parcels, they will be included automatically within the grant. The language imposes a definite geographical limitation on the operation of the automatic inclusion to either lands excepted from the leased lands or adjoining roadways, lanes, or rights-of-way.

The CAPL lease contains a similar provision in the granting clause.

Express Powers under the Grant

The granting clause also confers special rights that are related to the exploration for and production of the substances. Those enumerated in the standard (non-CAPL) clause are almost universal throughout Canada; they confer upon the lessee the exclusive right and privilege to "explore, drill for, win, take, remove, store and dispose of the leased substances and for the said purposes to drill wells, lay pipelines and build and install such tanks, stations, structures and roadways as may be necessary."

In considering the rights that are granted by the clause, it is necessary to distinguish between those that relate to the surface and those that might be described as necessarily incidental to the exercise of the *profit à prendre*.

Surface Rights

The granting clause in the older forms of lease purports to confer on the lessee the right to drill wells, lay pipelines, and install tanks, stations, structures, and roadways. These extensive powers have no practical effect, however, since they have been displaced by provincial legislation that precludes the lessee from utilizing them.[73]

---

73 The Alberta *Surface Rights Act*, R.S.A. 2000, c S-24, s 12, provides as follows:

12(1) No operator has a right of entry in respect of the surface of any land
  a) for the removal of minerals contained in or underlying the surface of that land or for or incidental to any mining or drilling operations,
  b) for the construction of tanks, stations and structures for or in connection with a mining or drilling operation, or the production of minerals, or for or incidental to the operation of those tanks, stations and structures,
  c) for or incidental to the construction, operation or removal of a pipeline,
  d) for or incidental to the construction, operation or removal of a power transmission line, or

For all practical purposes the lease does not grant any rights to use the surface, and the words that purport to do so should be omitted. Such rights can only be created by a separate agreement with the surface owner for which compensation is paid, or under provincial right of entry legislation, which gives the lessee the right to use the surface for the purpose of taking and disposing of the leased substances. Any right of entry, of course, will be subject to the compensation and other conditions imposed by the government agency.

The CAPL lease does not purport to confer any rights to use the surface.

Subsurface Rights

On the other hand, the subsurface rights are clearly within the power of the lessor to grant and indeed would accompany the grant of a *profit à prendre* in any event. As the Privy Council stated in the *Borys* case,[74] the right must follow the grant. The existence of the grant (or reservation of petroleum as was the case in *Borys*) necessarily implies the existence of the power to recover it and the right to work it.

---

e) for or incidental to the construction, operation or removal of a telephone line, until the operator has obtained the consent of the owner and the occupant of the surface of the land or has become entitled to right of entry by reason of an order of the Board pursuant to this Act.

(2) Notwithstanding anything contained in a grant, conveyance, lease, license or other instrument, whether made before or after the commencement of this act, and pertaining to the acquisition of an interest in a mineral, an operator does not thereby obtain the right of entry in respect of the surface of any land unless the grant, conveyance, lease, license or other instrument provides a specific separate sum in consideration of the right of entry of the surface required for his operations, that this subsection does not apply in a case where the operator, prior to July 1, 1952, has, for any of the purposes referred to in s.1, exercised the right of entry in respect of the surface of land in accordance with the provisions of a grant, conveyance, lease, license or other instrument.

There is legislation in other provinces to similar effect; see Saskatchewan, *Surface Rights Acquisition and Compensation Act*, R.S.S. 1978, c S-65, s 6(l); Manitoba, *Surface Rights Act*, C.C.S.M. c 5235, s 16-18; *Ontario Mining Act*, R.S.O. 1990, c M-14, s 79(2); British Columbia, *Petroleum and Natural Gas Act*, R.S.B.C. 1996, c 361, s 9(1).

74 *Supra* n 6.

Right of Surface Owner to Support

One limitation on the proposition that the granting of a *profit à prendre* necessarily carries with it the power to recover the substance may be found in the right of the surface owner to support. The right to support, which means the mineral owner cannot conduct his operations so as to cause the surface to subside, has long been recognized as a limitation on the dominant position of the mineral title. As to what constitutes the right to support, the classic statement seems to be that in *Humphries v Brogden*:[75] "The only reasonable support is that which will protect the surface from subsidence and keep it securely at its ancient and natural level."

An example of how the right to mine minerals could cause subsidence to the surface and thus be enjoined is found in *The Trinidad Asphalt Company v Ambard*,[76] where the owner of the asphalt had excavated right to the border of an adjoining property so that asphalt from the adjoining property seeped over the boundary and the surface subsided. Normally, however, there can be no suggestion that the withdrawal of petroleum or natural gas from formations thousands of metres below the surface will interfere with the right of support of the surface. There may be exceptional circumstances, such as shallow gas forming hydrates and thereby causing subsidence, which may create a situation where the surface owner would have some legal redress.

Geophysical Exploration

The right to explore for the leased substances is among the specific powers enumerated in the granting clause. Apart from drilling, the most common method of exploring for petroleum and natural gas is by seismograph. This involves the movement of mobile equipment, and vehicles, across the land, the drilling of shallow "shot" holes, and the temporary laying of wires. Small explosive charges are detonated in the "shot" holes, and the reflections from the subsurface formations are recorded. A right to carry out this type of work would probably be included in the specific power to "explore," but here again the situation is controlled by government regulation. In the prairie provinces

---

75 (1850), 12 Q.B. 739, 116 E.R. 1048.
76 [1899] A.C. 594, 68 L.J.P.C. 114 (P.C.).

there is a prohibition against any person conducting geophysical operations on privately owned land except with the consent of the owner.[77] The regulations also prescribe in detail the manner in which such operations are to be carried out.

Secondary Recovery

Secondary recovery to enhance production is widely used in the oil industry. Essentially, secondary recovery is the supplementing of original reservoir drive by the injection into the reservoir of water, gas, a mixture of both, or some other miscible substance, to maintain the pressure within the reservoir. The process involves several concepts that are outside the scope of the normal oil and gas lease and are governed by conservation legislation.

Because the lease grants rights with respect to "substances," it would seem logical to look to it as a source for the materials, i.e., water and gas that are to be injected into the reservoir. Water is a "substance" as referred to in the granting clause, and it is frequently produced in association with petroleum and natural gas. It would appear, therefore, that water so produced would be included in the grant, subject to the qualification that the lessor may not have title to the water and therefore could not grant any rights with respect to it.

Provincial legislation vests priority rights in water in the government.[78] In any event, water produced in association with oil and gas normally would not occur in sufficient volumes to maintain a secondary recovery scheme, so the operator must look outside the lease for his injection material.

Nor would the words of grant appear to confer upon the lessee the right to take gas and re-inject it back into the reservoir for pressure maintenance, at least without payment of royalty to the lessor. Any such injection is also, of course, subject to the provisions of existing provincial legislation dealing with conservation. The implementation of a secondary recovery scheme also requires the actual physical injection of the

---

77 *Exploration Regulations*, Alta. Reg. 214/1998, s 4; *Seismic Exploration Regulations*, 1999 R.R.S. c M-16.1, Reg. 2, s 39(2); *Geophysical Regulations*, Man. Reg. 110/94.

78 *Water Act*, R.S.A. 2000, c W-3; *Water Corporation Act*, S.S. 2002, S-35.01, s 7. The Manitoba Act exempts water obtained incidentally as a result of drilling for oil or the operation of an oil well from all references to "water" in the *Water Rights Act*, C.C.S.M. c W80, s 2.

substances into the reservoir. Normally, this is done by converting existing wells, either producing or suspended, into injector wells. This represents a substantial change in the status of the minerals owned by the lessor as they will no longer be produced. The power to inject substances into a formation underlying the lessor's lands is not expressly mentioned in the granting clause of the conventional lease, but it could be subsumed under the right to "win" the leased substances.

The CAPL lease specifically addresses this issue and confers upon the lessee "the right to inject substances into the said lands for the purpose of obtaining, maintaining or increasing production from the said lands, the pooled lands or the unitized lands and to store and recover any such substances injected into the said lands." Moreover, the recovery of any injected substance is included in the definition of "operations" that will continue the lease in force beyond the primary term.

Practically all secondary recovery schemes are conducted on lands that have been unitized, which greatly simplifies the problems that otherwise would occur under the lease. Unitization has such a profound impact on the lease that it warrants separate and detailed treatment; see *infra*, Chapter 10.

Underground Storage

Underground storage of natural gas, liquid petroleum, and condensate is a recognized means of storing large volumes at a low unit cost. Various types of underground caverns, including salt domes, have been used for this purpose. One of the best receptacles for underground storage is a depleted oil or gas reservoir, which raises the question: Does the lessee under an oil and gas lease acquire some ownership in the reservoir space itself, or does it remain the property of the mineral owner? Under a series of old English cases on mining it was established that the owner of a "mine" had ownership of the "whole containing chamber."[79] This holding in connection with mines was consistent with the principle of "outstroke," which is the right to excavate so much of the surrounding rock as may be necessary to build

---

79 *Proud v Bates* (1865), 34 L.J. Ch. 406. These and other cases are discussed in Stewart, *supra* n 68. See also Lyndon, "The Legal Aspects of Underground Storage of Natural Gas" (1961) 1 Alta. L. Rev. 543; McRae, "Granting Clauses in Oil and Gas Leases," *Second Annual Institute on Oil and Gas Law* at 43.

adequate passageways for the transportation of the mineral to the surface. This right, however, was connected with the grant of "mines," a grant not usually found in oil and gas leases. Since the minerals granted under the oil and gas lease are not "mined" but are withdrawn from the reservoir through a wellbore, it is not likely that the grant of such minerals would be held to also include the grant to the surrounding spaces. Nor is the right to underground storage among the enumerated specific powers.

As more and more depleted reservoirs become available for storage of gas, storage has come to play a significant role in the marketing of gas. Storage allows gas to continue to be produced in periods of relatively low demand and injected into storage, to be withdrawn during periods of heavy demand. At first underground storage was concentrated in Ontario, where the gas could be stored close to the major markets. The sheer size of storage facilities in the West, however, has made them an important marketing influence in their own right, particularly in levelling out the peaks and valleys of demand.

Ontario and British Columbia have taken the lead in legislating on the subject of gas storage. The *Ontario Energy Board Act, 1998*,[80] specifically authorizes the storage of gas in section 38:

38.(1) The Board by order may authorize a person to inject gas into, store gas in and remove gas from a designated gas storage area, and to enter into and upon the land in the area and use the land for that purpose. 1998, c. 15, Sched. B, s. 38(1).

(2) Subject to any agreement with respect thereto, the person authorized by an order under subsection (1),
  (a) shall make to the owners of any gas or oil rights or of any right to store gas in the area just and equitable compensation in respect of the gas or oil rights or the right to store gas; and

---

80 *Ontario Energy Board Act 1998*, R.S.O. 1998, c 15, s 38; British Columbia has enacted a special statute on the subject, *Petroleum and Natural Gas Act*, R.S.B.C. 1990, c 361, s 126–32; see also *Mining Act*, R.S.Q. 1995, c M-13.1. Alberta and Saskatchewan to date have confined themselves to bringing underground storage under the control of the respective regulatory boards, but have not legislated on private rights; see *Oil and Gas Conservation Act*, R.S.A. 2000, c O-6, and *Oil and Gas Conservation Act*, R.S.S. 1978, c O-2.

(b) shall make to the owner of any land in the area just and equitable compensation for any damage necessarily resulting from the exercise of the authority given by the order. 1998, c. 15, Sched. B, s. 38(2).

(3) No action or other proceeding lies in respect of compensation payable under this section and, failing agreement, the amount shall be determined by the Board. 1998, c. 15, Sched. B, s. 38(3).

The Act specifically authorizes the storage of natural gas but also provides that both the owners of the oil or gas rights or of storage rights and the owners of the surface shall be compensated in a fair, just, and equitable manner. The provisions of this Act were interpreted in *Wellington and Imperial Oil Ltd.*,[81] where the applicant sought to have payments made by the lessee, who had an order to store gas under the land, classified as being royalty payments for the undepleted reserves of gas left in the ground at the time storage operations commenced, rather than compensation under the Act for the storage privileges. The Ontario High Court held that it was barred by privative language in the Act itself from determining the question, which lay solely within the jurisdiction of a board of arbitration to be appointed under the Act. In the course of judgment, however, the court noted that, while the applicant lessor and Imperial Oil Limited as lessee had entered into both oil and gas leases and unit agreements concerning the lands, none of these documents contained a clause giving the lessee right to store gas. When interpreting the *Energy Board Act*, the court observed that "the consideration and construction of both oil and gas leases and unit operating agreements must have been within the contemplation of the legislature when it enacted"[82] the specific provision authorizing the storage of gas. Although it was not called upon to decide that precise point, it is clear from the decision that the *Energy Board Act* did confer the right to store gas and that such right would override any conflicting claims that might be advanced by the mineral or surface owners.

In British Columbia, the Minister of Mines and Petroleum Resources may designate certain areas as "storage areas" and may grant the right to explore for suitable reservoirs or structures for underground storage as well as a licence to store. The Act provided for agreement with the owner

---

81 [1970] 1 O.R. 177, 8 D.L.R. (3d) 29, [1969] O.J. No. 1438 (Ont. H.C.J.).
82 Ibid., at 35.

of the mineral rights or storage rights as to compensation or a determination of "fair, just, and equitable compensation" by the board of arbitration. If the surface is owned in freehold, the Act appears to make the written consent of the owner and lawful occupant of the land mandatory.

Although the granting clause of the CAPL lease does mention the right to "store," that right relates only to the right to store substances injected into the said lands "for the purpose of obtaining, maintaining or increasing production from the said lands." It does not grant the right to use the lands for storage purposes.

It has now become common practice to include the right to use underground storage along with the right to inject substances into the formation as specific provisions in unitization agreements. Since unit agreements, if signed by the lessor, can amend the affected leases, the rights under a lease could be extended. Query, whether this would still be the result if the lessor had not signed the unit agreement and the lessee had exercised his unilateral right to unitize the lands?

Salt Water Disposal

Large quantities of formation salt water are frequently brought to the surface in the production of oil and coalbed methane. The disposal of these unwanted volumes of salt water becomes a serious problem in logistics. Small and very carefully controlled volumes can be stored in surface pits, but the conservation legislation imposes strict limits on the amount that can be so dealt with, and the harmful effects of salt water leaking from surface pits create pressure to eliminate the privilege entirely. The commonest means of disposing of salt water is to inject it back into a formation, not necessarily the one from which it is produced. Frequently salt water will be trucked considerable distances to a well that has been converted to salt water disposal. There is a charge per barrel for the privilege of injecting the salt water. Clearly, such a right is not conferred under the lease, and here again a mineral operator desiring to use an existing well for salt water disposal or to drill a well for that purpose must deal with the owner of the mineral rights on the basis that such ownership includes the actual cavern or reservoir in which the minerals may be located.

If the water being disposed of was produced solely as a result of producing operations on the lands covered by the lease, it might be successfully argued that the lessee has the right under the lease to dispose of the water as being incidental to the production of the leased substances.

Other Versions of the Granting Clause

It frequently happens that a freehold mineral owner may have title only to natural gas.[83] Under these circumstances, the wording of the clause will grant and lease "all the natural gas and related hydrocarbons (except coal and valuable stone), all other gases, and all minerals and substances (whether liquid or solid and whether hydrocarbons or not) produced in association with any of the foregoing or found in any water contained in any reservoir." As discussed under the heading "Minerals under the Standard Clause," CAPL 99 has been designed to function either as a petroleum and natural gas lease or just as a natural gas lease.

Occasionally a lessee will seek to obtain rights above and beyond the right to explore for and produce the leased substances. For example, one form of lease contains this phrase: " ... and the exclusive right to use any well on the said lands for the injection of gas, air, water or any other fluids, whether obtained from the said lands or elsewhere, into the subsurface strata and the right to perform any operation necessary, incidental to or associated with any of the aforesaid operations of the lessee." If the grant were held to be effective, the lessee would have the right to inject foreign substances into the subsurface strata, thus removing any doubt that the lease grants the power to implement secondary recovery procedures. The language also seems designed to permit the use of a well for such non-producing activities as disposal of salt water. It stops short, however, of granting the express right to use the strata for storage of petroleum substances, and, bearing in mind the overall purpose of the lease, namely to explore for and produce oil and gas, it is doubtful if the language would be interpreted as including such a right.

Some versions of the granting clause that originally purported to bestow wide-ranging surface rights, i.e., the right to construct "power stations, treating and processing plants, dwellings for its employees and other structures and lines of communication," have largely disappeared. Presumably their disappearance is attributable to the fact that the lease in Canada does not grant the right to use the surface.

---

83 This situation is a direct consequence of *Borys v C.P.R., supra* n 6, which held that the reservation of "petroleum" did not include the natural gas occurring in a free state in the underground reservoir.

7 The *Habendum* and Interpretation Clauses

The Primary Term

The *habendum* clause, together with its provisos, is the heart of the lease. It sets forth the conditions under which the lease continues in force and thus accounts for much of the litigation that has swirled about the document. The *habendum* and its provisos define the primary term of the lease, the manner in which it may be extended, and what happens when drilling results in a dry hole or production ceases, both before and after the expiration of the primary term. Strangely enough, it also contains the provision that deals with drilling operations on the land.

Drilling has little relation to the primary or extended term of the lease, and why it was structured into the first proviso to the *habendum* in Canadian forms remains a mystery. True, a failure to comply with its terms may result in a termination of the lease, but this applies as well to other provisions that are written as separate and distinct clauses. Because of its importance and its lack of connection with the *habendum* the drilling proviso will be treated separately, in Chapter 7, under "Drilling," and in Chapters 14 and 15. A typical version of the *habendum* clause, complete with its provisos, reads:

> TO HAVE AND ENJOY the same for the term of ... ( ) years from the date hereof and so long thereafter as the leased substances or any of them are produced from the said lands or the pooled lands subject to the sooner termination of the said term and subject also to extension of the said term all as hereinafter provided.

> PROVIDED that if operations for the drilling of a well are not commenced on the said lands or the pooled lands within one (1) year from the date

hereof, this Lease shall terminate and be at an end on the first anniversary date, *unless* the Lessee shall have paid or tendered to the Lessor on or before said anniversary date the sum of ... Dollars ($ ...) (hereinafter called the "delay rental"), which payment shall confer the privilege of deferring the commencement of drilling operations for a period of one (1) year from said anniversary date, and that, in like manner and upon like payments or tenders, the commencement of drilling operations and the termination of this Lease shall be further deferred for like periods successively;

PROVIDED FURTHER that if at any time during the said ... ( ) year term and prior to the discovery of production on the said lands or the pooled lands, the Lessee shall drill a dry well or wells thereon, or if at any time during such term and after discovery of production on the said lands or the pooled lands such production shall cease and the well or wells from which such production was taken shall be abandoned, then this Lease shall terminate at the next ensuing anniversary date hereof unless operations for the drilling of a further well on the said lands or the pooled lands shall have been commenced or unless the Lessee shall have paid or tendered the delay rental, in which latter event the immediately preceding proviso hereof governing the payment of the delay rental and the effect thereof, shall be applicable thereto;

AND FURTHER ALWAYS PROVIDED that if at the end of the said ... ( ) year term the leased substances are not being produced from the said lands or the pooled lands (whether or not the leased substances have theretofore been produced therefrom) and the Lessee is then engaged in drilling or working operations thereon, or if at any time after the expiration of the said ... ( ) year term production of the leased substances has ceased and the Lessee shall have commenced further drilling or working operations within Ninety (90) days after the cessation of said production, then this Lease shall remain in force so long as any drilling or working operations are prosecuted with no cessation of more than Ninety (90) consecutive days, and, if they result in the production of the leased substances or any of them, so long thereafter as the leased substances or any of them are produced from the said lands or the pooled lands; provided that if drilling or working operations are interrupted or suspended as the result of any cause whatsoever beyond the Lessee's reasonable control, or if any well on the said lands or the pooled lands or on any spacing unit of which the said lands or any portion thereof form a part, is shut-in, suspended or otherwise not produced as the result of a lack of or an intermittent market, or any cause whatsoever beyond the Lessee's reasonable control, the time of such interruption or suspension or nonproduction shall not be counted against the Lessee, anything hereinbefore contained or implied to the contrary notwithstanding.

The clause confers upon the lessee the right to hold the grant for a specified number of years. This is known as the primary term. In the industry's early years the primary term was commonly for a period of ten years and many of the lease forms had "ten years" printed in the text. As the years went on and the sophistication of mineral owners increased, much shorter terms of two or three years become the norm. Under certain conditions, as when there has been extensive drilling in the area, the primary term may be as short as one year. The length of the primary term is a matter of negotiation between the lessor and the lessee, and the agreed-upon period will be typed into the blanks in the *habendum* clause. The lessee can hold the lease for the number of years specified in the primary term without either drilling (so long as he pays the delay rental), or production. Accordingly, the shorter the primary term, the sooner the lessee will be required to get the lands on production or lose the lease.

The reduction in the length of the primary term has led to the elimination of delay rentals in CAPL 99.

Extension of the Primary Term

A fixed primary term by itself would not serve the particular needs of an oil and gas lease. If the term were for a fixed period of years and nothing more, the lease could terminate during the height of production, a state of affairs that would be unacceptable from the lessee's point of view. Hence, words are included that continue the lease in force beyond the primary term if the leased substances are being produced. Like so many other features of the lease, this provision is a balance between the rights of the two parties. On the one hand, it continues the lease in force if there is production, so that the lessee is not deprived of whatever reserves might have been discovered, while the requirement that there be production guarantees to the lessor that he will get his lands back unless the lessee has done something by the end of the primary term to realize their potential. This result is achieved by the phrase "and so long thereafter as the leased substances or any of them are produced from the said lands or the pooled lands."

Since there is no way to predetermine the precise date on which production may cease, the length of such a term cannot be definitely established until after the event. Such uncertainty would be fatal to a conventional property lease, but not to a *profit à prendre*, which may be for an uncertain term.[1]

PanCanadian Petroleum Ltd. v Husky Oil Operations Ltd.[2] posed a direct challenge to the "thereafter" language of the *habendum*. The *habendum* clause read as follows:

> To have and enjoy the same for the primary term of Twenty five (25) years from the date hereof and so long there after as the leased substances or any of them, are produced from the said lands or the pooled lands, subject to the sooner termination of the said term, and subject also to the renewal of the said term, all is hereinafter set forth.

The primary term of the lease was for twenty-five years, which would end on 3 January 1992. The lease covered a vast tract in the Lloydminster area, and at the end of the primary term, more than one thousand wells were producing oil and some seventy were producing gas. Thus, there was no question that the leased substances were being produced from the said lands when the primary term expired. The lease, which in many respects was more in the nature of a sale of the property, also contained a right of renewal under which the lessee had the option to renew for a further twenty-five-year term exercisable for a period ninety days after the termination of the primary term. This meant that the right to renew would not vest for twenty-five years, which, at the date the lease was entered into, 3 January 1967, clearly offended the Rule against Perpetuities. Accordingly, if Husky could not rely on the "thereafter" provision, the lease would terminate because Husky could not renew the lease. In argument, PanCanadian parsed the *habendum* clause, and focused on the phrase "and subject also to the renewal of the said term," to suggest that the only way the primary term of twenty-five years could be extended was by renewal, which was invalid under the Rule. Husky countered by arguing that the term of the lease was twenty-five years and so long thereafter as there was production of the leased substances. As McMahon J pointed out: "Apart from explaining why the dispute arose, the perpetuities issue is not

---

1 *Berkheiser v Berkheiser*, [1957] S.C.R. 387, 7 D.L.R. (2d) 721, [1957] No. 22 (S.C.C.).
2 26 Alta. L.R. (3d) 203, [1995] 4 W.W.R. 40, 163 A.R. 367, [1994] A.J. No. 1017 (Alta. Q.B.).

relevant to the interpretation of the *habendum* clause."[3] The trial judge wasted little time in concluding that the term of the lease was for twenty-five years plus so long thereafter as the leased substances were produced. If there is continued production at the end of the twenty-five-year term, as there was, the lease would continue in force without renewal.

In reaching this conclusion, the learned trial judge considered earlier cases in which *habenda* similar to the one in the *Husky* case had been interpreted by the courts. In *Canada-Cities Service Petroleum Corp. v Kininmonth*[4] the *habendum* read "To Have and Enjoy the same for the term of 10 years from the date hereof, and so long thereafter as the said substances or any of them are being produced from the said lands, subject to the sooner termination of the said term as hereinafter provided."

Speaking for the Supreme Court of Canada, Martland J said: "At the end of the 10 year term the lease is extended if any of the substances are being produced."[5] McMahon J also referred to *Durish v White Resource Management Ltd.*[6] in which Bracco J (as he then was) held that a lease would be continued by production after the expiration of the primary term.

He also referred to *Esso Resources Canada Ltd. v Pacific Cassiar Ltd.*[7] where the trial judge held: "It is unquestionable that production from any one of the Kent wells would extend the primary term for so long as such well produced a leased substance." In addition to judicial decisions, the trial judge was also able to rely on the writings of various authorities to the same effect.

While one may safely say that it is "unquestionable" that production from the lands will extend the lease beyond the primary term, there may, however, be some question as to what amounts to production.

What Is Production?

The primary term is extended if the substances "are produced" in the case of the conventional lease, and production will also be the primary cause of continuing a CAPL lease in force. The intent seems clear enough, but there may be some borderline situations: Will actual production, no

---

3 Ibid. at 210.

4 [1964] S.C.R. 439, 47 W.W.R. (N.S.) 437, 45 D.L.R. (2d) 36, [1964] S.C.J. No. 24 (S.C.C.).

5 Ibid. at 441.

6 (1987), 55 Alta. L.R. (2d) 47, [1987] A.J. No. 804 (Alta. Q.B.). This was the first of a series of cases involving the same parties and the same lands.

7 (1984), 33 Alta. L.R. (2d) 175, [1984] 6 W.W.R. 376 (Alta. Q.B.).

matter how small and uneconomic, be sufficient, or is there some requirement that it be of economic and commercial value? Must there be production at the very moment the primary term expires? What happens when
production is interrupted or ceases altogether?

Production in Paying Quantities

The standard *habendum* clause requires that the substances "are produced" in order to extend the primary term. There is no minimum
quantitative limit. American courts in most of the important oil-
producing states interpret the word "produced" as "produced in paying quantities."[8] This engrafting of a quantitative requirement works
to the advantage of the lessor since it prevents the lease from being
extended without any worthwhile benefit to him by way of royalties.
So far this issue has not arisen in Canada in connection with the "are
produced" language. In view of the approach taken by the Canadian
courts on other aspects of the lease, it must be considered highly
unlikely that the words would be expanded to include any economic
or volume conditions. If an operator is prepared to physically produce
a well, regardless of profit or loss, it is submitted that a Canadian court
would hold that the "are produced" test had been met.

This issue may well come before the courts in the future since there
are many marginal wells out there that are seemingly produced for no
other reason than to maintain the lease in force. With the advent of new
techniques, primarily horizontal drilling and improved seismic, some
properties that were once written off may become valuable and worth
the lessor's, or more likely, the top lessee's, challenging the validity of
the lease. As will be discussed later, much the same situation exists
with respect to marginal wells and shut-in payments.

The occasional lease does refer to "production in paying quantities."
The Ontario courts dealt with a variation of this wording in *Stevenson v
Westgate*,[9] where the fixed term of the lease was for one year "and for
such longer period as oil or gas is found thereon in paying quantities."
The use of the verb "found" rather than "produced" deflects the pre-
cise applicability of the decision; nonetheless, the court had to concern

---

8 Summers, *The Law of Oil and Gas*, vol. 2 (Kansas City, Mo.: Vernon Law Book Company)
   at 213. Many American courts have also interpreted "found," "discovered," "obtained,"
   and *"produced" as meaning the same thing, namely, "produced in paying quantities."*
9 [1941] 2 D.L.R. 471, [1941] O.J. No. 22 (Ont. H.C.J.); varied [1942] 1 D.L.R. 369, [1941] O.J.
   No. 165 (C.A.).

itself with the implications of "paying quantities." Indeed, the trial judge appears to have treated "found" as synonymous with "produced." The dispute arose from this fact pattern. The lease was dated 13 October 1938. The lessee drilled two wells and produced some oil from them, but more drilling apparently was required to fully develop the property (the wells were shallow and one assumes there were no minimum spacing restrictions at that time). The lessee entered into a development agreement with a third party, but at this time the problem posed by a prior mortgage became critical. The mortgagee would consent to the lease only if the lessor agreed to assign his royalty, which he avoided doing, and the developer refused to perform the work until the mortgagee had consented to the lease. As a result of this impasse, operations, including production, were suspended. At the end of the year, the lessee was ordered from the land.

The trial judge ignored any distinction between "found" and "produced" and referred to "produced in paying quantities." During the year the lessees had produced $539.00 worth of oil and they had expended over $4,000.00. Most of their expenditures, however, were of a capital nature; the operating costs were only $228.00. It was held that the true test was the relation between the oil produced and the cost of running and operating expenses. Capital expenditures, such as the cost of drilling the wells, were not to be included in the calculation.

The Court of Appeal seemed to place more emphasis on the meaning of the word "found." Experts had testified at the trial that the wells could be produced profitably. "The situation that developed was this: oil had been found upon the property in marketable quantities."[10] It is clear, however, that the court agreed with the trial judge in excluding capital costs. "Oil had been found and it was possible to pump it in quantities that were more than sufficient for the then current charges."[11]

In *Northwestern Utilities Ltd. v Peyto Oils Ltd.*,[12] Lomas J was called upon to interpret the phrase "until such time as petroleum and (or) natural gas and [sic] paying quantities shall be received ... " (other references in the case make it clear that the word "and" should be "in"). The trial judge quoted with approval a passage from Williams and Meyers[13] to the effect that "paying quantities" is defined in two

---

10 Ibid. at 371 (C.A.).

11 Ibid. at 372 (C.A.).

12 49 A.R. 1, [1983] A.J. No. 987 (Alta. Q.B.).

13 The judge was quoting from the 1981 edition of *Oil and Gas Law*, looseleaf (New York: Matthew Bender, 1981).

contexts: firstly in relation to the *habendum*, and secondly for purposes of the covenants in the lease. For purposes of the *habendum*, paying quantities means production in sufficient quantities to yield a return in excess of operating cost even though drilling and equipment costs may never be repaid.

With respect to covenants in the lease, the term means production in quantities sufficient to yield a return in excess of drilling, development, and operating costs. Thus, the purchaser under the agreement was released from the obligation to make certain payments because the second test of what amounts to paying quantities had not been met.

It would seem therefore that a Canadian Court faced with a reference to "produced in paying quantities" in the *habendum* would opt for revenue versus operating costs, and exclude the cost of drilling and equipping the well.

Continuous Production Difficult to Achieve

A literal interpretation of the phrase "and so long thereafter as the leased substances are produced" would appear to require continuous and uninterrupted production. There are many circumstances under which production may be suspended or interrupted: a well may be shut down for reworking or maintenance; the permitted allowable may have been produced within a portion of the month and the well shut in for the balance of the period; an overproduction penalty may be imposed with the result that a particular well is shut down completely for a prolonged period; a road ban may make it impossible to transport production from a well site not connected to a pipeline. These are but a few of the circumstances, unrelated to the productive capacity of the well, which may lead to a temporary halt in production. There are many others. If a well is productive of gas, the peculiar conditions of the market could lead to an entire field being shut in for several months out of each year. A particular gas field may be connected to a local utility company that will produce it only during periods of great demand such as December, January, February, and March.

All of these reasons are in addition to the more ominous one where production ceases because of the physical characteristics of the well and the reservoir. If production dwindles owing to the deterioration or depletion of the reservoir, the lessee will be able to contemplate the ultimate loss of its lease with more equanimity than where the lease is terminated "accidentally" in the full flood of its producing capacity.

Production may cease or be suspended either during the primary term or after its expiration.

Cessation of Production during Primary Term

The second proviso to the *habendum* is sometimes known as the "dry hole" clause. It deals with the situation where the lessee drills a non-productive well or wells during the primary term, or where production ceases and the well is abandoned during the primary term. In the absence of the second proviso it would appear that the result under the usual form of conventional lease would be that the lease continues in force during the balance of the primary term without the requirement of either any further drilling or the payment of delay rentals. The *habendum* grants the lease for the specified primary term, subject to earlier termination if the lessee does not commence drilling or pay the annual fee for deferring same. In the case of a dry hole or of a well becoming unproductive, the lessee will have met the drilling commitment, and thus there should be no basis for terminating the lease prior to the expiration of the primary term. Nor would the lessee be liable for any further payments of the delay rental since the undertaking to commence drilling has been met. When the primary term has elapsed the lease would terminate for want of production.

The second proviso, however, makes it clear that in order to hold the lease, the lessee must either commence drilling operations or tender the delay rental by the next anniversary date. In effect, the proviso treats the drilling of a dry hole or the abandonment of a well during the primary term as if no drilling operations had in fact taken place.

The CAPL lease dispenses with the "dry hole" clause.

Cessation of Production after the Primary Term

If production comes to an end after the primary term, the lease will terminate. In *Krysa v Opalinski*[14] production continued for some years beyond the primary term, but eventually was halted because the wells could no longer produce on an economic basis. The wording of the "thereafter" portion of the *habendum* was held to result in an automatic termination.

---

14 [1960] A.J. No. 15, 32 W.W.R. 346 (Alta. S.C.T.D.).

Because of the wording "and so long thereafter as the leased substances or any of them are produced," the lease would automatically
come to an end if production ceased, even temporarily, after the expiration of the primary term. The third proviso deals with this situation and
continues the lease in force if the lessee takes steps to place the lands
back on production or if certain other conditions are met. While every
lease will contain some form of the third proviso, the individual language of the clause may render it inapplicable to the circumstances of
the case. In *Canada-Cities Service Petroleum Corp. v Kininmonth*[15] the third
proviso was held to be inapplicable, with disastrous consequences to the
lessee. Incredibly enough, the *Kininmonth* version of the third proviso
was still to be found in some lease forms in circulation years after the
decision was handed down. The *Kininmonth* language did not contain
the words "at the end of the said ten (10) year term," but referred only to
the cessation of production *after the* expiration of the primary term.

The lessee delayed drilling until very close to the end of the primary
term. When the ten-year period had expired, the well had encountered
production and was ready for a treatment that would open up the formation. This occurred during the months of March and April. The lease
was dated 11 May, and the usual road bans were in force, with the result
that the equipment required to treat the well could not be trucked to the
lease until after the primary term had expired. The work was eventually completed, and the well produced briefly in June and July before it
was shut down by a Conservation Board order because the lessee did
not have the proper spacing unit. This latter point is irrelevant for our
purposes; we need only concern ourselves with the situation as it
existed on 10 May, when the well was awaiting a fracturing treatment
and was not producing. Because the clause in *Kininmonth* referred to
"after the expiration of the said ten year term," Martland J declared that
it could not apply where there was no production when the primary
term expired. It could not mean that "even though no production has
been obtained within the ten year primary term, the lessee may thereafter carry on drilling operations on the land which, if successful, will
then serve to extend the lease for a further period during the continuance of such production."[16] The proviso quoted above, referred to by

15 *Supra* n 4.
16 Ibid. at 445.

the court as "the fifth paragraph," did not apply, and "without the fifth paragraph the lease would automatically terminate upon the cessation of production."[17]

In a later decision, involving an interpretation of the "thereafter" clause and its provisos, the Supreme Court seems to have abandoned its "hard line" approach and to attach unexpected weight to the intention of the lessee to place the lands on production. While the facts in *Canadian Superior Oil Ltd. v Cull*[18] were generally similar to the *Kininmonth* structure, the result was totally different. In the *Cull* case the *habendum* clause was for a term of ten years "and as long thereafter as oil, gas or other mineral is produced from the said land hereunder, or as long thereafter as Lessee shall conduct drilling, mining or reworking operations thereon as hereinafter provided and during the production of oil, gas or other mineral resulting therefrom."

The lease also contained a clause that extended the primary term if the lessee was engaged in drilling operations at the time of its expiration.

12. If Lessee shall commence to drill a well within the term of this lease or any extension thereof, Lessee shall have the right to drill such well to completion with reasonable diligence and dispatch, and if oil or gas be found in paying quantities, this lease shall continue and be in force with like effect as if such well had been completed within the term of years herein first mentioned.

Clause 7 of the lease was a combination of the standard form of the second and third provisos to the *habendum* clause.

7. If prior to the discovery of oil or gas on said lands Lessee should drill a dry hole or holes thereon, or if after the discovery of oil or gas the production thereof should cease from any cause, this lease shall continue in force during the primary term, if on or before the rental paying date next ensuing after the expiration of ninety (90) days from date of completion

---

17 Ibid.
18 [1972] S.C.R. 89, [1971] 3 W.W.R. 28, 20 D.L.R. (3d) 360, [1971] S.C.J. No. 91 (S.C.C.); affirming (1970), 75 W.W.R. (N.S.) 606, 16 D.L.R. (3d) 709 (Alta. C.A.); affirming (1970), 74 W.W.R. 324 (Alta. S.C., T.D.). I commented on the implications of this decision in Ballem, "The Continuing Adventures of the Oil and Gas Lease" (1972) 50 Can. Bar Rev. 423.

of dry hole or cessation of production Lessee commences drilling or reworking operation or commences or resumes the payment or tender of
rentals, or after the primary term if Lessee commences additional drilling
or re-working operations within sixty (60) days from date of completion
of dry hole or cessation of production, and if production results therefrom then so long as such production continues.

The dispute arose on this fact pattern:

1 The primary ten-year term would have expired on 30 December 1957.
2 The well had been spudded on 28 November 1957, and drilled
ahead until 23 December 1957.
3 On 24 and 25 December the well was cored and a drill stem test was
run, with results that led the lessee to believe the well should be
completed as an oil well.
4 Drilling was resumed and continued to total depth, which was
reached on 28 December, and a radioactive log was run on the same
date.
5 Production casing was set on 29 December and a Christmas Tree (the
wellhead equipment that controls production) was set on the well.
6 The drilling rig was released on 30 December 1957, and it took two
days for the rig to be dismantled and moved off the site.
7 A service rig (much smaller and less expensive to operate than a
drilling rig and commonly used for completion operations) was
moved onto the site and rigged up on 2 January 1958.
8 On 3 January it commenced completion operations, including the
recovery of dropped casing, the running of a radioactive log, and
perforations into the prospective formations. Production tubing
was run, and on 6 January the well was acidized – a process
designed to open up the formation and increase the flow.
9 On 7 January the well was swabbed, an operation where outside oil
is introduced into the well to stimulate the flow of substances, and
both load and formation oil began to flow and were discharged into
a disposal pit. The service rig was released on the same date.
10 By 7 January 1958, the well was capable of producing oil for the first
time – on this date the well had started to flow; the Christmas Tree
was shut to stem the flow and the service rig released and removed
from the site.
11 There was no equipment then ready on the site to handle the production, although some of the material was on the site but not

hooked up. On 8, 9, and 10 January a 500-barrel tank, a separator, and miscellaneous equipment were erected and installed. After this work was completed the well was reopened on 11 January 1958, and began to flow into the tank. Subject to the production allowable established by the Oil and Gas Conservation Board, the well produced continuously in paying quantities.

12 The oil that began to flow into the tank on 11 January, as was pointed out by the court, was probably a mixture of outside load oil, which had been introduced during the swabbing operations and only partially recovered during tests, plus some formation oil. For accounting purposes the lessee treated all of the oil produced on 11 and 12 January as paying back the load oil from other sources and treated production as having commenced on 13 January.

The lessor argued against the continued validity of the lease primarily on two grounds: that the lease expired at midnight 29–30 December 1957, because the lessee was not then engaged in *drilling* the well to completion, since total depth had been obtained and clause 12 referred to the right "to drill such well to completion." The trial judge, Sinclair J, held that the non-drilling operations such as perforating, acidizing, and swabbing constituted drilling the well "to completion," and the lease was thus extended during the continuance of these operations. Both the Appellate Division and the Supreme Court agreed with this conclusion.

The second ground of attack was that, if the well had been drilled to completion on 7 January 1958, at which time it was capable of producing, it terminated automatically according to its terms on that date since it was not produced until 13 January. Although the trial judge was prepared to include those operations necessary to place the well in a position where it was capable of production as being included in the phrase "drill ... to completion," he was not prepared to extend such phrase to include the installation of tanks and other surface facilities needed to treat and save the oil. Therefore, he agreed with the lessor's contention that the lease was extended only until 7 January 1958, and that there being no production for a period of several days thereafter, the lease terminated on 7 January by its own terms.[19]

---

19 The trial judge upheld the lease on the ground of estoppel created by a subsequent document. This point will be discussed *infra*, under "Estoppel." Neither the Appellate Division nor the Supreme Court found it necessary to deal with estoppel.

Both the Appellate Division and the Supreme Court of Canada concluded that, under the circumstances above described, the lease had never terminated. The senior courts were obviously impressed by the fact that the well produced and marketed its full quota of oil for the month of January and the lessee had received the royalty. The trial judge had rejected the production allowable argument on the basis that it could not work until the well had produced to the point where the restriction would come into play. In other words, if the well had produced its monthly quota and had been shut in at the time its primary term expired, Sinclair J would have relied on the previous production to continue the lease in force. But the Appellate Division went even further by holding that allowable production that took place *after* the end of the term but during the same month in which it expired was sufficient.

The Appellate Division also paid attention to the mechanics of completing a well; Johnson JA was troubled that there might always be a time gap, which would make it impossible to effectively extend the life of the lease by the use of a clause such as the one contained in the *Cull* lease. "Given a ready market for oil does the combined effect of these clauses require that production be taken the very moment that the well has been completed? I have said 'the very moment' for it must be realized that in every case there will be a period, however short, while the well is connected to the gathering systems and the valves are being turned on, when no production is obtained." He then answered his own question: "It is not reasonable, I suggest, to apply so stringent an interpretation. Wells are not permitted to produce constantly. The Conservation Board sets a quota for each well ... Considering the effect to be given to paragraph 2 of the lease the question is not whether the well was flowing at the exact moment that the term of the lease expired (in this case when the well was completed) but whether oil can be taken and marketed so that the lessor and lessee will be entitled to the full benefit of the well's production."[20]

The lessor had placed great reliance on a trio of Supreme Court of Canada decisions, in each of which the term of the lease was held not to have been extended. All three cases, *Canadian Superior Oil Ltd. v*

---

[20] (1970), 75 W.W.R. (N.S.) 606, 16 D.L.R. (3d) 709 (Alta. S.C., App.Div.).

Murdoch,[21] *Canadian Superior Oil of California, Ltd. v Kanstrup*,[22] and *Canadian Superior Oil Ltd. v Hambly*,[23] involved gas for which there was no currently available market and the failure to make timely payment of the suspended well royalty. The Supreme Court of Canada agreed with the ground on which the Appellate Division distinguished these authorities, namely, that in all three cases there had been no present intention on the part of the lessee to place the wells on production, and that since the suspended well royalty had not been made on time, the lease could not be continued beyond the primary term by reason of constructive production.

In the *Cull* situation all the courts found that the lessee had a *bona fide* intention to proceed diligently to place the well on production and that this intention was carried out with reasonable diligence and dispatch. The Supreme Court also relied upon the provision in clause 12 that "if oil or gas be found in paying quantities, this lease shall continue and be in force with like effect as if such well had been completed within the term of years herein first mentioned." Oil had been found and the court held that the language enabled the lessee to put the well into production and thereby continue the lease.

The *Cull* rationale should really be compared with that of the *Kininmonth* case rather than with those three decisions involving suspended gas wells and untimely payment of the suspended well royalty. The *Kininmonth* case dealt with an oil well that the lessee was unable to complete prior to the expiration of the primary term. In that case, however, it will be recalled that the language of the "fifth paragraph" (the approximate counterpart of the third proviso in the conventional form of lease and of clause 7 in the *Cull* lease) did not apply according to its language until after the expiration of the primary term. Accordingly, it could not be relied upon by the lessee. The *Cull* case, particularly the Supreme Court of Canada decision where Martland J placed great reliance on clause 12, illustrated what might have been the result in *Kininmonth* if the "fifth paragraph" had been worded so as to apply at the end of, as well as after, the primary term.

---

21 (1969), 70 W.W.R. (N.S.) 768, 6 D.L.R. (3d) 464 (S.C.C.) affirmed without written reasons the decision of the Appellate Division (1969), 68 W.W.R. (N.S.) 390.
22 [1965] S.C.R. 92, 49 W.W.R. (N.S.) 257, 47 D.L.R. (2d) 1, [1964] S.C.J. No. 54 (S.C.C.).
23 [1970] S.C.R. 932, 74 W.W.R. (N.S.) 356, 12 D.L.R., (3d) 247, [1970] S.C.J. No. 48 (S.C.C.).

Republic Resources Limited v Ballem[24] is another example of what happens when the lease does not permit drilling past the primary term. In the *Republic* case the third proviso, as in *Kininmonth*, referred only to the leased substances not being produced "after the expiration of the said primary term." The oil company delayed the commencement of drilling until a week before the expiration of the primary term, and the well was not completed until seven days after the term had expired. It was held that the third proviso could only come into play if production had ceased *after* the expiration of the primary term, and since there was no production during the primary term, the lease had expired on its own terms.

The gap that was fatal in both the *Kininmonth* and *Republic* cases and which caused much judicial soul-searching in *Cull* is expressly covered by the words "if at the end of the said _____ term," which are to be found in the most widely used form of the third proviso. It must be borne in mind, however, that many existing leases, extended beyond their primary terms by production, contain the old wording and, as mentioned earlier, some new leases with the defective language were still being entered into long after *Kininmonth*.

The most commonly encountered version of the proviso attempts to deal with two situations:

(a) That occurring at the end of the primary term, with no production but where the lessee is then engaged in drilling or working operations on the lands. The proviso continues the lease in force so long as such drilling or working operations are prosecuted with no cessation of more than ninety consecutive days and, if such operations result in the production of leased substances, so long thereafter as such substances are produced.

(b) Where the lease has been continued beyond its primary term and then production ceases. The lease continues in force if the lessee commences further drilling or working operations within ninety days after the cessation of such production, and remains in force provided that such drilling or working operations are prosecuted with no cessation of more than ninety consecutive days and for the duration of any production resulting therefrom.

---

24 17 Alta. L.R. (2d) 235, [1982] 1 W.W.R. 692, 33 A.R. 385, [1981] A.J. No. 559 (Alta. Q.B.).

Both situations are also covered by language in the third proviso that is similar to a *force majeure* provision, and provides that, if the drilling or working operations are interrupted or suspended as the result of any cause beyond the lessee's reasonable control, the time of such interruption or suspension or nonproduction shall not be counted against the lessee. There is a further application of *force majeure* in that, if the production is shut in or suspended or not produced as a result of a lack of or an intermittent market or any cause whatsoever beyond the lessee's reasonable control, then such time shall not be counted against the lessee.

In the first edition of this work, I discussed the possible meaning of the phrase "shall not be counted against the lessee," and speculated it meant that where *force majeure* applied, the time intervals of ninety days within which the lessee must carry out drilling or working operations would not begin to run. In *Kissinger Petroleums Ltd. v Nelson Estate*,[25] however, the Alberta Court of Appeal said: "The only meaning I can give this wording is that the time of non production is not to be counted ... It is the same as if the well had been completed and produced for the hiatus between completion and production is not to be counted. For the purposes of the clause, the well should be considered as producing from its completion."

Macdonald JA, in his dissenting opinion in *Canada-Cities Service Petroleum Corporation v Kininmonth*,[26] interpreted the words in the same manner. In *Kininmonth* the majority in both the Alberta Court of Appeal and the Supreme Court found that the cause of suspension was not beyond the lessee's reasonable control and thus were not called upon to examine the meaning of the phrase "shall not be counted against the lessee." Macdonald JA, however, found that the cause of suspension was a regulatory order that was beyond the reasonable control of the lessee. He was of the opinion that the time of suspension should not be counted against the lessee and that during the time of such suspension the lease continued to be in full force and effect.[27]

---

25 (1984), 33 Alta. L.R. (2d) 1, [1984] 5 W.W.R. 673, 13 D.L.R. (4th) 542, [1984] A.J. No. 2587
    (Alta. C.A.); affirming 26 Alta. L.R. (2d) 378, 14 E.T.R. 207, 45 A.R. 393, [1983] A.J.
    No. 814 (Alta. Q.B.). (Leave to appeal to Supreme Court denied.)
26 (1963), 44 W.W.R. (N.S.) 392, 42 D.L.R. (2d) 56 (Alta. S.C., App.Div.).
27 Ibid. at 409.

Since the third proviso of virtually every pre-CAPL lease contained the words "shall not be counted against the lessee," the *Kissinger* decision has far-reaching implications. If the well has been drilled over the end of the primary term and encounters production, or if the well produces beyond the primary term and then ceases production, the lease will be continued indefinitely until production resumes provided that the reason for the non-production is due to a lack of or an intermittent market, or any cause whatsoever beyond the lessee's reasonable control.

The third proviso deals with two situations: (a) where drilling operations are being carried on over the primary term and (b) where production ceases after the expiration of the primary term. However, even if a potentially productive well is drilled during the primary term, the situation could still be affected by the *Kissinger* rationale. If the well is shut in during the primary term, the lease will be continued until the expiration of the primary term because the drilling commitment has been satisfied. The lessee will, or should, make a shut-in payment on or before the end of the primary term in order to deem production and thus continue the lease in force. If a subsequent failure to make another shut-in payment could be treated as a cessation of production, the lease would nevertheless continue in force, since the third proviso would be applicable and time would not be counted against the lease.

Under the version of the third proviso that was considered in the *Kissinger* case, the interruption or suspension of operations or non-production must be by reason of a lack of or an intermittent market or a cause beyond the lessee's reasonable control. One version of the third proviso, in fairly common use in the conventional lease, eliminates the reference to market conditions and causes beyond reasonable control and simply states that if such interruption of operations or non-production is for any cause whatsoever in accordance with good oil field practice, the time of such interruption or suspension or non-production "shall not be counted against the lessee."

While there still has to be a "cause," "good oil field practice" would seem to leave a great deal up to the discretion of the lessee. Shutting in a well where there is a likelihood or possibility of drainage would clearly not be "in accordance with good oil field practice," but if that was not a factor, and no mechanical or operational damage was done to the well, how much latitude does the lessee have? Does the fact he doesn't like the current price for his product, or wants to defer drilling and meet his contractual commitment from other wells, or other fields, constitute a "cause in accordance with good oil field practice"? Possibly.

Still other versions of the proviso are to the effect that so long as the well is capable of production and compensatory royalties, equal to the delay rental, are paid in each year, the lease continues in force.

The following point will be discussed in more detail in Chapter 8, but before leaving the third proviso, it should be noted that shut-in clauses, regardless of whether "may" or "shall" is used, are optional. Thus, it would appear that so long as the conditions of the third proviso are met, there is a possibility that the lease may continue indefinitely without the necessity of the lessee making any payments whatsoever. If this were to occur, the lease would truly have gained immortality.

This seems to be the argument advanced by the plaintiff by counterclaim in *White Resource Management Ltd v Durish*.[28] Durish argued that the words in the third proviso "the time of such interruption or suspension or non-production shall not be counted against the Lessee, anything hereinbefore contained or implied to the contrary notwithstanding," together with the *Kissinger* case, meant that the non-payment of a shut-in royalty should not be counted against him. Mason J distinguished *Kissinger* because there the well was started within the primary term and completed after the anniversary date of the lease. That, according to the judge, was precisely the situation to which the third proviso of the *habendum* clause is directed. In the *Durish* situation, the well in question was drilled and completed within the primary term, and the third proviso accordingly was not engaged, and the shut-in wells clause governed. Having found that the third proviso was not applicable, it was not necessary for the court to interpret the meaning of the words "shall not be counted."

Since there was no shut-in payment in the *Durish* case, it does not eliminate the possibility described in the penultimate paragraph above that a shut-in payment made at the expiration of the primary term may engage the third proviso with its "time shall not count" language.

The third proviso states that if the drilling or working operations result in the production of the leased substances, the lease shall remain in force. There is no reference to deemed or constructive production that results from a shut-in payment. There are other references in the

---

28 (1998) A.R. 201, [1998] A.J. No. 1041 (Q.B.), but see *obiter* in *Kensington Energy Ltd. v B&G Energy Ltd.*, [2005] A.J. No. 1672. This case also stands for the proposition that shutting in a well that has become essentially a "dry hole" is not in accordance with good oil field practice.

habendum that do incorporate references to deemed production, and it was argued in the *Kissinger* case that because the reference was to "the production of the leased substances," actual production was required before the lease could continue in force. The Court of Appeal held that there may be deemed production even though the word "deemed" is not used, and therefore constructive production under the shut-in clause would be sufficient.

Some versions of this proviso refrain from expressing the period during which production may cease and rely simply on a reference to "a reasonable time." Certainly where the clause spells out a ninety-day period it is unlikely that the court would permit any longer periods, but it remains an open question as to what the court might interpret as constituting "a reasonable period." Much would depend upon the circumstances of the individual case. A well with a serious technical problem located in an isolated area might be granted a longer period of interruption than would a readily accessible well with only a minor breakdown. Factors such as weather conditions or spring break-up might also be taken into consideration.

The effect of a temporary cessation of production under a lease with no equivalent of the third proviso remains a matter of conjecture insofar as Canada is concerned. American courts take the approach that a temporary cessation of production will not terminate the lease. "The law is well settled that a temporary cessation of developments or operations under an oil and gas lease does not, as a matter of law, constitute an abandonment."[29] In *Frost v Gulf Oil Corporation*[30] the court held that "the lease in question does not say that it shall be in force so long as minerals are *continuously* produced."

This approach has enabled lessees to maintain a lease where the production has ceased for a period of months or sometimes even years. The courts apply the test of whether the cessation of production was for an "unreasonable" period of time. The decisive factor in whether or not the elapsed time was unreasonable seems to be the efforts, or lack of them, made by the lessee to restore production. If the lessee has acted in good faith and carried out operations designed to reactivate

---

29 *Wisconsin- Texas Oil Co. v Clutter* (1894), 268 S.W. 921 (1925, Tex. Ct. of App.).

30 (1960), 238 Miss. 775, 119 So (2d) 759. For a detailed review of the American authorities on this point, see Brown Jr., *The Law of Oil and Gas Leases*, vol.1 (New York: Matthew Bender, 1997) at section 5.09.

the wells or drill new ones, the American authorities seem disposed to continue the lease in force.

It is doubtful if this approach would commend itself to Canadian courts with their stricter approach to the language of the lease. The following passage from the Ontario Court of Appeal in *Stevenson v Westgate* may forecast the attitude of Canadian courts:

> The question whether respondents' rights under the agreement of October 13, 1938 continued beyond the expiration of one year depends upon the proper effect to be given to the words "for as much longer period as oil or gas is found thereon in paying quantities." While appellants are entitled to have a construction placed upon these words that will assure them of the continued operation of any well upon their land, so that they may be assured of a reasonable return so long as respondents continue to occupy, at the same time this is a business arrangement, and regard must be had to the reasonable requirements of the business. It is not the fair meaning of the agreement that without interruption respondents must produce a constant flow of oil in paying quantities, or lose their right to continue operating. Operation may be interrupted from causes not chargeable to respondents. There may be times in the course of the operations when it cannot be said that they are paying. In my opinion a more liberal interpretation must be placed upon the terms of the agreement than to say, "if there is any such occasion, the lease terminates."[31]

Because of the reference to "with no cessation of ninety (90) consecutive days," in the third proviso of conventional leases, it seems reasonable to suggest that the courts would import that time limitation in those cases where the lease is silent on the point.

The CAPL lease is very specific on the effect of cessation of production after the expiration of the primary term. The production of any leased substance is included in the definition of "operations," and the *habendum* provides that the term of the lease shall continue so long thereafter as operations are conducted with no cessation, in the case of each cessation of operations, of more than ninety consecutive days.

Thus, dealing strictly with cessation of production after the expiry of the primary term, if the hiatus lasts for more than ninety consecutive days, the lease will terminate. The issue can be complicated by the fact

---

31 *Supra* n 9 at 371, 372.

that the definition of "operations" includes activities other than pro-duction, such as repairing a well, which could continue the lease for at least a limited time, in the absence of production. The suspended wells clause, if applicable, could also continue the lease in force. This will be discussed in more detail when we come to shut-in well payments.

The limitation of ninety consecutive days would seem to make the position of the lessee very vulnerable. However, as might be expected, the CAPL lease contains a *force majeure* clause that, like the third pro-viso in conventional leases, modifies and ameliorates the effect of the *habendum*. The *force majeure* clause provides, insofar as it relates to the continuance of the lease, that if operations are interrupted or sus-pended or cannot be commenced as a result of *force majeure*, the lease shall not terminate during any such period of interruption, suspen-sion, or inability to commence caused thereby or for thirty days there-after. The thirty days is a grace period to allow the lessee to get operations under way once the *force majeure* no longer exists.

Force majeure is defined as "any cause beyond the lessee's reasonable control and, without limitation, includes an act of God, strike, lockout, or other industrial disturbance, act of any public enemy, war, blockade, riot, lightning, fire, storm, flood, explosion, unusually severe weather conditions, government restraints, including road bans, but shall not include lack of finances."

The causes of *force majeure*, with the exception of "road bans," designed to overcome the *Kininmonth* ruling that a road ban is not an act of *force majeure*, are virtually identical to the typical clauses of this type. Interestingly, they do not include any reference to market condi-tions, although that question might be covered off by the suspended wells clause as will be discussed in Chapter 8.

Reversion of Rights at End of Primary Term

Most leases currently in use, including CAPL 88 and 91, will continue the lease beyond the primary term with respect not only to all the lands covered by the lease, but also to all zones and formations, so long as there is a producing well, or a well capable of production, on the lands. More and more leases, however, now incorporate a modification of this result by a deeper rights reversion clause.

Basically, a deeper rights reversion clause provides that at the expi-ration of the primary term, or a specified period thereafter (three months is common), the rights to all formations below the deepest formation penetrated by a well on the lands, or on pooled or unitized lands, will revert to the lessor. This of course is greatly to the benefit of the lessor, since it frees up formations that could be of interest to other potential lessees in the future. Until the appearance of CAPL 99, there was no "standardized" version of the reversion clause. Typically, it would take the form of a proviso to the *habendum* and would read as follows: "Provided, however, upon the expiry of the primary term of this lease or 90 days after cessation of drilling operations, whichever is the later date, all formations below the deepest geological penetrated shall *revert* to the lessor" (emphasis added). The reference to the ninety-day period can have the effect of delaying the reversion. For example, if the rig was released a week after the expiration of the primary term (the lease having been continued by the drilling operation), the formations would not revert to the lessor until ninety days after the rig release.

Another type of clause requires the lessee to *surrender* the deeper formations.

> PROVIDED that if at the end of the primary term the said lands or any lands with which the said lands are pooled or unitized are capable of commercial production, the lessee shall *surrender* all formations within the said lands which lie below the base of the deepest formation which is capable of production, except that if any operation contemplated in clause 1(g)(i) is being conducted at the end of the primary term then the date of such surrender shall be extended to 90 days after cessation of such operation (emphasis added).

The reference to any operation in clause 1(g)(i) means drilling, reworking, injecting substances, and other activities designed to obtain or improve production from the lands.

The reversion of undrilled formations to the lessor at the end of the primary term seems both logical and equitable. A further refinement might be a clause that continues the lease in force only with respect to those formations that are productive, or potentially productive. While it is true that the non-productive formations above the deepest depth drilled have been drilled and rejected, it is also true that new theories and techniques are constantly being developed by explorationists, and a formation that may be dismissed today could be attractive tomorrow. One version that is occasionally encountered might arguably have this effect. Usually when leases are pooled to form a spacing unit, all the lands are pooled. More and more, however, pooling is limited to the producing formation, and in this instance the clause would enable the lessor to reclaim all of the lands except for the producing or potentially productive formations. It should be noted that the clause requires the lessor to give written notice.

> PROVIDED FURTHER, if at any time after the end of the primary term the lessee receives written notice from the lessor, the lessee shall surrender any of the said lands not comprised within a spacing unit on which operations are being conducted or deemed to be conducted.

A clause such as the one below would put the matter beyond doubt.

> PROVIDED FURTHER, the Lessee shall within 90 days after the end of the primary term or cessation of drilling operations, surrender all formations and zones comprised within the said lands except those that are productive or capable of production.

This should be coupled with an undertaking to amend the lessee's caveat, as discussed under the next heading.

The reversion provision in CAPL 99 provides that at the end of the primary term the lease shall expire as to all zones beneath the base of the deepest zone completed for and capable of production of the leased substances.

While leases may provide that deeper rights will revert to the mineral owner, this by itself will not tell the world what has taken place. It is in the interest of the lessor to make sure that the registry of his title shows the reversion. This will be discussed in the following section.

Caveats

Upon obtaining a new lease the lessee invariably will register a caveat to record its interest in the lessor's title. Typically, the caveat will contain a description of the lease, including its date. This would allow anyone interested in the property to make an educated guess as to the likely expiration of the primary term. Further enquiries from public sources could reveal the existence of a well on the lands. This could be the end of the matter, since the caveat will not indicate that certain rights have reverted to the lessor. A knowledgeable oil company or broker, aware of the increasing prevalence of reversionary clauses, might make further enquiries and learn that certain rights were available. However, this is a haphazard process and not one the mineral owner should count on. The lessee's caveat should be amended to show that from and after a certain date the lessee's rights under the lease are limited to certain formations. Alternatively, the original caveat might be withdrawn and a new one, limited to the remaining zones, substituted. This may not appeal to the lessee since it opens up the possibility of an intervening registration taking precedence. If there are no intervening relevant caveats, it should be acceptable.

In the normal course of events, it is not likely that the lessor will be aware that the rights have reverted. He may learn of it by chance, and, failing that, the necessary information is available to him. An enquiry directed to his lessee after the expiration of the primary term will set things in motion, or he can access the well information by contacting the appropriate regulatory authority.

Since we are dealing with the situation where a lease comes to an end, either partially or completely, it is appropriate to say a word or two about the removal of caveats generally. Upon the expiration of a lease the great majority of lessees will withdraw their caveat as a matter of course, and others will do so after some prodding. In the case of a recalcitrant lessee or, more likely, a lessee who no longer exists, the mineral owner can always serve a notice to lapse a caveat under the *Land Titles Acts* of the various provinces.[32]

While this remedy is available to him, a lessor should not be driven to these extremes and the lease should impose a clear undertaking on the part of the lessee to remove his caveat upon termination of the lease. A clause to accomplish this purpose could read as follows:

REMOVAL OF CAVEAT
In the event of the lessee having registered in the Land Titles Office or Registry Office for the area in which the lands are situated, this lease or any caveat or other document in respect thereof, the lessee shall withdraw or discharge the document so registered within a reasonable time after termination of the lease.

---

32 *Land Titles Act*, R.S.A. 2000, c L-4, s 138; *Land Titles Act*, R.S.B.C. 1996, c 250, s 293; *Land Titles Act*, R.S.S. 2000, c L-5.1, s 63.

A proviso could be added to deal with the situation where a lease has terminated but only as to certain formations. Something along the following lines should suffice: "Provided that in the event this lease shall terminate but only as to part thereof, the lessee shall take such steps as may be necessary to amend or replace any caveat or other document registered with respect to this lease to limit it to those parts of this lease that continue in force." Unaccountably, the CAPL lease does not contain a removal of caveat clause. While it may be that most lessees are cooperative about removing caveats and the mineral owner has the ultimate remedy of a notice to lapse, it is very important to him to have a clean title, and he should be entitled to a specific undertaking in that regard.

Before leaving the subject of caveats, it should be pointed out that in yet another *Durish v White Resource Management Ltd.* case[33] the Supreme Court handed down an important decision with regard to the effect of caveats under the Torrens system and where the priorities lie as between competing caveats. The court ruled that as between encumbrances, priority is determined by the date of the caveats. A dispute between a caveator and a registered owner is not one of priority. This appeal did not deal with the validity of oil and gas leases, but only with issues relating to the Land Title system and priorities thereunder.

Drilling

Having dealt with the primary term and its extension, we may now return to the first proviso and the lessee's position re drilling on the lands. The "standard" proviso quoted at the beginning of this chapter provides that, if the lessee has not commenced operations for the drilling of a well within the specified annual period or paid the specified delay rental, the lease will terminate. This type of provision is the one commonly found in conventional leases in Canada and is known as the "unless" drilling clause. The termination of the lease for failure to commence drilling operations on time, or make the payment, is clearly set forth: "This lease shall terminate and be at an end on the first anniversary date, *unless* the lessee shall have paid or tendered to the lessor on or before the said anniversary date the sum of ... dollars ... which payment shall confer the privilege of deferring the commencement of drilling

---

33 [1995] 1 S.C.R. 633, [1995] S.C.J. No. 14, 121 D.L.R. (4th) 577, [1995] 3 W.W.R. 609 (S.C.C.).

operations for a period of one year from said anniversary date" (emphasis added). It has been held time after time that under the clear language of the lease itself the termination is automatic unless one of the alternatives of drilling or payment has been fully complied with.

Indeed, the language is so clear on the point that there is no need to rely on the judicial authorities. There have been many judicial pronouncements on such niceties as to what constitutes the commencement of drilling operations, what amounts to proper payment, and what are the precise time limits within which such operations or payments must be commenced or made. These matters are fully reviewed in Part 5, "Involuntary Termination." The historical reasons that led to the widespread use of the "unless" type of clause in Canada are described in Chapter 2.

There is another type of drilling commitment that does not contain the built-in hazard of the "unless" type. Under this alternative the lessee is obligated to commence drilling operations *or* pay an annual sum of money; hence its name, the "or" clause. For some reason the "or" clause, although advantageous to the lessee, did not come into widespread use in Canada until the arrival of the CAPL lease. A typical "or" clause reads as follows:

PROVIDED, however:
(i) that if drilling operations are not commenced on the said lands within one year from the date hereof, the lessee shall not later than thirty (30) days after the expiration of the said one (1) year period, pay or tender to the lessor rental at the rate of $ ... per acre of the said lands, (hereinafter called "the annual acreage rental") as the annual acreage rental for the next ensuing year of the primary term and that similarly during successive years of the primary term, if drilling operations are not commenced, the lessee shall make like payments or tenders.

The "or" clause does not contain any words of automatic termination. The lessee is merely obliged to either commence drilling operations or pay a specified rental. Because there is no automatic termination, the obligation of the lessee to make the rental payment continues so long as the primary term exists, and no drilling operations have taken place, but this obligation can be terminated by the lessee through a positive act of surrender under a subsequent clause in the lease. The fact that the oil industry was reluctant for so many years to use the "or" version of the drilling clause is puzzling; the usual explanation was that people were accustomed to the "unless" type. Inasmuch as the average lessor has little understanding of what he is signing, one printed form looking much like another, this explanation was never altogether convincing.

For income tax purposes, the lessee is entitled to deduct delay rentals paid to freehold lessors as a Canadian Oil and Gas Property Expense (COGPE) at the rate of 10 per cent per year. Insofar as the lessor is concerned, the amounts received as delay rentals are regarded as proceeds of disposition and will reduce the lessor's COGPE pool, which ultimately will reduce his Canadian Development Expense (CDE) pool. If the CDE pool becomes negative, the amount received by way of delay rentals must be brought into the lessor's income. If the lessor has no COGPE and CDE against which the delay rentals can be offset, the proceeds must be taken directly into the lessor's income.

There are no obligations on the lessee under the "unless" clause to either commence drilling operations or make the payment. The lessee's position has been defined repeatedly by the courts as that of a person who has an option and not an obligation, but the result of this freedom of action can often be fatal to the lease. The annual payment made to defer the commencement of drilling operations is normally referred to as a "delay rental," the reference to "delay" recognizing that by such payment the commencement of drilling operations may be postponed, or delayed. The courts have also pointed out on many occasions that the payment is not a rent. "This sum was not paid as rent but was paid for the privilege of postponing the obligation to drill, ... obviously, the sum of money paid each year by the oil company to the appellants was not rent but was the purchase price of an extension of the time fixed for drilling. The payments had none of the characteristics of rent."[34]

The amount of the delay rental, left blank in the printed form to be filled in on execution of the document, is almost invariably computed at the rate of one dollar per acre, so that if the lease covers one quarter section, 160 acres, the amount of the delay rental will be $160.00 and $640.00 for a full section. One dollar per acre was at one time the standard rental under Alberta Crown leases and was the limit for permitted deductions from the lessee's income for both Crown and freehold leases. Although there is still a limit on the deductibility of rentals under Crown leases (currently $2.50 per acre, although the rental is

---

34 *Duncan v Joslin* (1965), 51 W.W.R. 346, 51 D.L.R. (2d) 139 (Alta. S.C., App.Div.).

currently $3.50 per acre), the limitation with respect to freehold leases disappeared in 1962. Because of the former cap on taxable deductions, the figure of one dollar per acre became universally accepted as the annual delay rental. Although the reason for limiting the annual delay rental to one dollar per acre per year has disappeared, it continues to be the standard rate and is, for all practical purposes, a "given." It is very much to the economic advantage of the lessee that the practice remains undisturbed.

CAPL 91 offers the lessee an alternative when it comes to payment of rentals. The lessee can pay either on or before the time at which the additional bonus consideration becomes payable a lump sum equal to an amount that would be calculated by multiplying the amount of rental due each lease year ($1.00 multiplied by number of acres) for the number of years in the primary term or he can make yearly payments for each year in the primary term during which operations are not commenced on the lands. Very often the lessee will opt to make the lump sum payment since it is a relatively small amount.

As discussed in Chapter 4, CAPL 99 has eliminated any reference to delay rentals.

Interpretation

The *habendum* is usually followed by an interpretation clause that defines the precise meaning of certain words and phrases that occur throughout the lease. Typically, the clause in conventional leases will define "commercial production," "spacing unit," "pooled lands," and "said lands." With the exception of the last named, these phrases relate to subsequently occurring clauses in the lease and will be dealt with in conjunction with them. The phrase "said lands" is defined as the lands described in the opening part of the lease, "or such portion or portions thereof as shall not have been surrendered."

The interpretation clause in the CAPL lease is much more detailed and substantive, and plays a significant role in how the lease functions. It defines, *inter alia*, "lease year" as ending at midnight of the day immediately preceding the next anniversary date. It also defines "leased substances," "*force majeure*," "offset well," and, importantly, "operations."

CAPL 99 also contains a definition of "Horizontal Well," which will be discussed in Chapter 9 on offset drilling.

8 Royalties, Suspended Well Payments, and Taxes

The Royalty Concept

The royalty is the means by which the mineral owner shares in the production of the substances from his land. Both the concept and the word "royalty" originated in England, where it designated the share in production reserved by the Crown in grants of mines and quarries.[1]

The royalty clause accomplishes its purpose by providing that a certain portion, normally expressed as a percentage, of the production shall be deliverable or payable to the lessor.

For many years the typical royalty was set at 12½ per cent, or a one-eighth share. In recent years, however, higher royalties in the order of 18 per cent or more have become the norm, and most printed forms of the lease in use today, including the CAPL lease, leave the royalty percentage blank to be filled in after the parties have negotiated the rate.

Legal Categorization of Royalty

Three Alberta test cases have made it abundantly clear that a lessor's royalty under an oil and gas lease can be an interest in land capable of supporting a caveat. The three test cases are indexed as *Scurry-Rainbow Oil Ltd. v Galloway Estate*[2] and involved a consideration of three different gross royalty trust agreements ("GRTAs") entered into with three

---

1 Brown, "Royalty Clauses in Oil and Gas Leases," *Sixteenth Annual Institute on Oil and Gas Law and Taxation*, at 139.

2 *Scurry-Rainbow Oil Ltd. v Galloway Estate* (1993), 8 Alta L.R. (3d) 225, [1993] 4 W.W.R. 454, [1993] A.J. No. 227 (Alta. Q.B.).

different trust companies. Under the GRTAs the mineral owners assigned their royalty or potential royalty under oil and gas lease to trust companies, who then sold units in the interest and filed caveats to protect the interest of the unit holders. The plaintiffs in all three actions were unit holders seeking a declaration that the GRTAs conveyed an interest in land sufficient to support a caveat.

Hunt J (as she then was) found all three GRTAs to be interests in land, holding that a lessor's royalty can be an interest in land in the form of a species of rent, or akin to a *profit à prendre*. The learned trial judge held that the categories of interests in land are not closed and it is not necessary that a particular interest fit into a pre-existing legal category in order to be an interest in land. She also found that whether or not the royalty reserved in a lease, in itself, amounted to an interest in land, a lessor's retention of the reversionary interest would be an interest in land capable of supporting a caveat.

The decision was upheld by the Court of Appeal,[3] although that court chose not to rely on the trial judge's findings with respect to a species of rent or a lessor's *profit à prendre*, but preferred her finding that a lessor's retention of the reversionary rights in the leased substances would be an interest in land capable of supporting a caveat. Dealing specifically with royalty, the unanimous court wrote: "3. In accordance with the terms of the GRTA in each test case, the lessor-settlor granted to the trustee a royalty carved out of the mineral owner's said interest in land and this supported the caveat filed by it." Another case involving the question of GRTAs as interests in land was *Scurry-Rainbow Oil Ltd. v Kasha*,[4] which was decided after the trial decision in *Galloway* but before the Court of Appeal decision. Lefsrud J held that the GRTA conveyed an interest in land that could be protected by caveat. On appeal, which was heard after the appeal decision in *Galloway*, the court flatly stated that, "barring very specific language manifesting a contrary intention," a freehold mineral owner's royalty under lease is an interest in land.[5]

---

3 *Scurry-Rainbow Oil Ltd. v Galloway Estate*, 23 Alta L.R. (3d) 193, [1995] 1 W.W.R. 316, [1994] A.J. No: 669 (C.A.); leave to appeal dismissed [1994] S.C.C.A. No. 475 (S.C.C.).
4 *Scurry-Rainbow Oil Ltd. v Kasha* (1993), 143 A.R. 308, [1993] A.J. No. 579 (Alta. Q.B.).
5 (1996), 39 Alta. L.R. (3d) 153 at 167, 135 D.L.R. (4th) 1, A.J. No. 462, O'Leary JA (Alta. C.A.). See also *Bearspaw, Chiniki and Wesley Bands v PanCanadian Petroleum Limited* (1999), 65 Alta. L.R. (3d) 353, [1997] 1 W.W.R. 41, [1998] A.J. No. 381 (Alta. Q.B.); varied [2000] A.J. No. 870, [2001] 2 W.W.R. 442 (C.A.). McIntryre J held that a royalty interest can be

The GRTA cases also involved a perpetuities issue, it being argued that because the payment of royalty was dependent on production of the leased substances, the interest did not vest and the rule was offended. This was met with the finding that while the enjoyment of the interest might be postponed, there was no postponement of the vesting of the interest itself.[6]

En route to finding that a lessor's royalty was an interest in land, the courts had to deal with an earlier decision of O'Leary J (as he then was) (the same judge who subsequently wrote the judgment of the Court of Appeal in *Kasha*) in *Guaranty Trust v Hetherington*,[7] wherein he found that the GRTAs in that case assigned only a contractual right to receive royalty payments and did not create an interest in land necessary to support a caveat.

In the final analysis, the result of the *Hetherington* case at the Court of Appeal level depended on the interpretation of this clause in the GRTAs: "25. The Owner hereby covenants and agrees with the Trustee that, in the event that any lease that may be in existence as at the date of this Agreement is *cancelled* for any reason or in any event that no lease is in existence as at the date of this Trust Agreement, he shall and will in negotiating any lease or other instrument for developing the said lands reserve unto the Trustee the full 12 ½% Gross Royalty hereby assigned to the Trustee" (emphasis added). The trial judge examined this clause and held that the royalty interest assigned by the GRTAs was not intended to be referable only to the specific royalty reserved in the leases in existence at the time the GRTA was created and that a contrary intention would give no meaning to the clause.

While the trial judge was prepared to interpret clause 25 as applying to royalties under all leases existing from time to time, he held that the right to receive royalty payments did not create an interest in land.

On appeal,[8] the court disagreed with O'Leary's interpretation of clause 25 and concluded that the royalty was limited to the one payable under the leases in existence at the time the GRTAs were created. In

---

considered an interest in land. In that case, the court also held that royalties to the Indian bands were not subject to deductions for "TopGas" financing charges and operating, marketing, and administration charges. Because of the special circumstances of leases on Indian lands, this latter finding has no application to freehold oil and gas leases. On appeal, *sub nom Stoney Tribal Council v PanCanadian Petroleum Ltd.*, 86 Alta. L.R. (3d) 147, [2001] 2 W.W.R. 442, [2000] A.J. No. 870, McIntyre J's decision was upheld.

6 *Supra* n 2 at 279.

7 (1987), 50 Alta. L.R. (2d) 193, [1987] 3 W.W.R. 316, [1987] A.J. No. 148 (Alta. Q.B.).

8 (1989), 67 Alta. L.R. (2d) 290, [1989] 5 W.W.R. 340, [1989] A.J. No. 472 (Alta. C.A.).

doing so, the Court of Appeal focused on the word *cancelled* and held that clause 25 was not ambiguous and would have become operable and would have substituted royalties payable under the new lease for those under the cancelled lease. However, the leases that existed at the time the GRTAs were granted were not cancelled but expired at the end of the primary term, and accordingly the limited circumstances that would trigger the clause never occurred, and its powers of substitution never arose.

This finding made it unnecessary for the court to deal with the other matters involved in the case, including whether or not the interest conveyed by a GRTA created a caveatable interest in land. In any event, it is clear from the appeal court decisions in *Galloway* and *Kasha* that a lessor's royalty is an interest in land. If the language of the GRTA brings the case within the very limited purview of *Hetherington*, the assignment of the royalty, while presumably creating an interest in land, may not apply to subsequent leases. It is also possible that the wording of a particular GRTA may not be applicable to the facts. For example, if the assigned royalty is expressed to be on all production "from any well or wells that may be drilled upon the said lands, or any part thereof," and the producing well was drilled not on the said lands but on lands with which they are pooled to form a spacing unit, the GRTA may not apply.[9]

Interest Carved out of Lessee's Estate

It is safe to say that an interest carved out of the lessor's estate will be an interest in land, but the cases dealing with an interest carved out of the lessee's estate generally arrive at a different result. Most overriding royalties derived from the lessee contain wording that refers to "all petroleum and natural gas and related hydrocarbon production, saved and sold." The courts uniformly have held that such language by itself does not create an interest in land since the interest does not attach until the substances have been separated from the land, i.e., "produced."[10] In

---

9 In this connection see *Shell Oil Company v Gunderson*, [1960] S.C.R. 424, 23 D.L.R. (2d) 81, [1960] S.C.J. No. 19 (S.C.C.) where Martland J held that a reference to a well "on the said lands" did not include a well on other lands with which the said lands had been pooled to form a spacing unit.

10 Generally, see Davies, "The Legal Characterization of Overriding Royalty Interests in Oil and Gas" (1972) 10 Alta. L. Rev. 232.

Emerald Resources v Sterling Oil,[11] where the gross overriding royalty is characterized as not being an interest in land, the interest holder cannot protect his position by registration of a caveat and his claim may be defeated by the rights of intervening third party purchasers.

A typical example of a lessee-created interest would be an overriding royalty granted to a geological consultant who introduced the oil company lessee to the "play."

In *Saskatchewan Minerals v Keyes*[12] Martland J doubted whether the use of the word "royalty" implied an intention to create an interest in land.[13] In light of the GRTAs cases, this observation can no longer stand.

In the *Bensette and Campbell v Reece*[14] case the language of the document was such as to confer a royalty in all the minerals that may be found in, under, or upon the said lands. The court relied particularly on the word "in" to find that there was an interest of some kind "in" the minerals. In other words, the grantee obtained an interest in the minerals *in situ* and this was held to be an interest in land.

In *Montreal Trust Company v Gulf Securities Corporation Ltd. et al.*[15] the document reserved "a sum representing the sale value as hereinafter defined, of two and one-half per cent (2½%) of all oil [and all gas] produced and saved by Assignee." The agreement did not use the word "royalty." The agreement also contained a specific disclaimer stating that it did not intend to create an interest in land. Bence CJQB reviewed the dissenting opinion of Laskin J and was also obviously influenced by the decision of the Saskatchewan Court of Appeal that had just been handed down in *Bensette*. Bence observed that if it were not for the express disclaimer in the document, he "possibly would have concluded, with some hesitation, that an interest in land in fact was created." This language amounts at best to much qualified *obiter dictum*.

In *Canco Oil & Gas Ltd. v R. of Saskatchewan*[16] the agreement referred to all petroleum natural gas and related hydrocarbons that are "produced,

---

11 3 D.L.R. (3d) 630, [1969] A.J., No. 2 (Alta. S.C., App.Div.).

12 [1972] S.C.R. 703, [1972] 2 W.W.R. 108, 23 D.L.R. (3d) 573, [1971] S.C.J. No. 136 (S.C.C.).

13 Ibid. at 717: Laskin J (as he then was) dissented and his opinion, which relied heavily on American authorities, that a royalty can be an interest in land has been borne out by the GRTA cases with respect to a mineral owner's royalty.

14 [1973] 2 W.W.R. 497, 34 D.L.R. (3d) 723 (Sask. C.A.).

15 [1973] 2 W.W.R. 617, 36 D.L.R. (3d) 57, [1973] S.J. No. 61 (Sask. Q.B.).

16 (1991), 89 Sask. R. 37, [1991] 4 W.W.R. 316, [1991] S.J. No. 22 (Sask. Q.B.).

saved and sold" from the lands. Normally this language would prevent the agreement from being held to be an interest in land, but the agreement also contained a provision that the covenants shall run with the land. Because of this language, Matheson J found that the grantor intended that the gross royalty should contain an interest in land.

It is interesting to speculate if the result of the overriding royalty cases might have been different had the GRTA cases been decided before them. It now seems abundantly clear that if the gross overriding royalty document contains a statement that it is to be a covenant running with the land, or an interest in land, it will be held to be sufficient to support a caveat.

The Royalty Clause

Regardless of the form it takes, the royalty clause in a lease will do the following:

(a) grant to the lessor a share or participation in the production of the leased substances;
(b) specify the rate of such share;
(c) provide that any sale by the lessee will include the royalty share;
(d) require the lessee to account for and remit payment for such share on or before a specified date; and
(e) allow the lessee to use a portion of the production required for operations under the lease without payment of royalty.

A typical royalty clause frequently found in conventional leases reads as follows:

Royalties:
The Lessor does hereby reserve unto himself a gross royalty of ... per cent of the leased substances produced and marketed from the said lands. Any sale by the Lessee of any crude oil, crude naphtha, or gas produced from the said lands shall include the royalty share thereof reserved to the Lessor, and the Lessee shall account to the Lessor for his said royalty share in accordance with the following provisions, namely:

The Lessee shall remit to the Lessor, on or before the 25th day of each month, (a) an amount equal to the current market value at the wellhead on the date of delivery of ... per cent of the crude oil and crude naphtha produced, saved and marketed from the said lands during the preceding month, and (b) an amount equal to the current market value at the wellhead on the date of delivery of ... per cent of all gas produced and marketed from the said lands during said preceding month.

Notwithstanding anything to the contrary herein contained or implied, the Lessee shall be entitled to use such part of the production of the leased substances from the said lands as may be required and used by the Lessee in its operations hereunder, and the Lessor shall not be entitled to any royalty with respect to said leased substances.

Time of Payment

The undertaking by the lessee to remit the royalty on or before the 25th day of the month following the month of production creates an unrealistically tight time frame and is seldom complied with in practice. In many instances, the lessee himself will not have received the proceeds of the previous month's production by that date.

This matter has been eased in the CAPL lease, which provides that the royalty shall be payable on or before the 15th day of the second month following the month of production.

In recent years some lessees have adopted the practice of making payments at quarterly or even longer intervals. The royalties are accounted for on a monthly basis, but the monthly payments are lumped together. While this practice is not in compliance with the terms of the lease, it seems to be generally accepted by lessors. It does not threaten the continued existence of the lease, unless a lessor gives notice of default.

Other Versions of the Royalty Clause

The type of clause whereunder the lessor reserves his royalty share is by far the most common. There are, however, clauses under which the lessee covenants to pay a royalty, as shown in the following example:

Royalty:
The lessee shall pay to the lessor as royalty:
a) per cent (%) of the current market value at the well of all petroleum oil produced, saved and marketed from the said lands.

The CAPL lease provides that "the lessee shall pay a royalty."

Yet another type of royalty clause provides for delivery of the royalty share. Delivery of the royalty in kind is limited to oil because of the complicated marketing arrangements required for the sale of natural gas. This type of clause has largely fallen out of favour but is still to be encountered in some conventional leases, particularly in Saskatchewan and Manitoba. An example is as follows:

ROYALTIES

As royalty, the Lessee covenants and agrees:

(a) to deliver to the credit of the Lessor, in the pipeline to which the Lessee may connect his wells, the equal _____ part of all oil produced and saved by the Lessee from the said lands, or from time to time, at the option of the Lessee, to pay the Lessor the current market value of such _____ part of such oil of the wells as of the day it is run to the pipeline or storage tanks, the Lessor's interest, in other cases to bear _____ of the cost of treating oil to render it marketable pipeline oil.

(b) To pay to the Lessor on gas and casinghead gas produced from the said lands (1) when sold by the Lessee, _____ part of the amount realized by the Lessee, computed at the mouth of the well, or (2) when used by the Lessee off the said lands or when preserved or treated for the manufacture of gasoline or other products, the market value, at the mouth of the well, _____ of such gas and casinghead gas.

Even with respect to oil, the lessee has the option under the clause to pay the lessor the present market value of the royalty share instead of delivering same in kind. Thus, the right of the lessor to have his oil delivered is more apparent than real.

The royalty clause in CAPL 88 requires the lessee to pay to the lessor royalty in an amount equal to the current market value at the wellhead of ... per cent of all the leased substances produced, saved and sold, or used by the lessee for a purpose other than its operations on the said lands, the pooled lands, or the unitized lands, which part is free of royalty. It provides that no royalty shall be payable with respect to any substance injected into and recovered from lands other than leased substances originally produced from the said lands for which a royalty has not been paid. The lessor is to bear its reasonable proportion of any expense incurred by the lessee for separating, treating, processing, and transportation, to the point of sale beyond the point of measurement.

The clause also provides that the royalty shall be inclusive of any prior disposition of any royalty or other interest in the leased substances and the lessor agrees to make all payments required by any such disposition out of the royalty received hereunder and to indemnify the lessee from its failure to do so. The lessee may elect to make such payments on behalf of the lessor and to have the right to deduct any such payments from the royalty and other payments under the lease. This provision is designed to protect the lessee from the possibility of having to pay double royalties (e.g., where a lessor may have previously disposed of a royalty interest by way of a GRTA or other disposition).

The royalty clause also provides that the lessee will make available to the lessor during normal business hours its records relating to the leased substances produced from or allocated to the said lands.

The royalty clause under CAPL 91 varies from that in CAPL 88 by omitting the reference to the lessor bearing its reasonable proportion of any expense incurred by the lessee for separating, treating, processing, and transportation, and substituting the following:

[I]n computing the current market value at the wellhead of all the leased substances produced, saved and sold, or used by the Lessee for a purpose other than that described in subclause (b) hereof, the Lessee may deduct any reasonable expense incurred by the Lessee (including a reasonable rate of return on investments) for separating, treating, processing, compressing and transporting the leased substances to the point of sale beyond the wellhead or, if the leased substances are not sold by the Lessee in an arm's-length transaction, to the first point where the leased substances are used by the Lessee for a purpose other than that described in subclause (b) hereof; provided further, however, that the royalty payable to the Lessor hereunder shall not be less than ... percent (...%) of the royalty that would have been payable to the Lessor if no such expenses had been incurred by the Lessee. In no event shall the current market value be deemed to be in excess of the value actually received by the Lessee pursuant to a bona fide, arm's-length sale or transaction. The royalty as determined under this clause shall be payable on or before the 15th day of the second month following the month in which the leased substances, with respect to which the royalty is payable, were produced, saved and sold, or used by the Lessee for a purpose other than that described in subclause (b). No royalty shall be payable to the Lessor with respect to any substance injected into and recovered from the said lands, other than leased substances originally produced from the said lands for which a royalty has not been paid or payable.

The CAPL 91 lease also provides a cap on deductions from royalty by providing that the royalty shall not be less than a stated percentage of the royalty that would have been payable if no such expenses had been incurred. The matter of allowed deductions from royalty will be discussed in greater detail below.

The CAPL 91 also provides that the current market value shall not be deemed to be in excess of the value actually received by the lessee pursuant to a *bona fide* arm's-length sale.

The royalty clause in CAPL 99 differs in some respects from its predecessors, and these differences will be pointed out as the occasion arises. One difference is that the cap on deduction from royalty shall be 50 per cent, or some other percentage negotiated by the parties, which figure is to be inserted in the blank provided and will replace the 50 per cent cap.

Right of Lessor to Take Royalty Share in Kind

The standard clause in the conventional lease *reserves* the royalty share to the mineral owner. Does he have the right to demand that his share of the leased substances be actually delivered to him, or must he be content with the proceeds from the sale of such royalty share? Under most circumstances, this point will have little practical application, for the average lessor will not have the inclination, or the means, to dispose of his share of production and is only too happy to have that particular chore assumed by the lessee. This is borne out by the declaration, nearly always found in the royalty clause, that any sale by the lessee shall include the royalty share thereof reserved to the lessor. Consequently, there can be no doubt that the lessee is under a duty to share any available market with the lessor,[17] although in the standard form this obligation is limited to "crude oil, crude naphtha or gas."

---

17 In the absence of such a provision, is the lessee under any duty to market the lessor's royalty share? In the United States the lessee may be under an implied duty to do so; *Wolfe v Prairie Oil & Gas Co.*(1936), 83 F 2d 434 (10th Cir.). In view of the strict construction placed on the terms of the lease by Canadian courts and their reluctance to import any terms into such a detailed document, the lessor would be well advised to ensure that his lease expressly imposes such an obligation.

Presumably the lessee is not obligated to market any leased substances that do not fall within such classes.[18] However, if the lessor insists on delivery of the substances themselves, can he succeed? It is entirely conceivable that if a lessor were itself an oil company with a ready market, and if the volumes were sufficiently large, it might seek to enforce such a right.

The lease is silent on the mechanics of any such delivery. It does not, for example, provide that if the lessor is to take his share in kind the lessee must provide surface storage and other facilities. This type of provision would normally be included if the lease contemplated such delivery; understandings of this nature are frequently encountered in operating agreements and overriding royalty agreements where both parties are oil companies. While their absence may indicate that the parties did not expect the lessor to take his share in kind, express reservation by the lessor of his share surely preserves whatever title he might have had to that portion of the substances. Such rights would necessarily include the right to take them into his own possession and dispose of them. The requirement that imposes upon the lessee a duty to share any market does not seem to derogate from this right of the lessor; there is no provision that requires the lessor to use the lessee as his exclusive marketing agent. Under the standard type of clause, therefore, a lessor, if he were so inclined, might insist successfully upon delivery to him of his royalty share, although he would be faced with the necessity of either installing his own storage and transportation facilities or entering into some agreement with the lessee to share the existing ones.

The clause, found in the CAPL lease as well as many conventional leases, that requires the lessee to *pay* the lessor his share as royalty would appear to exclude any right of the lessor to insist upon actual delivery of the substances, his entitlement being to a share of the proceeds of sale and nothing more.

Even the clause which stipulates that the lessee agrees to deliver the royalty share to the lessor may not in fact permit the lessor to obtain his share in kind. The delivery type clause almost always contains an option on the part of the lessee to pay the lessor the current market value of his royalty oil. Thus, the lessee is vested with the power to dispose of the lessor's share rather than delivering it.

---

18 This could give rise to some interesting questions: i.e., is the lessee obliged to market sulphur? See the discussion as to the substances covered by the grant, Chapter 6 *ante*.

Substances Subject to the Royalty

The typical royalty clause makes it clear that the royalty applies to all the substances granted by the lease. There is an all-inclusive reference to "the leased substances," which, by definition, includes all the minerals covered by the grant. If, as sometimes happens, different substances attract a different royalty rate or there are variations in the permitted deductions, the clause may be subdivided to provide separately for each substance. This can lead to some question as to whether an individual substance not specifically mentioned is included. Usually, however, the question is put to rest by an omnibus provision that embraces "all other minerals" or "all other leased substances."

Certain of the substances are excluded from the imposition of a royalty. This, however, does not relate to the nature or quality of the substances but rather to their use. The lessee is not required to pay royalty on substances that are used for the purposes of operations on the lease. The theory is that the lessor, having the benefit of production, should share in the cost an expense thereof. One way is to exclude substances used for such purpose from the computation of royalty. Additionally, a certain amount of loss on the surface after production is inevitable and unavoidable because of evaporation spillage, and other circumstances often referred to as "shrinkage." Accidents under which substantial quantities of production are lost prior to sale occur from time to time and the lessee seeks to ensure that the mineral owner will bear his share of such loss.

These objectives frequently are accomplished by specific provisions, but the same purpose may be served by a description of the substances to which the royalty applies. The ultimate disposition of the materials becomes the criterion by which the applicability of the royalty is determined. The leased substances are qualified as being "produced and saved," "produced, saved and sold," "produced and marketed," and other words designed to carve out from the royalty those substances which, although produced, are not sold by the lessee. Under the usual language, the production must actually be sold or marketed by the lessee before it becomes subject to the royalty. Good conservation practices, which are rigidly enforced by the regulatory bodies, also may require the return of gas to the reservoir when it is produced in association with oil. This recycling may be due to the necessity of maintaining reservoir pressure, or the absence of an existing market for gas. An operation of this type, where a substance is produced and then returned to the reservoir, does not produce any direct monetary return to the lessee. There are also circumstances under which non-commercial or uneconomic volumes of gas are produced in association with oil, and these small quantities are permitted to be flared and burned.

All these exclusions from the impact of royalty appear to be equitable. There are, however, circumstances under which substances, although not sold or marketed in the true sense, may be used in such a way as to confer a substantial benefit to the lessee. For example, gas produced from a lease may be injected in a secondary recovery scheme in a reservoir where the lessor has no interest, although the lessee may have a substantial interest. The substances may be used by the lessee as a fuel for a processing plant that it may operate and that processes substances other than or in addition to those produced from the lease. For internal accounting reasons, the lessee may not charge for the substances so used as fuel, and therefore such substances are not considered as having been sold or marketed.

The right of the lessee to use the substances free from a royalty to the extent necessary to produce the substances from the leased lands is normally covered by an express proviso in the royalty clause. Under such a proviso the lessee is granted the use of the leased substances for its operations "hereunder." The reference to operations under the lease would encompass the exploration and drilling for and the removal, storage, and disposal of the substances. There seems to be, although it is nowhere spelled out, an intention that such royalty-free substances are to be used on the lease itself and that any attempt by the lessee to use them off the premises would not qualify as being in relation to "operations hereunder." Presumably the lessee could use the substances, without payment of royalty, as fuel in a drilling rig on the lands, or to thaw the ground for the laying of flowlines to carry production from the lands (possibly only to the extent that such flowlines were located within the lands covered by the lease), or to fuel machinery and equipment for the same purposes and to operate treaters and dehydrators located on the lands and not used to treat or process substances from other lands. The qualifications that the substances must be "produced and marketed" or "produced and sold" before royalty attaches seems to go further and to exclude substances other than those used in "operations hereunder." Some leases cover this point with this language: "produced and marketed from the said lands or used off the said lands."

The CAPL lease provides that the royalty will attach to all the leased substances, produced, saved, and sold or used by the lessee for a purpose other than the use of such part of the leased substances as reasonably may be required and used by the lessee in its operations on the said lands, the pooled lands, or the unitized lands. If the leased substances are used for such purposes, no royalty attaches, but the use of such royalty free of production is limited to operations that, directly or indirectly, affect the lands under the lease.

The royalty clause in CAPL 88 and 91 provides that no royalty is payable with respect to any substance injected into and recovered from the said lands, other than leased substances originally produced on the said lands for which a royalty has not been paid or payable. In other words, substances injected into the reservoir pursuant to an enhanced recovery scheme that were not part of the leased substances do not attract royalty when produced. CAPL 99 achieves the same result by limiting the definition of "leased substances" to those included in the certificate of title.

Value for Computing Royalty

If the lessee, having marketed the royalty share, is to pay the lessor, there must be some yardstick for determining the value of such share. The lessor would not be sufficiently protected by simply taking his share of whatever the lessee received, since the lessee might be selling to itself or an associated company and hence might be satisfied with a depressed price. Thus, the standard reference to "the current market value." This qualification is designed to ensure that the lessor will receive the going price for his royalty share. Generally speaking, the market value of the leased substances is relatively easy to ascertain. Crude oil prices are posted and are widely reported in a number of publications. The price of by-products such as propane, butane, and sulphur, although not as visible, are readily ascertainable. Likewise, the price of natural gas, which is sold both under fairly long-term contracts and more and more frequently on a "spot" basis, is transparent and is also widely reported.

The use of the word "current" might pose a problem, particularly in the case of natural gas sold under long-term agreements. It is entirely possible that new contracts may contain more favourable prices than earlier ones that have been entered into with respect to the same area. What then of the situation where a lessor's royalty share is under an early, long-term contract, but other volumes of gas in the same immediate area have the benefit of a substantially improved price? Could it not be argued that the new price prevalent in the area represents "the current market value" and that the lessee must account to the lessor on the basis of the best possible price? Such an interpretation would create a very severe financial hardship on the lessee who receives the lower price, but it is one that could easily be held to be the plain meaning of the words. The only countervailing argument is one based on the fact that the current market value is to be determined "on the said lands" or "at the wellhead," and since the gas is already committed under the earlier contract and cannot be sold under any other arrangement, the price actually obtained represents the current market value "on the said lands" or "at the wellhead." Such a construction, however, appears somewhat forced, and a court might very well prefer the plain meaning of the phrase "the current market value" as meaning the best existing price paid in the area at any given point of time. The specific inclusion of the word "current" is difficult to reconcile with any other interpretation.[19]

The royalty clause in the CAPL lease also refers to "current market value."

Insolvent Lessee

The market price of oil and gas is subject to wild swings, and a prolonged period of depressed prices may lead to some lessees simply not having the funds to pay the royalty. What is the position of the unfortunate lessor when this happens? The default clause can't be used to terminate the lease since there is a well on the lands, which will prevent the lease from terminating. The lessor would seem to be much more than an ordinary creditor. He should be able to advance a claim that the royalty is subject to a constructive trust.

Sulphur

In the past, sulphur has been subject to abrupt and violent fluctuations in its price. For this reason, some leases that were entered into during the 1960s contained a royalty clause that required the lessee to pay a fixed-dollar royalty amount regardless of the actual price received by the producer: "To pay to the Lessor One Dollar ($1.00) per long ton (2,240 pounds) on all sulphur mined and marketed by the Lessee from sulphur deposits within or upon the said lands."

---

19 This problem is discussed in Rae, "Royalty Clauses in Oil and Gas Leases" (1965) 4 Alta. L. Rev. 323 at 327, 328, and by Brown, "Royalty Provisions of Oil and Gas Leases," *The Landman*, September 1964, 6.

This practice originated when the sulphur market was severely depressed and guaranteed to the lessor a certain fixed amount. The clause is still to be found in a number of old leases that remain in force. It has worked very much to the detriment of the lessor, since the price of sulphur has averaged a level much higher than that which would produce a royalty of $1.00 per long ton.

Point Where Value Determined

The point or place at which the royalty value is determined is an essential provision. The value of the leased substances, whether oil or gas, will vary in accordance with the point at which it is measured, increasing in value as it leaves the well and approaches the end consumer. Gas that has been treated and processed is obviously more valuable at the plant outlet where it is delivered to the pipeline than in its raw state at the well; similarly, oil refined into its various components is worth more as gasoline in service station tanks than as crude oil back at the lease. When it comes to determining the value of the lessor's royalty, the leases are virtually unanimous in providing that such value shall be determined "at the well" or "on the said lands," or even more specifically "at the mouth of the well."

The intention of the reference to "the well" or "the said lands" is to establish those points as the basis for measuring the value and to permit the lessee to deduct all costs subsequently incurred. The lessor's share is not subject to any of the costs of producing the substances and bringing them to the surface, but is burdened with its share of the costs beyond that point.

In *Skyeland Oils Ltd. v Great Northern Oil Ltd.*[20] the instrument was a gross overriding royalty, rather than a royalty pursuant to a lease. The language, however, was very similar in that the gross overriding royalty was to be "based upon the current market value at the time and place of production of the petroleum substances produced, saved and marketed

---

20 [1976] 5 W.W.R. 370, 68 D.L.R. (3d) 318 (Alta. S.C.T.D.). See also *Resman Holdings Ltd. v Huntex Limited*, [1984] 28 Alta. L.R. (2d) 396, [1984] 1 W.W.R. 693, [1983] A.J. No. 731 (Alta. Q.B.), which held that the payor of a gross overriding royalty "payable at the outlet valve to the pipeline" was entitled to deduct the cost of compressing, gathering, processing, and transporting the gas. The court seems to have treated "outlet valve to the pipeline" as being the same as "at the well." Presumably if the agreement had referred to "plant outlet valve" the result would have been different.

from the (said) lands." The trial judge held that the royalty should be calculated without any deduction for Crown or other royalties paid by the
lessor. It was conceded by counsel and declared by the court that the cost
of transporting the substances to a refinery or gas plant was properly
deductible before calculating the gross overriding royalty.

Like the price received for the product, the permitted deductions
should be relatively easy to determine. In principle, the costs between
the wellhead and the point of sale are deductible before computing the
royalty. Insofar as crude oil is concerned, the sale takes place either at a
pipeline connection at the wellhead or from storage tanks at or in the
vicinity of the well site. For many years the general practice in computing royalty on oil was to ignore any treating and surface storage costs
and to pay royalty computed on the actual selling price of the crude.
As I pointed out in previous editions, this results in a more generous
treatment of the lessor than would appear to be required by the clause
itself, and because of this industry practice, the interpretation of "current market value at the wellhead" did not come before the courts for
some considerable time.

As the costs for treating and storing crude steadily rose, lessees
began to look at their bottom line and to deduct these costs in calculating the royalty payable with respect to crude oil.

In *Acanthus Resources Ltd. v Cunningham and Sullivan*[21] the lessee
deducted substantial amounts for the cost of treating oil. Hart J found
that there was no ambiguity and that the royalty provision meant that
the lessor must bear his respective share of costs properly incurred
downstream of the wellhead to the point of sale.[22]

The Manitoba case of *Missilinda of Canada Ltd. v Husky Oil Operations
Ltd.*[23] also involved the matter of deductions from oil. The language in
the relevant clause provided that the lessee shall remit to the lessor,

---

21 (1998), 57 Alta. L.R. (3d) 9, [1998] 5 W.W.R. 646, [1998] A.J. No. 25 (Alta. Q.B.). This case
   is discussed in Baker and Crang, "Recent Judicial Developments of Interest to Oil and
   Gas Lawyers" (1999) 37 Alta. L. Rev. 439 at 471. The writers point out that proof of the
   amount of deductions claimed is essential.

22 The case was another Pyrrhic victory for the plaintiff in that the court found that Acanthus had not met the burden of proving the costs that it had been deducting and
   reduced the charge from the $8 per cubic metre that the lessee had been charging to
   $1 per cubic metre. The situation appears to be that a lessee, in calculating royalties on
   oil, can deduct all costs beyond the wellhead including treating and storage costs, but
   must provide satisfactory evidence as to the appropriateness of such costs.

23 206 Man. R. (2d) 13, [2005] 9 W.W.R. 764, [2005] M.J. No. 87 (Man. Q.B.).

"(a) an amount equal to the current market value at the wellhead on the date of delivery of seventeen and one-half (17½%) percent of the crude oil and naphtha produced, saved and marketed from the said lands during the preceding month."

The crude oil was not sold at the wellhead, but was transported downstream to a battery where water is extracted, stored, and eventually moved by pipeline to the point of sale. In holding that those costs were properly deducted, Keyser J applied the decision of Hart J in *Acanthus*.

On appeal, the result was upheld by a majority, but by a different route.[24] Huband JA agreed with the trial judge that "the wording in the lease at bar is clear," and then went on to state that the *meaning* of those words was obscure. The learned judge noted that there is no such thing as "market value at the wellhead." While each individual word was understandable, the overall meaning was impossible to discern without extrinsic evidence. Thus, in the view of the court, there was a latent ambiguity in the clause. A latent ambiguity is not observable on the face of the document; it becomes evident only when one attempts to apply it to the facts of the case. The court pointed out that extrinsic evidence was admissible not only to resolve a latent ambiguity, but also to assist the court in construing technical words or phrases as they are understood in a trade or industry.

Having found the clause to be latently ambiguous, the court applied extrinsic evidence (the writer's, in this instance) that industry practice was to deduct the costs of transportation, storage, and treating to resolve the ambiguity and allow the costs to be deducted.

The courts, whether relying on the meaning of the words themselves, or as interpreted with the aid of industry practice, have confirmed that costs incurred downstream of the wellhead can be deducted from royalties for crude oil.

In the case of gas, however, the matter can be more complicated, since it frequently involves transportation to a central, and costly, processing plant where the raw gas is treated to meet pipeline specifications. The conventional lease does not contain any guidelines for determining the amount of permitted deductions, and many questions remain unanswered. Is the lessee entitled to include a rate of return on the investment in the gathering pipelines and processing plant? On what basis should the capital structure be apportioned as between

---

24 212 Man. R. (2d) 252, [2007] 3 W.W.R. 613, [2007] M.J. No. 51 (Man. C.A.).

equity and debt? Are income taxes to be taken into account? What is the proper period of amortization of the investment? In practice, the average freehold lessor simply accepts the calculations and formulae used by the lessee and its accounting department. When the Crown or an experienced oil operator is the lessor, these matters are negotiated in great detail.

In Alberta, the regulatory authority and its predecessors have employed what was long known as the Jumping Pound formula, which enunciates certain principles that are to be used in determining the deductions.[25] (The formula's colourful name was derived from the location of an early Shell gas plant near a buffalo jump where Indian hunters drove the animals over a cliff to provide food and furs for their tribe.) Now known as the Gas Cost Allowance, it spelled out the method of calculating deductions under Crown leases, but it is also routinely used in connection with freehold leases. These principles may be summarized as follows: (1) the wellhead value can be determined by working back from the sale price; (2) the lessee is entitled to receive a return on invested capital; (3) income taxes were proper items to be allowed and included in the cost of operations; (4) intangible costs (interest charges, etc.) incurred prior to and during construction of the plant should be allowed as part of the cost of the plant; (5) depreciation should be allowed as an operating

---

25 The jurisdiction of the Energy Utilities Board to make such orders is found in section 10 the *Gas Utilities Act*, R.S.A. 2000, c 5. Pursuant to section 5(l) the board must be authorized by an order of the Lieutenant-Governor-in-Council before exercising its jurisdiction. See also *Rabson Oil Co. Ltd. v Shell Exploration Alberta Ltd.*, which is unreported, but the trial decision of Egbert J is reported in *Canadian Oil and Gas*, 2nd ed. (Bennett Jones Verchere and Bankes, eds.), vol. 1, Dig. 68. The decision of the Appeal Court is reported in Dig. 69 and is quoted in the judgment of Milvain J in *Calgary & Edmonton Corporation Ltd. v British American Oil Co. Ltd.* (1963), 40 D.L.R. (2d) 964 at 970. In the *Rabson* case the Court of Appeal reversed the decision of Egbert J and held that the province had the right to appoint a board with the power to interpret contracts "as necessarily incidental to its proper decision." In the *Calgary & Edmonton* case it was held that the board was not "the only competent tribunal" and that the courts continue to have jurisdiction over the interpretation of contracts. The board had indicated that it would not deal with contractual issues between the parties unless the contract was construed by the court. It would appear that the board is unlikely to participate in future determinations of permitted deductions, but the important thing is that the Jumping Pound formula has been established as a standard for such deductions. See also the 1992 case *Re Hydro Resources*, reported in *Canadian Oil and Gas, supra*, at Dig. 354.

charge. After enunciating the principles, the Energy Utilities Board made an order setting out the specific costs, charges, and deductions based on actual operating experience. The order favoured a capitalization of 50 per cent debt and 50 per cent equity.

Occasionally, a royalty clause will contain a specific provision to the effect that the royalty interest will *bear* its share of processing and other expenses. A typical provision reads as follows: "PROVIDED that the lessor's interest shall bear its proportion of any expense of treating petroleum oil to render it merchantable as crude oil, or of separating, treating, processing, compressing or transporting gas in connection with the marketing thereof." It may have been the use of the word "bear" or similar phraseology that led a few lessees in the late 1980s and early 1990s, when natural gas prices were depressed and some gas wells were operating at a loss, to actually invoice their lessors for a share of the loss. This was not by any manner of means a common practice, but it did happen, although the writer is not aware of any instances where these invoices were actually paid by the lessor. The attempt by a lessee to have the lessor pay for expenses, rather than have them deducted from royalty that would otherwise be payable, flies in the face of the concept of royalty where it is the lessor's royalty, and not the lessor himself, that is to bear its share of the expenses.

Similarly, since the royalties are payable on a monthly basis from each month of production, the lessee is not entitled to carry forward any losses from one month to the next and charge them against the lessor's royalty.

The reference to "on the said lands" could, under a given set of circumstances, lead to some results not contemplated by the lessee, particularly where gas is involved. The courts have construed "at the wellhead" as entitling the lessee to deduct all costs beyond the wellhead, including treating, separating, and dehydrating facilities on the lease, and storage either on the lease or at a central battery. An oil and gas lease sometimes covers very substantial areas of land since lessees prefer to include as much of the lessor's lands as possible under one lease. If plant facilities for the processing of gas were constructed within the area of the said lands, the wording suggests that the value for the purposes of computing the royalty would be at the outlet of such plant and that the lessee would not be able to deduct the costs of transportation and processing to such point. The reference to the well as the determination point would seem to be much more precise and accurate than a general reference to "on the said lands."

The three CAPL leases deal with the matter of deductions with increasing particularity. CAPL 88 provides that the lessee may deduct any reasonable expense (including a reasonable rate of return on investment) for separating, treating, processing, compressing, and transporting the leased substances to the point of sale beyond the wellhead. CAPL 91 provides for the deduction of "any reasonable expense incurred by the Lessee (including a reasonable rate of return on investment) for separating, treating, processing, compressing and transporting the leased substances to the point of sale beyond the wellhead ... " CAPL 99 adds "water disposal" to the list of permitted deductions.

The effect is to make every expense downstream of the wellhead deductible. This may be more onerous in the case of the natural gas lessor than the normal practice, which is not to deduct the costs of dehydration and compression. Knowledgeable lessors have objected to this express listing of permitted deductions and have succeeded in having the language deleted, which leaves it up to the parties to agree on the current market value at the wellhead. In light of the *Acanthus* decision, however, lessees can deduct all costs beyond the wellhead if the lease so provides. As is always the case, attention must be paid to the words themselves.

CAPL 91 broke new ground by imposing a limit on the amount of deductions that could be made with respect to a royalty. It does this by providing that the royalty shall not be less than a certain percentage of what it would have been if no deductions had been permitted. For example, if it is agreed that there shall be a 40 per cent cap on deductions, the proviso would state that the royalty shall not be less than 60 per cent of what would have been paid to the lessor if no expenses had been incurred by the lessee. As noted earlier, CAPL 99 provides for a 50 per cent cap unless the parties negotiate a different figure.

CAPL 88 and 91 incorporate a limitation on current market value. This is for the protection of the lessee and is often found in conventional leases as well. It provides that in no event shall the current market value be deemed to be in excess of the value actually received by the lessee pursuant to a *bona fide* arm's-length sale. The intent was to protect the lessee from having to pay royalties on monies he did not receive.

This language was omitted from CAPL 99 on the ground that it was unnecessary because the royalty only attaches when the substances are sold, which would equal the amount the lessee receives. CAPL 99 also deals with the situation where the lessee does not sell the leased substances pursuant to a *bona fide* arm's-length transaction. If this happens, the current market value at the wellhead shall be deemed to be the average market price in the area in which the lands are located, less all expenses permitted to be deducted therefrom.

Royalty Payable When Lessor Owns Less Than Entire Estate

The royalty clause reserves to the lessor or requires the lessee to pay the lessor a share of the leased substances produced and marketed "from the said lands." The wording appears to be remarkably straightforward and free from ambiguity. What is the situation where the lessor turns out to own something less than the entire mineral interest? For example, his interest may be determined to have been only an undivided 25 per cent rather than the whole. This situation is provided for in both the conventional and CAPL 88 and 91 leases by a separate clause on the following lines: "LESSER INTEREST: If the Lessor's interest in the leased substances is less than the entire and undivided fee simple estate therein, the royalties herein provided shall be paid to the Lessor only in proportion which such interest bears to the whole and undivided fee."

CAPL 99 addresses this situation by tying the royalty to the lessor's *undivided fee simple* interest in the lands. Thus, if the lessor's interest in the lands is something less than 100 per cent, the royalty will be automatically adjusted.

The Supreme Court of Canada has indicated that, even without such a clause, the lessee cannot be compelled to pay royalty upon oil that does not belong to the lessor. This statement, which is clearly *obiter dicta*, was made by Martland J in *Imperial Oil Limited v Placid Oil Co.*[26] In this case, the issue concerned the royalty payable under lands affected by the Saskatchewan *Road Allowances Crown Oil Act*, 1959, which provided that in every producing oil reservoir 1.88 per cent of the recoverable oil shall be deemed to be under road allowances, and the property of the Crown. Imperial, as the original lessee, took the position that it was required, despite the existence of the Act, to pay the freehold lessor his royalty on the basis of 100 per cent of the substances produced from the lands. The particular lease contained the lesser interest clause in the same form as set forth above. Imperial, concerned that it might unwillingly be in breach of the lease, was not content to rely on the protection

---

26 [1963] S.C.R. 333, 43 W.W.R. 437, 39 D.L.R. (2d) 244, [1963] S.C.J. No. 33 (S.C.C.).

of this clause, possibly on the ground that it might not apply to the situation created by the Saskatchewan Act. The Supreme Court held that the effect of the road allowance act was to make the specified percentage of 1.88 the property of the Crown. The court considered the effect of this upon the lease in the following passage: "Insofar as the lease is concerned, the obligation to pay royalty is upon the leased substances owned by the lessor and leased and granted by him to the lessee. The lessee cannot be compelled to pay royalty upon oil which does not belong to the lessor and this conclusion, which, I think, must follow, even apart from the provisions of clause 4 of the lease, is reinforced by the terms of that clause."[27]

The interesting portion of this passage is the statement that the lessee's obligation is to pay royalty only upon the substances owned by the lessor *even apart from the lesser interest clause.* Since the lease did contain such a clause, the observation is no more than *dicta,* but it is, nonetheless, remarkable. It seems to impart the concept of ownership into the royalty clause. The actual words used in the clause do not contain any reference to ownership, but only to production from the said lands. The view that the royalty is applicable only to the leased substances "owned" by the lessor seems to vary the express terms of a contract between the parties, particularly in view of the rule of capture. If the parties see fit to impose a royalty on all the substances produced from the said lands, then that result should not necessarily be altered by the subsequent discovery that the lessor may own something less than 100 per cent. If such a result were to be achieved, surely the proper method would be in an action for rectification on the ground of mistake. In most cases, the point may be academic because of the almost universal existence of the lesser interest clause. There may, however, be circumstances that lie outside the ambit of its language or where it is absent from the lease, and then the *obiter dicta* of Martland J would become very material.

As noted above, the ownership approach is reflected in CAPL 99.

Assignment of Royalty

A number of conventional leases include the following provision at the end of the royalty clause: "In the event the lessor or any prior owner of the minerals has, prior to this date, assigned all or any portion of the

---

27 Ibid. S.C.R. at 339.

aforesaid royalty, the lessee shall be entitled to pay the royalty payable hereunder to the assignee thereof to the extent the same has been assigned and such payment shall discharge the lessee's obligations hereunder in respect to the payment of royalty to the extent the same has been assigned." The purpose is to allow the lessee to recognize assignment or partial assignments of the royalty made by the lessor prior to the date of the lease. The classic example is a gross royalty trust created by the lessor or his predecessor.

A number of conventional leases contain language in the royalty clause whereby the lessor agrees that the royalty reserved and payable under the lease shall be inclusive of any prior disposition by the lessor of any royalty or other interests in the leased substances. In the absence of such a provision the lessee might run the danger of having to pay both the royalty under the lease and any prior disposition of royalty to which the lands were subject. If the prior disposition, whether by gross royalty trust or otherwise, is evidenced by a caveat on the title, it could be argued that the lessee took his interest in the lands subject to that prior disposition, and thereby became liable for it.

The CAPL lease incorporates such a provision as follows:

(c) The Lessor agrees that the royalty reserved and payable hereunder in respect of the leased substances shall be inclusive of any prior disposition of any royalty or other interest in the leased substances, and agrees to make all payments required by any such disposition out of the royalty received hereunder and to indemnify and save the Lessee harmless from its failure to do so; provided, however, that the Lessee may elect by notice in writing to the Lessor to make such payments on behalf of the Lessor and shall have the right to deduct any such payments made from the royalty, rental and suspended well payments otherwise payable to the Lessor.

Since CAPL 99 does not provide for delay rentals, there is no reference to "rental." The CAPL royalty clauses also give the lessor the right during normal business hours to examine the lessee's records relating to the leased substances produced from or allocated to the said lands. In the normal course of events, this right is seldom exercised by the average lessor, but in the event of a dispute or serious concerns it provides him with a valuable tool.

The assignment clause in the CAPL lease and most conventional leases provides that no assignment by the lessor shall be binding upon the lessee unless the assignment is for the entire interest of the lessor. The effect of this is that the lessee, in the event of a partial assignment by the lessor, can continue to deal exclusively with the lessor in all matters pertaining to the lease, including the giving of notices, and making of payments, including royalty payments. The assignment clause also provides that no assignment shall be binding on the lessee until forty-five days after it has been furnished with satisfactory evidence of the assignment. The CAPL lease further provides that the lessee may act on the assignment prior to the expiration of the forty-five-day period.

In the event of a change in the mineral ownership, the new owner should be sure to obtain an assignment of the lease and provide the lessee with a copy of the assignment in order to establish his right to the royalties.

No Automatic Termination for Failure to Pay Royalty

The royalty clause does not contain words of automatic termination. The obligation of the lessee under a conventional lease is to remit to the lessor on or before a specified day of each month an amount equal to the royalty share of the substances produced and sold in the previous month, or, in the case of the CAPL lease, in the second previous month. Since the lessee is obligated to make the payments by the specified date, failure to do so falls within the default clause discussed in more detail *infra*. In brief, if the lessee fails to remit royalty payments as required, the lessor may give a default notice and, unless the lessee commences to remedy such default within a specified period of time from receipt of such notice, the lease could then terminate. Most leases, however, provide that the lease will not terminate if there is a well on the lands. But the well must have the capability to produce. A well where the production has declined until the producing zone is "dry" for all practical purposes, and the surface equipment has been removed, will not qualify.[28]

In the absence of a default notice and the expiration of the period of grace without remedial action by the lessee, the failure of the lessee to pay the royalty would not terminate the lease. The *habendum* clause maintains the lease in force for the primary term and so long thereafter

---

28 *Kensington Energy Ltd. v B&G Energy Ltd.*, [2005] A.J. No. 1672, [2005] ABQB 734 (Alta. Q.B.). This case is also discussed in the sections dealing with the Canadian jurisprudential, approach, *ante*, and the shut-in well clause, *infra*.

as the leased substances are *produced*. So long as the substances are being produced, the lease is continued regardless of whether or not the royalty payments are made.

Entitlement to Royalties as between Life Interest and Remainderman

Entitlement as between a life tenant and a remainderman to royalties payable under an oil and gas lease remains a very nice question. The problem arises because of the fact that, like mines, the petroleum sub-stances to which the royalty attaches are removed from the land and are not replenished by nature as are growing crops. The underlying principle was described in *Campbell v Wardlaw*,[29] which held that the life interest was entitled to the whole produce and profits from the life estate but the substance of the estate is to be preserved and not destroyed. This principle, however, was always subject to the condi-tion that the settlor could indicate a contrary intention that the life estate was to enjoy the corpus of the estate. Hence, the exception in English law that a life tenant was entitled to the benefits from a mine that had been opened in the settlor's lifetime, it being inferred that it was his intention that the benefits continue to flow to the recipient. Similarly, a testator or settlor could expressly provide that minerals might or could be worked by the trustees, and the courts would be pre-pared to hold that it was his intention that his widow was to enjoy the benefits arising from their working.[30] In other words, the English courts were prepared to be guided by the intention of the settlor, where such intention could be identified.

Intention is also the determining factor for Canadian courts. In *Re Murray*[31] the testator had executed the oil and gas lease and had received delay rental payments in his lifetime, and the court concluded that he must have intended his widow should have received whatever income or benefit he would have received under the lease. The court quoted with approval a passage from *Re Kemeys-Tynte*: "So in this case, where mines have been let by the settlor before the will came into operation, the tenant for life under the will is entitled, in my opinion, to the rents and royalties as incident to the reversion of which he is tenant for life."[32]

---

29 (1883), 8 App. Cas. 641.
30 Ibid. Lord Watson at 650.
31 [1961] O.W.N. 189 (Ont. H.C.).
32 [1892] 2 Ch. 211.

In the leading Canadian case of *Hayduk v Waterton*[33] the lease was granted after the trust had been created, but the court looked at the intention of the parties at the time the trust was set up and found it was intended that "everything must go to the parents during their lifetime." Consequently, the life tenant, or "life renter" in the words of the document, was entitled to the royalties. The court also found that this intention among the parties still existed at the time the lease was entered into.

In *Re Moffat Estate*[34] the widow, who had a life estate, and her son, the remainderman, acting in their capacities as executrix and executor, joined in executing a lease and sought the opinion of the court as to which one of them was entitled to receive the monies (bonus payments, delay rentals, and royalties) payable under the lease.[35] McKercher J quoted *Campbell v Wardlaw*,[36] and also *Halsbury*, to the effect that a remainderman is not entitled to work the mines, and if he does, the tenant for life is probably entitled to have the proceeds invested and to be paid the income arising therefrom. The court followed this approach and held that the widow was entitled to have the proceeds from the lease accumulated and invested in trustee securities and receive the income therefrom. On her death the accumulated funds were to be paid to the remainderman.

In the *Moffat* case there was no indication that the testator intended his widow to share in the corpus of the estate. If a court finds such an intention, the life tenant will be entitled to the full benefit of the royalty. If not, the result would likely be as set forth in *Re Moffat*.

Apportionment

Somewhat similar is the problem of who is entitled to the royalty when the land covered by a lease has been subsequently conveyed by the lessor to separate owners and production occurs on one parcel but not on

---

33 [1968] S.C.R. 871, 64 W.W.R. 641, 68 D.L.R. (2d) 562, [1968] S.C.J. No. 66 (S.C.C.).

34 (1955), 16 W.W.R. 314 (Sask. Q.B.).

35 The court quoted extensively from Summers, *The Law of Oil and Gas* (Kansas City, Mo.: Vernon Law Book Company) to the effect that, while neither a life tenant nor a remainderman may separately execute a valid lease, they could do so jointly. Since the partners were acting in their capacity as personal representatives, this point appears to be irrelevant.

36 (1883), 8 App. Cas. 641.

the other. Is the owner of the parcel on which there is production entitled to the royalty exclusively, or must he share it with the owner of the other parcel?

The one Canadian decision on this point had a fact pattern that contained all the ingredients for the principle of apportionment. In *Re Dawson and Bell*[37] the lessor had granted a lease covering portions of two lots. During the primary term two gas wells were brought into production on one lot, but there was no drilling on the other. The lease, of course, was continued beyond the primary term by the presence of production. The lessor then died, and by agreement among his heirs-at-law the land was divided into two portions, one comprising the area on which the two wells were located. The question was whether the owner of the non-productive lot was entitled to any share of the royalty. The Ontario Court of Appeal applied English mining law to hold that the royalty "is the compensation which the occupier pays the landlord for that species of occupation which the contract between them allows."[38]

Once royalty had been equated to rent, the court applied long-established principles of English law to hold the right to receive the proportionate part of the rent passed under the grant of land. The owners of the freehold were entitled to have it apportioned, in the event of a subsequent subdivision of the freehold, notwithstanding that all of the oil or gas may be produced from only one portion. The division of the freehold did not have the effect of severing the *profit à prendre*.

The application of the English rule of apportionment really settled the matter, although the Court of Appeal also looked to the existing American authorities. As quite often happens, the court found that there were two conflicting lines of authorities, depending on whether the particular state took the view that a lease vested in the lessee an estate in the land only, or absolute title to the oil and gas in place.[39]

---

37 [1945] O.R. 825, [1946] 1 D.L.R. 327, [1945] O.J. No. 563. (Ont. C.A.)

38 *Reg. v Westbrook* (1847), 10 Q.B. 178, 116 E.R. 69.

39 Rae, *supra* n 19, points out that in applying the Texas cases, the Ontario Court of Appeal may have overlooked the fact that the Supreme Court of Texas subsequently reversed one of the decisions, overruled another, and distinguished the third of the three cases cited. Nonetheless, the apportionment theory seems to be firmly established in the states of California, Mississippi, and Pennsylvania, although the non-apportionment theory, according to Rae, is followed in the states of Arkansas, Colorado, Illinois, Texas, Kansas, Kentucky, Louisiana, Nebraska, New Mexico, Ohio, Oklahoma, and West Virginia. As McRuer JA pointed out, the American decisions are only useful insofar as they may expound the law consistently with the principles of English law.

The *Dawson and Bell* case is not binding on any courts outside the province of Ontario, so it is not possible to determine how widespread will be the Canadian acceptance of the doctrine of apportionment. It has an appeal to equitable considerations, and it has the support of English mining law. Some forms of leases finesse the problem by including, usually in the assignment clause, an express provision for apportionment of royalties. Such a clause was considered by the Alberta Trial Division in *Prudential Trust Company Ltd. v National Trust Company Ltd.*[40] The lease contained this provision: "If the leased premises are now or shall hereafter be owned in severalty or in separate tracts, the premises, nevertheless, shall be developed and operated as one lease, and all royalties accruing hereunder shall be treated as an entirety and shall be divided among and paid to such separate owners in the proportion that the acreage owned by each such separate owner bears to the entire lease acreage." The lessor entered into two agreements, subsequent to executing the lease, in which he disposed of portions of his royalty to two different owners. The Trial Division applied the provision of the entirety clause and apportioned the royalty among the two assignees. Because of the existence of this clause, McDermid J (as he then was) expressly refrained from deciding whether the rule of apportionment as applied in *Re Dawson and Bell* was in force in the province of Alberta.

Constructive Production and the Shut-in Well Clause

The shut-in well clause is one of the provisions of the lease that has been subjected to many changes and amendments over the years. It goes without saying that the changes were all designed to improve the position of the lessee. The shut-in clause is meant to deal with the situation where, for one reason or another, the lands cannot be put on production before the primary term of the lease will expire. If there is no production at the end of the primary term the "so long thereafter" language of the *habendum* clause would automatically terminate the lease. The failure to get the lands on production before the end of the primary term most frequently occurs when there has been a discovery of gas on the lands. Attaching a discovery of natural gas to a market can be a very time-consuming and difficult proposition, particularly if the

---

40 (1965), 50 W.W.R. 29, 47 D.L.R. (2d) 596 (Alta. S.C.T.D.).

discovery is not in the vicinity of an existing pipeline system, or if there is no current demand for gas over and above the existing supply. The shut-in clause was inserted in the lease to prevent the loss of a potentially productive property because of a temporary lack of market. Since the problem was normally encountered with respect to gas, the original form of the clause dealt only with discoveries of natural gas. In fact, the clause was originally referred to as a "capped gas well clause." A typical clause of this type provided: "Where all wells on the said lands producing, or capable of producing, gas only are shut-in, suspended, capped or otherwise not being produced as the result of a lack of or an intermittent market, lessee may pay as royalty the sum of $100.00 per well per year, and if such payment is made it will be considered that gas is being produced from the said lands." The effect of the payment is to create a constructive production. The well is deemed to be producing and the "thereafter" aspect of the *habendum* is satisfied, which continues the lease in force.

Because it refers to "gas only," the above clause clearly could not apply to an oil well, and there may be considerable question as to whether it would apply to a well that produces distillate, condensate, or sulphur along with the gas. This particular point has never been decided in Canada, although it was argued both before the Trial and Appellate Divisions of Alberta in *Canadian Superior Oil Ltd. v Paddon Hughes Development Co. Ltd. and Hambly*.[41] Here the well, in addition to encountering gas, also discovered volumes of heavy oil in deeper horizons. It was argued that, because of the presence of oil, although it might not have been economically expedient to produce it at that time, the well could not be considered as one producing "gas only." This point was not dealt with by the courts as the lease was struck down on other grounds.

It soon became apparent to the lessee that the shut-in clause, while invaluable under certain circumstances, was too restrictive in scope. Not only was its application limited to a gas well, but the cause of the well being shut in was tied to market conditions. The clause quoted above had another serious limitation in that it referred to "wells on the said lands." The Supreme Court has ruled that this phraseology means

---

41 (1969), 67 W.W.R. (N.S.) 525, 3 D.L.R. (3d) 10 (Alta. C.A.); affirming (1968), 65 W.W.R. (N.S.) 461 (Alta. S.C.T.D.). The issue was not raised before the Supreme Court of Canada, [1970] S.C.R. 932, 74 W.W.R. (N.S.) 356, 12 D.L.R. (3d) 247, [1970] S.C.J. No. 48 (S.C.C.).

that the well must be on the lands covered by the lease and that the presence of a well on lands with which the lease lands are pooled would not suffice.[42] The clause was amended to refer simply to "well or wells," which included oil wells in addition to natural gas wells, and expanded the reasons for the well being shut in to include not only market conditions but "any cause whatsoever beyond the lessee's reasonable control." A later refinement was to expand the description of the market to include not only the lack of or an intermittent market, but also an uneconomical or unprofitable market, and also made it clear that a well on lands with which the leased lands were pooled would satisfy the clause. A typical example of this type of what might be called an "intermediate" clause reads as follows:

> If at the expiration of any year during the primary term or any extended term of this lease and grant there be a well or wells upon the said lands, or upon lands with which the said lands and leased substances or any part or parts thereof have been pooled or unitized, or upon lands adjacent to the said lands and included in a spacing unit wherein the said lands or any portion thereof is comprised, from which leased substances are not produced as a result of a lack of or an intermittent or uneconomical or unprofitable market or any cause whatsoever beyond the lessee's reasonable control, the lessee may, on or before such anniversary date, pay to the lessor in the same manner provided for the payment of delay rental hereunder, as royalty, an amount equal to the annual delay rental payable hereunder, and if such sum is so paid, such well or wells shall be deemed to be a producing well or wells on the said lands under all the provisions of this lease and grant for the following twelve (12) month period. By like payment made in a like manner such well or wells shall be deemed to be producing for like periods successively.

In two instances Alberta courts have found that the lessee failed to establish the necessary market conditions and have struck down the lease. In *Blair Estate Ltd. v Altana Explor. Co.*[43] it was held that while the evidence supported the inference that the market provided by the lessee's major customer was intermittent, it did not demonstrate a lack of

---

42 *Shell Oil Co. v Gunderson*, [1960] S.C.R. 424, 23 D.L.R. (2d) 81, [1960] S.C.J. No. 19 (S.C.C.). This case is discussed in detail under "Termination of Productive or Potentially Productive Leases," *infra*.

43 (1987), 53 Alta. L.R. (2d) 419, [1987] A.J. No. 554 (Alta. C.A.).

an alternative market, namely, the discount *intra* Alberta market that existed at that time.

In *549767 Alberta Ltd. v Teg Holdings Ltd.*[44] the shut-in clause referred to "a lack of, or an intermittent, market or lack of transportation facilities or any other cause whatsoever beyond the lessee's reasonable control." The wells on two petroleum and natural gas leases did not produce any natural gas beyond the primary term and in fact had not produced for over twenty years. The lessee relied upon both the lack of transportation facilities and also that there was a lack of market. The lessee argued that since there were no transportation facilities available, the gas could not be processed and firm sales contracts could not be entered into. Deyell J accepted expert evidence that there was available capacity in the pipeline to which the wells could have been connected and also that there was sufficient processing capacity to process the gas on at least an 80 per cent firm basis. The trial judge also accepted expert evidence that if a producer was only given assurance that 80 per cent of the anticipated volumes could be processed, that producer would choose to enter into a firm contract for the 80 per cent and sell any additional gas on an interruptible basis. Having accepted evidence that it would have been economic to tie in and produce the wells, the court held that the lessee could not rely on the shut-in clause and the leases had expired. The *Teg* case is also interesting because it held that the onus was on the lessee defendants to show that they came within the clause that would have justified the non-production of the wells. The question of onus will be discussed under Chapter 19, which deals with litigating the lease.

In what would appear to be the definitive test to determine an economic and profitable market, a majority of the Alberta Court of Appeal in *Freyberg v Fetcher Challenge Oil & Gas Inc.*[45] held that it was "whether, based on information available at the time, a prudent lessee would have foreseen profitability."

Another form that is encountered more and more frequently entirely omits any reference to market conditions or causes beyond the lessee's reasonable control and simply provides that if wells on the said lands are shut in, the lessee shall pay a sum equal to the delay rental and the well will be deemed to be a producing well hereunder. An example of

---

44 172 D.L.R. (4th) 294, [1999] A.J. No. 321 (Alta. C.A.).
45 42 Alta. L.R. (4th) 41, [2005] 10 W.W.R. 87, 363 A.R. 35, [2005] A.J. No. 108 (Alta. C.A.).

this type reads as follows: "Subject to the provisions hereinbefore set forth, if all wells on the said lands are shut-in, suspended or otherwise not produced during any year ending on an anniversary date, the lessee shall pay to the lessor at the expiration of each such year, a sum equal to the delay rental hereinbefore set forth and each such well shall be deemed to be a producing well hereunder, provided that this clause shall not impose an obligation upon the lessee to make the payment of a sum equal to the delay rental unless all wells on the said lands are shut-in, suspended or otherwise not produced for a period of ninety (90) consecutive days in any such year." This type of shut-in clause materially strengthens the lessee's position, and, by the same token, weakens the lessor's position. Under the "intermediate" type described above, which is probably a reasonable balance between the rights of the lessee and the lessor, the lessee must meet certain tests before he is able to prolong the life of the lease by shut-in payments. For example, if a lessee has five gas wells in an area and has a sales contract that can be supplied by only three, he may not be in a position to simply shut in the other two and maintain the lease or leases covering those two wells by shut-in payments. In other words, the lessee can be made accountable, to some degree at least, to the lessor with regard to the marketing of the leased substances.

Nonetheless, there must still be a well on the lands. While the foregoing clause does not state it must be "capable of producing the leased substances," it must still be a "well." It seems logical that in order to qualify as a "well" it must be capable of production. This point was made in the *Kensington* case[46] where the shut-in clause was identical to the one quoted above, and simply referred to the wells being shut in. On the question of whether or not there was a well on the lands, the facts in support were weak in the extreme. A gas well was drilled on the leased lands during the primary term of a lease. Natural gas was encountered, but production did not commence until more than four years later. Shut-in payments were made throughout the entire time frame. Production continued for more than five years, and then the well was shut in. The evidence was that in the months preceding it being shut in, the well was unable to produce on a consistent basis and daily production had declined to only 4.5 mcf of natural gas. In the words of the trial judge, LoVecchio J, "it had become essentially a dry

---

46 *Supra*, n 28.

hole." When production ended, the surface equipment was removed, which helped to confirm that it was no longer a well. Since there was not a well on the lands, the lessee was not entitled to make a shut-in payment and the lease expired.

The shut-in, or suspended wells, clause in CAPL 88 and 91 requires that there be a well capable of producing the leased substances on the said lands, the pooled lands, or the unitized lands before the clause could be activated. There is no requirement that the wells must be shut in for market conditions or causes beyond the lessee's reasonable control.

The possibility of losing a lease by not being able to preserve it by making a shut-in payment is just about the only lever available to the lessor to force the lessee to actively market and produce the substances. There has been a considerable backlash against this clause, and the CAPL 99 lease has been radically amended to read as follows:

Shut-In Wells
(a) If, at the expiration of the Primary Term or at any time or times thereafter, there is any well on or in the Lands, the Pooled Lands, or the Unitized Lands, capable of producing leased substances, or any of them, and such well is shut-in, it shall be deemed that Operations are being conducted on the Lands, for so long as the said well is shut-in.
(b) If, at the expiration of any Lease Year after the Primary Term, production of Leased Substances for at least 720 hours has not been obtained during any such Lease Year from a well on or in the Lands, the Pooled Lands, or the Unitized Lands, the Lessee shall pay to the Lessor an amount equal to the Lease Payment (the "Shut-in Well Payment"), to be paid within 90 days after the expiration of any such Lease Year.

Subsection (a) provides that if there is any well on the lands, the pooled lands, or the unitized lands capable of producing and such well is shut in, it shall be deemed that operations are being conducted on the lands. The fact that operations are being conducted of course maintains the lease in force.

Subsection (b) is meant to deal with the situation where the lease is being held by a well that may be capable of production, but whose status as a valid economic well is questionable. If in any year after the primary term a well has not produced for at least 720 hours, the lessee shall pay an amount equal to the lease payment within ninety days after the expiration of a lease year. The effect of this provision is twofold: if the well produces for at least 720 hours it will maintain the lease without the necessity of a shut-in payment. If, however, it does not produce for 720 hours in any one year the lessee must pay an amount equal to the lease payment or lose the lease. The lease payment will be a considerable sum of money since it is the consideration received by the lessor for granting the lease. The result is that if the lessee wants to maintain the lease on the basis of a poorly performing well, he can do so, but only by the payment of a significant amount of money. The alternative is to let the lease lapse.

"Shall" or "May"

The early forms of the clause almost invariably provided that the lessee "may" pay a shut-in payment. It was clearly an option, and if he elected to make the payment, the lease was continued. The option aspect might be illusory in that a prudent lessee would not consciously elect to not make the payment and thereby lose a valuable lease. Nonetheless, it was framed as an option and certainly a lessee could not be forced to make the payment.

Gradually the use of "shall" in the place of "may" became more prevalent, and one frequently encounters it today, although "may" has by no means disappeared. Does the substitution of "shall" for "may" convert the option into an enforceable obligation of the lessee? The difference could be crucial because, if "shall" were to be construed as creating an obligation to make the payment, a lessee who had failed to make a proper payment could argue that the default clause in the lease would apply, with the result that he would be entitled to receive notice of default and a period of grace within which to correct the default and preserve his lease.

The meaning of "shall" in the context of a shut-in clause came before the courts in the first *Durish v White Resource Management Ltd.* case.[47] Natural gas leases were granted on two parcels of land on 27 May 1978. A well was drilled, production commenced, and notice was served on the lessor that the lands were being pooled for purposes of production. The well continued to produce until November 1985, when it was shut in because of a dispute between the lessee and the operator of the field concerning transmission and processing charges

---

47 (1988), 55 Alta. L.R. (2d) 47, [1987] A.J. No. 804 (Alta. Q.B.).

charged by the operator. The leases contained a clause that provided for termination of the lease if production ceased for more than ninety days, unless such cessation resulted from a cause that was "in accordance with good oilfield practice." Termination could also be avoided by the payment of a shut-in royalty:

Shut-in Wells:

Subject to the provisions hereinbefore set forth, if all wells on the said lands as [sic] shut-in, suspended or otherwise not produced during any year ending on an anniversary date, the Lessee shall pay to the Lessor at the expiration of each such year, a sum equal to the delay rental hereinbefore set forth and each such well shall be deemed to be a producing well hereunder, provided that this clause shall not impose an obligation upon the Lessee to make the payment of a sum equal to the delay rental unless all wells on the said lands are shut-in, suspended or otherwise not produced for a period of ninety (90) consecutive days in any such year.

Prior to the anniversary date of 27 May 1986, the lessor's royalty account was in a debit balance. In April 1986 that account was allegedly credited with a shut-in payment, which reduced the debit balance. However, no notice of the credit was given to the lessor, and it seems clear from the judgment that the court was highly skeptical that a credit had actually been made. In August 1986 the lessor advised the lessee that the lease had terminated as a result of a cessation of production. In January 1987 the lessee made further payments to the lessor allegedly representing past shut-in payments. Then the lessor brought an action to have the caveats removed from the titles on the basis that the lease had terminated due to non-production and failure to pay the shut-in royalty.

The well had been shut in by the operator because of the lessee's default in payment of revised transmission processing fees amounting to some $151,000. Bracco J (as he then was) was unable to find that the dispute between the operator and the lessee, even though relating to transmission and processing fees, came within the ambit of "good oilfield practice." There was no evidence that the revised fees made continued production impossible or unprofitable, and since the non-production could not be attributed to "any cause whatsoever which is in accordance with good oilfield practice," that argument could not support the leases. If they were to continue in force it would only be because of the operation of the shut-in clause.

The shut-in wells clause provided that "the Lessee shall pay to the Lessor at the expiration of each such year." If the clause required the lessee to pay the shut-in fee, the default clause would kick in and the lessee would be able to salvage the lease by making the shut-in payment. The trial judge analysed the basic structure of the lease and found all of the provisions of the *habendum* to be consistent with the premise that the lease automatically terminates unless the periods of interruption of drilling or non-production fall within those exceptions where such delays are not to be counted against the lessee. In this context he found that the use of the word "shall" does not alter the fundamental structure of the lease and the payment of the shut-in fee is not a covenant imposed as an obligation upon the lessee. He also commented on the fact that the shut-in fee is very modest and imposes no real impediment upon the lessee in deciding as to whether to continue the life of the lease or allow it to lapse. This, however, was clearly not the basis of his decision.

The court's finding that the use of the word "shall" created an option and not an obligation is in accord with the universal understanding of how the shut-in clause works. The CAPL lease also provides that "the Lessee shall pay," which creates an option, not an obligation.

The clause in *Durish* and in many conventional leases contained an exculpatory provision "that this clause shall not impose an obligation upon the lessee to make the payment" unless all wells on the lands are shut in or not produced for a period of ninety consecutive days in any year. This language and the reference to "obligation" seem more consistent with the clause being obligatory rather than optional. This point was not dealt with in *Durish*. Presumably the obligation that is referred to is the "need" for the lessee to make the payment if he wants to maintain the lease.

Having interpreted the shut-in clause in a manner consistent with the working of the lease, the learned trial judge then turned his attention to when payment would have to be made and examined the phrase "at the expiration of each such year." He quoted the definition of "at" in Black's Law Dictionary, 4th edition, to the effect that "at" is: "[a] term of considerable elasticity of meaning and somewhat indefinite ... As used to fix a time, it does not necessarily mean *eo instante* or the identical time named, or even a fixed definite moment. But 'at' may often express simple nearness and proximity, and consequently may denote a reasonable time." This led him to the view that the payment of the shut-in fee may be paid on the anniversary date of the lease year or within a reasonable time either before or after such anniversary date. In the event, the lessee tendered a payment on 16 January 1987, which was accepted by the lessor but credited to past shut-in payments allegedly in arrears for previous years. The court found that payment on 16 January 1987 was not within a reasonable time of the 27 May 1986 anniversary date and struck down the lease on that basis.

This finding may have reduced Bracco J's interpretation of "at" into *obiter*, and the point was not dealt with in the Court of Appeal. Unlike his interpretation of "shall," it seems completely at variance with the context of the oil and gas lease. Virtually every lease, including CAPL, contains a provision that "time is of the essence," and certainly time is of the essence in the oil industry, where as the courts have pointed out on more than one occasion, fortunes can change drastically overnight. The courts have consistently ruled that payment of the delay rental must be made on time in order to maintain a lease with the "unless" drilling clause, and even a delay of one day has been held to be fatal.[48] While it is true that a shut-in clause does not contain the words of termination that are to be found in the "unless" drilling clause, payment of the shut-in royalty is nevertheless the means by which a lessee avoids the termination of his lease. The lessor should not be left waiting for whatever a reasonable time might be to know whether or not the lease on his land has terminated, leaving him free to deal with it.[49]

The trial decision was upheld in the Court of Appeal,[50] which expressly agreed that the shut-in clause granted an option to the lessee to extend the term of the lease after shutdown of production, but did not oblige him to do so. Therefore, the default clause had no application.

Shut-in Payments during the Primary Term

The shut-in clause invariably provides that payment may or shall be made if there is a shut-in well on the lands or the pooled lands. Some versions, like the second form quoted above, expressly provide that if there is a shut-in well "at the expiration of any year during the primary

---

48 *Canadian Fina Oil Ltd. v Paschke* (1957), 21 W.W.R. (N.S.) 260, 7 D.L.R. (2d) 473 (Alta. S.C., App.Div.). For a colourful, and accurate, account of how the value of mineral rights can fluctuate almost overnight, see Porter JA at 263.

49 Ibid.

50 (1988), 63 Alta. L.R. (2d) 265, [1988] A.J. No. 1162 (Alta. C.A.).

term or any extended term" of the lease, the payment may or shall be made. What is the situation with respect to the shut-in payment when the lessee drills a potentially productive well, say in the second year of a five-year primary term, and the well is shut in for a reason that satisfies the clause? Does the lessee have to make the payment in each year of the primary term? The answer seems to be that he does not, except for the payment at the expiration of the primary term. By drilling the well, the lessee has satisfied the drilling commitment, and thus the first proviso of the *habendum*, which would terminate the lease in the absence of drilling or the payment of a delay rental, is not activated. Since the well is not a dry hole, the second proviso would not be applicable either. This does create a discrepancy between the *habendum* and the shut-in clause, which contemplates a payment regardless of whether the lease is in its primary term or beyond.

The one payment that must be made is the one that falls at the expiration of the primary term. If this payment is not made, there will be no deemed production and the lease will terminate on its own terms.[51]

The CAPL lease avoids any possible conflict between the shut-in clause and the *habendum* by making the suspended wells clause come into effect "at the expiration of the primary term or at any time or times thereafter."

The Shut-in Clause and the *Habendum*

The shut-in clause works in conjunction with the *habendum*. In most instances the connection will be with the basic *habendum* itself, which gives the lessee the right to "Have And Enjoy" the lease for the specified number of years in the primary term "and so long thereafter as the leased substances are produced from the said lands or the pooled lands." By creating a constructive production the shut-in clause meshes with the *habendum* and the lease is continued.

The shut-in clause can also interact with the third proviso of the *habendum*, which typically comes into play under two sets of circumstances:

---

51 *Can. Superior Oil of Calif. Ltd. v Kanstrup*, [1965] S.C.R. 92, 49 W.W.R. (N.S.) 257, 47 D.L.R. (2d) 1, [1964] S.C.J. No. 54 (S.C.C.). *Canadian Superior Oil Ltd. v Paddon Hughes Development Co. Ltd. and Hambly*, *supra* n 41, is an example of the primary term being extended when the lessee is engaged in drilling operations at the end thereof. The result is still the same; however, the payment must be made at the expiration of the extended primary term or the lease will terminate.

(a) when there is no production at the end of the primary term but the lessee is engaged in drilling or working operations, or (b) when production ceases after the expiration of the primary term. If the operations under (a) result in a well that is capable of production but cannot immediately be placed on production, a shut-in payment will continue it in force. Similarly, if the lease is beyond its primary term and production ceases and the well is still capable of production, a shut-in payment will maintain the lease.

Kissinger Petroleums Ltd. v Nelson Estate[52] involved the interaction of the shut-in clause and the third proviso. The well was drilled over the end of the primary term, which made the third proviso applicable. McDermid JA, who wrote the unanimous decision of the Alberta Court of Appeal, posed the question: Was the lease continued by the words, "the time of such ... non-production shall not be counted against the lessee"? He concluded that the time of such non-production is simply not to be counted and the lease would be continued in force.

If that interpretation were to be applied literally, there is a possibility that a lessee who fits within the third proviso might be able to ignore the making of shut-in payments and yet have his lease continued indefinitely. This unexpected result can be illustrated in the following manner: A well is drilled over the primary term, is potentially productive, but cannot be produced for reasons that satisfy the shut-in clause. Because the well was drilled over the primary term, the third proviso becomes applicable and the time of non-production does not count against the lessee. If one were to treat a failure to make shut in payments as amounting to non-production, the lack of payments would appear not to be fatal to the lease.

In the *Kissinger* case, however, the court went on to consider the payment that had been made and to hold that it was validly made. This step would have been unnecessary if the court was of the view that the "time shall not count" provision was applicable to a shut-in payment situation. The court found that the shut-in clause provides for a royalty to be paid while the well is not being produced, although McDermid JA admitted to some difficulty in interpreting the shut-in clause as so providing

---

52 (1984), 33 Alta. L.R. (2d) 1, [1984] 5 W.W.R. 673, 13 D.L.R. (4th) 542, [1984] A.J. No. 2587 (Alta. C.A.); affirming 26 Alta. L.R. (2d) 378, 14 E.T.R. 207, 45 A.R. 393, [1983] A.J. No. 814 (Alta. Q.B.). (Leave to appeal denied.) The trial decision is criticized in Desbarat & Carson, "Recent Developments in the Law of Interest to Oil and Gas Lawyers" (1985) 23 Alta. L. Rev. 183 at 188.

because it contained the word "may." In other words, the lessee was not obliged to make the payments in the event of non-production.

Since there *was* a shut-in payment in the *Kissinger* situation, the question of whether or not a payment is necessary to maintain the lease when the third proviso is applicable must be considered as still open. It would seem to be an untoward result if a lessee who postponed drilling the well until almost the end of the primary term and thus brought himself within the third proviso could still maintain his lease even if he failed to make the payments, while a lessee who drilled and completed the well during the primary term would be faced with the necessity of making the payments or losing his lease.[53]

Query: The shut-in clause in *Kissinger* refers to "well or wells," not to a well "capable of production" as is commonly found in these clauses. Would the result have been different if the well in *Kissinger* had to be "capable of production"? Bracco J's interpretation of "at" could be relevant in this regard.

The phrase "the time of such ... non-production shall not be counted against the lessee" was also raised in the 1998 *Durish v White*[54] case, but the court held that the proviso only applied after the expiration of the primary term, and in this case the well had been drilled and completed during the primary term.

Existence of a Well as a Condition Precedent

Shut-in clauses universally provide that if wells on the said lands are shut in, the lessee may or shall pay a sum of money and, if he does so, the well will be deemed to be producing. This would lead one to expect that a well or wells must be in existence and shut in as a condition precedent to the payment being made.

The American authority, Eugene Kuntz,[55] describes the dilemma of a lessee faced with making a payment to extend the term of his lease: "If

---

53 Note: The lessee who failed to make the payment after the expiration of the primary term might argue that this amounted to a cessation of production, thereby bringing his lease within the third proviso and freeing him from the necessity of making further payments to maintain his lease. However, such an interpretation would stretch the meaning of the third proviso beyond all reasonable bounds.

54 [1998] A.J. No. 1041, 230 A.R. 201 (Alta. Q.B.).

55 *A Treatise on the Law of Oil and Gas*, vol. 4 (Cincinnati: Anderson Publishing Co., 1962) at 38, para. 46.5.

he pays in advance, there is no way of identifying the payment as a shut-in gas royalty because there is no shut-in gas well. It is unreasonable to assume that the parties contemplated that the lessee make payment simultaneously with the physical act of shutting in the well. It is submitted that the shut-in gas royalty clause should be construed to permit the lessee to tender a shut-in gas royalty after he has reasonably made the decision that the well must be shut-in – but before he has taken the final act of shutting-in the well." The learned author is clearly of the opinion that a well must have reached the stage where the lessee has reasonably made the decision that the well will be shut in, or in other words, that it is potentially productive but cannot be produced immediately.

The issue of whether or not a well must be in existence at the time the payment is made was squarely raised by the factual situation in the *Kissinger* case.[56] The lease was dated 6 March 1970, and was for a primary term of ten years. The lessee commenced the drilling of a well on 1 March 1980, a few days prior to the expiration of the primary term. On 4 March 1980, the lessee sent a payment equivalent to the delay rental to the depository bank. As of midnight on that date the well was drilling ahead and was only two-thirds of the way to total depth. No testing had been conducted, nor had any oil or gas been encountered at that time. The well reached total depth on 9 March 1980, and a drill-stem test was carried out on 10 March. This test established that the well was capable of commercial production. On the following day, 11 March, the lessee, Kissinger, advised the lessor that the well had been "cased" as a gas well and referred to the payment of $640.00 that was credited to the lessor's account at the depository bank, stating that the payment "will act as the shut-in royalty payment as per Clause 3 of the subject lease."

It was argued by those who attacked the validity of the lease that the payment was invalid because it was made before there was a shut-in well on the land. The Alberta Court of Appeal held that there was nothing to suggest that a payment made by a lessee in advance of the completion of the well, and in anticipation that the well will be capable of commercial production, is not in compliance with the shut-in royalty clause when, upon completion of the well, it is designated as a shut-in royalty payment and accepted as such by the lessor.

---

56 *Supra* n 52.

A number of conclusions can be gleaned from this finding. A well need not have reached the stage where it has been tested and found to be potentially productive, and the subsequent designation of the payment as a shut-in royalty may be essential. Since this had been done in the *Kissinger* situation, the court stated that it did not have to decide what the position would be if the lessor refused the payment.

The designation of the payment as a shut-in royalty involves the principle of appropriation, which normally requires the payor to appropriate the payments at the time they are made.[57] This restriction was not applied in the *Kissinger* decision where the designation followed the payment by several days.

In *Kissinger* the well had at least been commenced and was drilling ahead. Can a lessee validly make a payment before the well has even been commenced? The *Kissinger* rationale would not appear to go quite this far, since it mentions "anticipation" that the well will be capable of commercial production. On the other hand, the Kissinger well had neither reached the target depth nor been tested at the time the payment was made. Thus, the "anticipation" could have been little more than a fond hope.

The above discussion deals with the timing of the initial payment. There may also be some question as to the time when subsequent payments are to be made. Much will depend on the wording of the individual clause. Some provide that if wells are shut in during any year ending on an anniversary date, the lessee shall pay "at the expiration of each such year." Does this mean that the lessee must wait until the last day of the year to make the payment? Other clauses provide that the payment may be made "on or before such anniversary date." Here, the lessee is clearly not limited to one date since he may make the payment "before" the anniversary date. The reference to "anniversary date" may itself raise some questions. Anniversary date is frequently referred to in the *habendum*, and there it clearly refers to the anniversary of the date of the lease. Presumably, it would have the same meaning when it is used in the shut-in well clause, but it might be argued that it should relate to the anniversary of the expiration of the

---

57 *Camco v Northwind Industries* (1982), 36 A.R. 585, [1982] A.J. No. 810 (Alta. Q.B.); *Cory Brothers and Company, Ltd. v The Owners of the Turkish Steamship "Mecca,"* [1897] A.C. 286 (H.L.).

extended term of the lease, i.e., the date on which a well drilled over the primary term was completed, or the date on which production ceased after expiration of the primary term. Conceivably, these new expiration dates could create new anniversary dates, although that does not appear to have been the intention of the draftsman.

The trial judge's interpretation of "at" as meaning a reasonable time before or after in the *Durish* case could become relevant to this issue. However, it was not adopted by the Court of Appeal and seems inconsistent with the way in which a lease works.

How long does a well have to be shut in before the shut-in clause applies? Some clauses refer to the well being shut in at the expiration of any year, while others refer to wells being shut in or not produced during any year, ending on an anniversary date. Under the latter type of clause it is conceivable a well having been shut in for a very brief period during a given year may require a payment to be made. However, most clauses of this type provide that the lessee need not make the payment unless the well has been shut in for a period of ninety consecutive days in any year.

It is obvious that the shut-in clause gives a great deal of protection to the lessee. Indeed, if the *Kissinger* rationale is applied, he is given an unreasonable amount of protection, particularly in those instances where the clause simply requires the well to be shut in regardless of the reason why. The clause means that a lease can be maintained in force indefinitely without production and, in some instances, without any limitation on the lessee's discretion on whether or not to produce the well. There must, however, be a well.

Canadian lease forms do not contain any obligation on the part of the lessee to develop a market for the leased substances, and it is highly questionable that Canadian courts would imply any such term. In *Freyberg v Fletcher Challenge Oil & Gas Inc.*[58] The trial judge found that there was an implied term to produce the well in the secondary term, thus bringing it under the protection of the default clause. The Alberta Court of Appeal overturned this finding and held there was no such implied term.

---

[58] 323 A.R. 45, [2002] A.J. No. 1173 (Alta. Q.B.); reversed 42 Alta. L.R. (4th) 41, [2005] 10 W.W.R. 87, 363 A.R. 35, [2005] A.J. No. 108 (Alta. C.A.); leave to appeal refused [2005] S.C.C.A. 167. *Freyberg* is analysed in Part 5, "Involuntary Termination."

Responsibility for Taxes

Most leases attempt to allocate the responsibility for taxes that may be
levied against the ownership of the minerals and the operations conducted on the lands. Generally, the lessor is made responsible for the
taxes arising out of his interest (the royalty share) in production
obtained from the lands and his ownership of mineral rights. He is also
charged with the responsibility for payment of such taxes as may be
levied against the surface of the lands if he owns same.

The lessee is charged with responsibility for the taxes levied in respect
of its operations on the said lands and its interest in production.

From the point of view of the lessor, the most significant tax is the
provincial tax imposed on his ownership of the actual mineral rights.
In Alberta, for example, the tax is based on revenue from production
and is very substantial. Because the lessor is the registered owner, the
government collects the tax from the lessor, but the lessee normally
will undertake to reimburse the lessor for a share of such taxes equal to
the lessee's interest, i.e., the percentage that is left after deducting the
royalty percentage from one hundred. While the lessor specifically
agrees to pay and discharge the taxes levied against his interest, his
continued failure to do so may result in a situation where his mineral
interest may eventually be taken from him.[59] Most, but not all, conventional leases allow the lessee to pay the taxes under such circumstances
and recover the expenditure from payments due under the lease.[60]

In the conventional lease responsibility for taxes is allocated by these
two standard clauses, which are self-explanatory:

TAXES PAYABLE BY THE LESSOR
The Lessor shall promptly satisfy all taxes, rates and assessments that
may be assessed or levied, direct or indirectly, against the Lessor by reason of the Lessor's interest in production obtained from the said lands, or
the Lessor's ownership of mineral rights in the said lands, and shall further pay all taxes, rates and assessments that may be assessed or levied
against the surface of the said lands during the continuance of the term
hereby granted or any extension thereof if and so long as the said surface
of the said lands is or continues to be owned by the Lessor.

---

59 *Freehold Mineral Rights Tax Act*, R.S.A. 2000, c F-26.
60 The standard clause that does this is discussed in Chapter 9, *infra*, under "Encumbrances."

TAXES PAYABLE BY THE LESSEE

The Lessee shall pay all taxes, rates and assessments that may be assessed or levied in respect of the undertaking and operations of the Lessee on, in, over or under the said lands, and shall further pay all taxes, rates and assessments that may be assessed or levied directly or indirectly against the Lessee by reason of the Lessee's interest in production from the said lands. The Lessee shall on the written request of the Lessor, accompanied by such tax receipts, statements or tax notices as the Lessee may require, reimburse the Lessor for _____ of any taxes assessed or imposed on the Lessor during the currency of this Lease by reason of the Lessor being the registered owner of the leased substances or being entitled to become such owner.

The blank in the immediately preceding clause is meant to be filled in by a figure that is the equivalent to the lessee's interest after deduction of the royalty.

The two clauses in CAPL 88 and 91 that deal with taxes make no mention of ownership of surface and deal only with the lessor's interest in production of leased substances or the lessor's ownership of leased substances. The lessor has to pay the taxes that are levied against him by reason of his interest in the production of leased substances or his ownership of leased substances, while the lessee is to pay all taxes levied against it by reason of its interest in the production of leased substances. If requested by the lessor, the lessee is to reimburse the lessor for a percentage of the taxes paid by the lessor equivalent to the lessee's interest in the lands, i.e., that percentage which remains after deducting the royalty percentage from 100 per cent.

CAPL 99 requires the lessee in the first instance to pay all the applicable taxes with the right to require the lessor to reimburse it for the royalty share. A separate clause in both the conventional lease and CAPL dealing with the discharge of taxes and encumbrances gives the lessee the right to pay and discharge any taxes incurred by the lessor, and to reimburse itself from payments due under the lease. This provision enables the lessee to protect itself against loss of its interest due to the lessor's failure to pay taxes.

9 Drainage – Offset Drilling and Pooling

The ambulatory nature of oil and gas raises both the hazard of drainage and the economic advantage of producing the substances through a minimum number of wells. Drainage can occur whenever a well in the vicinity of the lands is placed on production. As the pressure in the reservoir is reduced the substances may begin to migrate towards the producing wellbore.

Protection against Drainage

Loss of production through drainage can be counteracted by drilling a well on the leased lands and placing it on production. This is the purpose of the offset drilling clause – to impose upon the lessee an obligation to drill if certain conditions are met. The offset drilling clause has undergone many modifications over the years and contains a number of specialized and complicated provisions. Nonetheless, the basic purpose of the clause remains the same: to protect the lessor against loss of the oil and gas underlying his land through drainage. The best approach to understanding the operation of the clause is to consider the basic ingredients found in the early forms of the clause.

The following clause is typical of the early versions:

> In the event of commercial production being obtained from any well drilled on a spacing unit laterally adjoining the said lands and not owned by the lessor, then unless a well has been or is being drilled on the spacing unit of the said lands laterally adjoining the said spacing unit on which production is being so obtained and to the horizon in the formation from which production is being so obtained, the lessee shall within six (6)

months from the date of said well being placed on production, commence or cause to be commenced within the six (6) month period aforesaid operations for the drilling of an offset well on the spacing unit of the said lands laterally adjoining the said spacing unit on which production is being so obtained, and thereafter drill the same to the horizon in the formation from which production is being obtained from the said adjoining spacing unit; PROVIDED that, if such well drilled on lands laterally adjoining the said lands is productive primarily or only of natural gas, the lessee shall not be obligated to drill an offset well unless and until an adequate and commercially profitable market for natural gas which might be produced from the offset well can be previously arranged and provided.

The clause is designed to protect the interest of the mineral lessor and at the same time avoid placing the lessee in an uneconomic position with regard to the drilling of a well. It does not impose an absolute drilling obligation, but is conditional upon the fulfilment of certain prerequisites, namely:

(a) The well that creates the obligation must have encountered "commercial production." This is one of the terms defined in the interpretation clause and means such output from a well as, considering the cost of drilling and production operations and the price and quality of the leased substances, would commercially and economically warrant the drilling of a like well in the vicinity thereof after a production test of thirty days. This requirement ensures that the creating well must have encountered production in economic volumes that were maintained for at least a thirty-day period.

(b) The creating well must have been located on a spacing unit laterally adjoining the leased lands. This condition is based on the theory that no significant drainage will occur over greater distances. "Spacing unit" is another defined term and means the area allocated to the well for the purpose of drilling for or producing the leased substances under the existing conservation and production laws. The provincial conservation laws permit a very substantial variation in the size of a spacing unit; it may range from a quarter section to several sections depending on the type of substance and reservoir conditions. The requirement that the spacing unit must be "laterally adjoining" is virtually universal. A diagonal offset, which occurs when the producing spacing unit corners on the leased lands, will not activate the clause.

Alberta has enacted legislation[1] which provides that, where a well is drilled and produces oil or gas from a drilling spacing unit that laterally adjoins a drilling spacing unit subject to an oil and gas lease that contains an offset drilling provision, then the well that creates the obligation shall be deemed, regardless of its actual location on the drilling spacing unit, to give rise to the offset obligation. This legislative provision is meant to take care of the situation that may arise where a "drilling spacing unit" under the Act consists of several sections of land comprising several leases. In such a case, the producing well could be located on one lease with another lease, comprising part of the drilling spacing unit, intervening between the well and yet another lease with an offset clause.

(c) The creating well must be on land not owned by the lessor. This requirement is justified on the theory there would be no actual monetary loss to the lessor if the creating well were situated on his lands, even if not included within the subject lease, as all the petroleum substances drained from the leased lands would be recovered to his possession through the other well. A lessor, if he were so inclined, could circumvent this limitation by simply transferring the rights to a relative or other "friendly assignee."

The standard clause contains a modification of this limitation under which the offset will accrue with respect to land owned by the lessor unless the land is also leased by the lessee. This variation, although the logic behind it is not readily apparent, can only be beneficial to the lessor since it widens the applicability of the obligation.

CAPL 88 and 91 achieve the same result by defining "offset well" as meaning "any well drilled on any spacing unit laterally adjoining the said lands, which spacing unit does not include lands owned by the lessor or, if owned by the lessor, not under lease to the lessee."

CAPL 99 replaces "drilled" with "producing" to deal with the complications caused by horizontal wells.

The use of "include" means that not all of the lands in the spacing unit that creates the offset need to be owned by the lessor. If he owns only a portion of the lands, the offset will not be created.

CAPL 99 makes it clear that only a well drilled subsequent to the date of the lease can create an offset. It is possible that the same result

---

1 *Oil and Gas Conservation Act*, R.S.A. 2000, c O-6, s 98.

would flow from the definition of "offset well" in other forms of leases as meaning any well *drilled* on any spacing unit. The reference to "drilled" may well mean that the well must have been drilled after the lease of the adjoining lands was entered into, but the express reference in CAPL 99 puts it beyond doubt.

The definition of "offset well" in CAPL 99 is a marked departure from all previous forms in that for the first time it includes a reference to a spacing unit *diagonally adjoining* the lease lands, as well as laterally adjoining the lands. Previous offset clauses were confined to spacing units laterally adjoining the lands on the premise that significant drainage would only occur when the offsetting well was on a laterally adjoining space unit. CAPL 99 recognizes that drainage can also occur from a well on a diagonally adjoining space unit.

Termination on Failure to Drill Offset Well

Failure to comply with an offset drilling obligation, unlike the drilling commitment, does not lead to automatic termination of the lease. It may ultimately result in termination if the lessor sets in motion certain procedures. Most leases contain a provision under which the lessor may give the lessee written notice of a default, and, if the lessee fails to commence to remedy such default within a specified period of time, the lease will terminate. Since the offset clause creates an obligation on the part of the lessee and not a mere option, failure to drill constitutes a default. Therefore, if the lessor gives notice and the required period of time elapses without remedial action, the lease will terminate.

The requirement of notice and a period of grace in which to remedy the default before termination of the lease flows from the language of the document itself. The point was tested before a Canadian court on one occasion and the court reached the same conclusion.[2] The validity of the lease was attacked on the ground that the covenant to drill offset wells goes to the very root and substance of the contract, and thus a breach of the covenant entitled the lessor to treat the lease as having been terminated. The Saskatchewan Court of Appeal rejected this argument and held that the failure to drill the offset well was a default that required notice under the default provision before the lease could be terminated.

---

2 *Madison Oils Ltd. v Kleiman*, unreported, 1966 (Sask. C.A.), digested in *Canadian Oil and Gas*, 2nd ed. (Bennett Jones Verchere and Bankes, eds.), vol. 1, Dig. 68.

The question of what amounts to a notice under the default clause could give rise to some confusion and difficulty. A clear-cut written statement identifying the well that creates the offset and a demand requiring the fulfilment of the obligation poses no difficulty. But what of a letter that merely complains of the drainage and does not specifically require the lessee to remedy the situation? Does this amount to an effective notice under the default clause? The lessee would be well advised to treat it as such; otherwise, it might find itself in a position where the remedial period is deemed to have elapsed. It is clear, however, from the wording of the default clause that the notice must be in writing.

The notice of default does not have to be in the prescribed form. In *True North Land Services v Hamilton*,[3] the court held that the purpose was to provide the lessee with sufficient notice so that it is able to rectify the default. The court struck down the lease on the ground that the lessee had not drilled the well pursuant to the offset clause.

This case is also interesting because the offsetting well had been drilled prior to the date of the lease under attack, but had not been placed on production until after that date.

An Ontario case, *Ewing v Francisco Petroleum Enterprises Inc*,[4] also involved the question of what constitutes a proper notice of default. The Ontario *Gas and Oil Leases Act*[5] provides that a lease could be declared null and void when the lessee is in default and fails to cure the default within thirty days of receiving notice. It was held that a letter from the lessor's lawyer threatening an application under the Act was proper notice. The court also commented that the lessee knew the lessor was dissatisfied with the way the lease was being managed, but this was in the nature of an aside and not necessary to the decision.

CAPL 99 makes it clear that the offset-creating well must be drilled after the date of the lease. The other two CAPL leases may achieve the same result by referring to a well "drilled" on the adjoining spacing unit.

Virtually every form of default clause requires the lessee to commence to remedy the default within the specified time. Accordingly, the default will be cured provided the lessee commences to drill the well within the specified period; it is not necessary that the well be completed within that time.

---

3 Bennett Jones Verchere and Bankes, *Canadian Oil and Gas*, 2nd ed., vol. 1 (Toronto: Butterworths, 1997) at Dig. 408.
4 [1996] O.J. No. 2348 (H.C.J. Gen. Div.).
5 R.S.O. 1990, c G-3, s (2)(1)(f).

At this juncture it may be useful to look at some of the basic features of the offset clause and point out the unresolved questions and issues that could arise under it. A basic (earlier) form of the clause can be paraphrased:

> If commercial production is obtained from a well on any laterally adjoining spacing unit, then unless there is already a well on the lands covered by the lease and to the same horizon or zone, the lessee shall within six months of the offsetting well being placed on production, either commence, within such six months, operations for the drilling of a well and thereafter drill to the producing horizon, or surrender the lands.

The offset clause creates an obligation that brings the default clause into play. This provides that where the lessee is in breach of any obligation, the lessor shall, before bringing any action or declaring any forfeiture, give the lessee notice of the default, and if the lessee fails to commence to remedy the default within ninety days from receipt of the notice, the lease will terminate. The clause also contains a proviso that the lease will not terminate if there is a well capable of production on the leased lands, in which event the lessor's remedy is limited to damages.

The first thing to be noted is that the well that creates the offset must be capable of commercial production. This is a defined term and means production that, after a production test of thirty consecutive days, would, after considering all relevant costs, economically warrant the drilling of a well in the vicinity thereof.

One of the questions that arises is that of timing. The obligation is to commence to drill a well within six months of the offsetting well going on production. But the default clause requires notice from the lessor, and the default is cured if the lessee commences to take remedial action within ninety days. If there is no well producing from the same horizon on the leased lands, and the lessee fails to commence remedial action within ninety days, the lease is terminated.

Things become more complicated if there is a well on the leased lands and the lessor's remedy is limited to damages. As is often the case, years might pass before the lessor becomes aware of the existence of an offsetting well. He gives notice but the lessee takes no steps to remedy the breach. At what point in time are the damages to be assessed? Back when the obligation first arose? Or when notice, was received? The lessee is not required to commence drilling until ninety days after notice in order to maintain the lease. Should not damages be determined as of the same point in time? If so, the damages could be minimal if the production has declined.

What is the situation where, by the time the lessor gives notice, production from the offsetting well has declined to the point where it is no longer commercial? Should the lessee be compelled to drill to preserve his lease?

What about the situation where 3D seismic indicates that the productive horizon does not extend into the leased lands? Should the lessee be required to drill a dry hole to preserve the lease?

Even if there is no well on the leased lands, if the lands form part of a unit that contains wells drilled to the offsetting horizon, the offset obligation will not arise because unit wells are deemed to be on the leased lands. The same would seem to hold true even if the unit wells were not producing from the same horizon but had been drilled to, or through, it.

The foregoing are merely some of the issues that could arise under the basic parameters of an offset clause. These parameters are still applicable to many leases that remain in force, but the clause, like many other parts of the lease, has continued to evolve.

Alternatives to Drilling the Offset Well

While the early version of the offset clause that basically required the lessee to drill the offset well or lose the lease is still encountered in existing leases, later, more sophisticated clauses provided the lessee with alternatives to drilling.

The lessee could, in lieu of drilling, surrender that portion of the said lands comprised in the offset spacing unit. If the lands to be surrendered have a well capable of production in commercial quantities, the zone from which such production is taken is excepted from the requirement to surrender the lands. The CAPL lease takes this a step further by providing that the surrender "shall include but may be limited to the zone or formation from which production is being obtained from the offset well."

The lessee also has the option of paying a compensatory royalty commencing on the last day of the six-month period, which royalty shall be equal to a royalty that would have been paid if the leased substances produced from the offset well were actually produced from a well on the said lands.

The compensatory royalty is to be the same as would be paid to the lessor if the leased substances were being produced from the leased lands. The offsetting production is deemed to have commenced on the last day of the six-month period. CAPL 99 also provides that where information with respect to the offsetting well is restricted pursuant to any Regulations and such information is unknown to the lessor, the date of deemed production is to be three months after the information is made public. Unlike those leases that provide for damages and do not include the option of paying compensatory royalty, the time when royalty becomes payable is defined. What is the situation if there is more than one offsetting well? The clause in the conventional lease gives the lessee the option to base the royalty on the closest wells. The CAPL leases provide for averaging where there are more than one producing well.

As in the earlier clauses, the obligation to drill an offset well does not arise if during the six-month period the offsetting well ceases to be capable of regular commercial production, and if the offsetting well is productive of natural gas the obligation does not arise until there is an adequate and commercially profitable market for natural gas.

The offset clause in the CAPL lease confers the same options on the lessee and also provides that the lessee may pool or unitize that portion of the said lands which comprises or is included in the spacing unit laterally adjoining the spacing unit of the offset well. This would enable the said lands to participate in the production from the offsetting well and thereby eliminate the need to drill the offset well.

The CAPL lease also provides that the offset obligation will not arise if all or part of the spacing unit on the said lands laterally adjoining the offset well have been pooled or included in the unit in which the production is from the same zone or formation from which production is being obtained from the offset well.

The option of paying a compensatory royalty is an interesting one. If production from the offsetting well, while meeting the "commercial" test, is not all that exciting, paying the royalty could be an economic way to maintain the lease. It also delays the need to commit to an expensive drilling operation and gives the lessee time to assess the performance of the offsetting well.

Horizontal Wells and the Offset Clause

The offset clauses in conventional leases and CAPL 88 and 91 assume vertical wells, that is, where the productive zone is located in the same spacing unit where the well was spudded. Horizontal drilling, however, has proven to be very effective and is increasingly common when the conditions are right. A horizontal well starts out as a vertical well; in many cases an existing wellbore is re-entered, and then the drill bit is diverted so it drills horizontally. This technique increases the amount of the formation that is accessed by the well, and under ideal conditions can increase a well's productive capacity by many multiples. It also can, and often does, mean that the well extends beyond the bounds of an individual lease or spacing unit. Furthermore, the zone or formation from which production is obtained may lie outside the lease where the well has been spudded.

For example, let us suppose a well is spudded on a spacing unit laterally adjoining a spacing unit to the south, which is under lease to A. After the well to the north has reached a certain depth, horizontal drilling is commenced, and the well extends beyond the spacing unit and encounters a productive formation in a spacing unit under lease to B to the north of the spacing unit where it was spudded. Who has the benefit of the offset obligation? The lessors of the leases laterally adjoining the unit under lease to B, or is it A's lessor?

Since the well was drilled, or at least spudded, on the spacing unit laterally adjoining A's lands, it could be argued that, strictly speaking, the offset obligation would arise under his lease, even though there was no production from the laterally adjoining spacing unit.

CAPL 99 addresses the problem created by a horizontal well and provides that the offset obligation accrues under the lease covering lands laterally adjoining the lands which contain the productive formations. It does this by defining an offset well as "producing" from a laterally adjoining spacing unit. Since the productive zone in a horizontal well can laterally adjoin lands under a number of leases, multiple offset obligations may be created.

Coalbed Methane and the Offset Clause

Coalbed methane wells do not fit comfortably within the parameters of the offset drilling clause. Most importantly, drainage, the *raison d'être* of the clause, is not a significant factor in CBM production. Also, effective production of CBM requires a density of wells substantially higher than is the case for conventional natural gas. Four wells per a section of 640 acres (256 hectares) is the norm, and smaller spacing units can be obtained on application to the appropriate regulatory body. Normally, the CBM operator will proceed on a project basis and will assemble the rights to a significant area before commencing a drilling program. For these reasons, the usual practice is to exclude coalbed methane wells from the operation of the offset drilling clause. For example:

"**Offset Well**" means any well, excluding wells producing coalbed methane, coal gas, coal bed gas, coal seam gas and all other forms of natural gas found in, derived from or directly related with coal seams, drilled subsequent to the effective date hereof and producing leased substances from any spacing unit laterally or diagonally adjoining the said lands, which spacing unit does not include lands owned by the lessor, or, if owned by the Lessor, not under lease to the Lessee.

Damages for Failure to Drill an Offset Well

The question of termination or non-termination may not be of too much importance to the parties. Presumably the lessee will refuse to drill under conditions where it has reason to believe that the reserves are of little commercial value. For example, the offsetting well after producing satisfactorily for the thirty-day period may start to produce excessive volumes of water, cease production altogether, or a neighbouring dry hole or other discouraging geological information may dampen enthusiasm for the prospect. Under such circumstances the lessee would be quite happy to forget about the lease, while its mere surrender would confer a doubtful benefit upon the lessor. The question then becomes whether the lessor can collect damages against the lessee, and, if so, in what amount.

The offset clause in the CAPL lease and the more modern forms of the conventional lease gives the lessee a number of options in the event of an offsetting well, including the payment of compensatory royalty and surrender. Because the act of surrendering would comply with the lessee's obligations under the offset clause, there would be no basis for damages and the lessor's rights would be limited to termination of the lease.

Earlier forms of the offset clause, however, imposed an absolute obligation to drill the offset well, and in that case the lessee could be liable for damages in addition to losing the lease.[6]

While the lessor may be able to claim damages, the quantum of those damages is likely to be minimal. The pattern was set in *Cotter v General*

---

6 *Albrecht v Imperial Oil Ltd.* (1957), 21 W.W.R. (N.S.) 560 (Alta. S.C.T.D.).

Petroleums Ltd. and Superior Oils, Ltd,[7] which did not involve the offset clause but did contain an obligation to commence drilling a well within a specified time. The trial judge in the *Cotter* case awarded damages based on the cost of drilling,[8] but this was repudiated by the Supreme Court. Cartwright J reviewed the circumstances and held, "I do not think that the cost of drilling is the proper measure of damages."[9]

The *Cotter* case has been treated as eliminating the cost of doing the work as the measure of damages. The same trial judge who had used the cost of drilling as the measure of damages in *Cotter* was once again faced with the problem a few years later. In *Prudential Trust Company Ltd. and Wagner v Wagner Oils Limited*[10] the obligation arose under a lease, although not under the offset clause. The lease form in question was quite unusual in that it contained an absolute commitment to drill. The defendant refused to drill, and the geological evidence at the trial was most discouraging on the prospects of success for any well. The trial judge, McLaurin J, stated:

> If it were not for the Cotter decision, I would be disposed to fix the damages at some substantial amount, probably the cost of drilling a well. I still see nothing unfair in visiting a defaulting party with damages in this amount. The whole foundation of legitimate promotional efforts in the exploitation of oil is based on the assumption that the parties will not renege on such deals. However, the Cotter case has established that such damages must not be awarded, but it does hold that nominal damages are recoverable even though no nominal damages were fixed in that case.
>
> As to damages, I assume that I would be loyally following the Supreme Court of Canada by fixing some relatively inconsequential amount. I accordingly fix damages at $500.00.[11]

Both the *Cotter* and *Wagner* decisions were applied in *Albrecht v Imperial Oil Ltd.*,[12] which involved the breach of an offset drilling clause in a petroleum and natural gas lease. The creating well produced satisfactorily during the thirty-day period, but shortly thereafter water

---

7 [1951] S.C.R. 154, [1950] 4 D.L.R. 609 (S.C.C.).

8 [1949] 1 W.W.R. 193, [1949] A.J. No. 21 (Alta. S.C.T.D.).

9 [1951] S.C.R. 154.

10 (1954), 11 W.W.R. (N.S.) 371 (Alta. S.C.T.D.).

11 Ibid. at 374.

12 *Supra* n 6.

began to intrude into the formation and led to the abandonment of the well within seven months after it had been placed on production. The plaintiff claimed damages for drainage of petroleum substances during the productive period of the creating well. In the light of evidence given by geological experts, the trial judge found that royalty payments that the plaintiff might have received from any production drained from his land would not exceed the trifling sum of $11.50. The main contention, however, arose over the claim for damages for breach of contract. Evidence at the trial indicated that the cost of drilling a well would amount to $40,000.00, with an additional $4,000.00 for production equipment. The court accepted geological evidence to the effect that a well on the plaintiffs land would be non-productive. Riley J rejected out of hand the cost of drilling the well as a basis for determining the damages, citing the *Cotter* and *Wagner* precedents.

American authorities, to the effect that the measure of damages for failure to drill an offset well is the amount of royalty the lessor would have received had the well been drilled, were quoted with approval. The geological evidence had, in the view of the court, affirmatively disproved that the plaintiff would have received any royalty whatsoever had the well been drilled on his land.

The plaintiff was not totally deprived of damages, however. The court correctly held that the *Cotter* case did not necessarily restrict the plaintiff to nominal damages. Once again the difficulty lay in establishing damages as a matter of evidence. The plaintiff had led evidence to the effect that, prior to the first well going to water, there had been offers of substantial cash considerations plus commitments to drill immediately; that the plaintiff had gone to the defendants and offered to purchase the lease back for the sum of $10,000.00; that they had been offered $3,000.00 for each one point of royalty – an offer they did not accept; and that, had the defendants spudded in the well on the plaintiff's land, each one point of the plaintiff's royalty would have increased in value to $6,000.00. The court felt that at the material time the plaintiff possessed a valuable asset. Riley J pointed out that the plaintiff had apparently refused the offer of $3,000.00 a point and that there was some doubt as to whether concrete offers in the amount of $6,000.00 per point would have been made if the well had been spudded, or accepted by the plaintiff if made. Indeed, the spudding in of the offset well would seem to affect only the possible increase in value of the points from $3,000.00 to $6,000.00. Nonetheless, the plaintiff was deprived of an opportunity to sell the whole or a portion of the points at an attractive price. Without attempting any detailed mathematical analysis, the court awarded damages in the sum of $6,000.00 for a loss of the opportunity to sell, plus $11.50 for the drainage claim.[13]

This case is interesting as an example of how a court, while inhibited by geological evidence that downgrades the property, nonetheless may conclude that the lessor is entitled to something more than purely nominal damages.

While it was not cited in the *Albrecht* decision, an earlier Ontario case had developed a similar approach. In *Carson v Willitts*[14] the Ontario Court of Appeal declined to base damages on the cost of drilling, but was prepared to grant the lessor damages on the basis of a loss of a sporting or gambling chance that valuable oil or gas would be found if the drilling was performed.

Sunshine Exploration Ltd. v Dolly Varden Mines Ltd.[15] involved a mining operation in which the defendant failed to carry out the work it had agreed to do. This failure was conceded to have terminated the agreement, and the sole issue was reduced to the quantum of damages. Not surprisingly, the defendant relied heavily on *Cotter* to contend that only nominal damages should be awarded. The Supreme Court, however, distinguished *Cotter*, where the consideration had not passed to the defendant since they had not exercised the option, nor had they been granted the sublease. In the *Sunshine* case, the defendant had received consideration in the form of the transfer of the one-half interest in the mining properties, the withdrawal of the notice of default, waiver of performance of the originally required work, and an extension of the term of the first development period. The Supreme Court held that the

---

13 This decision and its predecessors are analysed in Ballem, "Damages for Breach of Drilling Commitment" (1957) 35 Can. Bar Rev. 971; Bjornson, Boyd, Bredin, Brown, and MacWilliam, "Problems in Development of Leased Lands" (1965) 4 Alta. L. Rev. 302 at 306; see also Sychuk, "Damages for Breach of an Express Drilling Covenant" (1970) 8 Alta. L. Rev. 250.

14 (1930), 65 O.L.R. 456, [1930] O.J. No. 132, [1930] 4 D.L.R. 977 (Ont. C.A.); see also *Krantz v McCutcheon* (1920), 19 O.W.N. 161, [1920] O.J. No. 248 (Ont. C.A.). In *Medalta Potteries Ltd. v Medicine Hat*, [1931] 1 W.W.R. 217 (Alta. S.C.T.D.), purely nominal damages of $5 were awarded in a case that had some aspects of the failure to drill situation, but the plaintiff was required to have incurred expenditures as a condition to receiving a benefit under the breached contract. This feature makes it clearly distinguishable from the oil and gas lease, where the lessor is not required to do anything other than receive the benefit of having the well drilled on his property.

15 [1970] S.C.R. 2, 8 D.L.R. (3d) 441 [1969] S.C.J. 62 (S.C.C.). The possible effect of this decision is discussed in Ballem, "Some Second Thoughts on Damages for Breach of a Drilling Commitment" (1970) 48 Can. Bar Rev. 698.

proper measure of damages was the cost of performing the work that the defendant obligated itself to perform.

The grounds for distinguishing *Cotter* would not appear to apply to the obligation to drill an offset well under the lease, since consideration will have passed as the lessee will have received the lease and the benefit of the very substantial rights granted by a lease. However, the Supreme Court in *Sunshine* went on to find that the work that the defendant had agreed to perform would have been of value and of substantial advantage to the mining properties. In the case of an offset obligation under a lease the chances are that geological evidence would have largely discounted the value of having the well drilled, with the result that the damages would be minimal.

While it was not the legal issue before the court, compensatory royalty was involved in a Supreme Court of Canada decision in *Storthoaks (Rural Mun.) No. 31 v Mobil Oil Canada Ltd.*[16] Mobil, after drilling a successful offsetting well, elected to pay compensatory royalties and sent monthly cheques to the municipality. After two dry holes were drilled immediately to the south of the leased lands, Mobil wrote to the municipality surrendering the lease insofar as it related to the lands subject to the offset obligation. For some reason, Mobil's accounting department was not notified of the surrender, and monthly royalty cheques continued to be sent to the municipality for some years until the mistake was discovered and Mobil requested a refund of the overpayment in the amount of some $31,000.

It was held that Mobil was entitled to the repayment because the monies were paid under a mistake of fact, and the knowledge of one of its employees that the lands had been surrendered was not material because he did not know it was not being acted upon. The municipality advanced the interesting argument that Mobil, having elected to make the compensatory royalty payments, could not later elect to surrender the drilling unit and terminate its obligations. Martland J opined that the submission would have some weight had it not been for a general right of surrender given to Mobil by a subsequent clause that "notwithstanding anything herein contained" entitled Mobil to surrender any part of the lands at any time.

---

16 29 D.L.R. (3d) 483, [1972] 5 W.W.R. 90, [1972] S.J. No. 95 (Sask. Q.B.); reversed, 39 D.L.R. (3d) 598, [1973] 6 W.W.R. 644 (Sask. C.A.); affirmed, 55 D.L.R. (3d) 1, [1975] 4 W.W.R. 591, [1975] S.C.J. No. 70 (S.C.C.).

Pooling

Both oil and gas wells can drain the substances from a certain area within the reservoir. The drainage area will vary with the substances in question – gas being much more fugacious than oil – and the characteristics of the reservoir. Because of this, it would be economic folly to drill wells in a pattern denser than that required to effectively drain the reservoir. Conservation legislation and regulations uniformly provide for a limit on the density of the drilling patterns for both drilling and production purposes. In Alberta, for example, the normal drilling spacing unit for an oil well is a quarter section of 160 acres (64.7 hectares), while the normal drilling spacing unit for a gas well is one section of 640 acres (259 hectares). This reflects the greater ability of gas to move through the reservoir. The legislation also provides for expansion or contraction of the normal spacing unit in response to reservoir conditions.

The conservation legislation also provides, generally, that before an operator can obtain a drilling licence he must prove that he has the appropriate rights with respect to the entire spacing unit. A similar situation exists when an operator applies for a licence to produce. This can create problems for the lessee, particularly in the case of a gas well. A quarter section, 160 acres, which is the typical farm or ranch, is the most commonly encountered type of freehold mineral title in the West. Because of this, the great majority of petroleum and natural gas leases cover a quarter section; normally this will be sufficient for oil drilling purposes, but inadequate in gas areas. The pooling clause is designed to cover this situation.

POOLING

The Lessee is hereby given the right and power at any time and from time to time to pool or combine the said lands, or any portion thereof, or any zone or formation underlying the said lands or any portion thereof, with any other lands or any zone formation underlying the same, but so that the lands so pooled and combined (herein referred to as a "unit") shall not exceed One (1) spacing unit as hereinbefore defined. In the event of such pooling or combining, the Lessor shall, in lieu of the royalties elsewhere herein specified, receive on production of the leased substances from the said unit, only such portion of the royalties stipulated herein as the surface area of the said lands placed in the unit bears to the total surface area of lands in such unit.

Drilling operations on or production of the leased substances from, or the presence of a shut-in or suspended well on any land included in such unit shall have the same effect in continuing this Lease in force and effect as to all the said lands, as if such operations or production were upon or from the said lands, or some portion thereof, or as if said shut-in or suspended well were located on the said lands or some portion thereof.

The pooling clause empowers the lessee to combine the lands with the adjoining lands but only to the extent of one "spacing unit," which is defined in the interpretation section as the area allocated to a well for the purpose of either drilling or producing under the existing conservation laws. Therefore, if a lease covers a quarter section in a gas area, the lessee can enter into pooling arrangements with the holders of the leases covering the remaining three quarter sections and obtain a licence to drill a well.

The clause also makes the necessary adjustment to royalty, by providing that the royalties shall be apportioned on the basis of the ratio the surface area covered by the lease bears to the entire surface area comprised within the unit. If, for example, there were four leases, each comprising 160 acres, each owner would be entitled to a royalty based on one-quarter of the production of a gas well regardless of where such well might be located within the spacing unit.[17]

For the purpose of continuing the lease in force, it is essential to equate operations on the pooled lands to operations on the lands covered by the lease. That is the purpose of the final sentence in the clause, which provides that drilling operations, production, or the presence of a shut-in or suspended well on any land included in the unit shall have the same effect insofar as the lease is concerned as if the same had taken place upon the said lands. This is a necessary step in preserving

---

17 See *Lickacz v Magna Petroleums Ltd.*, 160 A.R. 193, [1993] A.J. No. 1056 (Alta. Q.B.), the facts of which were fully set out in the section dealing with the rule of capture, *ante*. Miller J held that a 1952 amendment to the *Oil and Gas Conservation Act* that established spacing units of one section for gas wells did apply to a lease granted in 1948 and a gas well drilled on the lands many years later. Accordingly each owner of the four quarter sections was entitled to 25 per cent of the royalties. The trial judge also opined that if he was wrong about the conservation legislation being retroactive, he would not hesitate to use the concept of equitable pooling. The Court of Appeal upheld the decision but ruled out the concept of equitable pooling on the ground that the conservation legislation covered the point. 162 A.R. 180 (Alta. C.A.).

the lease, and its importance was vividly dramatized by *Shell Oil Company v Gunderson*,[18] which is discussed in detail in Part 5 dealing with "Involuntary Termination," *infra*. In the *Gunderson* case, the lease covering the quarter section on which the well was not located did not make any reference to shut-in or suspended wells, but referred only to drilling operations on, or production of leased substances from, any of the leased lands included in the unit. The existence of a capped gas well on another quarter section within the section comprising the spacing unit and the tender of a capped gas well royalty to the lessor were held by the Supreme Court of Canada not to be sufficient to extend the primary term. Since the pooling clause contained no reference to suspended or shut-in wells, there was no basis for extending the definition of "said lands" within the lease, and thus it was only the presence of a suspended or shut-in well on the actual lands covered by the lease, plus the appropriate payment of a capped gas well royalty, that would have preserved the lease.

The omission of any reference to suspended wells in the pooling clause was a common feature of virtually every lease entered into until at least 1961. Similarly, the early form contained additional language, long since dropped, that also created difficulties for the lessee. The original form contained these words: "when such pooling or combining is necessary in order to conform with any regulations or orders of the government of the province of or any other authoritative body, which are now or may hereafter be in force in relation thereto."[19] It sounds innocuous enough, but its effect was to make pooling virtually impossible to achieve. In *Shell Oil Company v Gibbard*[20] the Supreme Court of Canada held that the effect of such wording was that pooling could only be accomplished when necessary to conform with the regulations. In the view of the court this condition could only be met when there was an affirmative and specific requirement that the lands be pooled. There is, of course, no such requirement in the conservation rules.[21]

---

18 [1960] S.C.R. 424, 23 D.L.R. (2d) 81, [1960] S.C.J. No. 19 (S.C.C.)

19 See discussion in Mullane and Walker, "The Pooling Clause and the Effects of Unitization on the Oil and Gas Lease" (1966) 4 Alta. Law Rev. 250.

20 [1961] S.C.R. 725, 36 W.W.R. (N.S.) 529, 30 D.L.R. (2d) 386, [1961] S.C.J. No. 51 (S.C.C.).

21 This is subject to an exception in that legislation provides for compulsory pooling under certain circumstances where the parties cannot agree. The sections of the acts that provide for such compulsory pooling also stipulate that operations, or production, or the presence a shut-in well within the unit shall have the same effect as if they

The conservation regulations, however, do provide that, before a well can be placed on production, the operator must have the right to produce from the entire spacing unit. This requirement that it may be necessary to include the leased lands with other lands in order to obtain the approval of the Conservation Board to a spacing unit and to obtain a production permit was not judged by the Supreme Court to amount to the type of regulation or order that would activate the pooling clause.

If the pooling clause spells out the reason for pooling, this may be sufficient even if there is no affirmative regulation or order requiring such pooling. In *Canadian Superior Oil of Calif. Ltd. v Kanstrup*[22] the lease originally did not contain a pooling clause. During the term of the lease, however, the lessee wrote the lessor requesting the addition of a pooling clause. The letter contained the new clause, which was identical in all respects with the one in the Gibbard lease. After reciting the clause, the letter from the lessee went on to explain why it was required. It was pointed out that the area within which the leased lands were located was a gas area and that the spacing unit was 640-acres. The lessee wrote that it desired to pool the quarter section covered by the lease with the remainder of the lands in the section for the purpose of forming a spacing unit to drill a well. The lessor signed a copy of the letter, acknowledging and agreeing to the amendment of the lease. The Supreme Court of Canada said that under these circumstances it was prepared to hold that the lessee intended the clause to be construed as providing for pooling to enable it to establish a 640-acre spacing unit and to obtain a licence from the Conservation Board to drill a well. Since the lessee had stated the purpose for which it wished to pool the lands, the pooling clause was thereby effective even in the absence of any affirmative order or regulation. It should be noted,

---

were carried on or located on the lands covered by the lease. For Alberta, see the *Oil and Gas Conservation Act, supra* n 1, s 80(7). The question as to whether a lease with an unenforceable pooling clause can be pooled on a compulsory basis remains open. Section 80(2)(c) requires the applicant to state that an agreement to pool cannot be made on reasonable terms. Can this statement be made when the lease contains a pooling clause, albeit a defective one? The point was not in issue in the *Gibbard* decision. See also *Mines and Minerals Act*, C.C.S.M. c M162, s 1720; *Oil and Gas Conservation Act*, R.S.S. 1978, c O-2, ss 30–33; and Bankes, "Compulsory Pooling under the Oil and Gas Conservation Act of Alberta" (1997) 35 Alta. L. Rev. 945.

22 [1965] S.C.R. 92, 49 W.W.R. (N.S.) 257, 47 D.L.R. (2d) 1, [1964] S.C.J. No. 54 (S.C.C.).

however, that the circumstances in the *Kanstrup* case on this point are unique and not likely to be repeated. The special conditions arising from the fact that the lessee stated the purpose of the pooling clause makes it clearly distinguishable under most circumstances and does not derogate from the original interpretation of such a pooling clause as expressed in *Gibbard*.

For all practical purposes, then, the pooling clause contained in virtually every lease entered into until the early 1960s is totally ineffective. The more modern forms of the conventional lease overcome these two drawbacks by omitting the reference to orders and regulations and conferring an unfettered power to pool, and by including a specific reference to the presence of a suspended or shut-in well.

Is Written Notice Required?

Some leases provide that "upon written notice to the Lessor, the Lessee may pool." Where this wording is present it seems inescapable that written notice is necessary for an effective pooling. The majority of pooling clauses, however, omit the specific reference to a written notice, and the question arises as to whether a formal written notice is required.

The answer, according to the Supreme Court, is "no." In the *Gibbard* case Locke J expressly disagreed with the opinion of Johnson JA in the Alberta Court of Appeal that a formal written notice of the election of the lessee to pool was necessary.[23] However, he did go on to point out that there was sufficient evidence that the lessee had pooled the lands because of an application it had made to fix a special spacing unit, and letters to the lessor enclosing royalties that would be applicable if the pooling had been effective. While it clear that a formal written notice is not required, must there be something that will indicate to the lessor that his land has been pooled? Or was the court merely looking for evidence that the lessee had an intention to pool?

In *Gas Initiatives Ventures Ltd. v Beck*[24] Moore J (as he then was) applied *Gibbard* to hold: "The fact that there was no notice of pooling is immaterial."[25]

---

23 *Supra* n 20, S.C.R. at 732.

24 [1979] 3 W.W.R. 741 (Alta. S.C.T.D.); reversed on appeal by consent, [1981] 2 W.W.R. 603, 122 D.L.R. (3d) 768 (Alta. C.A.)

25 Ibid. at 754. This finding would not seem to be affected by the subsequent disposition of the case when it was reversed by consent on appeal.

The pooling clause in the CAPL lease provides that after pooling the lessee shall give written notice to the lessor describing the extent to which the said lands are being pooled and describing the spacing unit with respect to which they are pooled.

Working Interests Must Agree to Pool

The pooling clause confers upon the lessee the unilateral right to pool the land with other lands to form a spacing unit. While the consent of the lessor is not required, it is obvious that there must be agreement to pool among the holders of the leases covering the other lands. Normally this will be achieved by the parties entering into a written agreement that pools the land for the purpose of drilling or producing, and allocates production among the tracts. Since a pooling agreement covers only one spacing unit, the allocation will almost invariably be on a simple surface acreage basis.

While a written pooling agreement is the normal practice, what happens if the agreement has not been executed by the critical time, i.e., the time at which the lease would expire if not pooled? The point was addressed in the *Gas Initiatives* case,[26] where the parties had agreed to pool prior to the expiry of the primary term of the subject lease. The agreement was typed at that time and specified an effective date that was long before the end of the primary term, but the actual execution of the formal agreement did not take place until some time after the primary term had expired. The Alberta Trial Division held that the failure to execute the formal agreement until after the primary term did not invalidate the agreement to pool. Thus, it can be said that something less than a completely executed agreement will suffice, although there must be evidence to establish that the parties had reached agreement. In the *Gas Initiatives* situation there was a typed document. It should be noted, however, that the subsequent disposition of this case, when it was reversed on appeal by consent, makes it somewhat suspect as a precedent.

A number of points concerning the requirements of a pooling agreement arose in *Paddon Hughes Development Co. v Pancontinental Oil Ltd.*[27] This case involved four issues:

---

26 *Supra* n 24.
27 (1992), 2 Alta. L.R. (3d) 343, [1992] 5 W.W.R. 106, [1992] A.J. No. 488 (Alta. Q.B.). This was the second of the three *Paddon Hughes v Pancontinental* cases involving leases in the same spacing unit.

(a) whether an option to lease had been validly exercised;
(b) whether a pooling agreement had been validly and timely entered
     into;
(c) whether there could be an oral agreement to pool, and;
(d) whether if one lease failed the others would also fail because there
     was no valid pooling of the spacing unit.

As discussed earlier in the section dealing with options, Rooke J found
that a late exercise of an option to lease that was accepted and signed
by the lessor was valid either as an accepted late exercise of the option
or the creation of a new lease. The issue under (c) will be dealt with
under the next following heading.

The defendant, Pancontinental, held freehold leases on the east half
of a section; the Crown leases on the west half were held by Amoco.
The primary term of the first freehold lease in the southeast quarter
expired at midnight, 20 June 1989. Pancontinental spudded a well on
15 March 1989 on the northeast quarter. Amoco and the defendant
orally agreed on 24 April 1989 (after the well turned out to be a prolific
gas well) to pool the section. The first draft of the pooling agreement
was prepared three days later and was expressed to be retroactive to
the date of the oral agreement. A formal written pooling agreement,
declared to be effective 24 April 1989, was found by the judge on the
balance of probabilities to have been executed in counterpart by the
various lessees on 20 June 1989, and delivery of the executed copies
was completed by 27 June 1989.

There was no doubt that a valid pooling agreement existed by 27 June
1989. However, to maintain the validity of the earliest freehold lease, the
pooling agreement must have been in effect before midnight on 20 June
since there was no well on the southeast quarter. Rooke J found on what
he described as "tenuous" evidence, but uncontradicted, that the written
pooling agreement had been executed on 20 June.

The plaintiff then argued that the pooling agreement is a deed that
requires physical delivery, and the counterpart execution pages were
not fully delivered until 27 June. Rooke J held that even if the agreement were a deed, rather than a mere contract for consideration,
"delivery" could be by oral communication rather than physical delivery of the document.

The most important part of the judgment, however, is that Rooke J
found that there was a valid, "if basic," oral pooling agreement in place
on 24 April 1989. (He expressly assumed there was no other impediment

to validity, such as the *Statute of Frauds*, as no such point had been argued before him.) He held that the same principles that applied in the *Gas Initiatives* case, where there was a letter agreement followed by a more formal agreement, applied here. He quoted *Home Oil Co. v Page Petroleum Ltd.*,[28] where Laycraft J (as he then was) wrote: "The incorporation of the essential terms of an agreement into a more detailed and formal agreement at a later time is a common feature of commercial life. On some occasions the final agreement is expressed to be 'subject to' the terms of the contemplated formal agreement in which case there is no completed contract until the formal agreement is in fact executed ... In other cases, such as the present, however, the parties are bound temporarily by the preliminary agreement which is to be replaced by the more detailed formal agreement which it contemplates."[29] Holding that this was exactly the case before him, Rooke J held there was a binding oral agreement to pool to be replaced by a more detailed formal agreement at a later time. He also found there was substantial performance on both sides, including a package of well information, an invoice for the costs of drilling and casing the well, an AFE (authority for expenditure) to complete the well, and numerous other communications between the lessees.[30] He found that this performance supported the existence of a binding oral agreement, but did not specifically find that it was the kind of part performance that would satisfy the *Statute of Frauds*.

The trial judge expressly did not rule on the *Statute of Frauds* issue. Since a pooling agreement is part of the claim of title to a lease, one is left to wonder if an oral pooling agreement, without any part performance, is sufficient.

Can There Be a Valid Pooling of Less Than a Spacing Unit?

The pooling clause confers upon the lessee the power to pool or combine the lands with other lands, but the power is limited to the extent that the lands so pooled or combined cannot exceed one spacing unit, which is defined as the area allocated to a well for drilling or producing. Normally, this area will be a quarter section in the case of an oil well and a

---

28 [1976] 4 W.W.R. 598 (Alta. S.C.T.D.).

29 Ibid. at 603, 604.

30 Rooke J also relied on *Calvan Consolidated Oil & Gas Co. v Manning*, [1959] S.C.R. 253, 17 D.L.R. (2d) 1, [1959] S.C.J. No. 9 (S.C.C.).

full section for a gas well. The purpose of this limitation is to prevent the pooling clause from being used as an indirect means of unitizing.

While there is no doubt that the pooling power is limited to a maximum of one spacing unit, can it be validly used to pool an area that is less than a spacing unit? For example, if only three-quarters of a section are pooled for the production of gas, is that a valid pooling that will continue a lease covering one of the three quarters in force? It is not suggested that the pooling has to be simultaneous; the question will arise when all of a spacing unit is not pooled at the critical time.

"Pooling" and "pool" are words of art in the oil industry; they are used to denominate the bringing together of small tracts sufficient for the granting of a well permit under the applicable spacing rules.[31] The well permit or licence will authorize drilling or producing a well as the case may be. Since the purpose is to bring together or "pool" parcels of land to permit drilling or producing, it would seem that anything that falls short of that cannot be a "pooling."

American decisions, on balance, seem to favour the view that the pooling must be complete.[32] The first time the issue was raised in Canada was some *obiter dicta* by Johnson JA in *Gibbard*, where he stated that he did not think "a pooling which becomes ineffective as to part can be considered valid as to the balance."[33] This observation was prompted by the fact that the lease covering the Gunderson quarter section had lapsed,[34] leaving only three quarters covered by valid leases. In *Gibbard* the dispositive point at issue was that the pooling was not necessary in order to conform with government regulations, so the learned judge's comments are clearly *obiter*. Presumably, if a pooling becomes ineffective because a part fails, it would also be ineffective if it never comprises the entire unit.

---

31 Williams and Meyers, *Manual of Oil and Gas Terms*, 6th ed. (1984), 652.
32 In *Whelan v Placid Oil Company* (1954), 274 S.W. (2d) 125, 4 O.&G. Rep. 442 (Tex. Ct. Civ. App.), the court held that the lessors who had signed a pooling amendment were bound by their contract even though the owners of the other half-interest had not signed the agreement. This appears to be an instance where the parties are made to fulfil the agreement they have signed. Two Louisiana decisions, *Viator v Haynesville Mercantile*, 6 O.&G. Rep. 67 (1956), (Louisiana) and *Union Oil Company of California v Touchet*, 5 O.&G. Rep. 1117 (1956), (Louisiana), held that where one tract member had not pooled, the unit was invalid. See also *Eleventh Annual Institute on Oil and Gas Law*, 360.
33 (1961), 34 W.W.R. (N.S.) 117 (Alta. S.C., App.Div.). See also Angus, "Voluntary Pooling in Canadian Oil and Gas Law" (1955–61) 1 Alta. L. R. 481, 490.
34 *Shell Oil Co. v Gunderson*, [1960] S.C.R. 424, 23 D.L.R. (2d) 81, [1960] S.C.J. No. 19 (S.C.C.).

There is also *obiter* to the same effect in *Paddon Hughes Development Co. Ltd. v Pancontinental Oil Ltd.*,[35] which in the introduction to the judgment contains the statement that:

1 This is a case where the plaintiff, a third party to two purported agreements (to one of which it became a successor in title), seeks to have the agreements declared to be of no force and effect. If either agreement is so declared, it will have the "domino" effect of invalidating three freehold petroleum and natural gas leases under which the defendant claims the right to continue to produce natural gas on a one-quarter section of mineral lands to which the plaintiff now holds fee simple title to all mines and minerals (except coal).

In the agreed statement of facts, it was acknowledged that the lease under attack must have been validly issued for the other leases to have been continued beyond their primary terms by pooling; if it was not there would not be a one-section spacing unit. Thus, counsel for Pancontinental conceded that there could not be a valid pooling of less than a full spacing unit. What effect this had on the judge's statement is unclear, but it meant that the point would not have been argued at trial.

The same point arose in the third *Paddon Hughes* case,[36] where O'Leary JA, writing for the majority of the Court of Appeal, stated matter-of-factly, "If either of the Bishop or Thatcher leases is found to have terminated for late payment of delay rental in 1985, the pooling notice was ineffective to preserve the other leases beyond their primary term."

Since the majority went on to find that the delay rental payments were not late, the statement is *obiter*, but it is a good indication of how the courts would hold if the matter were raised directly before them.

Termination of Pooling, Voluntary and Otherwise

Very few pooling agreements contain any reference to the term during which they will remain in force. Their purpose is to permit the drilling and production of a well, which does not lend itself to a fixed term since the period during which production will continue cannot be predicted

---

35 (1992), 2 Alta. L.R. (3d) 343, [1992] 5 W.W.R. 106, [1992] A.J. No. 488 (Alta. Q.B.).

36 *Paddon Hughes v Pancontinental*, 67 Alta. L.R. (3d) 104, [1999] 5 W.W.R. 726, 223 A.R. 180, [1998] A.J. No. 1120 (Alta. C.A.); [1998] S.C.C.A. No. 600 (leave to appeal dismissed).

with any certainty. Most pooling clauses are silent on the matter of terminating pooling, although one form used by a major oil company includes the express power to dissolve a pooled unit where no operations are being conducted on the unit.

Even without this provision, it is probable that the lessee has an implied right to terminate a pooling. The clause that gives him the right to pool unilaterally is not restricted in its scope, except for the limitation of one spacing unit, and would seem to carry with it the right to terminate.

In practice, termination of a pooling is not likely to cause any conflict between lessor and lessee. Since they both have an interest in the tract, their interests in maintaining the pooling or dismantling it should be mutual. Nor would a lessee be motivated to terminate a pooling unless the well turned out to be dry or production from the spacing unit ceased.

A change in circumstances may cause an involuntary termination of pooling. If a well, originally designated by the conservation authority as a gas well and thus requiring a full section as the spacing unit, were to be reclassified as an oil well, which requires only a quarter section, it would seem that the pooling of all four quarter sections would no longer be effective. Production from the reclassified oil well would no longer be attributed to those quarter sections and, if the leases covering those lands were beyond their primary term, it is probable that a court would find them to have terminated.

The result might be different if the lessor and lessee had entered into a separate agreement pooling the lands and agreeing that production would be allocated. However, the usual arrangement does not involve an agreement but merely a unilateral act on the part of the lessee.

Involuntary de-pooling may also occur in a domino fashion if a lease covering lands that comprise a portion of the pooled unit is found to have terminated or lapsed, as in *Gunderson*.

The lessee of lands within a pooled unit that has been involuntarily terminated for one of the reasons outlined above could find himself in a position where his lease has been terminated for reasons over which he has no control, i.e., a regulatory agency reclassifying a well, or a lease not owned by him being struck down by the courts. If this results in automatic de-pooling, his own lease could fall for want of allocated production or the deemed presence of a well under the pooling agreement. It would seem equitable for the lessee to have a period of grace within which to take steps to maintain his lease by entering into new pooling arrangements or by conducting operations on the lands.

These points are expressly covered in the CAPL lease, which (a) gives the lessee the right to terminate pooling on written notice to the lessor; (b) deals with the situation where the spacing unit is varied or terminated by any statute, regulation, order, or directive of any governmental agency; (c) provides that if the pooling is terminated or invalidated by reason of the termination or expiration of a lease covering any lands, other than the said lands, within the spacing unit, or any other cause beyond the lessee's reasonable control, and the lease would otherwise terminate, it shall nonetheless continue in force for a period of ninety days after the lessee receives notice that the spacing unit has been varied or terminated, or the pooling has been terminated or invalidated. The term of the lease may be extended further pursuant to other provisions of this lease, including the commencement of operations within the said ninety-day period.

Pooling by Zone or Formation

The pooling clause grants to the lessee the right to pool the lands or any portion thereof or any zone or formation underlying the said lands or any portion thereof. The right to pool the lands, in the absence of a deeper rights reversion clause, allows the lessee to retain control over the non-productive formations that may be unexplored and potentially valuable. Although pooling may be limited to a specific formation, production from that formation will hold the lease in force as to the other formations and any other lands that are covered by the lease, even though they are not included in the pooled unit.[37] This result flows from the fact that any production, deemed or actual, from any part of the leased lands will continue the lease as to all the lands granted.[38]

---

37 *Esso Resources Canada Ltd. v Pacific Cassiar Ltd.* (1984), 33 Alta. L.R. (2d) 175, [1984] 6 W.W.R. 376 (Alta. Q.B.) lends support to this proposition, although the *Esso* case dealt with the effect of unitization rather than pooling.

38 This is not necessarily so in some American jurisdictions, where the effect of pooling by formation has been construed as dividing the leased premises into unitized or non-unitized areas. Under these circumstances the lessee has been required to pay delay rentals to maintain the lease in force even with production from the unitized acreage. *Fremaux v Buie* (1968), 212 So. (2d) 148 (Louisiana C.A.).

Horizontal Drilling and Pooling

Under virtually every pooling clause, pooling shall not exceed one spacing unit. Spacing units for oil wells are commonly, although by no means always, set at 64.7 hectares (160 acres). A horizontal well can extend well beyond the boundaries of such a spacing unit. However, by definition, spacing unit means the area allocated to a well from time to time as prescribed by or under a statute, regulation, order, or directive of any government or any governmental agency. Thus, if the appropriate governmental agency or authority grants a greater area as a spacing unit for the drilling of the horizontal well, that greater area will become the spacing unit that cannot be exceeded. If no such area has been allocated to a horizontal well, the definition of "spacing unit" means the areas that would have been allocated to one or more vertical wells on the lands containing the productive sections of the horizontal well. In the case of horizontal wells, the key factor is where the production comes from, not where the well is drilled.

Agency

Implementation of a pooling clause may create the possibility of a principal and agent relationship between lessor and lessee.[39] If so, the lessee will owe to the lessor that very high duty, amounting to a trust, that an agent must render to his principal. These responsibilities and how they may apply to an oil and gas lease are discussed in connection with unitization. If the act of pooling does in fact create the relationship, the lessee would be in a much better position to discharge an agent's duties than would be the case under unitization, since pooling involves a much smaller area of land, fewer parties, and less possibility of a conflict of interest.

---

39 "Problems in Development of Leased Lands," *supra* n 13, 302.

10 Unitization

Modern forms of the conventional lease and the CAPL lease expressly grant the right to unitize by including the leased lands or any portion thereof in a Unit Agreement. As will be seen later in this chapter, unitization profoundly affects the lease, but before describing these effects, we will briefly describe unitization itself.

What Is a Unit?

Hydrocarbon substances are accumulated in underground traps of various types. These traps prevent the further migration or dispersion of the substances and may be referred to as "reservoirs," "pools," or "fields." Regardless of what they are called, each accumulation will have a finite geographical area, which may be just a few sections of land, or many square miles, in extent. Each field is a homogeneous whole, with the substances free to move within it. From an operational point of view it makes good engineering and economic sense to operate a field as an entity without regard to any artificial distinctions created by different ownerships. Since the average freehold lease will comprise a quarter section of land, a field will include many different ownerships and individual leases within its boundaries.

If the parties enter upon an arrangement under which a field or pool is to be operated as a common unit without regard to the boundaries imposed by lease ownership, then the field will be described as having been "unitized." Any arrangement that ignores lease boundaries must create fundamental changes in the relationship between a mineral lessor and lessee.

Unitization Clause

Unlike pooling, which is limited to one spacing unit, unitization encompasses the entire pool and thus is limited by geological and not geographic features. The unitization clause, which is invariably found in the same clause that grants the right to pool, gives the lessee the right to include the lands in a unit agreement. The basis and terms of the unitization, including the manner of allocating production among the various tracts and the terms of any unit agreement, are to be in the sole discretion and determination of the lessee, exercised *bona fide*, and are binding upon the lessor. The unilateral right of the lessee to determine all matters pertaining to the unit agreement is necessary because otherwise the power to unitize might be held to be unenforceable on the grounds that it would be void for uncertainty. The parameters of any future unitization agreement would be totally unknown at the time the lessor executed the lease. By expressly conferring discretion on the lessee to determine the terms of the future unitization agreement, the clause avoids the possibility of being struck down for uncertainty.

Advantages of Unitization to the Lessor

The principal advantage that a lessor obtains from unitization is that of security. Instead of relying on the continued production from one well on his lands for royalty revenue, he shares in a number of wells, effectively spreading the risk. Unitization also lends itself to the implementation of secondary recovery measures, which are designed to improve the economics of the operation and to increase the ultimate recovery of the substances.

Operating economies made possible by unitization should filter back to the lessor in the form of reduced deductions from his royalty. Only those savings that relate to above-ground operations are of any benefit to the lessor since his royalty is not subject to deductions for drilling or lifting costs. There is no doubt that unit operation facilitates economies in gathering and processing costs, mainly through the construction of one large central plant, instead of several smaller ones, and the avoidance of duplication in gathering flowlines.

Advantages of Unitization to the Lessee

The real beneficiary of unitization is the working interest owner, the lessee. In the first place, the lessee's economic stake is much greater, usually in the ratio of six or higher. The lessee obtains the same benefits as the lessor by allocation of reserves and production over a number of wells and properties with its greater assurance of continued revenues. The benefits of enhanced recovery accrue to the working interest owner as well as the lessor, multiplied by a greater interest in the minerals.

It is in the area of cost saving, however, that the lessee reaps the greatest benefits. The unique feature of unitization, in contrast to all other types of joint-venture associations, is that under unitization it is not necessary to drill and produce wells in order to preserve individual leases. Wells can be located and drilled to achieve optimum production and recovery with the least number; thus, one very substantial area of savings is in the diminished number of wells required. The reduction in drilling and well operating costs accrues solely to the lessee.

There is a secondary economic advantage to the lessee that is not available to the lessor. The unit facilities, gathering flowlines, processing plants, and compressor facilities are financed so as to yield a satisfactory rate of return on the invested capital. Although the primary reason for the construction of the facilities is to process the substances and make them marketable, the fact remains that investment in such facilities is an attractive proposition with a built-in profit factor.

Unit Agreement

A brief analysis of a unit agreement will illustrate the changes that unitization imposes upon the lessor-lessee relationship. Both working and royalty interests enter into a unit agreement. Execution is by counterpart and all parties become bound by the one agreement. In addition, the working interests will enter into a unit operating agreement among themselves, but this document is confined to the manner in which the joint working interests will be operated and does not affect the royalty or mineral owner. In the western provinces the unit agreement will be the model form prepared by the Petroleum Joint Venture Association.

Unitized Zone

It is not the entire leased substances that are unitized; normally unitization embraces only the productive horizons or zones. Thus, the unit agreement will define the unitized zone or zones as being a specific formation or formations within the unit. Similarly, the substances that are unitized will be only those in the unitized zones.

Effect of Unitization

The model agreement provides that, upon the interests of each royalty and working interest owner being unitized, the unitized zone shall be treated as though it had been included in a single lease executed by the royalty owners as lessors and by the working interest owners as lessees and as if the lease had been subject to the unit agreement. This is the fundamental effect of unitization, and thereafter individual lease boundaries may be disregarded for all operational purposes.

Production of Substances

Each lease subject to the unit agreement is continued in force by operations or production from the unit, regardless of whether or not such operation or production takes place on the leased lands. This is achieved by a clause, rather similar in effect to the pooling provision under a lease, which states that operations conducted with respect to the unitized zone or production of the unitized substances shall be deemed conclusively to be operations on, or production from, all of the unitized zone in each tract, and shall continue in force and effect each lease as if such operations had been conducted on and a well was producing from each tract.

Once a lease is included in a unit, any and all operations anywhere within the unit have the effect of continuing the lease in force. Moreover, the entire lease and not just the unitized zone will be continued. This is the only result that is consistent with the wording of the lease and has also received judicial sanction in *Voyager Petroleums Ltd. v Vanguard Petroleums Ltd.*[1] This case also stands for the proposition that if the lessor does not execute the Unit Agreement and there is no unitization clause in the lease, the lease will not continue in force.

Not only does production from the unitized zone continue the lease in force with respect to all zones, it also continues the lease with respect to lands that are not included in the unit. In *Esso Resources Canada Ltd. v Pacific Cassiar Ltd.*,[2] the lease covered both a large portion of the east

---

1 (1982), 17 Alta. L.R. (2d) 212, [1982] 2 W.W.R. 36, 47 A.R. 14, [1982] A.J. No. 629 (Alta. Q.B.) (this point was not raised on appeal).

2 (1984), 33 Alta. L.R. (2d) 175 (Alta. Q.B.), [1984] 6 W.W.R. 376 (Alta. Q.B.); reversed, 45 Alta. L.R. (2d) 1, [1986] 4 W.W.R. 385, 28 D.L.R. (4th) 104, [1986] A.J. No. 408 (Alta. C.A.).

half and the entire west half of a section. The east half was included in a unit but not the west half. Subsequently another party took a lease on the west half and registered a caveat. The trial judge held that the unit production allocated to the east half would maintain the lease in force with respect to all the lands included in the lease, and this finding was upheld by the Court of Appeal. This would not be the case with leases (such as CAPL 99) that have a deeper rights reversion clause.

The Court of Appeal went on to hold that since the caveat had not been registered against the west half, the subsequent lessee took priority pursuant to the *Land Titles Act*, which provides that a person taking a lease from the registered owner is unaffected by a prior interest that is not protected by caveat, except in the case of fraud.[3] The Court of Appeal found that the unitization agreement created new rights and pointed out that "without that agreement production from lands outside the leased lands would have no effect on the lease and failing production from the leased lands the lease would terminate at the end of the 10-year period."[4]

The obvious lesson here is that a lessee who entered into a unit agreement must register a new caveat on all of the lands covered by the lease. Without that, and despite the protection afforded by the unit agreement, he could stand to lose the lease to an intervening third party if there was no production from the leased lands not included in the unit.

Unit Tracts

Each individual lease comprised within the unit is treated as a separate tract. The unit agreement assigns a participation factor to each tract, which is that tract's share of ownership of production from the unit and its corresponding share of expenses incurred by the unit. The agreement provides that the unitized substances when produced shall be allocated to each tract in accordance with its tract participation and the amount so allocated is deemed conclusively to have been produced from the tract. This is so regardless of whether or not there was any production from the tract or whether the amount so allocated was greater or lesser than the amount actually produced from a tract.

---

3 In this connection see also *Pan American Petroleum Corporation. v Potapchuk and Scurry-Rainbow Oils Ltd.* (1964), 46 W.W.R. 237 (Alta. Q.B.); affirmed, 51 W.W.R. 700, [1964] A.J. No. 11 (C.A.); affirmed, 51 W.W.R. 767 (S.C.C.).

4 *Supra* n 2, 4 W.W.R. at 399.

Distribution within Tracts and Calculation of Royalty

The working interest owner (the lessee) is responsible for the distribution of each tract's allocated production to whatever other parties may be entitled to an interest in the tract. The production of unitized substances allocated to each tract becomes the basis on which royalty is payable under the lease, and the royalty owner (the lessor) of each tract agrees to accept payment of royalty so calculated in satisfaction of the royalty payable under the lease.

The model agreement also provides for an allowance, in calculating royalty on everything except crude oil, for the costs and expenses of processing, gathering, and compressing. The allowance is to include a reasonable return on investment. This provision is a more detailed statement of the royalty provision in the lease, which normally refers to value "at the well" or "on the said lands." To arrive at the value at the well of residue gas, it is necessary to deduct from the price paid at the outlet of a plant all the costs incurred in transporting it from the wellhead, processing it at the plant, and compression, if necessary to meet pipeline requirements.

Operations

The agreement authorizes the working interest owners to develop and operate the unitized zone without regard to the provisions or the boundaries of the individual leases. The working interest owners are also given the specific right to inject substances into the unitized zone and to convert any wells into injection wells. This power permits the institution of secondary recovery schemes and, if it is not an extension of the powers granted under the normal lease, at least makes the right an express one instead of possibly being implied as necessary or incidental in order to "win, take, remove the leased substances from the said lands."

Storage

The model agreement includes a specific provision granting the right to inject unitized substances for storage. This is clearly an extension of the grant contained in the usual lease. The storage is confined to unitized substances and does not confer the right to use the unitized formation for storage of substances produced outside the unit. The clause also delays the payment of royalty for any injected substances until they are recovered from storage and sold.

Use or Loss

The agreement authorizes the working interest owners to use whatever of the unitized substances, other than crude oil, are necessary for the operation and development of the unitized zone. They are specifically given the right to inject the substances into the unitized zone, e.g., for purposes of second recovery drives. No royalty is payable with respect to any substances so used or injected.

No Transfer of Title

Although the unitization agreement authorizes the common operation of the field, it is not to be construed as a transfer or exchange of any interest in the leases or in the unitized substances before production. In other words, each party retains title to its own interest, and execution of the unit agreement does not operate as an automatic cross-transfer of title.

Amends the Lease

The unit agreement substantially changes the terms of any lease. In *Alminex Limited v Berkley Oil and Gas Ltd.*[5] it was held that unitization only amends a lease to the extent it was specifically provided for in the contractual terms. Presumably to overcome this limitation, a clause in the unit agreement provides that each lease is amended to the extent necessary to make it conform to the agreement.

Lease Ratified

By executing the unit agreement a lessor, unless a court action has been commenced or is pending, ratifies and confirms the lease and agrees that no default exists with respect thereto and that the lease is in effect. Since the lease itself requires execution under seal and the unit

---

5 [1971] 4 W.W.R. 401 (Alta. S.C.T.D.); [1972] 6 W.W.R. 412 (Alta. S.C., App.Div.);
affirmed [1975] 1 S.C.R. 262, [1974] 1 WWR 288, [1973] S.C.J. No. 143 (S.C.C.).

agreement purports to amend and ratify the lease, the agreement should also be under seal.

Unit Operation in Ontario

Productive pools within Ontario tend to be of very limited areal extent. The reservoirs are small, sharply defined pinnacle reefs. The small amount of acreage comprised within a pool, plus the reluctance of an operator to drill until 100 per cent of the land has been leased, results in one lessee owning all the rights within a reservoir. This situation in turn has given rise to the Unit Operation Agreement.

The only signatories to an agreement of this type are the lessee and the individual lessors. All the lands comprising the unit area are described in a schedule attached to the agreement, and another schedule lists the leases held by the lessee in the unit area. The list is further broken down into the acreage within each lease that is included in the "participating section" of the unit area, and that which is included in the "non-participating" depends on whether the land is within or outside the limits of the reservoir. Although the documentation stops short of establishing one overall agreement, it clearly envisages common operation of the unit area. The lessee is to endeavour to have similar agreements executed by all other lessors in the unit area and "this Agreement together with any such other agreements entered into and executed shall be interpreted and treated as a common agreement by the Lessors and the Lessee for the purpose of developing and obtaining production of the leased substances from those portions of the unit area." Insofar as the lease is concerned, the unit operation agreement has many of the effects of the conventional multi-party unitization agreement. The royalty is allocated on an acreage basis (if non-participating acreage is retained, the lessor receives an annual payment of a stated sum per acre); payment of the royalty is deemed to be production from the lease; the lessee is given complete discretion in operating the unit area, and is given the right to carry out secondary recovery procedures, to inject substances and exercise similar powers.

The lease is deemed to be amended to the extent necessary to carry out the agreement, and is expressly ratified and confirmed.

The arrangement contemplated by the unit operation agreement works only when there is just one working interest owner. If it became necessary to enter into a multi-party unitization arrangement in Ontario, it is likely that the model agreement, or a variation thereof, would be utilized.

Titles Committee

The working interest owners, i.e., the lessees, appoint a titles committee to investigate the ownership of the working interests and the royalty interests in all tracts and each working interest owner is entitled to be represented thereon. The lessees are required to submit to the committee such title data and information as the committee may reasonably require. The titles committee is to report the results of its investigation to the working interest owners and to make recommendations with respect to approval of title to the various tracts.

This can be a hazardous process for a lessee with a skeleton, such as a late delay rental, in the closet. There is always the danger that the fatal flaw may be exposed and acted upon by a third party. For this reason, companies sometimes indemnify their tracts into the unit rather than have them subjected to scrutiny.

Compulsory Unitization

Where the lease grants the lessee the right to unilaterally unitize, this does not pose a problem. It is otherwise, however, where the lease does not grant this right or where the particular clause may be unenforceable because of uncertainty of terms.

The economic and conservation advantages of unitization are so substantial that four of the five provinces where freehold mineral rights are of importance have decreed that it may be imposed compulsorily. The *Ontario Energy Board Act, 1998*[6] authorizes the board to require and regulate the joining of various interests within a field or pool for the purpose of drilling or operating wells. Saskatchewan provides that, upon the application of any interested party or the Minister of Mineral Resources, the Oil and Gas Conservation Board may hold a hearing and order that a field or pool is to be operated as a unit.[7] The Saskatchewan Act further provides that, if a unit is formed, then any production allocated to a tract shall be deemed to have been actually produced from that tract and that all operations within the unit area are deemed to have been carried on within each tract. In 1966 the Saskatchewan legislation was amended to recognize a voluntary unitization as well as compulsory unitization imposed by the board, and the

---

6 S.O. 1998, c 15, Sch. B, s 41.
7 *Oil and Gas Conservation Act*, R.S.S. 1978, c O-2, s 30.

voluntary form has been more commonly followed since that date. In Manitoba the board, upon its own motion or upon the application of a working interest owner, may make an order for compulsory unitization.[8] There is the usual statutory protection of the lessee's interest in that production or operations within the unit area are deemed to take place on each tract.

Section 115 of the British Columbia *Petroleum and Natural Gas Act*[9] provides that if the minister receives an application for a unitization order, the minister may make an order binding on all owners of interests in the unit area.

Alberta does not provide for compulsory unitization. At one time, the *Conservation Act* did contain a fully articulated part setting out the way in which parties could apply to have the Conservation Board impose unitization. But that part was never proclaimed, and remained in limbo. Then the board and the industry agreed there was no need for it, and the sections were dropped from the Act. Thus, unitization can be achieved in Alberta only by agreement among the parties.

Although there is no compulsory unitization in Alberta, section 79 of the *Oil and Gas Conservation Act*[10] directs the board to encourage unitization, and as Lucas and Hunt[11] point out, it can indirectly promote unitization by using its powers to impose production penalties, or to increase allowables, or require implementation of enhanced recovery schemes.

Void for Uncertainty

What follows is a fuller discussion of why it is necessary for the lessee to have the unilateral right to determine the terms of the unit agreement. There are many fundamental elements of a unitization agreement that are totally unknown at the time the lease is executed. The general terms of the model unit agreement are certainly ascertainable, but no one will know the extent of the unit area, the unitized zone or the unitized substances, or the formula for the determination of tract factors. As long as it expressly confers discretion on the lessee to determine the terms of the future unitization agreement, the clause should

---

8 *Oil and Gas Act*, C.C.S.M. c O34, s 126.

9 R.S.B.C. 1996, c 361, s 115.

10 R.S.A. 2000, c O-6.

11 *Oil & Gas Law in Canada* (Calgary: Carswell, 1990) at 215.

not be held to be void for uncertainty. In *May & Butcher v The King*,[12] Viscount Dunedin said, "Of course, it may leave something which still has to be determined, but then that determination must be a determination which does not depend upon the agreement between the parties." He went on to say, "For instance, it is a perfectly good contract as to price to say that the price is to be settled by the buyer."

Since the lessee has sole discretion over the terms of the unit agreement, the same result should follow.

The closest judicial analogy to the unitization clause is the Supreme Court decision in *Calvan Consolidated Oil & Gas Company Ltd. v Manning*,[13] where the letter agreement provided that if certain lands were to be developed by the parties themselves, rather than being sold or farmed out, they would enter into an operating agreement, the terms of which were to be mutually agreed upon. If agreement could not be reached, there was to be arbitration by a single arbitrator pursuant to the *Arbitration Act* of Alberta.

Even though the letter agreement contemplated a subsequent agreement between the parties, it was held to be valid and enforceable because of the arbitration clause. The court was influenced by the following factors:

(a) There were several possible ways the parties could have dealt with the land.
(b) They did not know their ultimate intentions, so it was not reasonable to require them to provide in detail for a contingency that may never arise.

The above statements are a glass slipper fit for the unitization scenario. Unitization is a contingency that may never arise. The terms cannot be set out in detail because much will depend upon the nature of the unit and the other parties to the unit agreement.

Early forms of the unitization clause did not confer the right on the lessee to unilaterally determine the terms of the unit agreement. If the lessor was not prepared to voluntarily execute the unit agreement, the void for uncertainty argument could cause a problem for the lessee.

---

12 [1929] All E.R. Rep. 679 (H.L.).
13 [1959] S.C.R. 253, 17 D.L.R. (2d) 1, [1959] S.C.J. No. 9 (S.C.C.).

Rule Against Perpetuities

Since unitization is an event that will happen in the future, the clause might be attacked on the ground that it offends the rule against perpetuities. In Alberta, the province where the contractual right to unitize can be crucial, the *Perpetuities Act*[14] establishes a perpetuity period of eighty years, and if the contract provides for the acquisition of an interest at a time later than eighty years, then the interest may be acquired up to eighty years and not thereafter. Thus, for all practical purposes, the clause cannot be rendered ineffective by application of the rule. Furthermore, the Act contains a "wait and see" provision that holds a contract to be presumptively valid until actual events prove that the interest is incapable of vesting within the perpetuity period.[15]

Duty of Care

One area where the lessee's *bona fides* could be put to the test is in the allocation of tract factors. The participation percentage in the unit that is allocated to a tract will determine how much production is allocated to the tract and consequently how much royalty the lessor will receive. The allocation of tract factors is negotiated by the lessees as working interest owners, and it is quite common for a lessee to have interests in a number of tracts. A lessee with interests in several tracts within the unit may be willing to make concessions with respect to one tract in the expectation of receiving more favourable treatment for others.

In addition to acting *bona fide* the lessee may well be in a fiduciary position with respect to the lessor when it comes to entering into a unit agreement. The clause grants the lessee complete discretion as to the contents of the unit agreement. The lessee will possess detailed information about such matters as reserves, deliverability, pay thickness, and other geological and engineering factors that go into the determination of the tract factors. None of this information will be available to the average lessor.

The most authoritative statement on what it takes to create a fiduciary relationship is the following passage from the judgment of Wilson J in *Frame v Smith*.[16]

---

14 R.S.A. 2000, c P-5.
15 Ibid. s 4(l).
16 *Frame v Smith* [1987] 2 S.C.R. 99, 42 D.L.R. (4th) 81, [1987] S.C.J. No. 49 (S.C.C.). This view was expressly approved by the Supreme Court in *Lac Minerals Ltd. v Int'l Corona*

Relationships in which a fiduciary obligation have been imposed seem to possess three general characteristics:
(1) The fiduciary has scope for the exercise of some discretion or power.
(2) The fiduciary can unilaterally exercise that power or discretion so as to affect the beneficiary's legal or practical interests.
(3) The beneficiary is peculiarly vulnerable to or at the mercy of the fiduciary holding the discretion or power.

It would be hard to imagine a more precise description of the relationship between a lessee and a lessor under the unitization clause.

In *Manning v Calvan Consolidated Oil & Gas Company Limited and Imperial Oil Limited (No. 2)*,[17] Manning, having been assured by the Supreme Court of Canada in the earlier case[18] that the letter agreement between himself and Calvan was binding, alleged that Calvan was in breach of trust. The letter agreement granted Calvan the power to deal "as you see fit" with the Crown Permits. This is directly comparable to the lessee's power to unitize at its sole discretion, and the properties, while not freehold leases, were B.C. Crown Permits that granted similar rights with respect to oil and gas. Calvan, in negotiating a deal with Imperial Oil Limited under the power granted by the letter agreement, did not consult Manning at any stage of the negotiations. The result of the negotiations may be summarized as follows: the agreement involved three Permits, two of which were owned outright by Calvan and in one of which Manning was entitled to an undivided 20 per cent interest. The dispute arose over the allocation of work credits that would be earned by the exploration activities to be carried out by Imperial on the lands covered by the three Permits. The work credits replaced the requirement to pay rental fees to the government, and credits earned on one Permit could be allocated to others. The agreement negotiated by Calvan provided that work credits would be applied to the two Permits that were solely owned by it.

The trial judge found that Calvan was in breach of trust in the negotiations with respect to the treatment of the work credits. The trial judge observed that "it is well settled that a trustee must deal with

---

Resources Ltd., [1987] 2 S.C.R. 574, 61 D.L.R. (4th) 14, [1989] S.C.J. No. 83 (S.C.C.). See also Maddaugh and McCamus, *The Law of Restitution* (Aurora: Canada Law Book, 1990).

17 As digested in Bennett Jones Verchere and Bankes, *Canadian Oil and Gas*, vol. 1, 2nd ed. (Toronto: Butterworths, 1997) at Dig. 155.

18 *Supra* n 13.

property of a *cestui que trust* as he would prudently deal with his own; he must not make a profit or gain an advantage over the *cestui que trust* by the use of his office as trustee."

A lessee acting under a unitization clause with other working interest owners in a field would appear to occupy this position vis-à-vis the lessor. As always in the law, responsibility walks hand in hand with authority. While the unitization clause provides that the discretion conferred on the lessee is to be exercised *bona fide*, the existence of a fiduciary relationship may well impose a higher duty.

11 Administrative and Procedural Provisions

The pooling and unitization clause marks the end of what might be called the substantive portion of the lease in that it deals with the actual grant of the minerals and what may be done with them. The remaining clauses, for the most part, constitute the machinery for administering the lessor-lessee relationship. Because of their "boilerplate" nature, these provisions in both the conventional and the CAPL lease display, for the most part, a remarkable degree of uniformity. That does not mean, however, that they do not have an important role to play in how the lease functions, and whether or not it continues in force.

Operations

Oil and gas are inflammable, explosive, and volatile. In a word, they are dangerous substances. Under the lease, the lessee is given the entire management and control over the operations connected with these substances.

The relationship between lessor and lessee is such as to create a duty on the lessee to protect the lessor against damage. The lessor retains a vested interest in the minerals; he is entitled to a royalty and, if the minerals are lost or dissipated through the negligence of the lessee, the lessor has suffered damages. There are three areas in which the negligent conduct of the lessee may cause damage to the lessor: (a) wasting of the reserves; (b) if the mineral owner is also the surface owner, his property may be damaged by escape of the substances or by the surface operations of the lessee; (c) the lessor may suffer personal injury as a result of an accident at the well.

What is the standard of care required of the lessee? The common law is deliberately unspecific in this field, saying only that the standard of conduct is that of the reasonable man.[1] In each case the court must take the objective test and apply it to the facts before it. The element of foreseeability plays an important role. For example, would a reasonable man foresee the possibility of damage or injury in a particular situation? The magnitude and nature of the risk also are factors. For operations under an oil and gas lease, the standard of care of the reasonable man would be that employed by a reasonable and prudent oil operator. The fact that oil and gas are highly dangerous substances would necessarily impose a greater degree of care. Gas in the distribution system of a utility company has been classified by the Privy Council as a "dangerous thing" imposing strict liability upon the utility company.[2]

The typical "operations" clause in effect imports the common law duty of care: "Conduct of Operations: Lessee shall conduct all its operations on the said lands in a diligent, careful and workmanlike manner and in compliance with the provisions of law applicable to such operations, and where such provisions of law conflict or are at variance with the provisions of this Lease, such provisions of law shall prevail." The CAPL lease replaces "provisions of law" with "provisions of any statutes, regulations, orders or directions of any government or governmental agency," but the effect is the same.

The reference to "diligent, careful and workmanlike manner" obviously demands an objective standard by which it can be determined whether the operations were in fact "careful and workmanlike." The first question that the court must address itself to is whether the operations of the lessee complied with those methods and precautions that would be utilized by other operators within the oil industry. This, of course, requires expert testimony, but in most instances should be reasonably easy to establish since, over the years, the industry has built up a vast body of experience and operational techniques.

While the practice and custom of the industry will be of great importance in determining the liability of an operator and whether in fact the lessee was negligent, the matter does not necessarily end there. The lessee may be able to establish that its operations conformed in all

---

1 Heuston and Buckley, *Salmond and Heuston on the Law of Torts*, 21st ed. (London: Sweet & Maxwell, 1996) at 222.
2 *Northwestern Utilities Ltd. v London Guarantee and Accident Company Ltd.*, [1936] A.C. 108 (J.C.P.C.).

respects with those used by the industry under identical conditions, but the court might still hold that the practice of the industry was not the standard of care that should have been employed by a reasonable and prudent operator, bearing in mind the dangerous nature of the substances.

Strict Liability

The dangerous nature of the leased substances raises the possibility that the operator-lessee may be faced with absolute liability for any damage regardless of negligence. If there is to be absolute liability, it will be found in that area of law generally known as the Rule in *Rylands v Fletcher*,[3] which has been paraphrased by Salmond as follows: "The occupier of land who brings and keeps upon it anything likely to do damage if it escapes is bound at his peril to prevent its escape, and is liable for all the direct consequences of its escape, even if he has been guilty of no negligence."[4]

This rule has been extensively applied, distinguished, discussed, and refined by the courts in the intervening years.[5] It would seem, however, that the operations of a lessee in drilling or producing fulfil most, if not all, of the requirements for the application of the modern version of the rule. Certainly, the substances are dangerous; there may be some difficulty over the requirement of accumulating the substances, or bringing them upon the land; but there is the undoubted fact that by producing the well, the lessee may cause substances to migrate onto the land from adjoining properties. Where secondary recovery with the injection of water or other substances is used to drive the petroleum substances towards the wellbore, the element of accumulation would seem to be clearly established. Moreover, subsequent cases seem to substitute the aspect of escape for accumulation.[6] The element of escape would certainly be present under situations where damage is caused to the lessor's person or property, surface or underground. One of the refinements of the rule draws a distinction between natural and non-natural user of land and holds that the use must be non-natural before the liability is absolute. It has been argued that "an ordinary, reasonable and

---

3 [1868] L.R. 3 H.L. 330, 37 L.J.Ex. 161, [1861–73] All E.R. Rep. 1 (H.L.).
4 *Supra* n 1 at 355.
5 Ibid. at 359–77.
6 *Read v Lyons*, [1974] A.C. 156, [1946] 2 All E.R. 471 (H.L.).

proper operation to produce oil and gas should not be considered a non-natural user of the land."[7] This is similar to a refinement to the effect that the rule does not apply to the land itself or to things that are the product of natural forces operating in geological time, such as outcrops of rock. However, while a person may not be liable for *allowing* the escape of such things naturally on his land, he is responsible for *causing* their escape. It is clear from the nature of the operation itself that the lessee actively causes the escape of dangerous substances. Thus, there remains a strong likelihood that the lessee who causes the escape of petroleum substances from their underground location is under a strict liability for any resulting damage.

If the parties are in a voluntary relationship with each other, such as that of lessor and lessee, they can reduce the measure of care or skill that one of them might otherwise be forced to attain.[8] The importation of a standard of care stated to be "in a diligent, careful and workmanlike manner" may have the effect of excluding the absolute liability that might otherwise be imposed under *Rylands v Fletcher*, particularly in view of a subsequent clause in the lease that excludes any implied covenant or liability.

In the case of substances such as oil and gas, however, the distinction between absolute liability and that imposed under a standard of care concept may be of little practical significance. "Liability for inherently dangerous chattels is strict in all but name, since the standard of care is so stringent as to amount practically to a guarantee of safety."[9]

Surface Damage

The concept of strict liability, or compensation regardless of negligence, is embodied in the standard clause on surface damage: "COMPENSATION: The Lessee shall pay and be responsible for actual damages caused by its operations to the surface of, and growing crops and improvements on, the said lands." The undertaking to reimburse the lessor for actual damages caused by operations under the lease is independent of any element of liability. It applies only when the mineral lessor is also the owner of the surface. To some extent it may be a

---

7 Bennett Jones Verchere and Bankes, *Canadian Oil and Gas*, vol. 1, 2nd ed. (Toronto: Butterworths, 1997) at para. 8.11.

8 Fleming, *The Law of Torts*, 9th ed. (Sydney: LBC Information Services, 1998) at 121.

9 *Supra* n 1 at 359–77; *Adelaide Chemical Co. v Carlyle* (1940), 64 C.L.R. 514 (Aust. H.C.).

duplication of the documentation under which the surface rights are obtained. As mentioned in the discussion of the granting clause, surface rights in western Canada at least are not acquired under an oil and gas lease, but under a separate document known as a surface lease or, in the event of a failure to agree, by expropriation under the applicable provincial acts. The surface lease most commonly encountered in Canada contains a clause virtually identical with the one quoted above. If the rights are obtained by expropriation, the tribunal is empowered to award compensation for damage to the surface of land.[10]

The CAPL lease does not contain a similar provision since the matter will be dealt with in the surface lease.

Indemnification

The lessor, as registered owner of the lands, has a direct connection with the events and likely would be joined as a defendant by any third party suffering damages as a result of operations carried out under the lease. The lessor is indemnified against this event by the standard clause: "INDEMNIFICATION: The Lessee shall indemnify the Lessor against all actions, suits, claims and demands by any person or persons whomsoever in respect of any loss, injury, damage or obligation to compensate arising out of or connected with the work carried on by the Lessee on the said lands or in respect of any breach of any of the terms and conditions of this Lease insofar as the same relates to and

---

10 *The Surface Rights Act*, R.S.A. 2000, c S-24, s 12; *Mines and Minerals Act*, C.C.S.M.
c M162, ss 146, 157; *The Surface Rights Acquisition and Compensation Act*, R.S.S. 1978, c
S-65. An oil and gas operator may be liable to a landowner in the absence of either an
oil and gas lease or a surface lease on the grounds of nuisance, trespass, or negligence.
In *Phillips v California Standard Company* (1960), 31 W.W.R. 331 (Alta. S.C.T.D.), an
operator was held liable for damages to a water well occasioned by seismograph work
along the road allowance bordering the plaintiff's lands. This action was founded in
nuisance and not trespass since the latter required a physical entry on the plaintiff's
lands. In *McWilliams v Carlton Royalties Ltd.*, [1938] 2 W.W.R. 351, [1938] 3 D.L.R. 793
(Alta. S.C.T.D.), the operator was held liable to the landowner for damages occasioned
by drilling mud escaping from a sump where it had been collected during the drilling
of an oil well. In *Kopf v Superior Oils Ltd.* (1951), 4 W.W.R. (N.S.) 682, [1952] 2 D.L.R.
572 (Alta. S.C.T.D.), the document in question was headed "Instructions for Surface
Lease" and signed by the parties. It was held to constitute the requisites for a valid
lease and thus could be specifically enforced. It did not, however, contain a covenant
to pay damages for destruction of the surface. The court was not prepared to imply
such a covenant, but awarded damages on the basis of a tort, rather than by contract.

affects the said lands." The wording of this clause is wide and generalized. It would appear to protect the lessor against all third party liability arising from the lessee's work under the lease, and by the use of the word "loss" indemnifies the lessor not only against the amount of the claim asserted by an injured third party, but presumably against any out-of-pocket expenses, such as legal costs.

The indemnification clause in the CAPL lease expands the reference to said lands to include the pooled or unitized lands and provides that the indemnity will not apply if the loss, injury, or damage was caused by the act or omission of the lessor, its agents, employees, or contractors.

Information and Records

The information to which the lessor is entitled under the lease is sparse indeed. Under the standard clause the lessee is obliged only to provide: "RECORDS OF PRODUCTION: The Lessee shall make available to the Lessor during normal business hours at the Lessee's address hereinafter mentioned the Lessee's records relative to the quantity of leased substances produced from the said lands." Since the lessor's royalty share is computed on production, actual or allocated, the right to inspect the lessee's production records would seem to be the least that he is entitled to do. It is noted that the above clause merely refers to "the lessee's records relative to the quantity of leased substances." Presumably the lessor has to take the lessee's records as he finds them. It would be preferable to expand this clause by imposing upon the lessee an obligation to keep full and adequate accounts of all production from the said lands and to make those records available.

This is the only reference in the entire lease to information, records, or data to which the lessor may be entitled. The lease is silent on any information relating to drilling operations on the lands. It sometimes happens that an aura of secrecy shrouds these operations as the lessee will not want to disclose any information that would impair its ability to acquire a good land position in the area. But "tight-hole" conditions are the exception rather than the rule and could be adequately provided for by express exceptions. Most drilling information is a matter of public record, and there is no reason why the lessee should not provide the lessor with a condensed, general version of it. A mineral owner has more than a passing interest in whether a well is a potential producer or a dry hole. In view of the traditional industry attitude towards exploration information, however, this will likely prove to be a difficult concession to win from a lessee. A few owners of extremely large tracts of minerals require such information to be provided, but their bargaining position is much different than that of the average mineral owner.

The obligation of the lessee to provide information under the CAPL lease is found in the clause dealing with royalties, and provides that the lessee shall make available to the lessor the lessee's records relating to the leased substances produced from or allocated to the said lands. CAPL 99 provides that the lessee will make available to the lessor or its authorized representative the lessee's production and financial records relating to production from the leased lands.

Encumbrances

Since the lessor is the registered owner of the lands, he can by an express act or by omission create charges, liens, and defaults that encumber the interest in the land and could eventually lead to the extinction of his title and the defeat of the lessee's interest. Obviously, the lessee cannot stand idly by while its title may be defeated by the act or omission of the lessor. The lessee's right to take action under such circumstances is expressed as follows:

DISCHARGE OF ENCUMBRANCES
The Lessee may at the Lessee's option pay or discharge the whole or any portion of any tax, charge, mortgage, lien or encumbrance of any kind or nature whatsoever incurred or created by the Lessor and/or the Lessor's predecessors or successors in title or interest which may now or hereafter exist on or against or in any way affect the said lands or the leased substances, in which event the Lessee shall be subrogated to the rights of the holder or holders thereof and may in addition thereto at the Lessee's option, reimburse itself by applying on the amount so paid by the Lessee against the rentals, royalties, or other sums accruing to the Lessor under the terms of this Lease, and any rentals, royalties or such other sums so applied shall, for all purposes of this Lease, be deemed to have been paid to and received by the Lessor.

Even in the absence of the above clause, the lessee would have the right to redeem, at least with respect to a mortgage: "Any person entitled to an estate carved out of the mortgagor's estate is entitled to redeem, subject, of course, to any paramount equities which affect the estate."[11] The lessee under a mineral lease, being the owner of a *profit à prendre*, has an interest sufficient to exercise the right of redemption. In Saskatchewan, a mineral lessee who has redeemed a mortgage has the right by statute to have the mortgage assigned, rather than discharged.[12]

The clause enlarges this right of redemption to include any tax, charge, mortgage, lien, or any kind of encumbrance. It also subrogates the lessee to the rights of the holder or holders thereof and allows the lessee to reimburse itself from rentals, royalties, or other sums accruing to the lessor. This right of reimbursement would appear to be inconsistent with, in the case of a mortgage, the statutory right to require a transfer of the mortgage. If the lessee demanded and obtained such a transfer, that would appear to extinguish any right of reimbursement from proceeds due under the lease.

The right of reimbursement also extends to rentals due under the lease. Presumably the reference is to the "delay rental" defined in the first proviso to the *habendum* clause. Since the term "delay rental" is expressly defined as meaning a payment that might not be considered a rental, in a strict legal sense, the reference should be amended to expressly include the term "delay rental as defined." In view of the extreme strictness that the courts have used in determining whether or not a delay rental has been properly paid and the disastrous consequences of any failure to do so, a prudent lessee would be well advised to continue making delay rental payments and not seek reimbursements from those payments, even though the clause expressly provides that the rentals shall be deemed to have been paid to and received by the lessor.

CAPL 88 and 91 cover off this possibility by defining "rental" as meaning either the lump sum covering the entire primary term or the annual amount paid to defer the commencement of operations in any lease year during the primary term. Since CAPL 99 has eliminated the delay rental as such, there is no definition of "rental." The right of reimbursement has been extended to expressly include shut-in payments.

---

11 *Tarn v Turner* (1888), 57 L.J. Ch. 452; affirmed 39 Ch. D. 456 (C.A.).
12 *Land Titles Act*, R.S.S. 1978, c L-5, s 136(2).

Surrender

The lessee has a unilateral right to surrender.

SURRENDER

Notwithstanding anything herein contained, the Lessee may at any time or from time to time determine or surrender this Lease and the term hereby granted as to the whole or any part or parts of the leased substances and/or the said lands, upon giving the Lessor written notice to that effect, whereupon this Lease and the said term shall terminate as to the whole or any part or parts thereof so surrendered and the rental, royalty or otherwise, shall be extinguished or correspondingly reduced as the case may be, but the Lessee shall not be entitled to a refund of any such rent theretofore paid.

The right to surrender is much more important in an "or" type of lease during the primary term than in the more typical "unless" form. If the lessee under an "or" type did not have the right to surrender, then it would remain liable for each yearly rental during the primary term, regardless of whether or not it had any real desire to maintain the lease in force. With the right of surrender, the lessee can avoid constantly accruing liability for yearly rentals, provided it is prepared to give up its interest in the lease.

The right of surrender granted to the lessee can be fragmented both as to area and zone. If the lessee desires, it may surrender any portion of the said lands or the leased substances. The right to surrender a portion of the acreage covered by the lease clearly emerges from "or any part or parts of ... the said lands," while the reference to "leased substances" is meaningful only if it refers to geological zones or formations. If there is partial surrender on an area basis, there is provision for a corresponding reduction of the rental, but this result would not seem to follow in the case of a surrender by zone. In the latter case there is no mechanism for determining the proper apportionment of rental as among the surrendered and retained zones.

The clause in the conventional lease also contains a confusing reference to royalty: "the rental, royalty or otherwise." Royalty, per se, cannot be reduced by a partial surrender as it depends on the actual quantity of production from the land and nothing else. One could guess that the reference is meant for a suspended well payment, which would in fact be reduced as it tracks the delay rental payment and would be reduced automatically.

The lessee cannot escape liability for already accrued obligations by the act of surrender. By the express wording of the clause, the lessor is not required to refund any rent that may have been advanced. Here again, the word "rent" seems to be a misnomer and the reference should be to a delay rental.

Another type of surrender clause that is frequently encountered makes a specific reference to a surrender by zone or formation:

SURRENDER

Notwithstanding anything herein contained the Lessee may at any time or from time to time by written notice to the Lessor, surrender this lease and the term hereby granted as to the whole or any part or parts of the leased substances or the said lands, including any zone or formation therein, and the Lessee shall thereby and thereupon be released from all obligations accrued or to accrue respecting the leased substances and/or the said lands so surrendered excepting accrued royalty and money obligations for which specific provision is made in this lease, and the delay rental, royalty or otherwise shall be extinguished or correspondingly reduced, as the case may be, but the Lessee shall not be entitled to a refund of any such amounts theretofore paid.

The surrender clause in CAPL 88 and 91 expressly provides that if the lessee surrenders all or any part of the said lands by zone or formation the rental shall not abate. There is no reference to "rentals" in CAPL 99 since no delay rentals are payables.

Removal of Caveats and Registered Documents

The lessee will protect its interest under the lease by registration in the appropriate land titles office. Usually the registration takes the form of a caveat, but occasionally the lease itself will be registered. As a matter of mechanics, the lease provides that upon its termination any such caveat or registered document will be withdrawn or discharged from the lessor's title: "REMOVAL OF CAVEAT: In the event of the Lessee having registered in the Land Titles Office for the area in which the said lands are situated this Lease or any caveat or other document in respect thereof, the Lessee shall withdraw or discharge the document so registered within a reasonable time after termination of this Lease."

A mineral owner should ensure that any registration is discharged. Otherwise the title would indicate that the lands are subject to an existing lease and so discourage any new attempts at leasing. Similarly, if the deeper rights clause applies, the lessor should take steps to ensure the appropriate adjustments are made to the caveat.

As discussed earlier, and again in Chapter 19 on litigating the lease, provincial legislation provides a mechanism by which the mineral owner can cause a caveat to be lapsed and removed from his title.

Unaccountably, the CAPL lease does not contain a removal of caveat clause. If necessary, the procedure described in the preceding paragraph will force an unwilling lessee to comply.

Removal of Equipment

Once the lease has been terminated, ordinarily the lessee has no further status with respect to the said lands and any further entry would amount to trespass. However, some machinery, equipment, and other materials used for drilling, production, or other operations may still be on the lands at the time of termination. The lease confers the right to enter and remove such equipment for a period of time after termination: "REMOVAL OF EQUIPMENT: The Lessee shall at all times during the currency of this Lease and for a period of Six (6) months from the termination thereof, have the right to remove all or any of its machinery, equipment, structures, pipelines, casing and materials from the said lands." The clause that grants the right to remove equipment and materials fits the situation where production has ceased and the lessee is salvaging whatever equipment may be of value. Different considerations would apply, however, where the lease has been terminated while the lands are still productive. Conservation laws would step in to prevent the lessee from abandoning the well and removing equipment under such circumstances. The rights of the lessor and lessee where a productive lease has been terminated are discussed in Chapter 17, *infra*, under the heading, "Who Owns the Well?"

The clause in CAPL 88 and 91 is to the same effect as the one quoted above, differing only in that it contains a specific reference to "whether placed upon, within or under the said lands."

The CAPL surface lease grants the lessee the same right to remove all equipment, fixtures, casing in wells, pipelines, and everything else the lessee may have placed on the land. Presumably for this reason, CAPL 99 does not contain a removal of equipment clause.

Procedure in the Event of Default

The lease contains machinery for dealing with defaults by the lessee in the performance of any obligation thereunder. Such default does not result in automatic termination since the lessee is granted a time within which to remedy such default. The clause provides a grace period of ninety days.

> DEFAULT
>
> In the case of the breach or non-performance on the part of the Lessee of any covenant, proviso, condition, restriction or stipulation herein contained which ought to be observed or performed by the Lessee and which has not been waived by the Lessor, the Lessor shall, before bringing any action with respect thereto or declaring any forfeiture, give to the Lessee written notice setting forth the particulars of and requiring it to remedy such defaults, and in the event that the Lessee shall fail to commence to remedy such default within a period of Ninety (90) days from receipt of such notice, and thereafter diligently proceed to remedy the same, then except as hereinafter provided, this Lease shall thereupon terminate and it shall be lawful for the Lessor into or upon the said lands (or any part thereof in the name of the whole) to re-enter and the same to have again repossess and enjoy; PROVIDED that this Lease shall not terminate nor be subject to forfeiture or cancellation if there is located on the said lands a well capable of producing the leased substances or any of them, and in that event the Lessor's remedy for any default hereunder shall be for damages only.

The first thing to be noted about the clause is that it relates only to covenants, provisos, conditions, restrictions, or stipulations. In the early cases involving termination for failure to pay delay rental on time, this clause was relied upon by the lessee as requiring both a notice of default and time to remedy it and preserve the lease. The courts rejected this approach and held that, since under the "unless" type of lease the lessee was not obligated to pay the delay rental, it could not be treated as coming within the scope of "covenant, proviso, condition, restriction or stipulation."[13] The default clause has been held not to

---

13 *East Crest Oil Company Ltd. v Strohschein*, [1952] 2 D.L.R. 432, 4 W.W.R. (N.S.) 553 (Alta. S.C., App.Div.). See also *Chipp v Hunt* (1955), 16 W.W.R. (N.S.) 209 (Alta. S.C.T.D.).

apply to the shut-in well clause even when the clause says "the Lessee shall pay."[14]

Similar provisions are also to be found in most surface leases.

If a lessee is in breach of a clear-cut obligation under the lease, such as to pay royalty on actual production, the lessor must follow a set procedure to enforce whatever rights he may have. He must first give written notice to the lessee specifying the particulars of the default and requiring the lessee to remedy same. The lessee then has ninety days from the receipt of the notice to commence to cure the default. It is important to note that the lessee is not required to complete any remedial action within the ninety-day period, but only to *commence* such action, and thereafter to diligently proceed with the corrective measures. If the lessee does not commence to remedy the default within the ninety-day period, the lease will terminate unless a well capable of production is located on the said lands. In such event the lessor's remedy is limited to damages and the lease will not be terminated.

The default clause plays a legitimate role in the structure of the lease. It prevents automatic termination for a purely technical or nominal breach and gives the lessor a means of enforcing compliance with the terms of the lease.

Variation of the Default Clause

One version of the default clause contains an additional proviso that gives the lessee the opportunity to dispute that it is in default and have the matter adjudicated by the courts: "PROVIDED That if the Lessee shall dispute such default this lease shall not be forfeited or cancelled until it shall have first been finally judicially determined that such default exists, and after such final determination, the Lessee shall have been given a reasonable time therefrom to comply with any such covenant, proviso, condition, restriction or stipulation." Under this proviso the lessee's obligation to remedy a default does not begin to run until there has been a final judicial determination that a default exists.

---

14 *Durish v White Resources Management Ltd.* (1987), 55 Alta. L.R. (2d) 47, [1987] A.J. No. 804 (Alta. Q.B.); affirmed, (1988), 63 Alta. L.R. (2d) 265, [1988] A.J. No. 1162 (Alta. C.A.). Also, see discussion under "shall" or "may," *ante.*

The CAPL Default Clause

The default clause in the CAPL lease departs from the traditional "any covenant, proviso, condition, restriction or stipulation." Subsection (a) of the default clause provides as follows: "If, before or after the expiry of the primary term, the Lessor considers that the Lessee has not complied with any provision or obligation of this Lease, including but not limited to a failure to give notice or to pay in the manner specified any rental, suspended well payments, royalty or other sums for which specific provision is made in this Lease, the Lessor shall notify the Lessee in writing, describing in reasonable detail the alleged breach or breaches. The Lessee shall have thirty days after receipt of such notice to: ... " The significance of this departure is that it specifically brings failure to make delay rentals, and shut-in well payments, within the ambit of the default clause and gives the lessee the opportunity to remedy the failure to make such payments. The clause also gives the lessee the opportunity to have the question of whether or not there has been a default determined by the courts. The period of time during which the lessee must commence to remedy the breach or commence a court action has been reduced from the customary ninety days to thirty days.

The clause further provides that the performance of any act by the lessee to remedy the alleged breaches shall not be deemed an admission by the lessee that it has failed to perform its obligations. If the lessee fails to remedy or commence to remedy the breach within the thirty-day period or thereafter fails to continue diligently to remedy the breach, and if legal proceedings have not been commenced, the lease will terminate. If the lessee elects to try the matter in court, the lease will not terminate until the existence of such breach has been finally judicially determined, nor will it terminate if the lessee within thirty days of such judicial determination has remedied or commenced to remedy the breach and diligently continues to remedy the same.

If there is a well on the said lands, the pooled lands, or the unitized lands that is capable of producing the leased substances, or on which operations are being conducted, the lessor's remedy will be for damages only. The reference to "operations" means that even if the well is not then capable of production, but is being drilled or otherwise worked on, the lease will not terminate. Under the circumstances where most breaches are likely to occur, any damages awarded to the lessor are not likely to be substantial. The real prize is to get the mineral rights back free of the lease.

Relief against Forfeiture

In the event of a dispute between the lessor and the lessee as to whether or not the lessee is in breach of an undoubted obligation and covenant under the lease, a notice of default can put the lessee under considerable pressure. If the alleged breach is not remedied, or commenced to be remedied, within a short period of time, frequently thirty days, it could result in termination of the lease, particularly if there is no well on the lands. If the lessee is unable or unwilling to meet the lessor's demands, he may lose the lease. Despite this, and if the circumstances are such that the alleged breach is out of all proportion to the value of the lease, the lessee may be able to seek relief from forfeiture.

A good example of when relief against forfeiture will apply is *Alwell Mechanical Ltd. v Royal Bank of Canada*,[15] a decision of the Alberta Court of Appeal. The issue was whether the court should exercise its undoubted jurisdiction to relieve against forfeiture. The case involved the rental and possible purchase of a restaurant and motel. During the course of the lease the appellant had put more than $400,000.00 of improvements on the property. The arrears of rent at the date of the hearing amounted to some $90,000.00.

Laycraft CJA, speaking for a unanimous court, held that if the termination of the lease were permitted to stand, the apparent windfall to the respondent would be so out of proportion to the amount of arrears that a court of equity ought to intervene.

It is easy to visualize circumstances where the alleged breach would be out of proportion to the loss of an oil and gas lease, which could lead a court to exercise its jurisdiction to relieve against forfeiture. Needless to say, there can be no guarantee that an application for relief against forfeiture will succeed. It should be treated as a possible second line of defence for the lessee when the default clause would otherwise terminate the lease.

If the alleged breach relates to the payment of monies, the lessee may elect to pay the disputed amount under protest. This would cure the alleged default, and the lessee would still be in a position to bring an action in restitution to recover the monies.

---

15 (1986), 41 Alta. L.R. (2d) 8, [1985] A.J. 732 (Alta. C.A.).

Default in Ontario

By the *Gas and Oil Leases Act*,[16] the province of Ontario has provided a procedure whereby a lessor or any other person with an interest in the land may apply to a judge of the county court for an order declaring the lease void. If it were not for this legislation, which is unique to Ontario, the lessor could only bring such an action before the provincial High Court. Indeed, in view of the restrictions contained in the Act, a lessor would be well advised to ignore the route offered by the legislation and proceed in the normal course of litigation. The *Gas and Oil Leases Act* provides that an application may be made (a) where the lessee has made default under the terms of a lease by failing to commence to drill and has failed to pay rentals in lieu thereof, or (b) where the lessee is in default under some other provision of the lease and the default has continued for two years, or, if the default has continued for less than two years, the lessor has given notice and a thirty-day grace period and the lessee has not cured the default within the thirty days.

The effect of the Ontario legislation has been reviewed at the Supreme Court of Canada level in *Modde v Dominion Glass Co. Ltd.*[17] where, under an "unless" form of lease, two delay rental payments were late by several months. In the first instance, payment was made by cheque with an attached counterfoil and the lessor cashed the cheque, and signed and returned the counterfoil. In the subsequent year the late payment was also made by cheque forwarded to the lessor. The lessor cashed the cheque, but did not sign or return the rental receipt acknowledgment attached to it. Subsequently, the lessor sought to have the lease set aside and, unfortunately for him, elected to follow the procedure under the Act. In the Supreme Court of Canada, Spence J noted that the jurisdiction of the county court judge was solely statutory and that the statute specifically refers to the failure to drill or pay rent as a default. If it was a default, then it could be waived. Section 6 of the Act specifically entitled the judge to take into account any payment accepted after the making of the application, and the court agreed with the Ontario Court of Appeal that "*a fortiori* he is entitled to take into account one made before."

Because the application was made under the statute, the many judicial decisions holding that there was no duty upon the lessee to either

---

16 *Gas and Oil Leases Act*, R.S.O. 1990, c G-3.
17 [1967] S.C.R. 567, 63 D.L.R. (2d) 193, [1967] S.C.J. No. 45 (S.C.C.).

drill or pay rental and therefore no breach to waive had no application. Since there was a statutory duty, it could be, and had been, waived by the lessor and the lease was preserved.

Scholtens v Sydenham Gas and Petroleum Co. Ltd.[18] was a successful application made under the Ontario *Gas and Oil Leases Act*. In this case there had been a history of two tardy annual payments, which had been accepted by the lessor. In the third year, however, the rental was not paid on the due date, 29 July, and the application was made on 31 July. Subsequently, the lessees tendered a cheque for the rental, but it was returned uncashed. Since the lessor had not accepted the payment made after the application was brought, section 6 of the Act did not apply and the judge therefore was not required to take the act of tender into account. The ordinary law applied and the county court judge relied on both the *East Crest* and *Langlois* decisions to hold that the lease was void.

In *Ewing v Francisco Petroleum Enterprises Inc.*[19] the applicant sought a declaration under the Act that the lease was void because of failure to make royalty payments. The notice of default was not in the form provided for in the Act, but the court ruled that the respondent had received adequate notice and was well aware of the nature of the default. The respondent volunteered to pay the arrears, but the court ruled that it could not take this into consideration since the Act prohibited consideration of tenders and payments after the application had been commenced.

Warranty of Title and Covenant of Quiet Enjoyment

The heading of this clause in most conventional leases refers only to "quiet enjoyment." This can be misleading since the actual clause includes a warranty of title as well.

QUIET ENJOYMENT
The Lessor covenants and warrants that he has good title to the leased substances and the said lands as hereinbefore set forth, has good right and full power to grant and demise the same and the rights and privileges in manner aforesaid, and that the Lessee, upon observing and performing the covenants and conditions on the Lessee's part herein contained, shall

---

18 Unreported, 30 October 1963, Beardall J (Ont. Co. Ct.), digested in *Canadian Oil and Gas*, 2nd ed., vol. 1, Dig. 173.
19 [1996] O.J. No. 2348 (H.C.J. Gen. Div.).

and may peaceably possess and enjoy the same and the rights and privileges hereby granted during the said term and any extension thereof
without any interruption or disturbance from or by the Lessor or any
other person whomsoever.

The language of the clause imposes an absolute liability for title failure
upon the lessor. If title failed, the lessee could sue him and be awarded
damages that could be of staggering proportions. It is unlikely the
average lessor realizes that by signing a lease he has undertaken such a
potentially enormous liability. There are no recorded instances where a
lessee has attempted to invoke such a right against a lessor, but there is
no doubt that such a claim could be advanced. The warranty title on
the part of the lessor seems inconsistent with the practice followed in
the industry, whereby the lessee normally investigates any freehold
mineral title with great care. If the bonus consideration under a lease is
for a relatively insignificant amount, the lessee usually relies upon the
current certificate of title. Before undertaking the expense of drilling a
well, however, or paying a substantial bonus consideration, the lessee
should, and usually does, conduct a historic search of the lessor's title.

The balance of the clause amounts to an unqualified covenant for
quiet enjoyment. The language goes beyond the type of covenant usually encountered in landlord-tenant relationships since it is unqualified
and applies not only to interruption or disturbance by the lessor or
anyone claiming under him, but also from any person whomsoever.
Since the covenant for quiet enjoyment was imported from the law of
landlord and tenant, one would expect it to have the same scope under
the oil and gas lease.

The acts of interference must be physical[20] and a breach of the covenant may be restrained by an injunction. The effect of the covenant is
very similar to the legal principle that a person shall not derogate from
his own grant. A typical example of a breach of the covenant would
occur if the lessor erected a fence around the well site and attempted to
prevent the lessee from gaining access to the well. The split between
surface rights and grants of mineral rights may create some confusion
in this area, and the lessee should have the covenant in both the oil and
gas lease and the surface lease.

---

20 *Browne v Flower*, [1911] 1 Ch. D. 219.

The inclusion of "or any other person whomsoever" broadens the application of the covenant and makes the lessor responsible for disturbance of the lessee's quiet enjoyment even by strangers. This appears to be an unjustifiable extension of his responsibility, and it is suggested that the lessor should not be liable for interference except by himself and those claiming through him. Indeed, many quiet enjoyment covenants add "claiming through or under the Lessor" after "whomsoever."

Under a conventional lease of land, a covenant for quiet enjoyment would be implied if there were no express provisions. Although an oil and gas lease is not a lease in the proper sense of the word, it is likely that such a covenant would be implied in the absence of an express provision, subject always to the effect of the entire agreement clause discussed *infra*. The covenant exists only during the term of the lease and is ended upon its termination. The sometimes energetic actions by lessors to establish that a lease has lapsed are not in any way violations of the covenant for quiet enjoyment, but are merely attempts to define the legal status of the lease.

The CAPL lease has a similar provision.

Further Assurance

"COVENANT FOR FURTHER ASSURANCE: The Lessor and the Lessee hereby agree that they will each do and perform all such acts and things and execute all such deeds, documents and writings and give all such assurance as may be necessary to give effect to this Lease and all covenants herein contained."

The intent of the foregoing clause is clear, but there is a question as to its scope. It is obviously designed as a curative measure and is one of the fundamental covenants that are now implied by statute under the English property law. Presumably it would assist the lessee in cases such as these: If the land were misdescribed, the lessor could be required to execute a document remedying such defect. Where the seal has been omitted, the lessor may be compelled to affix one. The counterargument to this is that, if, for example, the seal were not affixed, the document would not be an effective grant. Therefore, the covenant never came into existence. More likely, however, the covenant would be enforced between the two parties. The covenant will not assist the lessee where the act of further assurance is to be done by someone other than the lessor. For example, if the homestead or dower affidavit has been improperly taken, the covenant could not be used to force the lessor's spouse to remedy the defect.

Assignment

Both parties have a virtually unrestricted right to assign their interests in the lease.

> ASSIGNMENT
>
> The parties hereto may each or either of them delegate, assign, sub-let or convey to any other person or persons, corporation or corporations, all or any of the property, powers, rights and interests obtained by or conferred upon them respectively hereunder and may enter into all agreements, contracts and writings and do all necessary acts and things to give effect to the provisions of this clause; PROVIDED that no assignment of royalties or other moneys payable hereunder shall be binding upon the Lessee, notwithstanding any actual or constructive notice or knowledge thereof, unless and except the same be for the entire interest of the Lessor in all of the said sums remaining to be paid or to accrue hereunder, nor then until Thirty (30) days after the Lessee has been actually furnished at its address hereinafter set forth with evidence satisfactory to the Lessee of such assignment of the entire interest of the Lessor in all the sums aforesaid, including, if effected by voluntary act, the original or a certified copy of the instrument effecting such assignment; PROVIDED FURTHER that in the event that the Lessee shall assign this Lease as to any part or parts of the said lands, then the delay rental shall be apportioned amongst the several leaseholders rateably according to the surface area of each, and should the Assignee or Assignees of any such part or parts fail to pay the proportionate part of the delay rental payable by him or them, such failure to pay shall not operate to terminate or affect this Lease insofar as it relates to and comprises the part or parts of the said lands in respect which the Lessee or its Assignees make due payment of rental.

The first portion of the clause sets forth the untrammelled rights of either party to assign without the necessity of consent from the other. The provisos, however, reflect the lessee's preoccupation with making the payments required to keep the lease in force. As has been demonstrated repeatedly, proper payment of the delay rental is critical to the continued existence of the lease. An assignment of the lessor's interest in the lease can create situations where the lessee may inadvertently pay the rental to the wrong person. The outstanding example of this difficulty is to be found in *Langlois v Canadian Superior Oil*,[21] where the lease was dated 12 October 1948, and there was an assignment by the lessor during one of the years of the primary term, namely, on 14 June 1954. Notice of this assignment was received by the lessee on 14 September of that year, and on the same day the lessee sent a change of depository agreement to be executed and returned by the new assignees. This agreement signed by the assignees was returned to Canadian Superior with a letter dated 30 September 1954, and on 5 October 1954, the lessee returned a copy of the depository agreement duly executed by it. In the meantime, on 1 October 1954, the lessee sent its cheque payable to the depository bank for the credit of the former lessor. The amount of the cheque was duly credited to his account, so the new assignees did not receive any payment. This failure to make proper payment was held to terminate the lease by virtue of its own terms.

The first proviso to the assignment clause is designed to avoid this unhappy result. It attempts to do this by providing that no assignment of royalties or other monies "shall be binding upon the lessee" regardless of any notice that the lessee may have, unless it is for the entire interest of the lessor in all of the sums to be paid. In addition, it does not become binding until a period of thirty days after the lessee has been furnished with evidence of the assignment. Such evidence, moreover, must be satisfactory to the lessee. Many leases, including the CAPL lease, specify forty-five days.

The first requirement that the assignment be of the entire amount of the monies payable is meant to protect the lessee against the hazards of fragmented payments. Reading this condition in the light of the opening portion of the assignment clause, it would appear that, while the lessor may assign a portion of the interest covered by the lease, the assignment of any monies payable thereunder can be only of the entire amount if it is to bind the lessee.

The second condition of the proviso allows the lessee a period of time to get its records in order.

It is relatively easy to determine the purpose that the first proviso is meant to achieve, but the imprecision of the language is troublesome. The proviso states that, unless and until the conditions are met, no assignment "shall be binding upon the lessee." What is the situation

---

21 (1957), 23 W.W.R. 401, 12 D.L.R. (2d) 53 (Man. C.A.).

where the thirty-day period has not expired but the lessee, being fully
aware of the assignment and of the identity of the new assignee, makes
payment to him rather than to the original lessor? Can that be considered a good payment? Can the lessee, in effect, elect to be bound by the
assignment despite the language of the proviso? It would appear that,
if the date for the payment of a delay rental occurs during the thirty-
day period, the lessee in order to be secure must pay the assignor.
There is also considerable elasticity in the thirty-day period; it starts
when the lessee "has been actually furnished" with evidence satisfactory to it of the assignment. Presumably the use of the word "furnish"
means that the lessee must be in receipt of the evidence before the
thirty-day period starts to run. There is also a note of uncertainty inasmuch as the evidence "must be satisfactory to the lessee." The further
reference to the original or certified copy of the instrument creating
such assignment is an indication that this would be evidence satisfactory to the lessee. Would something less than that be evidence satisfactory to the lessee? Would an uncertified copy of the instrument be
satisfactory evidence? Presumably it would, but under the wording of
the clause one could not be certain. Although the test is expressed to be
a subjective one in that the evidence must be satisfactory to the lessee,
a court would probably be prepared to substitute an objective standard
and hold that under certain circumstances the evidence should have
been satisfactory to the lessee.[22]

The whole thrust of the proviso is to avoid the hazards of a faulty
payment when an assignment is made near the anniversary date. The
draftsman attempts to achieve this objective through the broad-brush
approach of making the assignment not "binding" until the requirements have been met. Inasmuch as the parties to a contract can make
law for themselves so long as they do not infringe on legal prohibitions
or public policy,[23] a court might interpret this language to accomplish
the desired result. In view of the strictness that the courts have

---

22 See *California Standard Company v McBride* (1963), 38 D.L.R. (2d) 606 (Alta. S.C.,
   App.Div.), where the court held that a receipt that postponed payment until "the company's solicitors being satisfied that my title to the mines and minerals covered by the
   said Lease is valid and that the said Lease is a valid and subsisting agreement and that
   they form a first charge against the title to the said mines and minerals" did not make
   the instrument void for uncertainty. The document required payment when the lessor
   produced, as the court found he had, a good title.
23 Guest, *Anson's Law of Contract*, 26th ed. (Oxford: Clarendon Press, 1979) at 1.

employed in interpreting an oil and gas lease, one cannot be too sanguine that the words would be so interpreted. Surely it would be preferable to provide that any payment made to the lessor during the thirty-day period would be deemed conclusively to be proper payments within the meaning of the lease.

The second proviso is the other side of the coin and likewise is directed towards payment of the delay rental. It deals with assignments by the lessee of a portion of the lands, and in such event apportions the delay rental among the several leaseholders according to their respective shares of the surface area. For example, if the lease covered a full section and a quarter section was assigned to a third party, then the original lessee and the assignee would be responsible for the payment of delay rentals in the ratio of three to one.

It should be noted that the only allocation is one based on surface acreage. There is no mention of assignment by zone or formation. Under such an assignment the original lessee must continue to make payments directly to the lessor and seek reimbursement from the assignee. The assigning lessee's position is further protected by providing that, if the assignees of any part or parts of the lands fail to pay their proportionate part of the delay rental, this does not operate to terminate or affect the lease insofar as it relates to those portions where proper payment was made. The objective is clear, but one must be skeptical as to whether a partial payment can maintain a lease partially in force. The drilling proviso to the *habendum* clause is explicit as to the precise sum of money that must be paid and what happens if it is not. The payment of the delay rental is an option that the courts traditionally interpret with great strictness. This approach, together with the demonstrated reluctance to treat the grant and term clauses as being modified or amended by subsequent provisions,[24] makes it at least questionable if a partial payment could be effective. The lessee should rely on it only as a last resort under conditions where it is too late to make a full and timely payment.

The assignment clause in CAPL 88 and 91 provides that while no assignment by the lessor shall be binding on the lessee, notwithstanding any actual or constructive notice or knowledge thereof until forty-five

---

24 *Shell Oil Company v Gunderson*, [1960] S.C.R. 424, 23 D.L.R. (2d) 81, [1960] S.C.J. No. 19 (S.C.C.); see also *Canadian Superior Oil Ltd. v Kanstrup*, [1965] S.C.R. 92, 49 W.W.R. (N.S.) 257, 47 D.L.R. (2d) 1, [1964] S.C.J. No. 54 (S.C.C.), where the court refused to treat the *habendum* as being modified by the *force majeure* clause.

days after it has been furnished with evidence of the assignment, all payments made within the aforesaid period to the party who would have been entitled to the payment in the absence of the assignment shall be deemed to be valid payment. The lessee is free to act, however, on the assignment prior to the expiration of the forty-five days, and payments or tenders made in accordance with the assignment shall be deemed to have been made in accordance with the terms of the lease. This language is not found in the assignment clause in CAPL 99, but is contained in the manner of payment clause.

Manner of Payment

The lessor becomes entitled to a payment of money for a variety of reasons under the lease. Payments under the lease include: delay rental, royalties on production, suspended wells, reimbursement of taxes, and sometimes compensation for damages caused by operations. The delay rental payment is particularly critical since it may involve an automatic termination of the lease. The drilling proviso to the *habendum* requires that the lessee, in order to defer drilling operations, "shall have paid or tendered to the lessor." The use of this language by itself would seem to require the lessee to seek out the lessor personally and to pay him, or make tender, in cash. Virtually every form of lease relieves the lessee from this onerous burden by a special provision relating to the manner in which payment may be made.

MANNER OF PAYMENT
All payments to the Lessor provided for in this Lease shall, at the Lessee's option, be paid or tendered either to the Lessor or to the depository named in or pursuant to this clause, and all such payments or tenders may be made by cheque or draft of the Lessee either mailed or delivered to the Lessor or to said depository, which cheque or draft shall be payable in Canadian funds at par in the bank on which it is drawn. The Lessor does hereby appoint _____ as the depository for the receipt of all moneys payable under this Lease, and the Lessor agrees that said depository and its successors shall be and continue as his agents for the receipt of any and all sums payable hereunder regardless of changes of ownership (whether by assignment, succession or otherwise) of the said lands or of the leased substances or of the rentals or royalties to accrue hereunder. The Lessor may at any time designate a new depository by giving written notice to the Lessee specifying the name and address of

such new depository; PROVIDED that only a bank or trust company in Canada may be designated as depository, that only one depository shall be designated at any one time as aforesaid, and that the Lessee shall not be required to recognize any change of depository until the expiration of forty-five (45) days from the receipt by the Lessee of the notice in writing aforesaid. If any depository designated by the Lessor shall at any time resign or fail or refuse to act as depository and a successor depository shall not be designated as aforesaid within ten (10) days thereafter, or if any moneys payable hereunder become payable to more than one person and the persons to whom said moneys are payable shall fail to designate one depository hereunder, then the Lessee may at its option designate a bank or trust company in Canada as depository hereunder, which depository shall be entitled to charge its usual fees, and said bank or trust company shall be the depository to all intents and purposes as if originally designated herein by the Lessor.

The clause affords the lessee considerable latitude in the method by which a valid payment can be made under the lease. It can be made by cheque or draft, and it can be either mailed or delivered.

Time of Payment

The phrase "either mailed or delivered" seems straightforward enough, yet for a number of years there was considerable judicial uncertainty as to the effect of mailing a payment. Delivery was clear enough, the payment must be made or tendered to the lessor by the appropriate date, but what is the situation when the lessee, as it commonly does, uses the mail to make payment? Is it sufficient that the payment is mailed in a timely fashion or must there be an actual receipt of the payment by the lessor or the depository prior to the expiration of the time period? The issue was first put in question by the Alberta Appellate Division, which, in *Canadian Fina Oil Ltd. v Paschke*,[25] stated that, while the phrase conferred the privilege of making payment by mail, nevertheless the payment must *arrive* within the stipulated time.

---

25 [1956] A.J. No. 12, 19 W.W.R. (N.S.) 184 (Alta. S.C.T.D.); affirmed (1957), 21 W.W.R. (N.S.) 260, 7 D.L.R. (2d) 473 (Alta. S.C., App.Div.).

After an interval of nearly fourteen years, this statement was categorized by the Alberta Appellate Division as *obiter dicta* and was not followed. In *Texas Gulf Sulphur Company v Ballem*[26] the court held that the
mailing of a cheque prior to the expiration of the time period was
equivalent to making payment directly to the lessor or to the depository and, so long as the mailing was done by the required date, the
lease would be continued in force. This approach was subsequently
affirmed by the Supreme Court.[27] The same conclusion was reached in
*Paramount Petroleum and Minerals Corporation Ltd. and Bison Petroleum
and Minerals Ltd. v Imperial Oil Ltd.*,[28] where a Saskatchewan court held
the words to mean that mailing by itself constituted compliance with
the payment requirements of the lease.[29]

The doubt that for so many years clouded the effect of mailing led to
an amendment, which provided that a payment that is mailed by
depositing it in a mailbox or post office at least forty-eight hours prior
to the required date shall be deemed to have been received by the
addressee in sufficient time. This rather complex provision cures the
uncertainty that existed after the *Paschke dicta*, but has been rendered
unnecessary by the *Texas Gulf v Ballem* decision.

CAPL 88 and 91 provide that any payment mailed to the lessor shall
be deemed to have been paid four days after being mailed, excluding
Saturdays, Sundays, and holidays.

CAPL 99 provides that payment shall be made on the date of mailing.

---

26 (1969), 70 W.W.R. (N.S.) 373 (Alta. S.C.T.D.); reversed, 72 W.W.R. (N.S.) 273, 17 D.L.R.
   (3d) 572 (Alta. S.C., App.Div.). The trial judge, Riley J, had followed Porter JA's decision (arguably *obiter dicta*) in *Paschke* that the payment must arrive in the stipulated
   time.
27 *Texas Gulf Sulphur Co. v Ballem*, [1971] 1 W.W.R. 560n, 77 D.L.R. (3d) 640n (S.C.C.).
28 73 W.W.R. (N.S.) 417, [1970] S.J. No. 37; supplementary reasons [1970] S.J. No. 87
   (Sask. Q.B.).
29 American authorities hold that "proper mailing" prior to the expiration of the critical
   period is sufficient. Summers, *The Law of Oil and Gas*, vol. 2 (Kansas City, Mo.: Vernon
   Law Book Company, 1954) at para. 344: "An oil and gas lease may provide for the
   payment of delay rentals by the mailing of a cheque, draft or other form of remittance
   to the Lessor. In such a situation the postal service is made the Lessor's agent to
   deliver the remittance, and proper mailing, although it is never delivered, constitutes
   payment."

A much shortened version of the manner of payment clause was at issue in *Paddon Hughes Development Co. Ltd. v Pancontinental Oil Ltd.*[30] This clause simply stated that all payments to the lessor were to be paid at the lessor's address in San Francisco. As originally written the clause contained, *inter alia*, wording to the effect that "payments which are mailed, such payments shall be deemed to be received by the Lessor as of the date of mailing ... " This wording was deleted in the abridged version. In affirming Rooke J's decision, the Alberta Court of Appeal found that the agreement contemplated payment by mail. The notice clause in the lease contained the lessor's zip code, and payment by mail was consistent with commercial reality having regard to the small sums (delay rental in the amount of $53.34) and the distance between the parties. The next question was when was the payment made? The court followed *Texas Gulf Sulphur Co. v Ballem*[31] to hold that the payment was made on the day it was mailed to the lessor.

The question of when the actual mailing took place was also raised in the *Paddon Hughes* case. Contrary to the lessee's normal practice, two rental payments were sent by regular mail. The receipt of the payment in both instances was acknowledged well after both the anniversary date and what would have been the normal transit time between Calgary and the two destinations, Edmonton and San Francisco.

The issue boiled down to a matter of evidence, and the trial judge, after finding that the onus rested on the plaintiff who was attacking the lease (onus in connection with the validity of a lease will be discussed in greater detail in Chapter 19, "Litigating the Oil and Gas Lease"), found that because the lessee was aware of the importance of the leases, and despite the fact that the mailing procedure in the two cases differed from the lessee's normal procedure, the payments had been timely mailed.

The court having been forced to examine external evidence and draw conclusions about the lessee's intentions underlines the importance of sending payments by registered mail.

---

30 33 Alta. L.R. (3d) 7, [1965] 10 W.W.R. 656, [1995] A.J. No. 811 (Alta. Q.B.); affirmed 67 Alta. L.R. (3d) 104, [1995] 5 W.W.R. 726, 223 A.R. 180, [1998] A.J. No. 1120 (Alta. C.A.); [1998] S.C.C.A. No. 600 (leave to appeal dismissed). This case is commented on by Bankes and Quesnel, "Recent Judicial Developments of Interest to Oil and Gas Lawyers" (2000–1) 38 Alta. L. Rev. 320.

31 72 W.W.R. (N.S.) 273, 17 D.L.R. (3d) 572 (Alta. S.C., App.Div.); affirmed [1970] 1 W.W.R. 560n, 17 D.L.R. (3d) 640n (S.C.C.).

Tender Sufficient

In order for a payment to be valid, it is not necessary that it be accepted by the lessor or the depository. It is sufficient if it is tendered, whether mailed or delivered.

Sufficiency of Payment

Payments may be in the form of cheque or draft of the lessee, and such cheque or draft must be payable in Canadian funds at par in the bank on which it is drawn. A post-dated cheque is a "cheque" for the purpose of the lease. It must not be post-dated later than the anniversary date of the lease.[32] Since the courts regard deferment of the drilling commitment by payment of a delay rental to be in the nature of an option, it is imperative that the payment be for not less than the precise amount required. For example, if the bank deducted even a small handling charge, this could jeopardize the payment. An overpayment would be valid, but any short-fall would make the payment ineffective.[33]

The issue of the sufficiency of a payment was raised but not effectively dealt with in *Paramount Petroleum and Mineral Corporation and Bison Petroleum & Minerals Ltd. v Imperial Oil Ltd.*[34] In this case the lessors were residents of the United States and the lessee deducted and withheld the non-resident withholding tax from a payment of the delay rentals. In the result, the sum of money received by the lessor was 15 per cent less than the amount of delay rental specified in the lease.

Unfortunately, from the point of view of clarifying the law, the real attack on the lease was what the plaintiffs conceived to be a late pay-ment of the delay rental. The issue as to the sufficiency of the payment

---

32 *Freyberg v Fletcher Challenge Oil & Gas Inc.*, 323 A.R. 45, [2002] A.J. No. 1173 (Alta. Q.B.).

33 See, generally, discussion in DiCastri, *The Law of Vendor and Purchaser*, vol. 2, 3rd ed. (Toronto: Carswell, 1989) at 616–21; *Mus v Matlashewski* (1944), 52 Man. R. 247, [1944] 3 W.W.R. 358, [1944] 4 D.L.R. 522 (Man. C.A.). The insignificance of the deficiency is immaterial; *Carlson v Jorgenson Logging Company Ltd.* (1952), 6 W.W.R. (N.S.) 298, [1952] 3 D.L.R. 294 (B.C.S.C.); proper payment is a condition precedent to an option. Brown, *The Law of Oil and Gas Leases*, vol. 1, 2nd ed. (New York: Matthew Bender & Co., 1997) at paras. 7.07–7.08, examines the American authorities and concludes that where the failure to make payment of the proper amount is due to the fault of the les-see, "there is a strong probability that the lease will be held to have terminated."

34 73 W.W.R. (N.S.) 417, [1970] S.J. No. 37; supplementary reasons [1970] S.J. No. 87 (Sask. Q.B.).

was not mentioned in the pleadings and was raised for the first time in written argument following the trial. The Saskatchewan trial judge treated the contention as being merely "an afterthought on the part of the plaintiffs," and declined to give effect to it as the defendant had not had the opportunity to meet it with appropriate evidence. The court did not, however, decide on the merits of the argument itself, although Johnson J did indicate that, if pressed, he would have upheld the lease on this point because the lessor had signed partial assignments containing a covenant that the leases still subsisted and gave notice of these assignments to Imperial. This aspect of the case is discussed more fully in Chapter 18, which deals with estoppel.

It would seem arguable that, since the lessee is required by the *Income Tax Act* to make such a withholding, it should not be penalized for complying with the law of the land. Nonetheless, until the matter has been finally resolved by the court of last resort, a lessee would be well advised to make payment in such amount that a non-resident lessor receives not less than the full amount specified in the lease. This, of course, constitutes an overpayment, but the uncertainty of the other course makes it a sensible precaution for the lessee.

The CAPL lease specifically deals with the matter of withholding tax for non-residents by providing that the non-resident lessor agrees that the lessee may deduct income, withholding, or other taxes from any payment to the lessor in compliance with the provisions of the *Income Tax Act*, tax agreements, treaties, or other statutes of Canada or its provinces, and the timely remittance of the balance of the payment shall be deemed to constitute full performance in respect of such payments.

Depository

The manner of payment clause clearly contemplates that the lessor will appoint a depository by filling in the blank. If, however, the lessor refuses to designate a depository, all payments will have to be made to the lessor at the address specified in the notice clause. If the lessor designates a depository then he would appear to have lost the right to require payments to be made to him directly, for he agrees the depository and its successors will continue to be his agent for the receipt of all monies payable under the lease.

The clause limits eligible depositories to banks or trust companies in Canada, but in practice credit unions and treasury branches are frequently named. The lessor may designate a new depository by giving written notice to the lessee. The clause also provides that there shall also be only one depository and that any change in the depository shall not be recognized by the lessee until forty-five days after receipt by it of notice. This is another reflection of the lessee's justifiable anxiety regarding the critical payment of delay rentals. It is an attempt to avoid any confusion and possible error that might occur if a depository were changed near the due date. The lessee is not compelled to wait out the forty-five days before acting on the change of depository; the change may be recognized prior to the expiration of the forty-five-day period.

The lessor can terminate the appointment of a depository but only by designating a new one. If a depository resigns or falls or refuses to act, and the lessor does not designate a replacement within ten days, the lessee has the option to designate a depository. Similarly, if more than one person becomes entitled to payments under the lease and such persons fail to designate one depository, the lessee may do so. A depository, although designated by the lessee, shall nevertheless be entitled to charge the lessor its usual fees.

Depository as Agent

The depository is expressly made the agent of the lessor for the receipt of any and all sums payable under the lease. The agency, however, is confined to the receipt of sums. "It was the duty of the bank merely to receive and deposit, nothing more."[35] For practical purposes, the net effect of this provision seems to be that the lessee could not be held responsible for any delay by the depository in crediting the amounts paid to the lessor's account. For example, if the lessee elected to deliver a payment to the depository on the last day, then such payment would be effective, even if the depository did not actually credit the sums so paid to the lessor until a subsequent date. The question does not arise when the payment is mailed, as that act by itself constitutes payment.

The manner of payment clause in CAPL 88 and 91 works a variation on this by providing that any payment mailed to the lessor or to his depository shall be deemed to have been paid four days (excluding Saturdays, Sundays, and statutory holidays), after deposit in any mail-box or post office. The provision applies to payments made either to

---

35 *Texas Gulf Sulphur Company v Ballem* (1969), 70 W.W.R. (N.S.) 373 (Alta. S.C.T.D.); *Rostad v Andreassen* (1953), 7 W.W.R. (N.S.) 709, [1953] A.J. No. 3 (Alta. S.C.T.D.).

the lessor or to the depository and changes the "postal rule" that mailing amounts to delivery. CAPL 99 specifies the date of mailing.

Notices

The following clause sets forth the procedure for giving notice between the parties: "NOTICES: All notices to be given hereunder may be given by registered letter addressed to the Lessee at _____ and to the Lessor at _____ or such other address as the Lessor and the Lessee may respectively from time to time appoint in writing, and any such notice shall be deemed to be given to and received by the addressee Three (3) days after the mailing thereof, postage prepaid." It requires registered mail, specifies the official address of both parties, and provides for a constructive receipt, since such notice shall be deemed to be given to and received by the addressee three days after the mailing thereof with the proper postage. Many clauses provide for a seven-day period. The device of "deeming," sometimes also used in the manner of payment clause, has certain drawbacks. A question may arise if a notice is actually received prior to the expiration of the specified period, a very likely possibility, as to which date controls, actual or deemed receipt? The point is more than academic since some time periods, such as the grace period for default, commence only from receipt of notice. Furthermore, the "deemed" concept may have the weakness that it can be offset by absolute evidence of no receipt.

The clause refers only to "notices" and makes no mention of payments. Inasmuch as there is a specific clause dealing with payments, it may be sufficiently clear that there are two separate procedures: one for notices and one for payments. However, since both notices and payments are likely to be mailed, a cross-reference excluding any conflict seems desirable as a matter of draftsmanship.

Proving yet again the seemingly endless combinations of facts and circumstances that can arise in connection with the oil and gas lease, this question arose in one of the *Paddon Hughes v Pancontinental* cases.[36] The lessor insisted on the deletion of the wording in the manner of payment clause to remove all references to mailing, so that it read that all payments were to be paid to the lessor at his street address in San

---

36 *Supra* n 30.

Francisco. Since the manner of payment clause did not contain a provision for mailing, could the notices clause be invoked with its deemed receipt after seven days provision?

The problem was that the letter enclosing the cheque was sent by ordinary rather than registered mail. Would this constitute compliance with the notices provision? The trial judge did not deal with this issue, as he found on the evidence that the payments had been mailed on time. The appeal court, in a majority decision, upheld this finding on the ground that a Court of Appeal must not interfere with a trial judge's conclusions on matters of facts unless there is a palpable or overriding error.[37] The adoption of that strict standard of review can have the effect, in many cases, of turning the trial court into the court of last resort.

The notices clause in the conventional lease refers only to mailing. Today, of course, communication by e-mail or fax is the rule rather than the exception. This could cause complications because of the general rule that where there is instantaneous communication between principals the contract is made when the acceptance is received.[38] To be safe, notices should always be sent by mail in a timely fashion.

The notices clause in the CAPL lease expressly deals with the points discussed above. It provides that all notices and communications shall be in writing. Notices may be served personally by delivering them during normal business hours. They may also be served by telegraph or telecommunication or by any other method by which written and recorded messages may be sent, and the notice shall be deemed to be received when actually received by a party if received within normal working hours, or at the commencement of the next business day following the transmission thereof, whichever is the earlier, or by mailing them first class. Notices that are mailed shall be deemed to be received at noon, local time, on the earlier of the actual date of receipt or the fourth day – the tenth day in the case of CAPL 99 – (excluding Saturdays, Sundays, or statutory holidays) after the mailing thereof. In CAPL 88 and 91, any possible conflict between the notices and the manner of payment clauses is avoided by providing that nothing in the notices clause shall affect the method of the payment of monies as set out in the lease.

---

37 *Supra* n 31.
38 *Brinkibon Ltd. v StahagStahl m.b.H.*, [1983] 2 A.C. 34 (H.L.).

Personal Information

Increasing concern over the dissemination of personal information has led many lessees, both oil companies and land agents, to address the matter and obtain the consent of the lessor and impose limits on the use thereof. This is done by adding a schedule along the following lines:

Schedule ( )

Attached to and forming part of a Petroleum and Natural Gas Lease and Grant dated the _____ day of _____, _____.

PERSONAL INFORMATION CONSENT

By providing personal information to the Lessee, the Lessor consents to the Lessee's collection, use, retention and disclosure of that information for any and all purposes and uses as permitted or contemplated under the above-described Lease and as needed to comply with any legal requirements. The Lessee may retain this information so long as is reasonable to fulfill those purposes.

_____
Lessor

Entire Agreement

The lease attempts to confine the parties to the four corners of the document itself. "ENTIRE AGREEMENT: The terms of this Lease express and constitute the entire agreement between the parties, and no implied covenant or liability of any kind is created or shall arise by reason of these presents or anything herein contained." It has long been recognized, however, that an exclusionary clause cannot operate unless the contract itself has actual vitality. For example, this clause would not apply if the lease were executed on the condition that it was not to be effective until a certain event had occurred and that condition had not been fulfilled. In *California Standard Co. v Chiswell*[39] a petroleum and natural gas lease including such a clause was executed by both parties. Immediately afterwards the parties signed another agreement, which recited that the bonus consideration under the lease was to be made

---

39 (1955), 14 W.W.R. (N.S.) 456, [1955] 5 D.L.R. 119 (Alta. S.C.T.D.).

upon the successful completion of foreclosure proceedings now pending under an agreement for sale. The lessors were in fact the vendors under an agreement for sale which was then in default. An action for foreclosure was launched against the purchaser, but this action was settled. The entire agreement clause was held to be ineffective to exclude the collateral agreement between the parties that made the lease conditional upon the successful completion of foreclosure proceedings. The court quoted *Molsons Bank v Cranston*:[40] "There is a plain answer to this contention. It is that the clause relied on is not binding on any one unless and until the document itself becomes operative. The rule against contradicting a written document applies, of course, only to an agreement which has actual vitality, and not to one which is in a state of suspended animation, ineffective and undelivered. No such rule of evidence can be set up until the legal relation of the parties has been established; and if the condition relied on is unfulfilled, the whole agreement fails." Consequently, the clause could not exclude a collateral agreement that constitutes a condition precedent to the very existence of the lease itself.

Parol evidence has been allowed where the collateral agreement neither adds to nor varies the written agreement, but deals with a matter truly collateral to it. In *California Standard Co. v McBride*,[41] an oil and gas lease provided that time was of the essence and also contained a warranty of title. There was in fact a defect in title. The parties signed a collateral receipt acknowledging payment of a deposit with the payment of the balance subject to the company's solicitors being satisfied as to title. This was admissible since it dealt with the consideration for entering the lease, which was a collateral matter. The Appellate Division also said the fact that the matter could properly have been included in the main agreement did not render the collateral agreement inadmissible.

In *Paddon Hughes Development Co. Ltd. v Pancontintental Oil Ltd.*[42] O'Leary JA interpreted the "entire agreement" clause as being designed to prevent any terms being added to the lease by one party later claiming that there were additional terms agreed to but not reduced to writing. He went on to state, however, that it cannot prevent the court from asking what words in the lease actually mean. That is simply a matter of interpreting the term that is already part of the written agreement.

In his dissenting judgment, Côté J held that the "entire agreement" clause excludes implied terms from the contract. He was unable to find

---

40 44 O.L.R. 58, 45 D.L.R. 316, [1918] O.J. No. 9 (Ont. C.A.).
41 *California Standard Co. v McBride* (1963), 38 D.L.R. (2d) 606 (Alta. S.C., App.Div.).
42 *Supra* n 30.

a distinction between implying a term and interpreting a contract to find a term that is not express.

In addition to negating any implied covenant, the CAPL entire agreement clause provides that "this lease supersedes and replaces all previous oral or written agreements, memoranda, correspondence or other communications between the parties relating to the subject matter hereof."

This provision, of course, will only take effect when and if the lease itself came into force. Nor would it exclude any matter that was truly collateral to the lease, as in *California Standard Co. v McBride*.

Conservation and Other Applicable Legislation

Nor can the entire agreement clause exclude the effect of conservation legislation. Indeed, such legislation expressly overrides the provisions of any lease, in the event of a conflict.[43] In view of the express application and overriding effect of conservation legislation on the relationship between the parties to an oil and gas lease, the statement that the lease itself constitutes the entire agreement between the parties has been categorized as misleading.[44] It would be more accurate if the lease contained an express acknowledgment that it could be subject to, and its terms varied by, applicable legislation. As now written, it could mislead a lessor who could not be expected to be alive to the scope and application of conservation legislation and regulations.

This result is achieved in the entire agreement clause in the CAPL lease, which provides "the parties recognize that the terms of this Lease may be modified or affected by statute, regulation, order or directive of any government or governmental agency."

---

43 See, for example, *Oil and Gas Conservation Act*, R.S.A. 2000, c O-6, s 3, which provides that the Act applies to every well in Alberta and to any product obtained or obtainable therefrom, notwithstanding any terms to the contrary in any lease of grant from the Crown or from any other person; s 9, which provides that any terms or conditions to a contract or other arrangement that conflict with the Act, the regulations, an order of the Board, an order of the Public Utilities Board or an order of the Gas Utilities Board, are unenforceable, and do not give rise to any cause of action by any party against any other party to the contract. There are also other provisions, notably those dealing with pooling, ss 80–90, which may materially vary the express terms of the lease.

44 Dea, "A Look at the Lease from the Lessor's Point of View" (1965) 4 Alta. L. Rev. 208. The author describes circumstances under which a misunderstanding on the part of the lessor as to the application of conservation legislation to his arrangement with the lessee could lead to a severe deterioration in the lessor-lessee relationship.

The entire agreement clause is buttressed by the provision that the lease can only be amended in writing. Time is also to be of the essence.

Implied Terms

There are circumstances where it could be to the advantage of one of the parties, sometimes the lessee, other times the lessor, to supplement the terms of the lease with provisions not to be found in the document itself. Most situations will be covered by the express terms of the lease, but, for example, the covenant to market the leased substances, or to continue developing the property after a lease is being maintained by production, are not. Insofar as the oil and gas lease is concerned, however, it seems safe to say that implied terms are a non-starter.

In *Freyberg v Fletcher Challenge Oil & Gas Inc.*[45] one of the arguments advanced by the defendant lessee was that there was an implied term of the lease to produce the gas in the secondary term, if not excused by the lack of a suitable market. If there was such an obligation, the default clause would be engaged, and since there was a well on the lands, the lease would be maintained and the lessor's remedy would be limited to damages. Romaine J accepted this argument and held that the default clause operated to maintain the lease in force.

On appeal,[46] it was held that the trial judge's implied term constituted an error in law.[47] She also erred in finding that "different equities" applied in the secondary term. Ritter JA cited a long line of familiar Canadian decisions holding that a lease will terminate when the lessee does not perform "in the sense of drilling, paying or producing, and any term is dependant [*sic*] on such performance."[48] The appeal court found that there was no need for an implied term. There being no obligation to market, the default clause could not operate to maintain the leases.

While it still could be argued that the appeal court decision does not completely preclude implied terms, its interpretation of the lease, buttressed by a long line of judicial authorities, would seem to rule that out for all practical purposes.

There is also the entire agreement clause, which expressly excludes implied covenants.

---

45 323 A.R. 45, [2002] A.J. No. 1173 (Alta. Q.B.).
46 42 Alta. L.R. (4th) 41, [2005] 10 W.W.R. 87, 363 A.R. 35, [2005] A.J. No. 108 (Alta. C.A.).
47 Ibid. A.R. at 50.
48 Ibid.

12 Other Versions of the Clauses and Additional Provisions

In addition to the variations that were mentioned in the discussion of the typical clauses, there are numerous other versions found in conventional leases that should be looked at, as well as additional terms not ordinarily found in the lease. Many of these provisions date back to the early forms of the lease and have long since fallen by the wayside. This does not mean they can be ignored, however. Under the right conditions, leases can display remarkable longevity, and the parties, and on occasion, the courts, can be called upon to deal with their provisions, no matter how antiquated they may be. The contents of this chapter do not apply to the CAPL lease, as all its terms are uniform and have been discussed in previous chapters.

Definition of Operations

As will be seen in the discussion under "Involuntary Termination," much difficulty has been occasioned by what constitutes "drilling" and other operations that may be carried out on the lands. The following definition of "operations" goes a long way towards solving this problem, although the second reference to "operations" seems to be circular and the meaning would be improved by the substitution of "any act." "Whenever used in this lease, the word 'operations' shall mean any of the following: drilling, testing, completing, reworking, recompleting, deepening, plugging back or repairing of a well in search for or in an endeavor to obtain or increase production of the leased substances or any of them, excavating a mine, production of the leased substances or any of them (whether or not in paying quantities), or operations for or incidental to any of the foregoing."

Where coalbed methane is the primary or potential target it is customary to include a specific reference to dewatering in the definition of "operations." With the exception of the wet Mannville formation, water in the host coal seams in western Canada has not been the huge problem it is in the United States. Nonetheless, where CBM is involved, the definition of "operations" will include something along the following lines:

> The extraction of water and substances produced in association therewith in an endeavor to obtain, maintain or increase production of any leased substances from the said lands, the pooled lands or unitized lands.

Or

> Operations relating to the dewatering of any coal strata, coal seams, coal beds or carbonaceous shales underlying the Leased Lands or any lands pooled or unitized therewith.

Even where specific provisions such as the above are not to be found in the lease, it would seem that the removal of water would be included as operations to obtain production. The express language puts the matter to rest.

The second step is to link the continuance of the lease to "operations." In *Canadian Superior Oil Ltd. v Crozet Exploration Ltd.*[1] the clause successfully maintained a lease in force even though by the critical date there had been no actual breaking of the ground by a drill bit.

Third Proviso to the *Habendum* and Obligation to Market

As was illustrated in the *Kissinger* decision,[2] the conventional version of the third proviso is ambiguous and difficult to construe. The language of the following version is coherent and, while preserving the lease for the lessee, imposes some obligation on the lessee to seek a market for the leased substances from the shut-in wells.

---

1 (1982), 18 Alta. L.R. (2d) 145, 133 D.L.R. (3d) 53, 34 A.R. 256, [1982] A.J. No. 672 (Alta. Q.B.). This case is discussed in detail in Chapter 14, in the section "Operator's Good Faith."

2 (1984), 33 Alta. L.R. (2d) 1, [1984] 5 W.W.R. 673, 13 D.L.R. (4th) 542, [1984] A.J. No. 2587 (Alta. C.A.); affirming 26 Alta. L.R. (2d) 378, 14 E.T.R. 207, 45 A.R. 393, [1983] A.J. No. 814 (Alta. Q.B.).

That if, at the expiration of the primary term or at any time or times thereafter, there is any well on the said lands, or on lands with which the said lands or any portion thereof have been pooled, capable of producing the leased substances or any of them, and all such wells are shut in, this lease shall, nevertheless, continue in force as though operations were being conducted on the said lands, for so long as the said wells are shut in. If no royalties are otherwise payable hereunder during a lease year within which such shut-in period or periods occur and during such lease year no operations are conducted on the said lands, then, at the end of such lease year the Lessee shall pay to the Lessor as royalty, an amount equal to the annual acreage rental hereinabove specified. The Lessee covenants and agrees to use reasonable diligence to produce and either utilize or market the leased substances capable of being produced from the said wells, but in the exercise of such diligence the Lessee shall not be obligated to install or furnish facilities other than well facilities and ordinary lease facilities of flow lines, separator and lease tank.

This version of the third proviso makes it clear that the presence of a shut-in well will continue the lease in force without limit as to time. If no royalties are payable during a given year and no operations are conducted on the lands in that year, the lessee shall pay the annual acreage rental. The *Durish* case[3] tells us that despite the use of "shall," making the shut-in payment is an option, not an obligation, on the part of the lessee and does not activate the default clause. The provision is notable in that it specifically recognizes an obligation on the part of the lessee to do something about marketing when the lease is beyond the primary term. The obligation is to "use reasonable diligence," which undoubtedly would be the test applied by the courts if an obligation to market were ever to be implied. The lessee's obligation to invest in plant and equipment as a result of its undertaking to market is limited to conventional well site facilities.

The limitation of the obligation to the circumstances where the term is prolonged by a shut-in well makes it much more restrictive than the covenant to market implied by the American courts, which hold that the implied covenants come into operation within a reasonable period after discovery of the substances. Certainly the wider obligation would be preferable from the lessor's point of view, as he will be anxious to

---

3 (1987), 55 Alta. L.R. (2d) 47, [1987] A.J. No. 804 (Alta. Q.B.); affirmed (1988), 63 Alta. L.R. (2d) 265, [1988] A.J. No. 1162 (Alta. C.A.).

obtain royalty revenue at the earliest possible moment. The lessee's failure to market becomes particularly galling to the lessor, however, when the primary term has expired and the lease is being maintained by a small annual payment. The above clause is a recognition of that concern.

Pooling by Formation

The standard pooling arrangement has the effect of maintaining the lease in force for all the lands covered by the lease so long as there is production from the pooled area, including zones and formations other than those from which the production is being taken. A persuasive argument can be made that the mineral owner should be entitled to have the non-producing (actual or constructive) formations returned to him after the expiry of the primary term. The following clause achieves that result. It should be noted that the lessee is not required to surrender his interest until after the end of the primary term, and only if there is not a well capable of producing on the leased lands.

> POOLING: Upon written notice to the Lessor, the Lessee may at any time and from time to time pool such geological formation or formations of the demised estate as may be necessary to form a spacing unit with other lands adjoining the said lands. In the event of such pooling, the production of the leased substances from the portion of the demised estate placed in such spacing unit shall be deemed to be that proportion of the total production from the spacing unit which the area of the said lands bears to the total area of the lands in such spacing unit, and the Lessor shall receive royalties on such proportion of total production. Drilling for, or production of, or the presence of a well capable of production in paying quantities of, any of the leased substances from any geological formation or formations included in such spacing unit shall have the same effect in continuing this Lease in force during the term of this Lease as to all the demised estate as if such drilling was on the said lands, such production was from the demised estate or such well capable of production in paying quantities was on the said lands; provided however that if at the expiration of the primary term none of the leased substances is being produced or is capable of production in paying quantities from the demised estate, from a well on the said lands, this Lease shall thereupon terminate except as to the geological formation or formations included in such spacing unit.

This is a forerunner of the deep rights reversion clause. It goes further than the typical reversion clause because the lessee retains only the formation that has been pooled.

De-Pooling

At least one form of lease wrestles with the problem of dismantling a pool once the pooling power under the lease has been exercised. The language is as follows: "The Lessee may dissolve any unit established hereunder by giving to the Lessor written notice thereof if at that time no operations are being conducted in the unit for unitized leased substances. Subject to the provisions of this clause, a unit once established hereunder shall remain in force so long as any lease subject thereto shall remain in force." Although the reference is to "unit," earlier references in the pooling clause established that a unit in this context means nothing more than that area allocated to one well for the purposes of production of the leased substances. This is the classic limitation on the pooling power and makes it clear that "unitization" in the sense discussed in Chapter 10, *ante*, is not involved. The power to de-pool can be used only when there are no operations under way. It could not, for example, be invoked if the well on the spacing unit was in actual production or was being reworked, drilled, or deepened. The language of this restriction is directed to physical operations and would not seem to apply to a constructive "deeming" of operations pursuant to the suspended well clause.

De-pooling could result in termination of the lease if it were to be done after the expiration of the primary term and with no well on the lands covered by the lease. The lessee would be aware of this consequence and most likely would de-pool only where there was a well on the lands.

It goes without saying that the provision could have no application to a compulsory pool formed by board order under conservation legislation. A pooling order could only be amended or rescinded upon application to the appropriate provincial board.

Gas Well Royalty – Ontario Form

A form of lease that is frequently encountered in the province of Ontario has unusual features with respect to the payment of royalty for gas wells.

GAS WELLS

There is hereby excepted and reserved unto the Lessor a royalty in respect of each gas well completed on the said lands and which is capable of producing gas in paying quantities, computed as follows:

WHEN A WELL IS CAPABLE OF PRODUCING AN AMOUNT EQUAL TO OR IN EXCESS OF	BUT LESS THAN	AMOUNT
10 cubic feet per day	500,000 cubic feet per day	$100
500,000 cubic feet per day	1,000,000 cubic feet per day	$150
1,000,000 cubic feet per day	2,500,000 cubic feet per day	$250
2,500,000 cubic feet per day	5,000,000 cubic feet per day	$350
5,000,000 cubic feet per day		$500

The aforesaid royalty shall be computed in advance each year from the time each such gas well shall have been completed. The first payment for each gas well shall be based on its open flow measurement at the time of completion, and said payment for the period between the time of completion and the 30th day of September next ensuing shall be calculated at the rates above set forth and shall be paid as soon as may be practicable. Subsequent payments for each such well shall be paid in advance on or before the 25th day of October in each year and shall be based on the last open flow measurement of such well taken by the Lessee. While the said royalty is so paid it shall be deemed that each such well is a producing well hereunder and that the leased substances are being produced from the said lands.

The clause contemplates the payment of a royalty from the time the gas well has been completed. Therefore, the royalty does not depend upon production and sale of the substances. The amount of the payment is based upon the capability of the well to produce and increases along with the potential daily volume. The specified annual amounts would be nominal in comparison to what the lessor would receive for a true royalty for gas actually being sold in the stated volumes. There is also the familiar provision that payment of the royalty amounts to production of the substances for the purposes of the lease.

The operation of this royalty clause can be understood only against the background that the lessee, prior to commencing production of a gas reservoir or pool, will enter into another agreement known as the Unit Operation Agreement, which, *inter alia*, replaces the gas royalty payable under the lease with one specified in the Agreement. Seen in this light, the gas royalty under the lease becomes the equivalent of a suspended gas well payment, which, instead of being at a flat rate as in western forms, is adjusted in accordance with the potential of the well. It should be noted, however, that the small royalties specified under the clause in the lease represent the only gas well royalties due to the lessor unless and until he enters into a Unit Operation Agreement.

Additional Clauses

Some leases touch upon matters not dealt with by the express terms of the usual clauses in conventional leases.

Use of Gas by Lessor

Astonishingly, some leases still grant the lessor the right to use gas for domestic purposes. The clause usually takes this form:

> If as a result of drilling operations of the Lessee on the said lands natural gas is produced which is not needed for the operations hereunder, which is surplus to any amounts which the Lessee may have committed to deliver under contract, and which is safe and suitable for domestic use as produced, the Lessee shall supply on the demand of and at the sole risk of the Lessor, free of charge, and not subject to the accounting of royalty by the Lessee, such surplus natural gas to the Lessor for domestic use only in his principal dwelling only on the said lands, and all necessary installations of the supply of the said gas shall be made by the Lessee at the sole risk and expense of the Lessor.

The conditions under which the lessor can call upon the lessee for a supply of free gas are very specific. The drilling that produces the natural gas must take place on the leased lands; the gas must be surplus to the operations carried on under the lease (which means gas over and above that required for fuel and other operating purposes); and it must be surplus to any amounts that the lessee may have committed to deliver under contract – i.e., the well or wells must be capable of delivering volumes of gas in excess of that sold by the lessee under contract; the gas by itself must be safe and suitable for domestic use as produced, which means that it does not require special processing. If all these conditions are met, then the lessee is required to supply natural gas for domestic use only in the lessor's principal dwelling, which must be located on the said lands. The lessee will make the necessary installations but at the sole risk and expense of the lessor.

Although this clause, or variations thereof, is found in many earlier leases, the right of the lessor has been invoked very occasionally. There are a number of reasons for this. Gas is a volatile explosive substance not designed to be handled by amateurs or by makeshift arrangements. Very often it will contain poisonous impurities such as hydrogen sulphide and carbon dioxide, which make it unsuitable for any use until it has been processed. In many instances it arrives at the surface under pressures impossibly high for domestic purposes. The clause is very specific that, while the lessee may install the equipment necessary for the supply of the gas, it is at the sole risk and expense of the lessor.[4] Furthermore, the use to which the lessor may put the gas is severely restricted. He can use it only for domestic purposes in his principal dwelling. There is no Canadian authority on the scope of this description, although there has been much litigation on the point in the United States. Brown lists the various interpretations that have been placed on this and similar phrases by American courts.[5] For example, the reference to a "dwelling house," which is not dissimilar to "principal dwelling," has been held to include "the cluster of buildings in which a man with his family resides and extends to such outbuildings as are within the curtilage."[6] Thus, a Canadian court might be invited to include a garage and any outbuildings that contain, for example, boilers and other heating apparatus for the home.

The only Canadian authority to date involved the interpretation of a clause, found in a memorandum of agreement, not a lease, whereunder the defendant obligated itself to supply gas "for domestic and farm purposes."[7] The defendant had neglected to determine how much gas the plaintiff was using for these purposes before entering into the undertaking. It turned out that the plaintiff's consumption was

---

4 The very concept of this clause would seem to offend against the spirit if not the letter of legislation such as the Alberta *Gas Utilities Act*, R.S.A. 2000, c G-5, for the safe construction and operation of gas distributing systems.

5 Brown, *The Law of Oil and Gas Leases*, vol. 2, 2nd ed. (New York: Matthew Bender & Co., 1997) at 10.10–10.11.

6 *United Carbon Co. v Conn*, 351 S.W. (2d) 189 (1961, Kentucky C.A.).

7 *Smith v Inland Gas & Oil Ltd. and Wainwright Gas Co. Ltd.* (1955), 14 W.W.R. (N.S.) 558 (Alta. S.C.T.D.).

remarkable since, in addition to the household requirements, she had gone into the business of hog raising on a substantial scale and, for that purpose, cooked large quantities of hog food in a gas-heated steam boiler located in one of the farm buildings adjoining the house. The court held that, since the plaintiff's farm operations were of this nature at the time the agreement was entered into, the defendant had obligated itself to supply natural gas for all the farming operations including the steam boiler. Practically every clause to be found in later leases circumvents this difficulty and limits the use of gas to domestic purposes in the principal dwelling on the said lands.

It is suggested that this clause is not appropriate to modern conditions and its use should be discontinued. It is a very limited benefit to the lessor since both the purpose for which free gas may be demanded and the conditions under which the demand may be made are limited. Nonetheless, it can be the subject of irritation between lessor and lessee and is an open invitation to install facilities that are hazardous and unsupervised. It may have had some utility in the past when domestic fuel was both difficult and costly to obtain in remote areas. Today, however, with widespread gas distribution systems and the extensive use of propane as a farm fuel, even this justification has largely disappeared.

Force Majeure

The phrase *force majeure* means a superior, irresistible force. In the context of contractual relations, it refers to intervening changes in circumstances that render it impossible for a party to perform his obligations. Virtually every lease contains some reference to *force majeure*; the conventional lease refers to it only in the context of an interruption or suspension of drilling, working operations, or production of the leased substances after the expiration of the primary term. The third proviso to the *habendum* clause provides that, if such interruptions or suspensions are the result of a cause beyond the lessee's reasonable control, then "the time of such interruption or suspension or non-production shall not be counted against the lessee." Many leases contain a more extensive application of *force majeure* in a separate clause.

FORCE MAJEURE
The performance of any of the obligations of the Lessee hereunder shall, notwithstanding anything contained in this Lease to the contrary, be suspended while and so long as the Lessee is prevented from complying with

such obligations in part or in whole, by strikes, lockouts, acts of God, severe weather conditions and/or action of the elements, accidents, laws, rules and regulations of any governmental bodies or agencies, zoning or land use ordinances of any governmental agency, acts or requests of any governmental officer or agent purporting to act under authority, delays in transportation, inability to obtain necessary materials in the open market, inadequate facilities for the transportation of materials or for the disposition of production, or other matters beyond the reasonable control of the Lessee whether similar to the matters herein specifically enumerated or not, or while legal action contesting the Lessor's title to said lands or the Lessee's right in said lands by virtue hereof shall be pending final adjudication in a court assuming jurisdiction thereof. Time consumed in cleaning, repairing, deepening, or improving any producing well or its necessary appurtenances shall not be deemed or construed as an interruption or discontinuance of the Lessee's operations under this Lease. The Lessee need not perform any requirement hereunder, the performance of which would violate any reasonable conservation and/or curtailment program or plan of orderly development to which the Lessee may voluntarily or by order of any governmental agency subscribe or observe.

There are several points to note in the foregoing clause. It refers only to the lessee's obligations. Admittedly the lessor's positive obligations – apart from the grant itself – are modest, being confined to paying taxes and executing such further documents as may be necessary to give effect to the lease. The obligation of the lessee is merely suspended; the lease is not terminated. There is a lengthy catalogue of specific events of *force majeure*, including many references to the acts of governmental agencies. The list is not exhaustive; there is an omnibus reference to "other matters beyond the reasonable control of the Lessee." The insertion of "reasonable" is an attempt to extend the application of the clause. There are matters that obviously could be remedied if cost were no object, but where no reasonable or prudent operator would incur the extra cost. In addition, the clause contains some features particular to petroleum situations. If the lessee cleans, repairs, or performs work on a well, such time shall not be deemed an interruption under the lease. This concept appears out of place in a *force majeure* clause; it is designed mainly to ensure that an interruption of production for any of the listed reasons will not terminate the lease. It is akin to the third proviso of the *habendum* and, as a matter of arrangement, seems more appropriate to those provisions that deal with the term of the lease and its continuance.

There is also a specific reference to conservation programs and development plans, whether voluntary or compulsory. The lessee is excused from performing any requirement of the lease if the performance would violate such programs or plans. The precise scope of this qualification is hard to determine; certainly it attempts to go further than the usual concept that observance of the applicable legislation cannot be a breach of contract. Here the clause also includes programs voluntarily initiated.

The unique importance of litigation over the lease is recognized by the inclusion of legal action over the lessor's title or the status of the lease as an act of *force majeure*. While the existence of litigation suspends performance of obligations by the lessee, it does not expressly extend the term of the lease should the primary term expire before the litigation has been resolved.

Ironically, the clause is totally ineffective in those areas where the risk of losing the lease is highest. Most of the circumstances that give rise to an involuntary termination of the lease have been characterized by the courts as options on the part of the lessee and not obligations. Hence, the *force majeure* clause is ineffective to prevent the termination of a lease by reason of the lessee's failure to drill, pay delay rental, or produce. Martland J, referring to an argument based upon a *force majeure* provision, said: "The answer to this argument is that, while the clause postpones obligations, in certain events, it does not purport to modify the provisions of the *habendum* clause. That clause imposes no obligation upon the appellant to produce oil, gas or other mineral from the Northwest Quarter. It only provided that the primary term could be extended if oil, gas or other mineral was produced. If none of these substances were produced within the primary term, the lease terminated at the expiration of that term."[8] While the clause cannot protect the lessee against the major hazards to be found in a lease, it does have a definite area of operation. If a lessor has given a default notice regarding an undoubted obligation, such as an offset well, the clause can prevent the period of grace from expiring – and with it the lease – if the delay in remedying the default is occasioned by an act of *force majeure*.

The courts can be expected to construe the language strictly and to be cautious in holding that a particular set of facts represents a cause

---

8 *Canadian Superior Oil of Calif. Ltd. v Kanstrup*, [1965] S.C.R. 92, 49 W.W.R. 257, 47 D.L.R. (2d) 1, [1964] S.C.J. No. 54 (S.C.C.).

beyond the lessee's reasonable control. The decision of the Alberta Appellate Division in *Canada-Cities Service Petroleum Corporation v Kininmonth*[9] is a good illustration of this approach. The *force majeure* language was contained in that proviso to the *habendum* clause dealing with interruption or suspension of drilling, working, or production of operations. For purposes of discussion, the court treated the proviso as though it applied to the facts of the case. The well had been commenced towards the end of the primary term in the spring of the year when the break-up of winter conditions annually required municipal authorities to impose bans on the travel of heavy equipment over certain secondary roads. In order to test and complete the well the lessee required heavy fracturing equipment, which could not be moved over the roads during the prohibited period. Before the road ban was lifted, the primary term expired. The court was of the opinion that the imposition of the road ban was not a cause beyond the lessee's control. There were several grounds cited for this view: that the particular road ban in question was invalid as it did not comply with the enabling legislation (although it is hard to see just why a lessee should be required to make a determination as to whether municipal resolution had been validly enacted); that the lessee might have applied for and obtained a permit to move the equipment over the municipal roads; that the annual imposition of road bans is of such a common occurrence that the lessee could and should have anticipated it and stockpiled the necessary equipment on the well site.

All this indicates that the lessee must discharge a very heavy onus before *force majeure* comes into play. In *Kininmonth* the proviso referred to "beyond the lessee's control." Query, whether "lessee's reasonable control" reduces the onus.

Compliance with Laws

"Laws, rules and regulations" are included among the events listed in the *force majeure* clause. Occasionally a lease will go into greater detail.

> Compliance with any now or hereafter existing act, bill or statute purporting to be enacted by Parliament of Canada, or Legislature of the Province

---

9 (1963) 44 W.W.R. (Alta. S.C., App.Div.) 392; the Supreme Court of Canada did not deal with this precise point since they held that the clause in which the *force majeure* language was embodied did not apply to the facts of the case as it was confined to production ceasing after the expiration of the primary term; [1964] S.C.R. 439, 47 W.W.R. (N.S.) 437, 45 D.L.R. (2d) 36, [1964] S.C.J. No. 24 (S.C.C.).

of _____ or any other law-making body, or with orders, judgments, decrees, rules, regulations made or promulgated by Parliament of Canada or Legislature of the Province of _____ or any other law-making body, boards, commissions or committees purporting to be made under authority of any such act, bill or statute, shall not constitute a violation of any of the terms of this lease or be considered a breach of any clause, obligation, covenant, undertaking, condition or stipulation contained herein, nor shall it be or constitute a cause for the termination, forfeiture, revision or revesting of any estate or interest herein and hereby created and set out, nor shall any such compliance confer any right of entry or become the basis of any action for damages or suit for the forfeiture or cancellation hereof, and while any such purport to be in force and effect they shall, when complied with by the Lessee or its assigns, to the extent of such compliance, operate as modifications of the terms and conditions of this Lease where inconsistent therewith.

Basically, clauses of this type reflect what would appear to be the situation in any event; the parties to a contract remain subject to the applicable legislation and regulations regardless of what may or may not be contained in the contract itself.

Like the *force majeure* provision, the clause will afford only scant protection against termination of the lessee's estate. Canadian courts can be expected to follow the traditional approach that the lease will be terminated by a choice or option of the lessee, and not a failure to fulfil an obligation or the exigencies of a law or regulation. The foregoing clause attempts to deal directly with the question of forfeiture and termination in the following phrase: "nor shall it be or constitute a cause for the termination, forfeiture, revision or revesting of any estate or interest herein." If the *Kininmonth* rationale is followed, one would expect the courts to give this provision a very limited scope on the basis that it was not the compliance with any "act, bill or statute" that caused the termination, but rather the choice or election of the lessee not to do that which would have been required to keep the lease in force, i.e., commence drilling, make timely payment, or put a well on production.

In any event, it would appear that only a positive, affirmative requirement by statute, regulation, or order would engage the protection of the clause. In *Shell Oil v Gibbard*[10] the fact that the Conservation

---

10 [1961] S.C.R. 725, 36 W.W.R. (N.S.) 529, 30 D.L.R. (2d) 386, [1961] S.C.J. No. 51 (S.C.C.).

Board required that a section of land be pooled to form a spacing unit before it would grant a permit to produce gas was held not sufficient to meet the test "necessary in order to conform with any regulations or orders of the Government of the Province of Alberta or any other authoritative body." The Supreme Court made it plain that only an affirmative stipulation that the lands must be pooled would meet the test.

Non-Forfeiture

Occasionally a lessee, possibly driven beyond endurance by the judicial hazards to the lease, will insert this type of clause: "This lease shall not be forfeited or cancelled for failure to perform in whole or in part any of its covenants, conditions or stipulations until it shall have first been finally judicially determined that such failure exists, and after such final determination, the Lessee is given a reasonable time therefrom to comply with any such covenants, conditions or stipulations." The purpose of the clause is abundantly clear. It is to afford the lessee complete protection against involuntary termination of the lease, regardless of circumstances. While such a clause has never been interpreted by Canadian courts, it is unlikely to be of much benefit to a lessee. It would be dismissed on the familiar basis that termination of the lease does not constitute a forfeiture and that those requirements which cause the lease to terminate prematurely are not "covenants, conditions or stipulations," but are options or elections on the part of the lessee.

Perpetual Renewal

Some leases contain a provision that, at the option of the lessee, can tie up a lessor's lands virtually forever.

> Always provided that on the expiration of the primary term hereof, if the leased substances or any of them are not then being produced from the said lands, the Lessee shall have and is hereby granted the sole and exclusive option to renew the within Lease for a further primary term of Ten (10) years to commence as of the date of termination of the within Lease, subject to the same terms, covenants and conditions as are herein contained including this covenant for renewal. This option shall be open for acceptance for a period of Thirty (30) days immediately following the

expiration of the primary term hereof, and may be exercised by notice in writing to the Lessor given in the manner herein specified, accompanied by the Lessee's cheque for the same amount as the cash consideration for this Lease.

The unrestricted right to renew, which is tucked away as a proviso to the surrender clause, is an ingenious attempt by the lessee to avoid termination at the end of the primary term, even in the absence of any production, actual or constructive. The right can be exercised even if there has been no drilling whatsoever on the lands during the entire primary term. In fact, this is the most likely circumstance under which the right to renew would be exercised, as it is unlikely that a lessee would desire to renew a lease over lands that had been disproved by a dry hole. The lessee has thirty days after the end of the primary term to exercise the right of renewal, and the bonus consideration is the same as the original payment given as consideration for the lease. Inasmuch as cash considerations for leases have increased substantially over the years, such a payment usually means a very poor bargain from the lessor's point of view.

The right conferred on the lessee to perpetually renew the lease without exploring the potential of the lands is, of course, extremely unfavourable to the lessor.

Automatic Termination

At the other end of the spectrum is a provision that results in termination of a lease after a period of consecutive non-production. It fits comfortably and logically in the suspended well clause and reads as follows:

( ) notwithstanding clause ( ), if at any time after the primary term, there are three consecutive lease years during which all wells on the said lands, the pooled lands, and the unitized lands, produce no leased substances, this Lease shall terminate at the end of the third such lease year as though the Lessee had given written notice to the Lessor surrendering the Lease pursuant to paragraph ( ).

This provision, which protects the mineral owner from having a non-producing lease continued in force indefinitely by shut-in well payments, is very much in the best interest of the lessor.

Use of Water

Underground Water

A number of leases, even though water is not included in the description of the substances under the granting clause, provide in the royalty clause that the lessee may have the use of water free of royalty. "Notwithstanding anything to the contrary herein contained or implied the Lessee, in its operations hereunder, shall have the use, free from royalty, of water, other than water from the Lessor's water wells or from the Lessor's artificial surface reservoirs, and of gas produced from the said lands."

The right to use water, somewhat misleadingly placed in the royalty clause, can be very significant in view of the enormous volumes that may be required for water injection schemes. The power to use water is limited to operations under the lease, and expressly excepts water wells and surface reservoirs used by the lessor. This exception makes it clear that the lessee does not have the right to utilize the lessor's domestic water supply and that the provision is obviously designed with deeper water rights in mind. The restriction to "operations hereunder" prohibits the lessee from transporting water for injection in a water-flood scheme being conducted on other lands. One may speculate that the true intent was only to enable the lessee to use water free of royalty for routine operations such as boilers, mud pits, and engine coolants, similar to the manner in which gas may be used for fuel. There appears, however, to be nothing to prevent the lessee from utilizing huge volumes of underground water for secondary recovery so long as the injection is performed on lands covered by the lease and the lands are within a water-flood project.

Surface Water

Frequently the wording of a royalty clause demonstrates that water and its possible use came as an afterthought to the draftsman as he dealt with the use of the leased substances for operational purposes. "The Lessee shall have free use of oil and gas from the said lands, and, where the Lessor is the owner of the surface, of water therefrom, except water from the Lessor's wells, dugouts, or tanks, for all operations hereunder and the royalties on the said substances or any of them shall be based on the net quantity after deducting any portion thereof so used for the Lessee's operations." This language clearly limits the lessee's right to use water to that which may be deemed to be attached to the surface rights and would not include the right to use underground water for purposes such as injection.

Disposal of Salt Water

In a seemingly endless quest to extend the rights granted under a lease, the right to use a well for the disposal of salt water is sometimes included. "DISPOSAL OF SALT WATER: The Lessor hereby grants to the Lessee the right to drill, maintain and operate on the said lands, wells for the disposal of salt water produced from the said lands, or other lands, subject to obtaining the consent of the Alberta Energy and Utilities Board; and for such purposes the Lessee shall have the right to use and occupy all or any part of the surface of the said lands subject to the terms and conditions herein elsewhere provided." Formation water is often produced with the leased substances. Disposing of it can be an embarrassment, particularly since conservation authorities are becoming ever more concerned about the surface damage that can be done by a saline solution. The obvious answer is to reinject the salt water underground, and an operator who produces water along with each barrel of oil is willing to pay for the privilege. Under the proper conditions it becomes economical to convert a depleted well to water disposal or even to drill one for that express purpose. Nevertheless, such a utilization of the underground characteristics seems removed from the purposes contemplated by a mineral owner and oil operator when they enter into a lease.

Disposal of salt water is a valuable service and one for which the lessee would receive compensation if the well was utilized by third parties. The right to use a well for such purposes should be a matter of separate negotiation between the operator and the mineral owner.

Injected Substances

The practice of injecting foreign substances into a formation in order to maintain pressure and reservoir drive could, under some circumstances, give rise to royalty problems since these substances are produced from the well. If the injected substance is water, as is quite commonly the case, the problem does not arise. Frequently, valuable hydrocarbons such as gas and propane are used. Sometimes a lease will attempt to deal with the situation. "AND FURTHER PROVIDED that no royalty shall be payable in respect to any substance whether similar to or dissimilar to leased substances not initially obtained from reservoirs or strata underlying the said lands which is injected into the reservoir or strata underlying the said lands and is subsequently produced therefrom and sold, regardless of whether the same is produced in conjunction with the leased substances or otherwise." One must applaud the intention of such a provision. The problems of identification, however, are formidable. How does one divide gas and liquid hydrocarbons appearing at the wellhead between *in situ* and injected hydrocarbons? Engineering techniques would cast some light, but any such division could be challenged in the courts. The problem transcends any one lease, but disappears under unit operation.

Cost of Treating Leased Substances

Some lease forms are not content to rely upon the computation of royalty as the value of the substances "at the well" or "on the said lands," but go into detail as to the deductions that may be made.

> PROVIDED THAT the Lessor shall bear his proportion of any expense of treating oil, gas, and liquid hydrocarbons to render same merchantable, or of absorption or other process by which products are recovered from gas, or of treating, boosting or transporting of gas or residue gas in connection with the disposal thereof. And Lessor shall bear its proportion of any expense of treating, processing, refining and manufacturing from other minerals produced, mined and marketed to render such minerals merchantable.

Although the proviso refers to the lessor *bearing* his proportion of any expense, this does not mean that he is required to pay out funds in the event expenses exceed revenues in any month. It means that the expense can be deducted in computing royalty.

Lessor to Defend Title

One lease form, notable for the unusual burdens it imposes upon the lessor, contains, in addition to a warranty of title, a commitment by the lessor to defend the title to the leased substances in the said lands, or at the lessee's option to permit the lessee so to defend.

And the Lessor agrees to defend the title to the leased substances in the said lands, or at the Lessee's option to permit the Lessee so to defend and the Lessee to that end may and is hereby authorized to bring or defend in the Lessor's name and at the Lessor's sole cost and expense, any action necessary or incidental to the defense of such title. In the event of default of payment by the Lessor, the Lessee shall have the right to pay the expenses and costs of any such action, and may at its option deduct any amount so paid by it from rentals and royalties payable to the Lessor herein.

The provision places an unjustified burden on the lessor, who may not be particularly anxious to defend his title to the minerals granted, but, nonetheless, could be made responsible for all the costs and expenses of so defending. The lessee's right to collect such costs and expenses appears to be limited to a right of reimbursement from rentals and royalties. The entire concept seems inconsistent with the normal lessor-lessee relationship.

Well Information

One sophisticated and substantial lessor with extensive mineral holdings has developed its own lease form. As might be expected, the lease contains much more in the way of protection of the interests of the lessor than is normally found in oil and gas leases. In particular, the form imposes very detailed requirements on the lessee with respect to furnishing information on any drilling performed on the lands. The lease contains in effect the same requirements as to information, data, testing, and access as oil companies normally require of each other in joint venture projects.

The advantage of such stipulations to a lessor with widespread mineral rights and operations is obvious. The average lessor has no need for such detailed information, but he does have a legitimate interest in knowing that a well or wells have been drilled on his lands and the results obtained.

There would seem to be no compelling reason why the lease should not obligate the lessee to advise the lessor of the fact that a well will be commenced on the land on or about a certain date and to advise the lessor in general terms of the status of such a well, i.e., abandoned, completed for production, or suspended to await a market or pipeline connection. The interest of the lessee could be protected by specifying that such abandonment or completion information need not be provided until the expiration of the period when it would become generally available by law, provided that the lessee took whatever steps are required to clothe the well with confidential status.

Right to Take Royalty Share in Kind

The average lessor is in no position to deal with the oil and gas as physical substances and is only too happy to have the responsibility for disposing of his royalty share assumed by the lessee. Some lessors, large-scale oil operators in their own right, however, may wish to dispose of the royalty share directly. One form contains the following provision:

> The Lessor shall have the option exercisable at any time and from time to time, on thirty (30) days' written notice to the Lessee, to take in kind, in lieu of the royalty payable under sub-clause (a) of this clause 4 in respect of crude oil and liquid hydrocarbons _____ Per cent (_____%) of all crude oil and all liquid hydrocarbons produced and saved from the demised estate, and on like notice may at any time and from time to time revoke its exercise of such option; if the Lessor so exercises such option, the Lessee shall at the Lessee's cost remove basic sediment and water from the Lessor's said share in accordance with usual oil field practice so that such share will meet pipe line, refinery or other market specifications in that respect and the Lessee shall provide at the Lessee's cost storage facilities for at least ten (10) days' accumulation of such share and shall deliver the same to the Lessor or the Lessor's nominee at the outlets of such storage facilities in accordance with the usual pipe line and shipping practices and free and clear of all charges, liens and encumbrances.

Under this provision the lessor has the option on thirty days' notice to take its share of crude oil and liquid hydrocarbons in kind. The thirty-day notice period coincides with the usual practice under which crude oil is sold through purchase contracts that have a thirty-day termination clause. This permits the lessee to cancel any existing contract under which it is selling the lessor's share and thus place itself in a position to make delivery to the lessor. If the lessor has exercised its option, the lessee is required at the lessee's cost to remove certain impurities and water from the liquids as required to meet pipeline specifications. This involves a basic form of treating and separating on the well site and requires vessels and equipment that the lessee would need for treating its own share. The lessee is also required to provide at its cost tankage sufficient to store at least ten days' royalty share.

As discussed *ante*, in Chapter 8, the standard royalty provision empowers the lessor to demand his royalty share in kind, although it does not spell out the right in express terms. If he did so, however, the burden and cost of treating the substances or storing them would fall upon the lessor.

There are, of course, clauses other than the foregoing that are found from time to time in leases. Their number is limited only by the imagination and ingenuity of the draftsman. But those discussed above are both the most important and most commonly encountered.

PART FOUR

The Top Lease

13 Top Lease

The judicial hazards that threaten the existence of oil and gas leases have given rise to a curious document known as a "top lease." The agreement is entered into when there is an existing lease on the property, and reflects the hope or expectation that the current lease will expire or be terminated while the mineral rights under the property still retain some value. The Supreme Court of Canada has succinctly defined a top lease as follows: "A top lease is one which takes effect upon the termination of a prior existing lease."[1] However expressed, the top lease makes the lessor's reversionary interest subject to the top lessee's right to take a lease.

The top lease arrangement may follow any one of a number of forms. The ones most commonly encountered are: (a) a conditional lease, (b) a right of first refusal, and (c) an option to take a lease.

Conditional Lease

Under this method the lease form is identical with the conventional lease, with the exception that it contains the following proviso:

> PROVIDED that this Lease and Grant shall not become effective until the Petroleum and Natural Gas Lease dated the ____ day of _____ A. D. made between _____ as Lessor, and _____ as Lessee, hereinafter called "the current lease," affecting the said lands, shall have terminated, expired or ceased

---

1 *Meyers v Freeholders Company Ltd.*, [1960] S.C.R. 761, [1960] S.C.J. No. 46 (S.C.C.).

to have any force and effect. Upon the current Lease having terminated, expired or having ceased to be of any force and effect, the Lease and Grant herein created shall become effective and the term shall be deemed to commence as of such date, hereinafter called the "effective date." The current Lease shall be deemed to have terminated, expired, or ceased to be of any force and effect upon that date determined as follows:

(a) If any court proceedings are commenced with respect to the current Lease, when the Court having final jurisdiction in the matter shall have determined that the current Lease has so terminated, expired or ceased to be of any force and effect;

(b) When the current Lease terminates, expires, or ceases to exist by any other happening or by operation of law, PROVIDED that if the current Lease shall not have terminated, expired, or ceased to be of any force and effect, within twenty-one (21) years after the death of the last surviving direct descendant, now living, of Queen Elizabeth II of the United Kingdom, the Lease and Grant herein created shall terminate and be at an end.

Within thirty (30) days after the effective date has been determined as aforesaid, the Lessee shall pay the Lessor the sum of ... ($ ...) provided that in the event a bona fide dispute exists as to the date on which this Lease and Grant commences, the Lessee's obligation hereunder shall be postponed until the resolution of such dispute.

Right of First Refusal

A typical clause of this type reads:

DOTH HEREBY grant unto the Grantee the sole and exclusive preferential and prior right to acquire from the Grantor any interest of the Grantor in the petroleum substances or any of them within, upon or under the said lands from time to time and at any time during the currency hereof, such rights being granted upon and subject to the following terms and conditions: If at any time during and throughout a period of ....
years commencing as of the date hereof, the Grantor shall receive or make a bona fide offer acceptable to both him and his offeror and/or his offeree as the case may be, to sell, transfer, lease, license or otherwise in any manner howsoever dispose of any interest in and to the petroleum substances or any of them within, upon or under the said lands or any part or parts thereof, or to renew or extend the term of any estate or interest in the said

petroleum substances, whether now or hereafter created, the Grantor shall forthwith advise the Grantee by notice in writing, as hereinafter prescribed, (hereinafter called the "Grantor's Notice") of all of the terms of such offer, whereupon the Grantee, or its nominee, shall have the first preferential and prior right for a period of thirty (30) consecutive days, (hereinafter called "the period of first refusal") commencing and including the first day following receipt by the Grantee of such notice, to acquire from the Grantor the interest so intended to be disposed of by the Grantor, as aforesaid, upon and for a consideration Ten (10%) Percent greater than that disclosed in such offer but otherwise on the same terms and conditions as are contained in the said offer.

Option

The top lease concept is probably best suited to the option. A top lease may be created by an option that becomes effective only when the current lease has terminated. The key provisions of a top lease in the form of an option are as follows:

- The lands are described and the consideration is acknowledged to have been paid.
- The optionee is given the sole and exclusive option irrevocable for the specified period to acquire a lease that will have been executed by the optionor with the date left blank.
- The term of the option will be, where there is an existing lease, the earlier of forty-five days from the receipt of notice that the lease has been cancelled, expired, or surrendered, or a period of specified months or years.
- When the option is exercised the optionor shall be bound to grant and the optionee shall be obligated to accept a lease in the form already executed by the optionor.
- The optionee shall have a period of time after exercising the option to satisfy itself as to the optionor's title.

A simpler form of option ignores any lease that may be existing:

The Optionor, being the owner of the Petroleum and Natural gas rights in and under the lands herein described, DOES HEREBY GIVE AND GRANT to the Optionee the sole and exclusive Option, irrevocable within the time herein limited for acceptance, to lease all the petroleum, natural gas and related hydrocarbons, all other gases, and all other substances (whether fluid or solid and whether similar or dissimilar and whether hydrocarbons or not) produced in association with any of the foregoing or found in any water contained in an oil or gas reservoir, excluding, however, coal and valuable stone, in and under all or any part of the following lands, including the interest of the Optionor in such substances within, upon or under any lands excepted therefrom or roadways, lanes or rights-of-way thereto adjoining.

From the top lessee's point of view, the option route would seem preferable to the other alternatives. The conditional lease suffers from the defect that it is binding upon the lessee when the existing lease comes to an end. Once that happens, the lessee becomes obligated to pay the stipulated bonus and to assume the obligations of the lease. From the lessor's viewpoint, the fact that the lessee becomes obligated to at least pay the bonus consideration upon termination of the existing lease may be very desirable.

The first refusal technique suffers from the deficiency that it requires the positive act of some party other than the grantee to activate the right. Before the grantee's right to acquire comes into force, there must be a *bona fide* offer involving a third party.

From a tactical point of view, the top lessee would be well advised to insert a provision obligating the mineral owner to participate (at the top lessee's sole risk, cost, and expense) in any legal proceedings that may be brought to challenge the validity of the existing lease. The courts may be disposed to look more favourably on a challenge to the lease that is joined in by the mineral owner rather than have him remain aloof from the struggle.

Interest in Land

The right to acquire a lease as expressed in the top lease arrangement has been characterized as an equitable contingent interest in land.[2] The

2 *Pan American Petroleum Corporation v Potapchuk and Scurry-Rainbow Oils Ltd.* (1964), 46 W.W.R. 237 (Alta. Q.B.); affirmed 51 W.W.R. 700, [1964] A.J. No. 11 (C.A.); affirmed 51 W.W.R. 767 (S.C.C.). This decision applied *Frobisher Ltd. v Canadian Pipelines & Petroleums Ltd.*, [1960] S.C.R. 126, [1959] S.C.J. No. 81 (S.C.C.), commented on by La Forest, "Real Property – Options – Rights of Pre-emption – Equitable Interest in Land – Personal Contractual Obligation – Rule Against Perpetuities" (1960) 38 Can. Bar Rev. 595.

fact that it is an interest in land makes a top lease registrable by caveat or otherwise under the various provincial registry systems. Since the top lease effectively ties up the reversionary interest of the lessor and authorizes the top lessee to call for a conveyance of a *profit à prendre,* it is difficult to see how it could be treated as anything but an interest in land.

Rule Against Perpetuities

A top lease postpones the actual acquisition of an interest to some time in the future. Does it offend the rule against perpetuities? The common law rule provides that any interest in property is void if there is a possibility that it might become vested after the perpetuity period has expired. The perpetuity period is life or lives in being at the time the contingent interest was created plus twenty-one years. The answer is that a top lease does not offend the rule.

In Alberta, the *Perpetuities Act*[3] stipulates that no disposition creating a contingent interest shall be declared void as violating the rule against perpetuities by reason of the fact that there is a possibility of the interest vesting beyond the perpetuity period. There is also a "wait and see" provision that every contingent interest that is capable of vesting within or beyond the perpetuity period is valid until actual events establish that (a) the interest is incapable of vesting within the perpetuity period, in which case the interest shall be declared to be void, or (b) the interest is incapable of vesting beyond the perpetuity period, in which case the interest shall be declared to be valid.

There is no legislation in Saskatchewan either abolishing or amending the rule, although the legislature once considered abolishing the rule, but did not do so. The Saskatchewan Court of Appeal, however, has decreed that the rule does not apply to top leases.[4] The trial judge held that although top leases did not offend the policy behind the rule, any modification was best left to the legislature and so held the top lease to be void. In allowing the appeal, the Court of Appeal stated: "Given the trial judge's conclusion and our concurring view that the object and purpose of the rule against perpetuities is not offended by the top lease in question, we are persuaded that this is an appropriate

---

3 *Perpetuities Act,* R.S.A. 2000, c P-5, ss 3 and 4.
4 *Taylor v Scurry-Rainbow Oil (Sask) Ltd.,* 170 Sask. R. 222, [1999] 5 W.W.R. 424, [1998] S.J. No. 589 (Sask. Q.B.); reversed 207 Sask. R. 266, [2001] 11 W.W.R. 25, 203 D.L.R. (4th) 38, [2001] S.J. No. 479 (Sask. C.A.).

case for this Court to intervene and determine that the top lease in question is not rendered void."[5]

In the result, top leases will not be struck down in Saskatchewan for offending the rule against perpetuities.

Personal Covenant

Some well-known *obiter dicta* by Martland J in *Prudential Trust v Forseth*[6] suggested that although the agreement might be void because of the rule against perpetuities, the optionee might be entitled to specific performance of the covenant to grant a lease even if the agreement offends the rule against perpetuities. Martland J was "not prepared to say that the assignment did not constitute a personal contract by Forseth."[7] However, in two subsequent cases, *Harris v M.N.R.*[8] and *Politzer v Metropolitan Homes Ltd.*,[9] the Supreme Court of Canada stated that if a contract creates an equitable interest in land (which an option contract most certainly does), such contract cannot also be considered as a "personal" contract that can be enforced. The same conclusion was reached by McMahon J in *PanCanadian Petroleum Ltd. v Husky Oil Operations Ltd.*[10]

The rule against perpetuities is no longer a problem, but there may be other situations where a hard-pressed lessee may be driven to advance the personal covenant argument. The foregoing decisions would seem to have closed the door on that faint hope.

Amending a Lease Subject to a Top Lease

Not only does a top lease overhang the current lease like a Damoclean sword, it also represents an ever-present obstacle to any attempt by the lessee to improve its status under the lease. The inhibiting effect of a

---

5 Ibid., 11 W.W.R. at 62 (per Tallis JA).

6 [1960] S.C.R. 210, 30 W.W.R. 241, 21 D.L.R. (2d) 507, [1959] S.C.J. No. 84, (S.C.C.). The same reasoning was also applied by the Supreme Court of Canada in *Prudential Trust Company Ltd. and Canadian Williston Minerals Ltd. v Olson Ltd.*, [1960] S.C.R. 227, 21 D.L.R. (2d) 603, [1959] S.C.J. No. 85 (S.C.C.).

7 Ibid. at 226.

8 [1966] S.C.R. 489, [1966] S.C.J. No. 28 (S.C.C.).

9 [1976] 1 S.C.R. 363, [1975] S.C.J. No. 37 (S.C.C.).

10 26 Alta. L.R. (3d) 203, [1995] 4 W.W.R. 40, 163 A.R. 367, [1994] A.J. No. 1017 (Alta. Q.B.).

top lease was strikingly illustrated in the *Potapchuk* case,[11] where the trial judge, Cairns J, analysed the impact of a top lease with great care. His judgment was followed by the two higher courts.

The *Potapchuk* fact pattern is a good example of how a top lease works. The lands were subject to a lease dated 16 January 1951, with a primary term of ten years plus the usual "thereafter" provision.

On 16 May 1956 (during the primary term of the original lease), the mineral owner granted to one Minnie Potapchuk an option with an attached petroleum and natural gas lease, irrevocable for five years, to lease the minerals. Potapchuk was in fact an employee of Canadian Pipelines & Petroleums Limited, and she assigned her interest to that company. A caveat with respect to the option was filed in the appropriate land registry office on 1 June 1956. The Canadian Pipeline company, on 9 May 1957, assigned its rights under the option agreement to the defendant Scurry-Rainbow, which registered a caveat on 18 July 1957.

The original lease suffered from a defective pooling clause, which, like the one that had been interpreted in *Shell Oil Company v Gunderson*,[12] did not provide that the existence of a non-producing gas well on some part of the spacing unit, other than lands covered by the lease, could have, with the appropriate payment, the same effect in extending the primary term as though the well were on the said lands. Pan American, the lessee by assignment from Shell Oil Co. of the current lease, realized its perilous position as a result of the *Gunderson* decision and was successful in obtaining from the lessor a letter dated 20 May 1960 (during the last year of the primary term), in which he consented to the pooling of his lands with the other three-quarters to form a spacing unit and agreed that, if production of natural gas was encountered and such production was not sold because of lack of market, he would accept as royalty the annual acreage rental and it would be deemed that, while such payments were made, production was being taken from the lands and that the payment would be treated as royalty. This, of course, materially improved the lessee's position under the lease since it could continue it in force by payment of a capped gas well royalty.

Armed with this amendment, the lessee drilled a well in August 1960 on lands other than the leased lands but within the section that had been pooled. This well was capped as a shut-in gas well. The

---

11 *Supra* n 2. The *Potapchuk* decision and its effect on amending the lease were extensively canvassed by Curran, "Effect of Amendments to Petroleum and Natural Gas Leases" (1965–66), 4 Alta. L. Rev. 267.

12 [1960] S.C.R. 424, 23 D.L.R. (2d) 81, [1960] S.C.J. No. 19 (S.C.C.).

primary term of the original lease expired on 16 January 1961. On 1 May 1961 (within the five-year option period), Scurry exercised the option and paid the option price. Scurry also, on 23 May 1961, registered a caveat in support of its lease. The mineral owner returned the bonus consideration to Scurry with a letter in which he stated he was not entitled to it because of the arrangements that had been made with respect to pooling and shut-in royalty payments with Pan American.

The case boiled down to a single issue: if the amendments to pooling and capped well payments were effective, then the original lease would continue in force. In order to succeed on its option, the plaintiff had to strike down the amendment that had been made during the primary term of the lease. The trial judge found that by registering its caveat in 1956, the claim of the plaintiff Scurry was protected as from that date from anyone else taking an interest, or bettering or increasing any interest already held in derogation of the claim of the caveator. He quoted and applied a passage by Anglin J from *Alexander v McKillop and Benjafield*:[13]

> But whatever its effect as notice (and I incline to the view that it must be deemed notice to every person who claims to have acquired, subsequently to its being lodged, any interest in the lands, or to have increased or bettered any such interest already held), inasmuch as it is the only means provided for the protection of unregistered interests and it was obviously intended by the legislature thus to afford adequate and sufficient protection for them, I am of the opinion that a caveat when properly lodged prevents the acquisition or the bettering or increasing of any interest in the land, legal or equitable, adverse to or in derogation of the claim of the caveator – at all events, as it exists at the time when the caveat is lodged.

The *Potapchuk* decision stands for the proposition that, once a lessor has granted a top lease and the top lessee records its interest on the registry system, the lessor and the original lessee are prohibited from doing anything that would lead to the acquisition or the bettering or increasing of any interest in the land that would be adverse to or in derogation of the claim of the top lessee.

While Cairns J did not go into specifics as to what would be an "acquisition or the bettering or increasing of any interest in the land, legal or equitable, adverse to or in derogation of the claim of the caveator," it is implicit in his judgment that anything that would have the

---

13 (1912), 45 S.C.R. 551, 1 W.W.R. 871 (S.C.C.).

effect of extending the term of the lease or increasing the chances of it being extended would be so considered.[14]

In fact, virtually every change or amendment that the original lessee would want to make in the lease would be directed to the improvement of or protection of the interest that it originally obtained in the lease, and thus automatically would be adverse to or in derogation of the interest under the top lease. The ramifications of the *Potapchuk* approach are far reaching indeed.

Priority of Registration

The *ratio* of the *McKillop* decision makes it clear that registration is all important. It is the rights that exist at the time that the caveat is registered that cannot be "bettered or increased." Under the Torrens system, which is in effect throughout most of the oil and gas areas in Canada, the usual procedure is to register the interest claimed under a lease by a caveat. The instrument of caveat normally would include a summary of the rights claimed under the instrument. The Supreme Court of Canada in *Ruptash and Lumsden v Zawick*[15] held that the rights were limited to those expressed in the caveat, regardless of what was conferred by the document itself.

What Is an Amendment to a Lease?

The net cast by the *McKillop* case is a wide one. It includes anything that affects the interest protected by an intervening caveat. In *Potapchuk* a letter agreement that changed the pooling provision in the original lease was ineffective because it would have one of the proscribed effects on the caveated top lessee's position. If a broadening of the pooling clause is not to be allowed, the fundamental changes that are worked in a lease by a

---

14 Curran, *supra* n 11, argues that the amendment in the *Potapchuk* case merely changed the mode of performance of certain covenants in the existing lease and gave the lessee the right to pool lands, pay royalties, and drill a well on a different basis than that provided in the existing lease. While that may be so, the fact that such changes also had the effect of permitting an extension of the primary term of the lease, where otherwise it would have terminated, obviously was regarded by the court as being "adverse to or in derogation of the claim of the caveator."

15 [1956] S.C.R. 347, 2 D.L.R. (2d) 145, [1956] S.C.J. No. 13 (S.C.C.). See also *Esso Resources Canada Ltd. v Pacific Cassiar Ltd.* (1984), 33 Alta. L.R. (2d) 175, [1984] 6 W.W.R. 376 (Alta. Q.B.), where the caveat stated that the lease could be extended by "production," which was held to include both actual and constructive production.

unit agreement certainly must be an even more serious derogation of the claim of the top lease. It will be recalled from the earlier discussion of unitization that the voluntary execution by a lessor of the unit agreement makes the then existing lease virtually impregnable. It would be hard to conceive of anything more "adverse to or in derogation of the claim" of the top lessee. The limitation of the ability to enter into subsequent unit agreements must be considered as one of the most serious probable effects of an intervening top lease upon the original lease.

If the unitization clause in the lease grants, as most now do, a unilateral right to the lessee to unitize the lands, the existence of a subsequent top lease should not prevent unitization since that right exists at the time the top lease was caveated.

An assignee of a caveated interest can claim priority through the original caveat.[16]

Top Top Lease

An original lessee who has been top leased will sometimes "top" the top lease with an option to take a new lease, or have a new lease become effective, on the later of the date of termination of the existing lease, or on the expiration of the top lease. The document is in effect a top top lease. One result of a top top lease is to make it possible for the original lessee to launch an attack on the top lease. Without some hold on the reversionary interest it would not confer much benefit on a lessee to have a top lease set aside on some grounds such as misrepresentation, mistake, or *non est factum*. To do so would only free the lessor to deal independently with the minerals, if the current lease had also been invalidated, or to himself attack the current lease in an attempt to get his mineral rights back.

The registration of the rights acquired under a top top lease by caveat or otherwise would also, in accordance with the *Potapchuk ratio*, effectively freeze the top lessee's ability to improve or alter its position.

Ingredients of a Top Lease

The top lease device is utilized under a number of different conditions. Primarily it is predicated upon the extinguishment of the existing lease

---

16 *Durish v White Resource Management Ltd.*, [1995] 1 S.C.R. 633, [1995] S.C.J. No. 14, 121 D.L.R. (4th) 577, [1995] 3 W.W.R. 609 (S.C.C.).

at some point in time, but there are many degrees of the urgency with which the existing lease is to be attacked. The top lessee may know of a fatal flaw in a particular lease and so enter into an arrangement whereby the lease will be challenged forthwith and, if the attack is successful, the top lessee will have the option, or may be bound, to acquire a new lease. Under such circumstances both the option fee and the bonus consideration for the lease are likely to be very substantial. On the other hand, an operator might seek a large number of top leases within a given area and thereafter challenge the validity of one or more of the current leases in the form of a test case, or may be content simply to have the option to take a new lease without seeking to set aside any existing leases.

Obviously there are many individual terms and conditions that might be negotiated between the parties. Generally, however, it may be stated that a top lease should at least cover the following points:

1 It should have the lease form attached to it, or incorporated as a part of the document.
2 The lease form should be filled out in all details, i.e., the bonus consideration, delay rental, primary term, royalty rate, and all other items should be stipulated. A time limit, beyond which the option will expire, should be specified.
3 The lease should be executed by the optionor with the date left blank to be filled in by the optionee on the effective date.
4 The right of the top lessee should take the form of an option. (Under certain circumstances a top lessee might feel justified in committing to take a lease upon the expiration of the current one, but normally the option route is preferred.)
5 The top lease should contain an undertaking by the optionor that he will not waive any default under, or consent or agree to any modification of, or grant any renewal or extension of, the term of the existing lease. This undertaking should be carefully worded so that it, in turn, cannot be said to be adverse to or in derogation of the claim of the original lessee. It would be advantageous to have the mineral owner agree to participate in any legal proceedings against the validity of the lease. The lessor should insist on being indemnified against any costs or liability arising from such participation.

Above all, the top lease must be caveated in order to freeze the lessor-lessee documentation.

PART FIVE

Involuntary Termination

14 Termination of the Lease

An apt, if irreverent, subtitle for this part would be "The Lessor's Guide to Lease-Breaking." Unquestionably, the conventional oil and gas lease has led a very hazardous existence. Many a lease has come to an untimely and unexpected end.[1]

There are a number of areas in which the lease has proved to be vulnerable.[2]

1 Commencement of drilling within the stipulated time
2 Payment of delay rental
3 Operations at the end of the primary term
4 Pooling
5 Payment of suspended well royalty
6 Interruption or cessation of production

The case law on these points is well established; nonetheless, the lease continues to be under almost constant attack in the courts. The stakes are high, the wording of individual clauses varies from lease to lease, and there is a wide range of fact patterns.

---

1 See Ballem, "The Perilous Life of an Oil and Gas Lease" (1966) 44 Can. Bar Rev. 523; "The Continuing Adventures of the Oil and Gas Lease" (1972) 50 Can. Bar Rev. 423; and "The Further Adventures and Strange Afterlife of the Oil and Gas Lease" (2006) 44 Alta. L. Rev. 426. For a criticism of the approach to the lease taken by Canadian courts, see Currie, "Recent Cases and Developments in Oil and Gas Law" (1971) 9 Alta. L. Rev. 452.
2 Where a third party takes an option or top lease, attacks the validity of the underlying lease, and settles the action for a monetary sum, such money is taxable income in his hands; *Pawnee Petroleums Ltd. v M.N.R.* (1972), 72 D.T.C. 1273 (Tax. Rev. Bd.).

When it comes to termination, the CAPL lease is pretty well bullet-proof. It is possible that there may be litigation involving the interpretation or performance of some of its provisions, but it is not likely that its validity can be successfully attacked. There may be a problem in CAPL 88 and 91 if the bonus consideration is paid late, but that pertains more to whether or not a condition precedent has been satisfied, rather than termination of an existing lease.

Under CAPL 99, the lease automatically terminates if payment is not made within the stipulated period (usually ninety days). Moreover, despite the fact that the lease has terminated, the lessee is responsible contractually to make the bonus payment. The only way in which it can avoid this liability is if there is a defect in the lessor's title. If, within the stipulated time period, there proves to be a defect in the lessor's title and the lessee gives notice of that defect and states he will not be making the payment, the lease will still terminate, but the lessee will not be obliged to make the payment. This provision is much more onerous on the lessee than the previous versions of the CAPL lease.

Commence Drilling

The most common type of conventional lease provides for automatic termination if the drilling deadline is not met.[3] "PROVIDED that if operations for the drilling of a well are not commenced on the said lands within one year from the date hereof, this lease shall terminate and be at an end ..."

The question as to whether drilling operations have been *commenced* within the required time becomes critical in a number of situations. The lessee may have elected in any year of the primary term to drill a well and not pay the delay rental. The primary term may be about to expire so that drilling can no longer be postponed. The lease itself may impose a definite time limit, without the option of deferment.

Even under the typical lease that does contain the right to defer by the payment of the delay rental, the time limit will expire eventually, and if the lease is to continue, drilling must be carried out prior to the end of the primary term. In a sense, the last year of the primary term is shorter than the preceding years insofar as drilling is concerned. During

---

3 Subject, of course, to the right to defer drilling by payment of a delay rental during the primary term.

any of the initial years all that is required is that the lessee shall have commenced drilling before the end of the year. In the last year, however, by virtue of the way in which the *habendum* clause is worded, mere commencement of drilling will not suffice since the lease is continued only if the leased substances are produced, either actually or constructively, from the said lands. It has become customary to ameliorate the effect of this by a further proviso that permits a lessee, when a well has been commenced prior to the end of the last year, to continue such drilling operations with a resulting extension of the lease if production occurs.

What Constitutes Commencement of Drilling Operations?

The critical question is always whether or not what has been done on the lands prior to the critical date amounts to the commencement of drilling operations. In the instances that have come before the courts to date the leases or agreements contained several different versions of the drilling requirement: e.g., "if operations for the drilling of a well are not commenced," "a well has not been commenced," and "commence drilling operations" are the ones most commonly encountered. Regardless of the individual variations in the wording, the courts uniformly have treated such phrases as though they read "commenced the drilling of a well."

The pattern began to emerge as early as 1909 in *Lang v Provincial Natural Gas and Fuel Co. of Ontario*,[4] where the lease provided "that if within six months from the date a well has not been commenced on said premises this lease shall be null and void." At the end of the six-month period the lessee had done the following things: placed a stake on the land at the spot where the well was to be drilled; erected a derrick; and moved onto the land an engine, belt-house, drive pipe, and casing.

The trial judge noted that in oil contracts, time is of the essence of the bargain and also that a strict rather than a lax reading of the agreement would be appropriate. He reviewed English and American building cases, which held that "to commence work" meant to "break the ground" and that excavation for the foundation represents "the commencement of the building" within the meaning of the law. He concluded that the phrase "to commence work" as used in these building cases did not include mere preparations for the execution of the work.

---

4 (1909), 17 O.L.R. 262, [1908] O.J. No. 50 (Ont. H.C.).

With these precedents as a guide, the court held that some breaking of the ground was essential to meet the test of commencement of a well. That element being absent, the lease was terminated.

In *Wulff v Lundy*,[5] the operative language was found in a sublease. The land was held under a petroleum and natural gas lease granted by the province of Alberta, and the original lessees entered into a sublease that contained the following clause: "The Lessees agree to commence operations on the said lease with a view to the drilling of a well on the lands on or before 15 June 1937, and will continue said operations until said well is completed, it being understood that the continuing shall be in accordance with the established practice of the field and having regard to unavoidable delays or other causes." A company was incorporated on 31 March 1937 to carry out the drilling venture, but for want of capital it was never in a position to allot shares or to commence operations.

On 31 May 1937, the parties entered into another agreement, which recited that, owing to the difficulty of financing the well drilling operations, extension of the drilling obligation was granted to 1 November 1937, "and that in case at the said November 1st conditions are such that there would difficulty and it would not be advisable to consider financing or the conditions in general are not real good the parties of the first part will on application by the parties of the second part give consideration to a further extension." There was another agreement dated 12 November 1937, which granted a further extension of commencing operations to 1 May 1938, and provided "in case the requirement of commencing operations are not complied with by 1 May 1938, that the said agreement ... be thereupon null and void." By May 1938, all that had happened was that the company had been incorporated and that a geological survey had been made. Both of these events had occurred prior to the first extension that had been granted on 31 May 1937.

The sublessees argued that the reference in the agreements to "operations" did not necessarily mean "drilling operations" and that they could include such things as incorporation of a company, surveys, and attempts to raise capital. The Alberta Appellate Division agreed with a statement in *Thornton's Law of Oil and Gas* that there was no reasonable distinction to be made between commencing "operations" or commencing "drilling operations" under an oil and gas lease that provided for the commencement of work within a specific time.

---

5 [1940] 1 W.W.R. 444, [1940] 2 D.L.R. 126 (Alta. S.C., App.Div.).

Dealing with the acts that the defendants contended amounted to "operations," the court held that the incorporation of a company and the carrying out of a geological survey could not meet the test. This conclusion was fortified by the fact that both of these events took place prior to the first extension agreement of 31 May 1937, and, if these acts by themselves had constituted "operations" within the meaning of the original sublease, there would have been no necessity for an extension.

Operator's Good Faith

A trio of cases has elevated the operator's true intent and *bona fides* to an all-important factor. In *Wetter v New Pecalta Oils Company Limited*[6] the lease was dated 8 April 1947, for a primary term of twenty-one years, but provided: "The Lessees shall commence drilling operations not later than one year from the date hereof (if not commenced by that date the lease to be null and void unless the lessees pay $1.00 per acre rental in advance, and if so paid the date for beginning drilling to be extended another year) and this same procedure shall be observed from year to year but not beyond 31 December 1950. This lease shall be null and void if no well has been commenced to be drilled on the said demised premises by that date." The rental was duly paid up to that point in time where drilling operations had to be commenced if the lease were to be preserved, namely 31 December 1950.

The lease also contained a requirement that the lessees pay to the lessor $200.00 per annum per well for surface rights at the time that drilling operations were begun. On 28 December 1950, the lessees paid this surface rental. On 30 and 31 December 1950, a bulldozer was operated on the land and a drilling site was surveyed. During the first week in January 1951 (after the critical date) a service drilling rig was moved onto the premises and it drilled to a depth of 300 feet, after which it was removed. It is significant that a service rig has only a limited capacity and could not have reached the depth of any prospective horizon.

The trial judge found there had been no default under the lease, but this finding was reversed on appeal. It is clear from the judgment of the Appellate Division that the court might have been prepared to concede that the bulldozer work could have qualified as being preliminary to drilling if the actual drilling had been properly and continuously

---

6 (1951), 2 W.W.R. (N.S.) 290, [1951] 3 D.L.R 533 (Alta. S.C., App.Div.).

prosecuted. The court pointed out, however, that the actual drilling took place in January 1951 (after the cut-off date) and lasted only a week before the rig was removed. This persuaded the court that the work done was merely a pretence to continue the lease.

O'Connor CJA adopted the language of Summers, *Oil and Gas*: "The general rule seems to be that actual drilling is unnecessary, but that the location of wells, hauling lumber on the premises, erection of derricks, providing a water supply, moving machinery on the premises and similar acts preliminary to the beginning of drilling, when performed with the *bona fide* intention to proceed thereafter with diligence toward the completion of the well, constitute a commencement or beginning of a well or drilling operations within the meaning of this clause of the lease."[7]

The same court, seventeen days later, handed down its decision in *Oil City Petroleums (Leduc) Ltd. v American Leduc Petroleums Ltd.*[8] The instrument was not a lease but an agreement that set forth the manner in which the lands were to be drilled and developed. In particular, it specified that if the first well produced in commercial quantities, a second well was to be commenced on the adjoining legal subdivision by a date fixed by reference to the production date of the first well. The agreement continued: "That in the event that the operator fails to comply with such terms or to continue such leases in effect or fails to drill within the time set out or limited thereafter (providing the owners shall not be in default hereunder) they shall be liable to the owners for such default, or, at the option of the owners, the owners may notify the trustees in writing and this agreement shall forthwith cease and determine in all its terms except as to those legal sub-divisions upon which commercial wells have been drilled ... " The time limit expired on 18 October 1950, and a notice of termination was given by the owners on 27 October 1950.

By the critical date of 18 October 1950, the operator had prepared the surface, drilled a 30-inch hole to a depth of 300 feet, cased it for a short distance, and placed a water tank on the drill site. It was admitted that the operator had not entered into any drilling contract. Although it does not appear from the written judgment, the rig that had drilled the 300-foot hole had been removed from the well site; this fact would tell heavily against the intention of the operator to proceed.

---

7 Summers, *The Law of Oil and Gas*, vol. 2 (Kansas City, Mo.: Vernon Law Book Company, 1954) at 349.
8 (1951), 2 W.W.R. (N.S.) 371, [1951] 3 D.L.R. 835 (Alta. S.C., App.Div.); affirmed [1952] 3 D.L.R. 577 (S.C.C.).

The Appellate Division examined these activities and concluded that, while they might "be regarded as a preparation to drill," by themselves they did not satisfy the test of "commencement of drilling."

This view was endorsed on appeal to the Supreme Court of Canada, which contented itself by observing: "I think that the small amount of drilling relied upon by the appellant company as an answer to the allegation of default against it in this respect is not to be taken seriously as a compliance with its obligations."[9]

There is one case in which the court decided in favour of a lessee who had done something less than breaking ground with a rig capable of drilling to the projected depth. *Risvold and Mallory v Scott and Granville Oils Ltd.*[10] was decided in 1938 and involved a resolute course of action that a modern-day lessee, more aware of the hazards, would be reluctant to follow. In the *Risvold* case, the covenant was contained in an assignment of a lease and the lessee undertook "that he shall and will commence the erection of a derrick, will install proper and adequate drilling equipment and machinery as soon as possible, and shall and will commence actional drilling operations on the said lands, but not later than the 31st day of December, 1936 A.D."

The presence of the word "actional" is unusual, but had no influence on the decision as the trial judge determined that the word did not add anything material to the words that followed, namely "drilling operations," so that the phrase became the usual "commence drilling operations."

The wording of the first covenant of the lessee to "shall and will commence the erection of a derrick, will install proper and adequate drilling equipment and machinery as soon as possible" was very broad and indefinite and for all practical purposes was discarded by the court, so that the entire issue turned on whether or not the lessee had complied with the covenant to commence drilling operations by the specified date.

On 31 December 1936, the following work had been done: a surface lease had been obtained, a cellar – a large hole about 10 feet by 12 feet and from 12 to 15 feet deep – had been dug and cribbed and completed with a runway, contracts had been let for the erection of a derrick, a drilling contract had been awarded, and certain other contracts for the

---

9 Ibid. D.L.R. at 578 (S.C.C.).

10 [1938] 1 W.W.R. 682, [1938] 2 D.L.R. 238 (Alta. S.C.T.D.). The test as to "commence drilling" discussed in this decision was expressly approved by the Saskatchewan Trial Division in *Kendall v Smith and Northern Royalties Ltd.*, [1947] 2 W.W.R. 609 (Sask. K.B.).

use of the required equipment had been entered into. By that time the lessors had become alive to the potential of the land and were following the progress of operations very closely. On 11 February 1937, they purported to cancel the lease and warned the lessees that they would continue operations at their peril. The basis of the cancellation was the failure of the defendants to commence drilling operations by the required date. There was a further exchange of correspondence asserting and denying the breach, culminating on 9 March 1937 in the commencement of the action for a declaration that the lease had been terminated. Among the relief claimed by the lessors was an interim injunction; this remedy was not pursued, although the defendant company continued its drilling operations.

Despite the perils of the situation, the lessees pressed on with commendable determination. As the court pointed out, the work was continued without intermission during the very severe winter weather in January and February 1937 and despite the fact that a storm of unprecedented severity blew down the defendants' derrick. The well was completed in September 1937 (long after the commencement of the action) and became a substantial producer.

Since this was one of the earlier decisions, there was little in the way of Canadian precedents to guide the court, and it relied upon and quoted extensively from that well-known American authority, Summers, *Oil and Gas*, notably the passage quoted previously in connection with *Wetter v New Pacalta*, which emphasized the good faith of the operator.

Evidence had been given at the trial by a number of witnesses as to what they understood by the meaning of the term "commence drilling operations" as used in the oil fields. Their understanding of the phrase, as might be expected, conflicted. It was analysed by the trial judge in this passage, and the uncertainty that it reveals is still relevant today:

> Evidence was given at the trial by various witnesses as to the meaning of the term "commencing drilling operations," as used in the oil fields with which they were familiar. Their evidence is conflicting but I think for the most part these witnesses are not close observers of expressions used. Mr. Adams says that neither erecting a derrick nor installing drilling machinery is part of a drilling operation. Mr. Muir says that neither drilling a cellar nor erecting a derrick is part of a drilling operation, although he said that if he were asked to estimate the cost of drilling a well he would include everything. Mr. Snyder, on the contrary, says that all these

are part of drilling operations. Mr. Davies, who is a petroleum engineer and geologist of long experience and therefore as an educated man more likely to weigh carefully expressions which he hears in the practice of his profession, says that in his opinion on the facts of the case the defendant company had commenced drilling operations before 31 December 1936.[11]

The decision of the court really turned on the question of *bona fides* as stressed by Summers. In the *Risvold* case there could be no doubt as to the good faith of the defendants. This had been proved by the fact that once having commenced operations they pursued them to completion despite adverse conditions and repeated warnings and threats from the plaintiffs as to the uncertainty of their position.

The obligation to "commence drilling operations" is expressed in broad and non-specific terms. For this reason the obligation is one that can be stretched to include almost any activity if the court is so inclined. It would appear that a Canadian court might find that there had been no default if (a) at least *something* had been done on the lands by the critical date and (b) the good faith of the lessee could be established. The manner in which the *bona fides* appear to be established is by the diligent prosecution of the drilling of a well to its completion. This is an expensive operation, and it would take a very courageous and determined lessee to continue drilling a well in the face of a challenge to its title. The diligent completion of a well would be a very effective defence by a lessee whose title was attacked after the fact. But a lessee whose status was questioned before being too deeply committed to the well might well conclude that it would be foolhardy to proceed until the question had been resolved.

In *Canadian Superior Oil Ltd. v Crozet Exploration Ltd.*,[12] the *habendum* continued the lease beyond the primary term "so long thereafter as operations, as hereinafter defined, are conducted upon the said lands." This was followed by a definition of "operations" as: "Shall mean any of the following: drilling, testing, completing, reworking, recompleting, deepening, plugging back or repair of a well in search for or in an endeavour to obtain or increase production of the leased substances or any of them (whether or not in paying quantities) or *operations for or*

---

11 Ibid. at 688.
12 (1982), 18 Alta. L.R. (2d) 145, 133 D.L.R. (3d) 53, 34 A.R. 256, [1982] A.J No. 672 (Alta. Q.B.).

incidental to any of the foregoing" (italics added). The primary term would have come to an end at midnight on 30 July 1980. By that time the following relevant steps had been taken:

1 On 24 July the survey of the access road and well site area was completed and work started on constructing the access road.
2 The selected well site was located on a slope of a hill, and for that reason, and also because of the substantial rains that had preceded these activities, which in turn raised the water level, the contractors were forced to haul onto the site 3,780 yards of gravel to build, stabilize, and level that site. Gravel was also hauled for and used in the building up of the access road from the nearest municipal road into the well site area. This hauling took place on or about noon on 28 July to on or about noon of the next day.
3 On 27 July sump pits were commenced, although it is not clear that they were completed on that date.
4 On 27 and 28 July the "rat hole" and "mouse hole" were drilled.
5 On 29 and 30 July a drilling rig was moved onto the site and located or pinned in a horizontal position ready to be hoisted to the vertical.
6 On 30 July the "rigging up" commenced. This process included erecting the substructure and drilling platform and generally putting the pieces together so as to be prepared to commence boring into the ground.
7 A well licence to drill this well was issued by the appropriate licensing authority of the province of Alberta on 30 July 1980, and was posted on the righouse on 31 July.
8 On 31 July the derrick was raised to the vertical position.
9 On 31 July, at 9:00 p.m., the well was "spudded-in," that is, the surface of the ground was broken by the rotating action of the drill bit. It must be noted that this, and all other matters above-mentioned as having occurred on 31 July, took place after the expiration of the five-year primary term.

Thereafter the well was continuously drilled to completion at a cost of $955,695.03 and became a producing oil well.

In reaching his decision Stratton J reviewed the relevant Canadian decisions including the first Ontario case, *Lang v Provincial Natural Gas & Fuel Co. of Ontario*,[13] and took the view that the Ontario judge did not

---

13 *Supra* n 4.

intend his words to be limited to the actual act of breaking the ground as the result only of the rotary action of the drilling bit. In Stratton's view the basic finding of the judge in the *Lang* case was that the terms of the lease imported that some work was contemplated upon and in the ground. Stratton went on to state: "Obviously, in the present situation, in preparing the Section 8 site for the 'spudding-in,' substantial work was done on the site and the ground was broken by reason of this work." This is an interesting observation and suggests that any breaking of the ground by digging sump pits, or possibly even bulldozing the site, might suffice.

The decision in the *Crozet* case turned upon the key words, namely "operations for or incidental to ... (drilling)." The trial judge quoted a dictionary definition of "incidental" as "subordinate, non-essential ..."; and "for" as "a preparation toward; having as goal or object; in order to bring about or further; so as to secure as a result."

The court had no difficulty in finding that the actions taken prior to 31 July constituted preparatory actions within the meaning of the *habendum* in the Canadian Superior lease and so upholding the lease. The court also held it was not necessary that the preparatory actions include the actual "spudding-in," that is, the breaking of the surface of the ground by the rotary action of the drill.

The court was careful to point out that not all preparatory work would be sufficient to extend the lease beyond the critical date. Not only must the actions be preparatory to come within the clause in the *habendum*, they must also pass the following additional tests:

1 The preparatory steps or actions must be taken in good faith with the intention of completing the drilling of an oil and/or gas well.
2 The preparatory steps or actions must be taken with reasonable diligence and dispatch tested by the principles of good oil field practice.
3 The preparatory steps or actions must not simply be minimal within the concept expressed by the Supreme Court of Canada in the *Oil City Petroleums (Leduc) Ltd. v American Leduc Petroleums Ltd.*[14]

If these tests were met, then the actions taken prior to midnight, 30 July 1980, did not have to include the actual "spudding in" of the well.[15]

---

14 *Supra* n 8.
15 *Supra* n 12, D.L.R. at 63.

Stratton J emphasized that the three additional tests set forth above would not necessarily be applicable in situations involving different wording than the key words "operations for or incidental to."

The *Crozet* case underlines the advisability of an express reference to operations that are incidental to the drilling of a well, appears to recognize that something other than an actual spudding in of the well will suffice, and, even where the reference to incidental operations is not present, emphasizes the importance of the lessee's good faith and diligence.

Relief from Forfeiture

The courts have an equitable jurisdiction to grant relief from forfeiture where the rigid exercise of the legal right would produce a hardship, if adequate compensation to the injured party can be made by some means other than forfeiture of the estate.[16]

There is an obvious application of this equitable remedy to oil and gas leases. A lessee may argue, and many have done so, that the termination of the lease for tardiness in commencing the drilling of a well or in payment of a delay rental is forfeiture of the type against which the courts should relieve. The point has been considered in numerous cases, dealing with failure to commence drilling on time or a late payment of delay rental. As discussed in Chapter 16, the argument appears to have been completely rejected in the delay rental situation, but it still may retain some vitality when it comes to the commencement of drilling operations.

In the *Risvold* case there was *obiter dicta* that the court would relieve against the forfeiture. This observation is clearly in the category of *dicta* since the trial court found that the defendants were not in breach of the drilling obligation. Ewing J went on to note that the defendant had proceeded in good faith and that the performance of a contract was not open to criticism. He coupled this with the fact that the plaintiff, with full knowledge that the work was proceeding, did not attempt to restrain the work by injunction. The circumstances of the *Risvold* case were extraordinary and not likely to be duplicated since the defendant company actually drilled the well to completion.

---

16 La Forest, *Anger and Honsberger Law of Real Property*, 3rd ed., vol. 1 (Toronto: Canada Law Book, 2006).

The Alberta Appellate Division conceded in the *Wulff* decision that the claim for relief from forfeiture gave "much difficulty." It pointed out, however, that the breach of an agreement to drill a well was no light matter and approved a statement from *Thornton's Law of Oil and Gas* that "neglect to sink the well cannot be compensated in damages." Accordingly, the court refused to apply the equitable remedy.

In *Wetter*, the trial judge, after holding that there had been no default, went on to state that he would have been prepared to relieve against forfeiture on condition that "a drilling permit was applied for forthwith; that within thirty days a rig be moved on the premises, that actual rigging be commenced and drilling operations be diligently prosecuted."[17] On appeal, however, relief against forfeiture was not given because the work relied upon as commencement of drilling was not, in the view of the court, performed with the *bona fide* intention to proceed with diligence.

Relief from forfeiture received its most thorough review, insofar as commencement of drilling was concerned, in the *Oil City* case, where the Alberta Appellate Division emphasized the nature of the oil business with its pressures of time. The drilling obligation was considered to be an essential term of the contract, and to deny relief to a party in breach of it could not be said to transgress any principle of equity. The court also noted that the evidence indicated a lack of financial ability on the part of the plaintiffs to carry out their obligation and that no proposal had been placed before the trial judge under which they could be granted a reasonable period of time within which to commence drilling. This portion of the Appellate Division's judgment is significant as it indicates at least a disposition, under proper circumstances, to grant an extension of time within which drilling operations could commence.

On appeal, the Supreme Court of Canada expressly left the question open: "With respect to the contention that that appellants should be relieved from the consequences of their default, I see no grounds, assuming but without deciding there is jurisdiction to do so, upon which relief should be granted."[18]

It must be noted, however, that the documentation in the *Oil City* case involved an agreement rather than a lease. The granting of an

---

17 *Supra* n 6 at 291.
18 [1952] 3 D.L.R. 577 (S.C.C.).

extra period of time within which to commence drilling would seem to be totally excluded by the precise wording of the "unless" clause. Nonetheless, when dealing with the commencement of drilling, the courts have been reluctant to totally reject – as they have in the case of delay rental payments – relief against forfeiture. There is a distinction between the two situations: payment of the delay rental is a definite act, it is either done or not done, whereas the commencement of drilling is a more indefinite concept and allows the courts a greater scope as to whether what has been done constitutes drilling operations. As will be seen, the courts have discarded the remedy with respect to delay rentals, as they regard the payment of delay rentals to be a mere option. The same may also be true of drilling, but the latitude to construe almost any form of activity as amounting to the commencement of drilling lays the groundwork for the application of relief from forfeiture, if the facts of the case so incline the court.

Notice of Default

Virtually every lease contains a clause that requires the lessor to give the lessee notice of a default and grants a period of grace to remedy it, before the lease can be terminated. The operation of this type of clause was discussed in Chapter 11, *ante*. The courts have refused to hold that a notice of default must be given before a lease could be terminated as a result of failure to commence drilling.[19] The ground for so refusing has been that the commencement of drilling by the required time is considered as essential by the parties. Put another way, it is clear from the language of the "unless" clause that the lease will terminate automatically if drilling operations have not been commenced. There is no default on the part of the lessee in failing to commence since there is no absolute obligation to do so; the only consequence is that the lease will terminate.

No Provision for Termination

Occasionally, one suspects more by accident than design, the document in question will impose an obligation to drill, but does not expressly provide for termination in the event the deadline is not met. In what appears to be the first Canadian case on drilling obligations,

---

19 *Wetter v New Pacalta Oils Co.*, *supra* n 6.

Docker v London-Elgin Oil Co.,[20] the drilling clause did not contain words of automatic termination: "Will commence operations upon the said premises on or before the 1st day of November, 1902, or will pay to the lessor or his assigns the sum of $6.00 per month from the date hereof until operations are commenced on the said premises provided that the said term hereby granted shall cease and determine if the lessee and his assigns shall wholly cease for the space of six months continuously to operate under this lease." The lessee did not commence operations on or before the first day of November 1902, but did pay to the lessor, who accepted the same, the monthly rent computed from the date of the lease down to 1 November 1902. After 1 November 1902, the lessee paid further sums up to at least January 1905 and paid into court additional sums to take care of arrears that may have accumulated prior to the trial.

The lease was upheld on the basis that the lessee had an option to do one of two things, either to make a commencement of operations or to pay the required rent. In effect, the lease was of the "or" type and did not terminate automatically for failure to carry out operations. The contract was silent as to any obligation to commence operations and merely provided that the lessee must pay the monthly sum of $6.00 until there be such a commencement of operations.

In *Wulff v Lundy*[21] one agreement which expressly declared that it would be null and void if operations were not commenced by the specified date was held to have been terminated by such failure. There was another agreement in the same case that covered different parcels of land and contained a drilling obligation, but did not provide expressly for termination in the event of a breach of such obligation. The Appellate Division held that the only remedy for breach of the second agreement would be for damages and that, since there were no provisions for re-entry or for determination or forfeiture in cases of default, the agreement should not be terminated.

Sometimes the parties, rather than use one of the more or less standard forms, will draft their own version of an oil and gas lease. The results are often bizarre. In *Reynolds v Ackerman*[22] the lease was set forth in two pages of typewriting and included this clause: "The lessee

---

20 (1907), 10 O.W.R. 1056 (Ont. H.C.); affirmed (1908), 11 O.W.R. 726 (Ont. C.A.).
21 *Supra* n 5.
22 (1960), 32 W.W.R. (N.S.) 289 (Alta. S.C.T.D.). (Although not reported until 1960, the actual decision was delivered orally in 1953.)

shall pay to the lessor for the said period of three (3) years of this lease the sum of Two Hundred ($200.00) Dollars upon the execution of this lease, (receipt whereof is hereby acknowledged). This lease shall be subject to renewal for a further term from year to year by the lessee paying to the lessor in advance, the sum of One ($1.00) Dollar per acre per year, provided that all the covenants of the lessee therein contained, shall have been fully done and performed."

The lease was completely silent on the question of drilling. There was no provision terminating the lease in the event of the lessee's failure to drill. The renewal provision was without limitation and would seem to permit the lessee to renew the term from year to year by paying rental in the sum of $1.00 per acre per year. This indeed was the precise effect that counsel for the lessee contended should be given to the provision. The trial judge, however, quoted the Supreme Court of Canada's decision in *Can. Department Stores Ltd. v Gourlay and Billing*:[23] "It has long been established that a covenant in a lease, which provides for a renewal of the term, in order to be valid must designate with reasonable certainty the date of the commencement and the duration of the term to be granted." Finding no limitation in the renewal clause, McBride J held it to be void for uncertainty; a lessee cannot overcome the necessity to commence drilling operations by simply neglecting to insert a time limit in the lease. In view of the precise language contained in the usual "unless" lease, the last three cases mainly have a curiosity value.

Intervening Legislation

The remaining case in this area illustrates what would seem to be a self-evident proposition, that a drilling obligation will not be enforced, nor the lease terminated, if to do so would contravene applicable regulations. In *Mercury Oils Limited v Vulcan-Brown Petroleums*,[24] the lessee was required to drill one well within a stipulated time limit and a second one within twelve months thereafter. If the lessee failed to drill the second well, it was to have been deemed to have abandoned the property. The lessee timely drilled the first well, but before it could begin the second one, new regulations were passed by the province of

---

23 [1933] S.C.R. 329, [1933] 3 D.L.R. 238 (S.C.C.).
24 [1943] 1 S.C.R. 374, [1943] 1 D.L.R. 369 (S.C.C.).

Alberta that prohibited the drilling of the second well because its location would have been too close to the first one. The lease contained a clause that all operations were to be carried on in strict compliance with the statutes and regulations. The Supreme Court held that the lessee's failure to drill, when prohibited by regulation, could not be construed as a default that would terminate the lease.

Conclusions

The cases to date make it clear that each one will be decided on its own particular facts. Although there are few guideposts, the following generalizations seem to be justified:

1 An actual breaking of the ground on or before the critical date by a drilling rig capable of drilling to a prospective depth is the best means of satisfying the test.
2 An actual breaking of the ground or "spudding" may not be required where some operations at least have been carried on at the drill site prior to the deadline and the well is thereafter diligently prosecuted. The hazards of this approach to the lessee are obvious.
3 The lease should provide that operations "incidental to" drilling will be sufficient.
4 The courts seem willing to apply equitable considerations in this area; witness their emphasis on *bona fides* and their reluctance to totally reject relief from forfeiture.
5 There must be at least some physical activity on the well site even if it falls short of an actual spudding.
6 Governmental regulations that prohibit the drilling of a well may be a defence available to the lessee but may be limited to those cases where there has not been a total failure of consideration, i.e., where there is already a producing well on the property.
7 An oil and gas document, such as a lease, that ignores any drilling obligation and provides for perpetual renewal without limitation most likely would be held void for uncertainty of term.

15 Deferring the Commitment to Drill

The second half of the "unless" drilling clause allows the lessee to avoid termination of the lease by payment of an annual sum in lieu of drilling.

> ... *unless* the Lessee shall have paid or tendered to the Lessor on or before said anniversary date the sum of .... ($ ....) Dollars (hereinafter called the "delay rental") which payment shall confer the privilege of deferring the commencement of drilling operations for a period of One (1) Year from said anniversary date, and that, in like manner and upon like payments or tenders, the commencement of drilling operations and the termination of this lease shall be further deferred for like periods successively. (emphasis added)

The right to defer drilling is, of course, limited to the primary term. In every year of the primary term except the last one the lessee is entitled to keep the lease in force without drilling by payment of the delay rental.

Automatic Termination

The cornerstone decision on delay rentals is *East Crest Oil Company Ltd. v Strohschein*,[1] which effectively demonstrated the lethal character of the "unless" clause. The facts were clear and agreed to by both parties:

---

1 (1951–52), 4 W.W.R. (N.S.) 70, [1951] A.J. No. 2 (Alta. S.C.T.D.); affirmed [1952] 2 D.L.R. 432, (1951–52), 4 W.W.R. (N.S.) 553 (Alta. S.C., App.Div.).

1 The lease was dated 13 September 1948, with a primary term of six years.
2 It contained an "unless" clause to the same effect as the one quoted at the beginning of this chapter.
3 There were no drilling operations on the lands at any material time.
4 The lessee paid the annual delay rental in accordance with the terms of the lease on 13 September 1949.
5 Delay rental was not paid to the lessor or the depository on 13 September 1950.
6 On 13 October 1950, the lessor's solicitor wrote to the oil company advising that the delay rental had not been paid when due and claiming that the lease was at an end.
7 On the following day the oil company replied that the failure to pay the rental was due simply to an oversight. The oil company also referred to the default provision of the lease and forwarded a certified cheque for the sum of $160.00 (the amount of the delay rental) plus exchange.

The Appellate Division adopted the colourful expression of the California court in *Richfield Oil Corporation v Bloomfield*[2] that the document "carries within its own phraseology an automatic termination which clicks." That click has been heard in many Canadian courtrooms in subsequent years.

The Time Period

The fatal results that flow from failure to make a proper payment of delay rental have created situations where the courts are called upon to make the most detailed analysis as to what constitutes a sufficient and timely payment. In *Canadian Fina Oil Ltd. v Paschke*[3] the validity of the lease depended upon the interpretation of the word "from," and a time interval of one day. The lease was dated 12 October 1953, and contained the following clause: "Provided that if operations for a drilling of a well are not commenced on the said lands within one year from the date hereof, this lease shall thereupon terminate and be at an end

2 229 P (2d) 838 (1951, California).
3 [1956] A.J. No. 12, 19 W.W.R. (N.S.) 184 (Alta. S.C.T.D.); affirmed (1957), 21 W.W.R. (N.S.) 260, 7 D.L.R. (2d) 473 (Alta. S.C., App.Div.).

unless the Lessee shall have paid or tendered to the Lessor the sum of three hundred and twenty ($320.00) dollars as rental which payment shall confer the privilege of deferring a commencement of drilling operations for a period of one (1) year ... "

The difficulty arose with the payment for the year 1955. On 12 October the lessee deposited in a post office at Calgary a registered postpaid letter addressed to the depository, which was the Bank of Nova Scotia at Stettler. This letter contained a cheque in payment of the delay rental and was received by the depository bank on 13 October at 3:00 p.m. The cheque was immediately returned by the lessor, who maintained that the payment was late and therefore the lease had expired. In concluding that the grant had commenced on the day of the date of the lease, namely 12 October, and had therefore ended on 11 October, Porter JA strikingly emphasized the importance of time in the oil and gas industry:

> Upon argument, counsel for the appellant was critical of the reference that the learned trial judge made to the fact that time is of the essence in the oil production business, taking the position that while that might be the particular knowledge of the trial judge, because of his experience at the bar, it could not be regarded as general knowledge, of which judicial notice could be taken. Perhaps it would be useful for the guidance of those who are not familiar with the background of the development of this country, to know that the oil and gas business has been carried on with a good deal of vitality in this province for more than 50 years, from Milk River to Peace River, and from the eastern boundary of the province to the eastern slope of the Rocky Mountains. In the course of that time the people of this province have seen hopes and values dashed when a few strokes of the bit found salt water where oil had been hoped for, whereas in the other fields they have seen what was in common parlance called "cow pasture" turned overnight from areas of hope alone, to reservoirs containing thousands of barrels per acre. It is implicit in the search for oil, and indeed in its production and marketing, that events affecting these activities can occur with great suddenness unpredictably. In consequence there are heavy shifts of value and necessary new, almost instant, reappraisals of ventures to be undertaken. These facts are common knowledge in this province.

> Bearing in mind these characteristics of the business, it is my view that the appellant would have been shocked if it had been told that it could not move on to the property on October 12, 1953, that indeed, having signed the lease, its presence on the land would have made it a trespasser

until the next day. This practical view is emphasized by the fact that the law does not know fractions of the day. That being so, it follows that this document was to all intents and purposes signed on the first instant of October 12.[4]

Because of the minute and often unexpected variations in wording among the various forms of lease, the existing decisions must be applied with great care. The clause in the *Paschke* case referred only to "within one year from the date hereof," and the Appellate Division was of the view that the period of time commenced on the date the lease was signed and accordingly terminated on the day previous, one year later. The typical "unless" proviso contains the same reference but states that the lease shall terminate on "the first anniversary date," and the time within which the payment must be made is also related to the anniversary date. Does the insertion of anniversary date grant the lessee one extra day? Would the lessee, in the *Paschke* situation, have the right to make payment on 12 October if the clause had referred to the payment being made "on or before the anniversary date"? The answer would seem to be yes.

The manner of payment clause in the lease also has a bearing on the time of payment. This clause was fully discussed in Chapter 11, *ante*, and permits payment or tender to be either "mailed or delivered." After some initial doubt, it has now been determined that the act of mailing itself is sufficient if done by the cut-off date.[5]

Industry practice is to mail the delay rental payment by registered mail, which provides proof that the payment was made in time. If industry practice is not followed and the payment is sent by ordinary mail and the circumstances suggest that the payment may not have been made until after the critical date, the matter becomes one of evidence and inferences.[6]

---

4 Ibid. 21 W.W.R. at 263.
5 *Texas Gulf Sulphur Company v Ballem* (1969), 70 W.W.R. (N.S.) 373 (Alta. S.C.T.D.); reversed (1970), 72 W.W.R. (N.S.) 273, 17 D.L.R. (3d) 572 (Alta. S.C., App.Div.); affirmed, [1971] 1 W.W.R. 560n, 17 D.L.R. (3d) 640n (S.C.C.).
6 *Paddon Hughes Development Co. Ltd. v Pancontinental Oil Ltd.*, 33 Alta. L.R. (3d) 7, [1995] 10 W.W.R. 656, [1995] A.J. No. 811 (Alta. Q.B.); affirmed 67 Alta. L.R. (3d) 104, [1999] 5 W.W.R. 726, 223 A.R. 180, [1998] A.J. No. 1120 (Alta.C.A.); [1998] S.C.C.A. No. 600 (leave to appeal dismissed).

Relief against Forfeiture

The argument that the termination of a lease for a late payment of delay rental is the sort of "forfeiture" that a court should relieve against was advanced in *East Crest Oil Oil Company Ltd. v Strohschein*.[7] The Appellate Division pointed out a fatal flaw in the argument: "that on the true construction of the lease now under consideration the question of relief from forfeiture does not, at the stage to which the document has become operative, arise. There is no forfeiture to relieve against. There cannot be default in neglecting to do something one is not bound to do."[8] The Manitoba Court of Appeal expressly adopted this view in *Langlois v Canadian Superior Oil of California Limited*.[9]

Notice of Default

The same kiss of death was administered to the argument based upon the clause that requires a notice of default and a period of grace before termination. As they did in the drilling cases, tardy lessees contended that the default clause compelled a lessor to give notice of default in delay rental payments and to permit the lessees to remedy same, before a lease could be terminated.

In the *East Crest* case, Ford JA said:

> As to the argument based upon the lack of notice under clause 18 (the default clause), quoted above, I am of the opinion, apart from what I have already said, that this clause has no application to the failure to pay delay rental. This clause, in my view, has its full force in respect to defaults arising under the second part of the lease. It can have no application to the first part which provides for the commencement and extension or continuation of the lease. The use of the word "ought" shows clearly that clause 18 refers to those provisions which bind the lessee and have no application to the failure to do something he may or may not do as he pleases. The clause deals with "default" and, as I have said, there is no default in not doing something one is not obliged to do. Authority for this interpretation is to

---

7 *Supra* n 1 (Alta. S.C., App.Div.).
8 Ibid. W.W.R. at 558.
9 (1957), 23 W.W.R. 401, 12 D.L.R. (2d) 53 (Man. C.A.).

be found in the decision of this Division in the *Wetter* case, *supra*, and is supported by the reasoning in the *Richfield* case, *supra*.[10] (words in parentheses added)

As it did with the relief from forfeiture argument, the Manitoba Court of Appeal subsequently adopted this rejection of the default clause.[11]

The logic seems irrefutable; the lessee in an "unless" lease suffers from a lack of obligations. In *Chipp v Hunt*[12] the default clause, unlike any of the other cases, contained a specific reference to "rental": "In case of default in payment of the rental or royalty payable hereunder, or in case of breach or non-performance on the part of the lessee of any of its covenants herein contained, Lessor may give Lessee Thirty (30) days written notice in case of default in such payment ... " The lease also contained a typical unless clause that does not create an obligation, but confers an option, upon the lessee. Nevertheless, the lessee in *Chipp v Hunt* must have been considerably encouraged by the specific reference to "rental" in the default clause.

The Alberta Trial Division followed the *East Crest ratio*, noting that "default" in the *New Century Dictionary* was defined in part: " ... failure to meet financial obligations; in law failure to perform an act or obligation legally required ... " This definition led the court to conclude: "It seems to me that, before clause 10, *supra*, could have any application, the plaintiff would have to be in default under the lease of an obligation that he is legally required to perform. I do not think that he could be in default in the payment of rental, until he had first obligated himself to pay such rental. So it is my view that clause 10 does not take the case out of the law as laid down in the *East Crest* case, *supra*."

The court was also prepared, if required, to reject that portion of the default clause which dealt with rentals, on the ground that it was repugnant to the earlier provision dealing with the payment of delay rentals. The principle of repugnancy was described by the Privy Council in *Forbes v Git*:[13] "The principle of law to be applied may be stated in few words. If in a deed an earlier clause is followed by a later clause which destroys altogether the obligation created by the earlier clause,

---

10 *Supra* n 1 at 559.
11 *Supra* n 9.
12 (1955), 16 W.W.R. (N.S.) 209 (Alta. S.C.T.D.).
13 [1922] 1 W.W.R. 250, [1922] 1 A.C. 256, 61 D.L.R. 353 (J.C.P.C.).

the later clause is to be rejected as repugnant and the earlier clause prevails." If the default clause imposed an obligation on the lessor to give notice of non-payment of the rental before the lease could be terminated, then in the view of the court, this clause could not be reconciled with the earlier "unless" clause, which imposed no obligation, and must be rejected.

In addition to the reasons advanced by the courts over the years, the "unless" clause specifically provides that the lease "shall terminate and be at end" if the lessee has not commenced drilling operations or paid the delay rental by the anniversary date. It is not necessary to go beyond these words to establish that an "unless" type lease will terminate if no drilling has taken place and the delay rental has not been paid.

Competitor's Well

One of the *Durish v White* cases[14] illustrates how far the parties are prepared to go to maintain a lease. The lessee under a disputed lease sought to use a well drilled by a rival lessee under a different lease to satisfy the drilling requirement. Mason J refused to accept that argument, holding that the lease was intended to secure the exploration of the property by the lessee.

Waiver

Under the circumstances of the typical late delay rental payment, it is not surprising that the proceeds are sometimes retained by the lessor. Normally the payments are directed to a depository bank, which will simply credit them to the lessor's account without inquiry, or the lessor may be unaware that the payment is late, or of the significance of it being late.

In *Rostad v Andreassen*[15] the lease required payment by 29 November 1951, but the lessee did not send the cheque until 11 December. It was addressed to the depository bank, which routinely credited the amount to the lessor on 13 December, and it was not until 20 December that the

---

14 [1998] A.J. No. 1041, 230 A.R. 201 (Alta. Q.B.). This case is discussed by Bankes and Quesnel, "Recent Judicial Developments of Interest to Oil and Gas Lawyers" (2000–1) 38 Alta. L. Rev. 294.

15 (1953), 7 W.W.R. (N.S.) 709 [1953] A.J. No. 3 (Alta. S.C.T.D.); affirmed (1953), 8 W.W.R. (N.S.) 717n, [1953] A.J. No. 14 (Alta. S.C., App.Div.).

lessor received notice from the bank that this had been done. He immediately made arrangements to have the payment returned to the lessee. The lessee contended that the acceptance of the cheque by the bank and its act of crediting the proceeds to the lessor amounted to a waiver.[16] The Alberta trial court refused to treat this as a waiver and noted that the bank had no authority to receive rents except in accordance with the lease and its actions could not bind the plaintiff lessor.

In the *Langlois* case,[17] after a defective payment (to a lessor who had assigned the lease) in one year had gone unchallenged, the lessee made a payment to the proper lessor, which was credited by the depository bank to his account. In the next following year a similar payment was also made by the lessee to the depository bank, and it was credited to the lessor's account and retained for several months before being returned. In the meantime, the lessor had discovered that the delay rental payment made in the previous year had been credited to his account, whereupon he sent the lessee a cheque for the equivalent amount. The attempted reimbursement did not take place until some sixteen months after the original payment had been made.

The court refused to treat these events as creating any sort of waiver or estoppel. It noted that if any representation had been made by the lessors, presumably by retaining the payments, the lessee did not in any way alter its position. It had incurred no detriment, which is one of the tests that must be satisfied before estoppel will be invoked.

Waiver in Ontario

The principle of waiver seems to be on a somewhat different plane in Ontario than in the western provinces. In the early case of *Maple City Oil and Gas Co. v Charlton*[18] the lease contained an "unless" clause and was attacked on a number of grounds. The court on its own initiative appears to have raised the issue as to a possible late payment. The trial judge, on the assumption that it was a late payment, was prepared to hold that the lessors had waived any forfeiture that might have resulted from failure to make payment within the proper time when

---

16 Waiver is really a branch of *estoppel*. The application of this equitable doctrine was extensively developed in those cases dealing with termination after the primary term. Because of its importance, estoppel is treated separately in Chapter 18, *infra*.

17 *Supra* n 9.

18 (1912), 7 D.L.R. 345 (Ont. H.C.).

the proceeds were actually withdrawn by the husband from the depository bank. In view of later decisions by higher courts, the authority of this case must be considered doubtful.

Lack of Good Faith by Lessor

A lessor cannot take advantage of a defective payment where he has actively thwarted the lessee's attempts to make proper payment. In *Imperial Oil Ltd. v Conroy and Berthiaume*[19] the defendant lessor had been successful in an action to have her surface title rectified to include minerals. Her predecessor in title had granted a lease to Imperial Oil Limited, which she vigorously repudiated upon acquiring title to the minerals. She refused to designate a depository and returned a delay rental cheque that had been tendered to her. Under these circumstances the court was not prepared to treat the lease as having lapsed through default in delay rental payment and held that the lessor could not take advantage of her own refusal to name a new depository and her rejection of the delay rental cheque. Nor could she be heard to complain of Imperial's acts following such a refusal and rejection. The judge was of the opinion that Imperial would not have been required to make a tender of the delay rental payment following the rejection, since any tender would have been "a useless formality."

Effect of Litigation

There is an area of uncertainty as to the precise circumstances of a challenged lease while the litigation is in progress. What happens if, for example, the lessee fails to make a delay rental payment while the case is proceeding through the courts? The chances of this occurring are not negligible as the lessee's files will most likely be in the hands of the lawyers, with some resulting confusion and disarray in the lessee's records. Is the fact that the lease is *sub judice* sufficient protection? Probably not, because the terms contained in the lease must be satisfied in a timely fashion regardless, or the lease will terminate.

There is also the situation where the primary term of a lease may expire before the litigation is finalized. It would be of little comfort to a lessee to be assured by the Supreme Court of Canada that the lease had

---

19 (1954), 12 W.W.R. (N.S.) 569, [1954] A.J. No. 21 (Alta. S.C.T.D.).

been valid at some previous point in time only to be met with a claim on the part of the lessor that it was now terminated by effluxion of time. The American case *Bingham v Stevenson*[20] affords the closest analogy. There the lessor had repudiated the lease and refused to accept rentals or to permit the lessee to drill for a period in excess of seven years. The primary term was held to have been extended by an equivalent period of time.

A default clause in the CAPL lease, which is also commonly found in conventional leases, provides that if proceedings have been commenced for a judicial determination as to whether or not there has been a breach by the lessee, the lease shall not terminate until the existence of the breach has been finally judicially determined, and gives the lessee 30 days after such final determination to remedy or commence to remedy the breach. While this would seem to adequately cover the situation where the primary term expires while litigation is still in progress, it is submitted it would not protect the lessees where a delay rental or shut-in payment was not timely made.

Conclusions

Payment is a straightforward, simple act, and the volume of litigation on the subject is surprising. The following conclusions may be derived from the decided cases:

- Time is of the essence; any gap, no matter how minute, between the expiration of the period and payment is fatal.
- Although the result may be modified by the particular language used in the clause, the careful lessee should treat the delay rental period as ending at midnight on the day previous to the date of the lease.
- If the lease provides for mailing or delivery, as most do, the act of mailing before the end of the critical day is sufficient compliance.
- If the mail is used, the letter should be registered. Single registration is sufficient. All that is required is proof of mailing.
- Payment must be made in full; any deficiency, however insignificant, likely would be held to be an ineffective payment.[21] This result may

---

20 (1966), 420 P. (2d) 839 (Mont. S.C.).

21 There is no Canadian authority directly on this point, but payment of the delay rental is regarded as an option and it is well-settled law that an optionee must comply strictly with all requirements of the option.

not follow where the deficiency is caused by a legislative requirement, such as the obligation imposed by the *Income Tax Act* to
withhold a designated percentage of certain type of payments to
non-residents.[22]

- Overpayment would not amount to a fatal defect; the lessee should
  pay an amount that will net the lessor the amount specified in the
  lease after deduction of the withholding tax.
- The lessor is not required to give a notice of default, as failure to pay
  is not an act of default on the part of the lessee.
- Relief from forfeiture is not available to the lessee, as termination of
  the lease for non-payment, or a defective or late payment, is not a
  forfeiture.
- The depository bank or trust company can receive the payment only
  in accordance with the terms of the lease, and the act of the depository in crediting the amount to the lessor does not bind the lessor so
  as to constitute a waiver of the defective payment.
- Even the retention of the funds by the lessor himself does not constitute a waiver.
- Ontario lessors should treat the *Gas and Oil Leases Act* with great caution. It is safe to use only when *absolutely nothing* has transpired since
  the act or omission that terminated the lease.

---

22 This question remains open; see *Paramount Petroleum and Minerals Corp. Ltd. and Bison
    Petroleum and Minerals Ltd. v Imperial Oil Ltd.*, 73 W.W.R. (N.S.) 417, [1970] S.J. No. 37;
    supplementary reasons [1970] S.J. No. 87 (Sask. Q.B.), and discussion in Chapter 11,
    ante, under "Sufficiency of Payment."

16 Termination of Productive or Potentially Productive Leases

When a lessee loses a lease through failure to make a timely commencement of drilling or payment of a delay rental, there may be some consolation in the fact that the true potential of the lands has been unexplored and remains undetermined. Also, the lessee's out-of-pocket expenditures may not be too burdensome since no costly drilling will have taken place.

It is otherwise with those leases that are terminated because the primary term has expired and the "thereafter" provision has not been engaged successfully. Here the lessee is faced with the loss of a valuable property and one, moreover, on which substantial expenditures will have been made.[1] Indeed, the lessee may be in the galling position of realizing that his estate inevitably must terminate and yet be helpless to avoid the oncoming end. Some of the decisions that have populated this judicial graveyard have already been analysed in those chapters dealing with the individual clauses in the lease. This was necessary in order to fully comprehend the evolution of the current form of the lease clauses. These may be referred to briefly in what follows, but only to the extent necessary to describe those areas that can bring about the involuntary termination of a lease.

In this chapter I will deal with the facts and lease terms that may lead to a lease being found to have terminated, and in the next chapter I will discuss what happens after that.

---

1 The stakes in litigation involving the oil and gas lease are normally very high, but few can match *Pan Canadian Petroleum Ltd. v Husky Oil Operations Ltd.*, 26 Alta. L.R. (3d) 203, [1995] 4 W.W.R. 40, 163 A.R. 367, [1994] A.J. No. 1017 (Alta. Q.B.), where the oil lease covered approximately 1.1 million acres in the Lloydminster area.

Operations at the End of the Primary Term

The lessee who delays drilling until the primary term has nearly expired is flirting with disaster. The final year of the primary term is more fraught with hazard than the others. Subject to the effect of the third proviso to the *habendum*, which will be referred to later, the primary term of the lease can be extended only by something that amounts to production.

Canada-Cities Service Petroleum Corp. v Kininmonth[2] is a classic example of what happens when drilling operations have been commenced but not completed by the end of the primary term. In this case it will be remembered that the clause in the lease that might have permitted operations to be continued was interpreted as not applying until *after* the expiration of the primary term. Therefore, it was as though the lease did not contain any provision extending the primary term while operations continued.

The lease was for a ten-year primary term commencing 11 May 1951. At the end of the primary term the lessee had drilled a well to a total depth of 7,200 feet and plugged it back to a shallower depth that was productive of oil. Before the well could be placed on production, a process to open up the formation, known as fracing, was necessary. This was held in abeyance because of a road ban, so that at midnight, 10 May 1961, when the primary term came to an end, the well was incomplete and there were no operations on the well site. The lease was held to have expired on that date because it could not be said that any of the substances were "being produced" at that time.

In *Republic Resources Ltd. v Ballem*[3] the lease contained a clause that was identical in all relevant aspects to that in *Kininmonth* and provided, "if at any time *after* the expiration of the primary term production of the leased substances has ceased" (emphasis added). At the expiration of the primary term the lessee was engaged in drilling a well, but production was not encountered until six days after the end of the primary term. Holmes J held that the clause did not extend the term of the lease if the lessee had not encountered production within the primary term.

---

2 [1964] S.C.R. 439, 47 W.W.R. (N.S.) 437, 45 D.L.R. (2d) 36, [1964] S.C.J. No. 24 (S.C.C.).
  See full discussion in Chapter 7, *ante*.
3 17 Alta. L.R. (2d) 235, [1982] 1 W.W.R. 692, 33 A.R. 385, [1981] A.J. No. 559 (Alta. Q.B.).

Clause Extending the Primary Term

Most leases today contain a provision similar to the third proviso to the *habendum* discussed in Chapter 7, *ante*, that purports to extend the primary term if certain operations, principally drilling, are taking place at the date on which the term would otherwise expire. While such clauses are generally given effect to, their operation is so restricted in the eyes of the court that the lessee cannot afford the slightest miscue. In *Canadian Superior Oil Ltd. v Hambly*,[4] the lease was dated 17 June 1948, for a ten-year primary term and included this clause: "12. If Lessee shall commence to drill a well within the term of this Lease or any extension thereof, Lessee shall have the right to drill such well to completion with reasonable diligence and dispatch, and if oil or gas be found in paying quantities, this Lease shall continue and be in force with like effect as if such well had been completed within the term of years herein first mentioned." Drilling operations commenced on 10 June 1958 (a week before the end of the primary term), and the well reached total depth on 17 July 1958. Drillstem tests were run and prospective formations were perforated. The drilling rig was released on 6 August 1958, and subsequently the test lines were reconnected and gas flow testing was conducted on 9 and 10 August, while well-site clean-up was done on 11 and 12 August; the "Christmas Tree" was painted on 12 August, and chained and locked on 13 August 1958. The well was a gas well with no immediate market, which brought the shut-in well royalty clause into operation. The lessee forwarded the shut-in royalty payment by letter dated 13 August 1958, which was received on 14 August 1958.

Under these circumstances the courts held that, while the clause did have the effect of extending the lease beyond its primary term, it did so only to that date upon which the well was drilled to completion and that the latest date on which completion could be said to have occurred was 6 August 1958. At that time there was no actual production and the shut-in royalty payment had not yet been made, so that there could be no constructive production. Under these conditions the lease must be considered as having terminated by its own terms.

---

4 (1968), 65 W.W.R. (N.S.) 461 (Alta. S.C.T.D.); affirmed (1969), 67 W.W.R. (N.S.) 525, 3 D.L.R. (3d) 10 (Alta. C.A.); affirmed [1970] S.C.R. 932, 74 W.W.R. (N.S.) 356, 12 D.L.R. (3d) 247, [1970] S.C.J. No. 48 (S.C.C.). The same result was achieved in *Canadian Superior Oil Ltd. v Murdoch* (1969), 70 W.W.R. (N.S.) 768, 6 D.L.R. (3d) 464 (S.C.C.).

If the well turns out to be an oil producer, the lessee must hustle to get it on production before the extended term expires. The difference between an oil and a gas well was demonstrated in *Canadian Superior Oil Ltd. v Cull*.[5] Some lapse of time between actual completion of the well and commencement of production is permissible; it seems to be sufficient if the well's production allowable is met for the month in which the well is completed. The trial judge examined the various drilling operations with great care and concluded that the well was "completed" on 7 January 1958 (beyond the primary term) when there was a "Christmas Tree" in place and the well could have produced oil except that there was no separator or tank battery on the land. Sinclair J was prepared to hold that the lease terminated on that date. The lessee had proceeded with reasonable diligence to install the separator and tanks so that, by 11 January, all necessary facilities were ready. The higher courts refused to treat the lease as having come to an end on 7 January and rejected the idea that production at the very instant the well was completed was necessary in order to continue the lease in force. Under the facts of the case both the lessee and the lessor got the full benefits of production (because the well produced its monthly allowable) and this was sufficient.

In *Canadian Superior Oil Ltd. v Crozet Exploration Ltd.*[6] Stratton J (as he then was) perceived the *Cull* case to "be somewhat of a liberalization of the absolute strictness of the rule enunciated in *Canadian Fina Oil* case." He also noted the case "does not allow the lease to expire merely by reason of production not being taken at the very moment that the well was completed. Short periods of inactivity or delay were accepted as being in accordance with good oil field practice."

Conclusion

Despite the fairly liberal construction adopted in the *Cull* case, a lessee would be ill advised to place itself in a position where it must rely upon this type of extension of the primary term. If the property justifies the expense of drilling, it should be done in sufficient time so that

---

5 (1970), 74 W.W.R. (N.S.) 324 (Alta. S.C.T.D.); affirmed (1970), 75 W.W.R. (N.S.) 606, 16 D.L.R. (3d) 709 (Alta. C.A.); affirmed [1972] S.C.R. 89, [1971] 3 W.W.R. 28, 20 D.L.R. (3d) 360, [1971] S.C.J. No. 91 (S.C.C.). See full discussion of this case in Chapter 7, *ante*.
6 (1982), 18 Alta. L.R. (2d) 145, 133 D.L.R. (3d) 53, 34 A.R. 256, [1982] A.J. No. 672 (Alta. Q.B.).

the well can be completed and placed on production or the payment of shut-in royalty made prior to the expiration of the primary term.

Shut-in Well Payments

Kissinger Petroleums Ltd. v Nelson Estate[7] has been fully discussed in Chapters 8 and 9, *ante,* and the reader is referred to those chapters for a description of its facts. Insofar as shut-in well payments are concerned, it held that a payment made in advance of the completion of the well, and in anticipation that the well will be capable of commercial production, complies with the shut-in royalty clause when, upon completion of the well, the prior payment is designated as a shut-in royalty payment and accepted by the lessor as such. The court did not have to decide what the position would be if the lessor refused payment. Query, what would have been the result if the lessee had not, subsequent to the well having been completed, designated the payment as being a shut-in-payment?

As marginal wells maintain leases year after year by the payment of shut-in royalties at the purely nominal cost of $1.00 per acre, more and more attention is being focused on the conditions under which such a payment can be validly made and thereby create constructive production. There are many versions of the shut-in or suspended well clause, and each one must be scrutinized very carefully to determine its effect. Some will require lack of or intermittent market or other clause beyond the lessee's reasonable control, or good oil field practice, some may require that the well he capable of production, while others merely refer to a well on the lands or the pooled lands.

One of the more bizarre attempts by the lessee to maintain a lease in force past the primary term by the payment of the shut-in royalty is *Young v Mesa Petroleum (N.A.) Co.*[8] In that case there was a lease with a primary term of ten years that provided for a delay rental of $50.00 annually if drilling had not taken place. It also contained the usual "thereafter" provision that would continue the lease beyond the primary term if there was production, including constructive production pursuant to the shut-in clause. The oil company paid the $50.00 annual

---

7 (1984), 33 Alta. L.R. (2d) 1, [1984] 5 W.W.R. 673, 13 D.L.R. (4th) 542, [1984] A.J. No. 2587 (Alta. C.A.); affirming 26 Alta. L.R. (2d) 378, 14 E.T.R. 207, 45 A.R. 393, [1983] A.J. No. 84 (Alta. Q.B.). (Leave to appeal to the Supreme Court denied.)
8 [1989] O.J. No. 1043, 16 A.C.W.S. (3d) 198 (H.C.J.).

fee during each year of the ten-year term but did not carry out any drilling on the lands. There were, in fact, two capped gas wells on the lands, which had been drilled and capped some seven and eight years prior to the subject lease being entered into. The lessee argued that the monies paid after the expiration of the primary term were, in fact, shut-in royalties because of the two wells, which, as the court pointed out, were capped before the lease was even entered into. The court rejected this contention and found that payments that had been delay rentals for the ten-year primary term could not, at the expiration of that term, "suddenly be converted into royalties" based on wells that had been drilled and capped long before the lease was entered into.

In *Blair Estate Ltd. v Altana Exploration Co.*,[9] a one-page judgment of the Alberta Court of Appeal, the issue turned on whether or not the lessee could rely on a lack of market or of an intermittent market to justify maintaining the lease by paying the shut-in royalty. The court found that the evidence supported the inference that insofar as its major customer, TransCanada Pipelines, was concerned, the market was, in fact, intermittent. However, there was also evidence of a different market described as being a discount commercial market and because of the existence of this alternate market, the lessee had not proved there was a lack of market to justify the extension of the primary term.

Insofar as shut-in royalties are concerned, the most important aspect of the *Durish*[10] case was that the expression "shall pay" in the shut-in clause did not create an obligation to make the payment, which, in turn, would have activated the default clause. The trial judge also found that a purported payment eight months after the anniversary date was not payment within a reasonable time. Query, whether a shut-in payment can be validly made within a reasonable time after the date on which the lease provides it is to be paid? The better view would seem to be that once the date on which the shut-in payment was to have been made had passed with no payment, there would be no production, deemed or otherwise, of the leased substances and the wording of the "thereafter" provision in the *habendum* would automatically bring the lease to an end. The Court of Appeal did not have to

---

9 (1987), 53 Alta. L.R. (2d) 419, [1987] A.J. No. 554 (Alta. C.A.).

10 *Durish v White Resource Management Ltd.* (1987), 55 Alta. L.R. (2d) 47, [1987] A.J. No. 804 (Alta. Q.B.); affirmed (1988), 63 Alta. L.R. (2d) 265, [1988] A.J. No. 1162 (Alta. C.A.). See also case comment, *Bankes* (1989), 63 Alta. L.R. (2d) 269.

consider whether or not a shut-in payment could be made within a reasonable time after the anniversary date, so a suggestion that it could be remains as dubious *obiter* at the trial court level.

The 1998 *Durish* case stands for the seemingly obvious proposition that where no shut-in payment was made, the lease expired by its own terms.[11] In argument, Durish submitted that since he was the contractual owner of both the reversionary mineral title and the lease in question, he had the right to make such payment to himself notionally, or not at all. This argument did not succeed.

The extent to which the extended well clause can be used to prolong the life of a lease indefinitely and to effectively sterilize the rights of the mineral owner is illustrated by *549767 Alberta Ltd. v Teg Holdings Ltd.*[12] This case, which was heard in 1997, involved two leases on which there were two capped gas wells, one of which had been drilled in 1973 and the other in 1976. Neither well was ever produced. Throughout this period, the shut-in royalty was paid to the lessor. The lessor brought an action claiming that the two leases had expired in 1987. The court fixed the lessee defendants with the onus to show that there was a lack of market or transportation facilities in order to preserve the leases. The defendants interpreted the phrase "lack or intermittent market" to be "lack of economic market." The court found the result to be the same. After hearing much expert testimony on the availability of processing at gas plants, the cost of tying in the wells, and the existing market conditions, Deyell J found that the defendants had failed to bring their failure to produce within "as a result of a lack of, or an intermittent, market or lack of transportation facilities or any other cause beyond the lessee's reasonable control." Accordingly, both leases were struck down.

When it comes to delayed production, *Freyberg v Fletcher Challenge Oil & Gas Inc.*[13] will be hard to equal. The natural gas lease was dated 13 November 1975. A successful natural gas well was drilled and tested on the leased lands in 1978, but no further operations were conducted until December 1998 when the well was completed and put on production. Shut-in well payments were made during the twenty-year period.

---

11 [1998] A.J. No. 1041, 230 A.R. 201 (Alta. Q.B.).
12 172 D.L.R. (4th) 294, [1999] A.J. No. 321 (Alta. C.A.); see also *supra* n 9.
13 323 A.R. 45, [2002] A.J. No. 1173 (Alta. Q.B.); reversed, 42 Alta. L.R. (4th) 41, [2005] 10 W.W.R. 87, 363 A.R. 35, [2005] A.J. No. 108 (Alta. C.A.). I discuss this case in Ballem, "The Further Adventures and Strange Afterlife of the Oil and Gas Lease" (2006) 44 Alta. L. Rev. 429.

The Alberta Court of Appeal found that the onus was on the lessee to prove that there was a lack of an economical or profitable market that would justify shut-in well payments. The test as to whether there was an economic or profitable market was if a prudent lessee, based on information available at the time, would have foreseen profitability.

Using this test, the court held that the lessee had failed to establish that there had not been an economic market for the gas, so the shut-in payments could not maintain the lease in force.

What qualifies as working operations was one of the many issues before the court in *Montreal Trust Co. v Williston Wildcatters Co.*[14] The question was what activities amount to working operations that will maintain the lease in force when the leased substances are not being produced on the said lands.

In *Williston* there was no production during the period January 1990 to the end of July, well after the expiration of the primary term. During that seven-month period when there was no production:

- The lessee had ploughed the snow to facilitate access to the well site.
- The field operator attended the well in March and thawed out the flow line and started the well, but the line froze.
- In May, a fence was built around the well to keep out cattle and a dugout was built for the surface owner to replace his dugout that had been contaminated by salt water from the well.
- During 1990, the lessee paid the surface lease rent and taxes and filed reports with the government, paid the mineral tax, and corresponded with the plaintiff.

The trial judge noted that there had been no decision on the point and ruled that "working operations" must be activities directed to bring about the production of oil. He found that the activities of the lessee within the relevant period did not meet that test.

He also held that the lessee could not rely on the proviso in the *habendum* that if the working operations were suspended as a result of any cause beyond the lessee's control the time of such suspension shall not be counted against the lessee. The lessee submitted that the winter

---

14 [2004] 3 W.W.R. 574, 239 Sask. R. 57, [2003] S.J. No. 523 (Sask. Q.B.); varied 254 Sask. R. 38, [2005] 4 W.W.R. 20, 243 D.L.R. (4th) 317, [2004] S.J. No. 541 (Sask. C.A.); leave to appeal refused [2004] S.C.C.A. 474 (S.C.C.).

weather and the imposition of road bans were causes beyond its control. The trial judge dismissed the weather conditions as an ongoing situation that the oil industry had learned to deal with, and road bans were not beyond the lessee's control in that it could have planned its operations around them. In making his ruling on the road bans, Gerein CJQB followed the precedent of *Canada-Cities Service Petroleum Corp. v Kininmonth.*[15]

In *Kininmonth,* the Court of Appeal upheld the trial judge's decision that the lease had terminated and agreed that the activities of the lessee did not constitute working operations. The Court of Appeal also agreed that in order to qualify, the work must be directed to the production of oil. The trial judge's conclusion that the winter conditions and road bans were common events that were dealt with routinely by the oil industry and thus were not a cause beyond the lessee's control was also approved. The court observed that road bans in the spring are well known and the courts are entitled to take judicial notice of that fact.

Pooling

The concept of pooling is straightforward. If the lands covered by a lease are less than a spacing unit allocated under the applicable legislation for drilling or production purposes, they may be pooled with other lands to make up the necessary acreage. Virtually all leases contain a clause that empowers the lessee to pool the lands under such circumstances. It will be recalled, however, from our discussion on pooling in Chapter 9 that many leases contain a pooling clause that is totally ineffective. In *Shell Oil Co. v Gibbard*[16] the Supreme Court of Canada held that the phrase "when such pooling, or combining is necessary in order to conform with any regulations or orders of the Government of the Province of Alberta or any other authoritative body, which are now or may hereafter be in force in relation thereto" authorized pooling only where there was an affirmative requirement by the government to do so. Since there are no affirmative requirements that will activate the clause, many leases in effect today do not authorize the lessee to pool the lands.[17]

---

15 [1964] S.C.R. 439, 47 W.W.R. (N.S.) 437, 45 D.L.R. (2d) 36, [1964] S.C.J. No. 24 (S.C.C.).
16 [1961] S.C.R. 725, 36 W.W.R. (N.S.) 529, 30 D.L.R. (2d) 386, [1961] S.C.J. No. 51 (S.C.C.).
   See full discussion of this case in Chapter 9, *ante.*
17 As to compulsory pooling, see Chapter 9, n 21.

Pooling is frequently encountered in conjunction with shut-in royalty. The lands will be pooled with other lands on which there is a well, or on which a well is to be drilled, and then an attempt will be made to pay on a suspended well basis and thereby create constructive production.

Sometimes, however, the language used in the lease will not allow the creation of constructive production through a combination of pooling and suspended well payment. In *Shell Oil Company v Gunderson*[18] the *habendum* clause provided "and so long thereafter as the leased substances or any of them are produced from the said lands."

The suspended gas well royalty clause read: "3. Provided no royalties are otherwise paid hereunder, the Lessee shall pay to the Lessor each year as royalty the sum of Fifty Dollars ($50.00) for all wells on the said lands where gas only or primarily is found and the same is not used or sold, and while the said royalty is so paid each such well shall be deemed to be a producing well hereunder." The last sentence of the pooling clause was: "Drilling operations on, or production of leased substances from, any land included in such unit shall have the same effect in continuing this lease in force and effect during the term hereby granted, or any extension thereof, as to all the said lands, as if such operation or production were upon or from the said lands or some portion thereof."

The lease comprised a quarter section within the same section of land that also included the quarter section covered by the Gibbard lease. No well was drilled on the Gunderson quarter section, but one was drilled on another quarter section, and capped as a gas well. Prior to the expiration of the primary term a pooling notice was given under which the Gunderson quarter section was pooled with the balance of the section that included the capped gas well. The suspended gas well payment was also tendered, which, the lessee contended, was sufficient to maintain the lease in force.

The court rejected this argument on the grounds that the *habendum* clause referred only to production "from the said lands," which were defined as being the particular quarter section covered by the lease. Thus, the well referred to in the suspended well clause could only be a well on the said lands. Nor could the last sentence of the pooling clause assist the lessee, because it referred only to "drilling operations" or "production." The payment of the suspended well royalty could not amount to constructive production because that clause was limited to "all wells

---

18 [1960] S.C.R. 424, 23 D.L.R. (2d) 81, [1960] S.C.J. No. 19 (S.C.C.). See also discussion in Chapter 9, *ante*.

on the said lands" and the well in question was not located on the said lands. Thus, the lease was held to have terminated – a result that must have astounded and dismayed those who had drafted the lease.

Canadian Superior Oil of Calif. Ltd. v Kanstrup[19] is another example where the language was not sufficiently precise to meet the exacting tests imposed by the court. The fact pattern in *Kanstrup* was the common situation where a lease covered a quarter section and a gas well had been drilled and capped on another quarter section within the one-section spacing unit. The original lease did not contain any provision for pooling, but by subsequent amendment the right to pool under certain conditions was granted. The pooling language appeared to have the same defect as in *Gibbard* inasmuch as it contained the reference to "necessary in order to conform with any regulations or orders … " The amending letter, however, did recite the purpose of the pooling and that it was necessary because of the fact that the spacing unit for a gas well was 640 acres. Under these conditions the court was prepared to concede that pooling had been achieved, but this was of little assistance to the lessee. The amending letter also contained this language: "Drilling operations on, or production of leased substances from any land included in such unit shall have the same effect in continuing this Lease in force and effect during the term hereby granted, or any extension thereof, as to all the said lands, as if such operation or production were upon or from the said lands, or some portion thereof."

The original lease contained a capped gas well royalty clause, which read in part as follows: "Where gas from a well producing gas only is not sold or used, Lessee may pay as royalty $100.00 per well per year, and if such payment is made it will be considered that gas is being produced within the meaning of Paragraph 2 hereof." Paragraph 2 provided for continuation of the lease by production. Martland J analysed the portion of the amending letter, quoted above, which dealt with those items that were meant to continue the lease in force and effect. According to the view taken by the court, it was only drilling operations on or production of leased substances from any land other than the quarter section that would be effective to continue the lease. He pointed out that it did not say that a non-producing gas well not on the leased quarter section was to be equivalent to a non-producing gas well on the northwest quarter so as to entitle the lessee to rely upon the provision. The result is a clear example of the literalistic approach in action.

---

19 [1965] S.C.R. 92, (1964) 49 W.W.R. (N.S.) 257, 47 D.L.R. (2d) 1, [1964] S.C.J. No. 54 (S.C.C.).

Absence of or Cessation of Production

It is axiomatic from the language of the lease itself that it will terminate if there is no production (actual or constructive) at the end of the primary term. In *Sohio Petroleum Company v Weyburn Security Company Ltd.*,[20] the drilling operations did not commence until one week prior to the expiration of the ten-year primary term and the well was completed some ten days after that term had expired. The well went on production and royalty was paid to the lessor. The Supreme Court of Canada remarked, almost in passing, that the lease had terminated because there was no production within the primary term.

The *Kininmonth* decision was followed in *Paramount Petroleum and Minerals Corp. Ltd. v Imperial Oil Ltd.*[21] to strike down a lease that had two wells on it. The primary term expired on 1 June and the wells were not placed on production until 6 July and 19 December, respectively.

As to cessation of production after the primary term, the reader is referred back to the discussion of *Williston* earlier in this chapter and also to *Krysa v Opalinski*[22] in Chapter 7. The only open question appears to be the effect of interrupted or suspended production, which was also discussed in Chapter 7.

Perpetuities

The rule against perpetuities provides: No interest is good unless it must vest, if at all, no later than twenty-one (21) years after some life in being at the creation of the interest.[23] If no life is identified, as is the normal case with oil and gas leases, twenty-one years becomes the perpetuity period.

If an instrument was executed in Alberta prior to the cut-off date of 1 July 1973,[24] it can be vulnerable to an attack based on the rule against perpetuities. In *Pan Canadian Petroleum Ltd. v Husky Oil Operations Ltd.*[25] the leases in question had been entered into on 3 January 1967.

---

20 [1971] S.C.R. 81, 74 W.W.R. 626, 13 D.L.R. (3d) 340, [1970] S.C.J. No. 65 (S.C.C.).
21 73 W.W.R. (N.S.) 417, [1970] S.J. No. 37; supplementary reasons [1970] S.J. No. 87 (Sask. Q.B.).
22 [1960] A.J. No. 15, 32 W.W.R. 346 (Alta. S.C.T.D.).
23 See Morris & Leach, *The Rule against Perpetuities*, 2nd ed. (Toronto: Carswell, 1962).
24 *Peretuities Act*, R.S.A. 2000, c P-5, s 25. After that date the "wait and see" and eighty-year perpetuity period became effective.
25 *Supra* n 1.

The leases were for a primary term of twenty-five years and so long thereafter as the leased substances were produced. In addition to the "so long thereafter" language, the *habendum* contained the phrase "subject also to the renewal of the said term." The renewal provision gave the lessee the option for "a renewal lease of the leased substances in the said lands for a further primary term of twenty-five (25) years ..." Since the right to renew would not arise until the expiration of the twenty-five-year primary term, the rule was clearly offended. This was confirmed in the decision.

There were two leases under attack, both covering vast tracts of land (1.1 million acres) in the Lloydminster area. One was an oil and gas lease and was the real target of the attack. There had been a great deal of drilling activity pursuant to this lease and at the end of the primary term the leased substances were being produced from literally hundreds of wells. The plaintiff, Pan Canadian, argued that the "subject to" provision qualified and limited the "so long thereafter" *habendum* clause. McMahon J found that the "so long thereafter" clause continued the lease in force as there was production at the end of the primary term and there was no need for Husky to rely on the renewal clause.

Unlike the oil and gas lease, no work had been carried out on the mineral lease and there was no production at the end of the twenty-five-year primary term. The right to renew being void because it offended the rule, this, less valuable, lease was held to have expired at the end of the primary term.

In Saskatchewan, where the common law rule has not been abolished nor modified by legislation, there has been speculation for years that certain agreements that at one time covered some two million acres in the province, and still affect more than one million acres, could be overturned on the basis that they offended the rule.

In the early 1950s a number of companies were formed to acquire freehold mineral rights to be cooperatively shared for the benefit of all participating members, and for this reason they were known as "mutual companies." At the time they launched their campaigns to acquire freehold mineral rights, most of the lands wherein they acquired an interest were already under lease to major oil companies.[26] This led to an

---

26 For a detailed description of this process and how it worked, see Shortt, "Distinctive Forms of Freehold Leases and Transactions in Saskatchewan," March 1997, (1997) *Insight – Insights into Conducting Oil and Gas Operations in Saskatchewan*, at Tab VI.

arrangement that amounted to a top lease and provided that the lease was to come into effect on the termination, cancellation, avoidance, or expiration of the existing lease. In some cases the mineral title was transferred to the mutual company, with the result that upon the expiry of the existing lease, the mutual company would then have ownership of the mineral estate free and clear of the expired lease. The consideration to the mineral owner was in shares of the mutual companies.

At the same time as the mutual companies were crisscrossing Saskatchewan acquiring assignments of minerals and top leases, Prudential Trust on behalf of various oil companies was also waging a similar campaign to acquire mineral rights. Basically, the Prudential options followed this pattern: (a) the mineral owner conveyed an undivided one-half interest in his petroleum, natural gas, and related hydrocarbons to the trust company, and (b) the mineral owner also granted Prudential an option to acquire a petroleum and natural gas lease for a term of ninety-nine years, the option to be exercisable upon the expiry of the existing lease. When the mineral owners belatedly realized that they had assigned one-half of their mineral rights rather than merely granting an option to lease, a number of challenges were launched against the agreements on the basis of *non est factum*. This is discussed in Chapter 5 under the heading "Non Est Factum," *ante*. After some success in the lower courts, the challenges based on *non est factum* were brought to an end by the Supreme Court of Canada decisions in *Prudential Trust Co. Ltd. v Forseth*[27] and *Prudential Trust Co. Ltd. and Canadian Williston Minerals Ltd. v Olsen*.[28]

Forty years later, the rule against perpetuities issue came before the Saskatchewan courts in *Taylor v Scurry-Rainbow Oil (Sask.) Ltd.*[29]

The *Taylor* case had the perfect fact pattern to raise the perpetuities issue. On 26 April 1949 one Henry Taylor, the owner of a half section of land in Saskatchewan, including the minerals, granted a lease to Imperial Oil for a primary term of ten years and with the usual "so long thereafter as the leased substances are produced" clause. There was no production and the lease expired on its own terms on 25 April 1959.

---

27 [1960] S.C.R. 210, 30 W.W.R. 241, 21 D.L.R. (2d) 507, [1959] S.C.J. No. 84 (S.C.C.).
28 [1960] S.C.R. 227, 21 D.L.R. (2d) 603, [1959] S.C.J. No. 85 (S.C.C.).
29 170 Sask. R. 222, [1999] 5 W.W.R. 424, [1998] S.J. No. 589 (Sask. Q.B.); reversed 207 Sask. R. 266, [2001] 11 W.W.R. 25, 203 D.L.R. (4th) 38, [2001] S.J. No. 479 (Sask. C.A.). Although the case is indexed as *Taylor v Scurry-Rainbow (Sask.) Ltd.*, the real plaintiff was Maxx Petroleum, the lessee under a second lease.

On 7 August 1950, the mineral owner entered into an agreement with Freeholders whereby he assigned the royalty under the lease to Freeholders and also agreed that if the Imperial lease should terminate for whatever cause within a period of forty-two years, all mines and minerals were to become subject to the terms of the Freeholders lease for a term of ninety-nine years.

On 3 May 1956, Taylor entered into another agreement with Imperial Oil that recited the original lease and referred to the Freeholders agreement and granted unto Imperial another lease that was to become effective on the date of the latest of the date of termination, cancellation, etc. of the original Imperial lease or the date of the expiration of the Freeholders agreement. It contained a proviso that if the said lease and the said agreement had not been terminated within seven years from the date hereof, this agreement would expire and be at an end, which took care of the perpetuities problem for that agreement. In effect, what Imperial had was a top top lease.

The next relevant document was entered into on 16 November 1993, when Taylor's son granted a petroleum and natural gas lease in favour of Maxx Petroleum.

The question before the court was whether or not the Freeholders lease dated 7 August 1950, with its proviso that it would become effective if the Imperial lease terminated within forty-two years, offended the rule against perpetuities. The trial court held that Freeholders lease was void because the forty-two-year contingency period violated the rule against perpetuities. That finding was reversed by the court of appeal, which looked at the policy behind the rule and found that it was not offended by the contingency lease. Thus, it was an appropriate case for the court to intervene and hold that the top lease was not rendered void by the rule.

Whether because of the court finding that the commercial realities of the oil industry do not offend the policy behind it, or by legislative modification of its applicability, it seems unlikely that the rule against perpetuities will play any significant role in the law of the oil and gas lease.

Confidentiality

The matter of confidentiality can be a very difficult one in dealing with oil and gas leases. In many transactions such as a proposed purchase or share acquisition or other business arrangement, it is usual and customary to enter into confidentiality agreements. In the case of oil and gas leases, however, this would not appear to be practical as the party carrying out due diligence would not want to be foreclosed from dealing in the area in which he was interested. It is also true that the oil and gas lease is particularly susceptible to attack.

Breach of confidence was raised in the *Taylor* trial in a counter-claim by Tarragon Oil and Gas Limited against the plaintiff, Maxx Petroleum. Maxx had been in negotiations with the plaintiff by counter-claim, Tarragon, which had acquired Scurry-Rainbow's interest in the Freeholders lease in 1993, with respect to farming in Tarragon's interest in the subject lands. A final agreement was prepared and sent to Maxx, and then a lawyer acting for Maxx attended at the offices of Tarragon to conduct a due diligence examination of the relevant documentation. Among the documents provided by Tarragon was the by now famous Freeholders lease of 7 August 1950.

On the same day that the lease was produced to Maxx, Maxx engaged a land company to obtain a petroleum and natural gas lease from the mineral owner. This was done and both that lease and the 1950 Freeholders lease covering the same half-section were assigned to Maxx on 3 February 1994.

The trial judge found that Maxx had breached its duty of confidence that arose when Tarragon showed them the lease. Gerein J held that the lease was provided for the sole purpose of carrying out the due diligence review and ruled that Maxx held an interest in the mines and minerals as trustee for Tarragon. It was urged on behalf of Maxx that at all relevant times the form of the Freeholders lease was on file with the Corporations Branch of Saskatchewan Justice and the caveat largely set out what was contained in clauses 1 and 2 of the lease. Thus, it was argued that the Freeholders lease was in the public domain and could not be the subject of a breach of confidence.

In answer to that contention, the trial judge pointed out that while this enabled one to speculate about the contents of the Freeholders lease, it was only a form that was on file and one could not be certain of the terms of the actual lease. This could only be discovered when Tarragon opened its files. The document was produced to enable Maxx to determine whether Tarragon had good title. It was not intended to provide information to Maxx so it could undermine Tarragon's position.

Having found a breach of confidence, the Trial Court struck down Maxx's lease. The Court of Appeal stated that the cross appeal was rendered moot since it found the Freeholders lease not to be void.

The issue of confidentiality also arose in connection with oil and gas leases in *Cinabar Enterprises Ltd. v Richland Petroleum Corp.*,[30] which was handed down on 28 July 1998. In that case the plaintiff had shown the defendant some documents and plats in connection with a possible purchase of the property by the defendant. The material showed that the well on the land had been abandoned. There was no reference to confidentiality on either side. The defendant acquired a new lease because it felt that the existing lease had expired. The trial judge found that the circumstances under which the information was imparted to the defendant did not have the necessary quality of confidentiality. More telling was the fact that, well before the meeting with Cinabar, Richland had obtained a township plat from Petroleum Information Canada Ltd. that showed the relevant well to be abandoned.

There was an interesting side bar in this case. The well had been abandoned by Cinabar's predecessor in title and was listed as abandoned. However, the reason it had been abandoned was that there was a leak in the production casing and it was venting gas to the surface. This led Cinabar to maintain that the well was capable of production, and Cinabar continued to make shut-in payments despite the existence of the new lease. This issue was not before the court, and the court specifically stated that the point remained undetermined.

---

30 (1998) 255 A.R. 161, [1998] A.J. No. 891 (Alta. Q.B.). See also *Guyer Oil Company Ltd. v Fulton*, [1972] S.J. No. 189, [1973] 1 W.W.R. 97 (Sask. Q.B.); affirmed [1976] 5 W.W.R. 356 (Sask. C.A.); affirmed [1977] S.C.R. 791, [1977] 4 W.W.R. 112, [1977] S.C.J. No. 27 (S.C.C.), where the claim of breach of confidentiality was unsuccessfully raised in the case of a geological consultant who had been retained by the plaintiff to "sit" a well. Subsequently the consultant (defendant) bid on and obtained Crown leases in the area. The court found that the evidence did not establish that the consultant had made use of confidential information.

17 Accounting for Past Production

Having decided that a lease with a history of production has terminated, the court will be called upon to determine the parties' right to the proceeds of that production. Sometimes the matter will be resolved by private treaty between the parties, with or without the encouragement of the court. But courts have been required to deal with the issue on numerous occasions.

Sohio Petroleum Company v Weyburn Security Company Ltd.[1] is a good starting point, although by no means the final answer, for this analysis. The facts that led to the termination of the lease are set forth in the previous chapter. For our present purposes it is sufficient to know that the well began to produce in November 1959 and the action to have the lease declared invalid was not taken until October 1966. Thus, there was a very considerable volume of production at issue. The lessor, in addition to seeking a declaration that the lease had terminated, also sought an accounting of past production.

The Saskatchewan Court of Appeal took a broad brush approach to the problem, relying heavily on equitable principles and *bona fides*:

> The court has jurisdiction to grant this relief on terms which will be just and equitable to all parties involved. The respondent, Sohio, proceeded under a mistake as to its rights, and did not knowingly take an unfair advantage of the appellant's lack of appreciation of its legal rights. The

---

1 *Sohio Petroleum Co. v Weyburn Security Co. Ltd.*, [1968] S.J. No. 114, 66 W.W.R. (N.S.) 155 (Sask. Q.B.); reversed 69 W.W.R. (N.S.) 680, 7 D.L.R. (3d) 277 (Sask. C.A.); affirmed [1971] S.C.R. 81, 74 W.W.R. 626, 13 D.L.R. (3d) 340, [1970] S.C.J. No. 65 (S.C.C.).

respondents were first aware that their position was challenged when the writ of summons was served upon them. At that time the revenue which they had received from the sale of the production exceeded the amount that they had expended. Under the circumstances, it would appear just and equitable to order the respondents to account for all benefits from production received by them after the date of service of the writ of summons upon them.[2]

This solution was expressly approved by the Supreme Court of Canada.[3]

While neither the Court of Appeal nor the Supreme Court of Canada referred to any American decisions, the result is generally similar to what would have been achieved in the United States. There, the lessee under an invalid lease is treated as a trespasser. The courts then seek to determine whether the lessee is an innocent or wilful trespasser. This inquiry in turn narrows down to the *bona fides* or lack of same on the part of the lessee. If, for example, the lessee had cause to know that the validity of the lease was challenged or likely to be challenged, and nonetheless proceeded to drill and take production, it would likely be classified as a wilful trespasser.

In the United States the classification of a lessee whose title ultimately fails has a profound effect upon the duty to account for past production. In both cases the lessee whose lease has expired must account for the minerals produced. The bad faith trespasser, however, is not entitled to set off against the proceeds from the sale of the minerals the cost of drilling and operating the well. The good faith trespasser, while required to account for past production, is generally allowed to deduct the cost of producing and lifting the minerals.[4]

Although the Court of Appeal decision in *Weyburn* had been handed down almost a year before *Paramount Petroleums and Minerals Corp. Ltd. and Bison Petroleum and Minerals Ltd. v Imperial Oil Ltd.*,[5] it was not referred to in the judgment of the latter case. In *Paramount* a lease was

---

2 69 W.W.R. 680, 7 D.L.R. (3d) 277 (Sask. C.A.). This aspect of the decision is discussed critically in Harrison, "Selected Cases, Legislation and Developments in Oil and Gas Law" (1972) 10 Alta. L. Rev. 391 at 405–7.

3 [1971] S.C.R. 81, (1970) 74 W.W.R. 626, 13 D.L.R. (3d) 340, [1970] S.C.J. No. 65.

4 *Marathon Oil Co. v Gulf Oil Corporation*, 130 S.W. (2d) 365 (1939), (Tex. Civ. Appl); *Shell Oil Co. v Dove*, 135 F 2d 365 (1943, 7th Cir.).

5 (1970), 73 W.W.R. (N.S.) 417, [1970] S.J. No. 37; supplementary reasons [1970] S.J. No. 87 (Sask. Q.B.).

held to have expired for lack of production at the end of its primary term, 1 June 1959. As a result of that finding, an accounting of past production was sought. The trial judge granted it, stating that the *Kininmonth* case had decided the rights of the parties by ruling that the lease expired at the end of the primary term. All the production had taken place after the lease had expired, and the fact that Imperial was unaware of its position until years after it brought the wells into production did not alter the situation. The judgment did not deal with the question of whether or not Imperial would be entitled to take drilling and completion costs into account. I am advised, however, that in the actual accounting worked out between the parties these costs were deducted and recovered.

In *Hill Estate v Chevron Standard Ltd.*[6] a mentally incompetent man executed a general power of attorney in favour of his wife. His wife was well aware that he was mentally incompetent when he fixed his "X" to the power of attorney. As attorney for her husband, the wife leased his mineral interest to an oil company's agent. Neither the agent nor the oil company (Chevron) knew of the mental incapacity, and the circumstances did not alert them. The husband died intestate. His daughter was appointed administrix. During the primary term of the lease Chevron paid the annual delay rentals and the estate deposited them. Since the lease was nearing the end of its primary term, Chevron decided to drill. The daughter learned of this and was also advised that the power of attorney was void rather than voidable. Her lawyer wrote Chevron, demanding that the lease be surrendered and the caveat be withdrawn. Chevron refused, and proceeded to drill for oil. The estate sued for return of the mineral rights and an accounting.

The trial judge found that both the general power of attorney and the lease were voidable rather than void, and therefore the lease was enforceable by Chevron, which had given fair consideration.[7] The trial decision was reversed on appeal, the court ruling that the law relating to contracts is different from that relating to a general power of attorney. A contract is binding upon a mentally incompetent person unless it can be demonstrated that the other party knew, or ought to have known, of the incapacity. In the case of a power of attorney, no consideration passes; there is no contract for value. Therefore, the power of attorney is void rather than voidable, and everything done under it is also void.

---

6 85 Man R. (2d) 67, [1993] 2 W.W.R. 545, [1993] M.J. No. 665 (Man. C.A.).
7 [1991], 74 Man. R. (2d) 162, [1991] M.J. 411 (Man. Q.B.).

The lease having been declared void, the estate was entitled to all the revenues generated by the sale of oil, both past and future. Chevron was not entitled to deduct its costs and expenses. It may be that the special circumstances of the case did not dispose the court to grant the equitable relief of allowing the lessee to recover the cost of the well.

Until the remedies hearing of *Montreal Trust Co. v Williston Wildcatters Corp.*[8] came along, it seemed that the most likely result where a lease was held to have terminated after producing the leased substances for a period of time would see the lessee required to account to the lessor for that production. If the equities so inclined the court, the lessee could recover its costs of drilling and operating from such proceeds.

In *Williston*, the lease came to an end in January 1990, although that was not finalized until 2002, when leave to appeal to the Supreme Court was refused. At the end of the trial on 2 November 2001, the parties entered into a consent order permitting the lessee to continue producing, with the proceeds being paid into court. The plaintiff lessor claimed the value of the production between the termination of the lease in 1990 and the consent order in 2001 to be in the order of $1,500,000, after allowing for the drilling and operating costs.

Rather than following the concepts of ownership and restitution, the trial judge opted to assess the damages suffered by the lessor. This led to a result radically different from *Weyburn*.

The trial judge began by noting that the usual measure of damages is that which will restore the plaintiff to its original position prior to the defendant's wrongful act. He also noted there were two rules to be considered in quantifying damages. The first rule, which is described as "severe" or "harsh," is that the plaintiff should receive the value of what was produced without any allowance for the cost of production. The second, milder, rule holds that in calculating the value of the produced goods, an allowance should be made for the cost of production. This is what the plaintiff lessor had asked for. It is similar to the result in *Weyburn* where the court, observing that the lessee had more than recovered its costs by the time the writ of summons was served, held that it would appear "just and equitable" for the lessee to account for all benefits from production received after the date of service of the writ.

---

8 [2004] 3 W.W.R. 574, 239 Sask. R. 57, [2003] S.J. No. 523 (Sask. Q.B.); varied [2005] 4 W.W.R. 20, 254 Sask. R. 38, [2004] S.J. No. 541; leave to appeal denied, [2004] S.C.C.A. No. 474. I commented on this case in "The Further Adventures and Strange Afterlife of the Oil and Gas Lease" (2006) 44 Alta. L. Rev. 429.

The trial judge seized on the just and equitable aspect to arrive at a result that Professor Bankes ironically terms the "really mild rule."[9] In reaching this "really mild" result, the judge noted that the lessor would not have developed the property itself; rather, it would have relied on a third party – presumably an operating oil company – to do so.

It should be pointed out that Montreal Trust was a purely nominal plaintiff, holding the mineral rights in trust for the unitholders. One of the unitholders in the trust was an operating oil company, but its witness testified that he was not interested in drilling on the property as the economic prospects were not very good. The court commented that even if another unitholder might have developed the property, it only meant that the development property would have gone to a third party, not the plaintiff.[10] In making this comment the court was assuming that the plaintiff could only have achieved participation by way of a lease. This is not necessarily the case.

There was evidence that the plaintiff – Montreal Trust – could have obtained a royalty of 18 per cent and a bonus of $6,400 for a lease at the time the subject lease had come to an end. Abandoning both the "harsh" and the "mild" rules, the court used this evidence to "restore" the plaintiff to the same position it would have been in before the trespass, and awarded the plaintiff the sum of $6,400 by way of bonus and increased the applicable royalty rate from the 12½ per cent specified in the lease to 18 per cent. This approach to fixing the amount of damages was approved by the Saskatchewan Court of Appeal, although as we shall see, the length of time during which it was applicable was shortened by the finding of leave and licence.

With respect, it is submitted that there is a great deal to be concerned about in this way of assessing the lessor's position and rights where a lease with a producing well has terminated. Once that has taken place it is the lessor, not the lessee, who owns the minerals. In the absence of bad faith on the part of the lessee, and following the *Weyburn* approach, it would seem equitable to apply a form of restitution, and allow the lessee to recoup its costs from the proceeds of production. The aspect of ownership appears to have been overlooked at both the trial and appellate levels. This point is also germane to the remedies

---

9 Bankes, "Termination of an Oil and Gas Lease, Covenants as to Title, and Assessment of Damages for Wrongful Severance of Natural Resources: A Comment on *Williston Wildcatters*" (2005) 68 Sask. L. Rev. 23.

10 *Supra*, n 8, S.J. at 11.

hearing in *Freyberg v Fletcher Challenge Oil & Gas Inc.*,[11] which will be discussed later in this chapter.

One of the major concerns with the *Williston* approach to damages must be that it inevitably will reach a different result depending on the circumstances of the lessor. If the lessor is an ordinary private citizen with no operating experience or capability, the damages would be limited to whatever bonus and royalty rate the court believed he could negotiate at the time of the termination. On the other hand, if the lessor happened to be an oil industry entity, the appropriate damages might well be the revenues less the cost of production.

Not only does the "really mild rule" lead to different results depending on the circumstances of the lessor, but it requires the court to speculate on what an individual lessor might or might not do. The fact that the mineral owner may not presently be involved in the oil industry does not preclude him from hiring independent contractors to operate the property. This is not an uncommon arrangement today. Just as importantly, it also requires the court to delve into the affairs of the plaintiff, a task for which it is ill equipped.

Even more disturbing is that the "really mild rule" could encourage the lessee to continue producing the well after the lease has been challenged, knowing that the financial consequences will not be severe. Indeed, it would be very much to a lessee's advantage to do so, as the result could end up being almost the same as if the lease continued to be valid. Indeed, if the bonus consideration and the royalty rate happen to be the same as were commonly obtained at the time the lease was held to have terminated, it would appear that the mineral owner would not be entitled to any compensation whatsoever. This, despite the fact that the lessee had enjoyed revenue from the production of minerals to which it had no legal title.

Aware that there could be concern over the potential of the "mild rule" to lead to abuse by a lessee, the Court of Appeal had this to say:

> Arguments that suggest that this will encourage trespassers to be careless as to whether they act legally or not should be instantly quelled: a trespasser who does so is almost certain to fall under the harsher head of damages due to their negligence or bad faith, and thus this option of damages is not even open to the Court.[12]

---

11 [2007] 10 W.W.R. 133, 77 Alta. L.R. (4th) 354, [2007] A.J. No. 576, 2007 ABQB 353 (Alta. Q.B.).

12 *Supra* n 8, S.J. No. 541 at para. 110.

This statement is meant to be reassuring, but is of little comfort to the mineral owner. The reader will be aware of the lengthy period of time that can elapse between the statement of claim and the final determination of the status of the lease. It can be as much as ten years or more. These years could well encompass the period of prime production from the lands. A lessee, knowing that the worst case scenario would require only an upward adjustment in the royalty rate and possibly some additional bonus, would be tempted to remain in possession and appropriate the production revenue to itself. Even if it was aware of the probability that the lease was no longer valid, and even if it used all available stratagems to prolong the judicial process, it could scarcely be charged with acting in bad faith. It would be doing nothing more than exercising its legal rights.

Signalta Resources Ltd. v Dominion Exploration Canada Ltd.[13] did not involve a lease, and the statements in question are *obiter.* They do, however, address the situation where a well is found to have been drilled and produced without the legal right to do so.

The plaintiff's claim that the defendant had drilled and produced a well from a formation that was included in a unit was dismissed. Although the plaintiff's claim was dismissed, Park J went on to set damages in case the dismissal was not correct. In that event the defendant would have been required to pay damages in the amount of all revenues from the well, but would be entitled to recover drilling, operating costs, and royalties from the well's revenues. Furthermore, those costs should be fully paid before the plaintiff is entitled to receive any payment from the revenues.

In setting the amount of the damages, which in effect amounted to restitution, the court noted that there had been no evidence of *mala fides* or questionable conduct on the part of the defendant.

Park J began his approach to damages by saying that they should be assessed on the mild rule as set out in *Williston.* Nonetheless, his analysis reached a result – restitution – that was much more equitable between the parties than the *Williston* "really mild rule." It should be noted that the court in *Signalta* did not have to concern itself with the

---

13   *Signalta Resources Limited*, Plaintiff, and *Dominion Exploration Canada Ltd. and Her Majesty the Queen in right of Alberta as represented by the Minister of Energy for the Province of Alberta*, Defendants, and between: *Dominion Exploration Canada Ltd.*, Plaintiff by Counterclaim, and *Signalta Resources Limited*, Defendant by Counterclaim, [2007] A.J. No. 1203 (Alta. Q.B.) (Notice of Appeal filed).

individual attributes of the parties since both the plaintiff and the defendant were operating oil companies.

Another Alberta court had to deal with the situation where the plaintiff was a private individual in the second (remedies) stage of the *Freyberg* case.[14] The court was called upon to determine the remedy the plaintiff was entitled to when the well continued to be produced after the lease had terminated for failure to produce into an economical and profitable market. The methodology and factors considered, however, were different from *Williston*. The trial judge, Kent J, found that the compensatory, rather than restitutionary, approach to damages was appropriate. Regardless of which approach is used, however, it appears that the facts will determine whether the "harsh" or "mild" rule will apply:

> Courts awarding a remedy based in restitution would often draw a distinction between the "mild" and "harsh" forms rules of damages. In instances where a defendant knowingly commits a trespass or otherwise acts with *mala fides*, the harsh rule may be applied. Under this rule, the courts will award a remedy based on the value of the material (here, gas) with the only allowable deduction being that expended to transport the materials to market. Alternatively, where the trespass in question is an innocent one and there are no other indicia of poor conduct or *mala fides*, then the "mild" rule will apply, meaning that the remedy will be based upon the value of the material taken, less any costs incurred by the trespasser for severance, production and marketing.

> The second approach awards damages on a compensatory basis. It does not focus on stripping the benefit of a trespass away from a wrongdoer, but rather on placing the plaintiff back into the position he or she would have been in but for the commission of the tort. Under this approach, in a case such as this, it may be that the plaintiff receives damages equivalent to the substance converted less the costs of production (the mild rule in the restitutionary approach) or something less. It depends upon the facts.[15]

In the course of her decision the trial judge analysed in great detail both the persona and circumstances of Lady Freyberg, and the conduct

---

14 *Supra*, n 11.
15 *Supra*, n 11, A.J. at paras. 99 & 100.

of the defendant lessees. She held that the conduct of the lessees was not such as to justify the imposition of the "harsh" rule, which would have resulted in Lady Freyberg receiving the proceeds of past production without any allowance for the costs incurred by the defendants.

Lady Freyberg's circumstances were in issue because of the evidence as to the possible options and courses of action available to her, such as farming out the property, or using her own company together with a contract company to operate the well. This evidence was introduced in an attempt to avoid the *Williston* finding that the only course open to the lessor would be to lease the minerals and thus be limited to an award of bonus and increased royalty rate. The court scrutinized her personal situation, and evidence pertaining to the well, and referred to "the slight possibility that she could go it alone."[16] One of the reasons that led the court to this conclusion was the fact that Lady Freyberg's lease did not include all of the lands covered in the spacing unit. Her interest was two-thirds of 637 acres of the 640 acres in the unit. The other one-third interest in the 637 acres was owned by NV Resources Ltd. The remaining three acres were owned by the County of Paintearth, which took no part in the proceedings. NV Resources had not contested the validity of the lease, and were not disposed to cooperate with Lady Freyberg. Indeed, NV Resources had granted a new lease to the defendants without remuneration. The court recognized that this obstacle could have been overcome by compulsory pooling under conservation legislation, but concluded that in any event these alternatives were not practical for someone in Lady Freyberg's circumstances.

The plaintiff's case was based on the tort of conversion, although trespass was also pleaded. The court pointed out that trespass could not apply where, as was the case here, the defendants had the right to take one-third of the gas under a new and valid lease from another mineral owner. It was not physically possible to extract only some of the gas, and the defendants also had the right to enter onto the lands under a surface lease. Therefore, there was nothing unlawful about bringing Lady Freyberg's gas to the surface. A tort of conversion however occurred when the defendants dealt with that gas by transporting it from the wellhead.

As an aside, it might be observed that the tort of conversion may be a better fit than trespass for the circumstances of continuing production under a terminated lease. Trespass is a remedy affording compensation

---

16 *Supra*, n 11, A.J. at para. 140.

for wrongful interference with possession.[17] Conversion is "taking a chattel out of the possession of another with the intention of exercising a permanent or temporary dominion over it."[18]

Not only does conversion appear to be a better fit, but it has a wider range of applicability to situations arising in connection with a terminated lease. For example, a natural gas lease covering 160 acres (64 hectares) in a section of 640 acres (250 hectares) that has been pooled is terminated, but the operator continues to produce unabated from the pooled section. While this may not be trespass in a technical sense, it is clearly conversion. This scenario is similar to the situation in *Freyberg*.

Having found that the defendant's conduct was not such as to justify the harsh rule, and that there was only a "slight possibility" that Lady Freyberg could "go it alone," the court applied the compensatory model, and pointed out:

> What that is will differ from case to case. The fundamental rule is that the quantum of damages should be in an amount to put the injured party in the same position, or as near to the same position as possible, as she would have been in, but for the tort. In some cases, where there has been conversion of minerals, that will mean that the injured party will receive the value of the minerals removed minus the costs of removing the minerals, resulting in an award equivalent to the mild rule, if damages were being awarded on a restitutionary basis. In other cases, if it is shown that the owner could not have removed the minerals on her own, the amount will be calculated in a different manner such as royalty and bonus payment.[19]

How then to determine the appropriate royalty and bonus payment? To answer this question, the court posed another one. If both sides had known conclusively in December 1999 (when the well went on production) that the lease was invalid, what agreement would they have reached? The court speculated how such a meeting might have gone, and outlined the bargaining position of both sides.[20] Kent J noted that while Lady Freyberg "is entitled to a significant amount of the production, she would not have left the notional negotiation table with everything less expenses." But "she would not have accepted a slightly increased royalty and expenses."

---

17 *Clerk & Lindsell on Torts*, 19th ed. (London: Sweet & Maxwell, 2006) at 1005.
18 *Black's Law Dictionary*, 8th ed. (St. Paul, Minn.: West, 2004) at 357.
19 *Supra*, n 11 A.J. at para. 131.
20 Ibid., at paras. 140, 141, and 142.

While the learned trial judge determined that the award should be in form of an increased royalty and bonus, and that both should be substantial, she required more evidence to assess the damages. She also invited the parties to agree on that calculation and to set up a future hearing date.

In the event, the parties negotiated a settlement of $2,250,000.00 and this was approved by the court in a consent judgment dated 12 December 2007. This is a vastly different result from *Williston* and included a "top-up" payment that took into account the value of past production. This is in keeping with the court's finding that Lady Freyberg was "entitled to a significant amount of the production."

The importance of Kent J's decision lies in the passage quoted above as to how damages, using the compensatory model, should be determined. It is to be noted that while there was only a "slight possibility that Lady Freyberg could 'go it alone,'" she was entitled to, and received, some compensation for past production.

All the decisions on the matter make it clear that *bona fides*, or lack thereof, on the part of the trespassing party will weigh heavily on the court's approach.

Rate of Interest

The court ruled that interest on the damages received by Lady Freyberg will be at the rate set by the *Judgment Interest Act*,[21] not the current business rate.

Leave and Licence

The defence of leave and licence figured prominently, especially at the Court of Appeal level, in the *Williston* case and was also considered in *Freyberg*. While rarely encountered, it is not entirely unknown in oil and gas law. *Wurstenberger v Royalite Oil Co.*[22] is a 1935 case involving drilling in the historic Turner Valley field where the defendant Royalite drilled on the plaintiff's land without any written authorization. In holding that Royalite's occupation of the land was lawful, McGillvray JA quoted Lord Russell in *C.P.R. v The King*:[23] "There was nothing but

---

21 R.S.A. 2000, c J-1.
22 [1935] 2 D.L.R. 177, [1935] 1 W.W.R. 461 (Alta. S.C., App.Div.).
23 [1931] 2 D.L.R. 386, [1931] A.C. 414 (P.C.).

original trespass, which, by dint of toleration over a period of time, became an occupation by leave and licence."

Royalite's drilling operation became known to the plaintiff some considerable time before he complained of the trespass, and he knowingly allowed the trespass to continue. This toleration could amount to a tacit consent where there was knowledge of the trespass without requiring it to cease.

The *Williston* trial judge, Gerein CJQB, rejected the leave and licence argument, but it found favour with the Saskatchewan Court of Appeal. That court agreed with the trial judge that the lease had terminated in January 1990 for failure to produce, but went on to hold that as a consequence of certain correspondence from the lessor in March and April of 1992 the defendant occupied the land with leave and licence. The court agreed with Gerein CJQB's approach to assessing damages, but held it only applied during the period January 1990 to 11 March 1992 when leave and licence took over.

The correspondence that led the court to find leave and licence was, firstly, a letter dated 21 March 1992, which stated:

> We would, therefore, request an Affidavit, sworn to by an officer of TDL, the operator at that time, setting out the status of operations during the period January 1990 to July 1990. If an Affidavit acceptable to ourselves is not forthcoming within 30 days of receipt of this letter, we will consider this lease to be terminated pursuant to its own terms and provisions therein.
>
> Until such time as this matter is resolved, we believe that it is inappropriate for the Trust to respond to any request from you with regard to further developments involving these lands.

Vancise JA noted that the letter did not instruct Williston to vacate the lands. On 11 April 1992 Montreal Trust sent a second letter in which it wrote as follows:

> **The unitholders are certainly not yet requiring that the operator vacate the property** should the Affidavit not be forthcoming. They would, however, consider granting a new lease on the property. This group recently granted a lease at a rate of 18% and this may be acceptable to them once again. I would be glad to forward an offer to my clients should your clients wish to submit one. [Emphasis added by the court.]

The court accepted that the phrase "not yet requiring that the operator vacate the property" was evidence that the lessor consented to the lessee's continuing to operate the well, while reserving the right to give notice to vacate in the future. Notice to vacate the land was never given.

While notice to vacate might not have been given, on 26 February 1993 a statement of claim was issued in which the plaintiff claimed an accounting but did not specifically plead trespass. The statement of claim was amended in 2000 to claim damages for trespass. The lessor continued to receive royalties based on the royalty rate of 12½ per cent specified in the lease.

The Appellate Court found that the correspondence from the lessor, together with its acceptance of royalties and its acquiescence in allowing the lessee to continue operating on the lands, and to drill a second well thereon, amounted to leave and licence, which justified the lessee's continued occupation of the land.

It is important to scope out the ramifications of this decision. There can be no doubt that it was the two letters from Montreal Trust on behalf of the mineral owners that persuaded the court to accept leave and licence. Notice to vacate the land was never given, and the lessors continued to accept royalty payments for many years. The court held that issuing and serving a statement of claim, even if it did include a claim for trespass either inferred or express, was not sufficient to revoke the leave and licence. The court noted that no request was ever made for the lessee to stop production or vacate the land. Instead, other letters were sent to the lessee requesting unpaid royalties and also requesting an increase in production.

Not surprisingly, leave and licence was also an issue in *Freyberg*. Kent J analysed the facts, especially the conduct of Lady Freyberg and her advisers, and held there was no basis for finding the plaintiff had granted leave and licence. While this was sufficient in itself to distinguish *Williston*, she went on, tellingly, to decline to follow it, and to disagree with the reasoning of the Saskatchewan Court of Appeal. Specifically, she rejected the Saskatchewan court's conclusion that there could be leave and licence before the issue of the validity of the lease was adjudicated with finality. In *Williston* the court had based this conclusion on the fact that the plaintiff would have received legal advice on the question before the decision, and the court would only provide more certainty that there had been a trespass. But as Kent J pointed out, it was only when the Supreme Court denied leave to appeal that the parties knew that the lease was invalid.

This lack of certainty continued until 10 November 2005 when the Supreme Court denied leave. At this point, Lady Freyberg would have known of her rights, and for the period of three months from then until 13 February 2006, when the well was shut in because of a demand from her counsel, the court found there was leave and licence. The finding that there was leave and licence during the brief period of production *after* it was determined that the lease was invalid demonstrates how important knowledge of this fact is in the eyes of the court.

Absence of knowledge that a lease has terminated is clearly crucial, although it may not always be dispositive of the issue. The court examined the conduct of Lady Freyberg during the relevant periods of time and found there was nothing to suggest leave and licence had been given to the defendants. She received legal advice, but, in contrast to *Williston*, did not acknowledge the lease, nor encourage the defendants to continue production, or to install additional equipment. She did cash royalty cheques and was aware that the well was producing, but, in the view of the court, that was not enough. There was also the fact that her English solicitor had advised the defendants that her acceptance of royalties was without prejudice. It seems clear from the judgment that, even without that qualification, cashing the royalty payments would not create leave and licence.

The only thing that Lady Freyberg did not do was to demand that the defendants stop producing her gas. The court's response to this was:

> In the face of clear pleadings which demanded compensation for all of the gas produced and the unrelenting pursuit of that claim through the courts, I do not accept that such a formality is required.

The *Freyberg* decision makes it clear that leave and licence requires a unique set of facts with overt actions and communications on the part of the lessor. By rejecting the proposition that it could apply before the parties knew with certainty that the lease had terminated, *Freyberg* severely circumscribed the circumstances under which the doctrine could apply.

What Leave and Licence Does

If successfully invoked, leave and licence is one way of delineating what happens in the period between the time the lease actually ceased to exist and the final judicial determination of that fact. It does not perpetuate the lease. By way of illustration, in the event estoppel was the reason the validity of a lease was upheld, that lease would continue in force and govern the relationship between the lessor and the lessee. Not so with leave and licence. The lease would no longer function; and leave and licence would be restricted to assessing the consequences of its demise.

Who Owns the Well?

When a lease on which a well has been drilled is struck down, the question of how to treat the well, and the costs associated with it, immediately arises. This question was addressed early in the development of the Canadian oil industry. In *Maple City Oil and Gas Co. v Charlton*[24] the well was drilled by the holder of a lease that was in the nature of a top lease as it was taken despite the existence of an earlier lease. The prior lease was upheld, but the Ontario High Court ruled that if the plaintiff (the successful lessee) took "the benefit of the work done and improvements made by the defendant company on the lands, it must be on terms of compensating that company therefore."[25] It should be noted that the plaintiff was the holder of the prior lease and that it was only if it wished to take advantage of the existence of the well that it was obliged to compensate the company that had drilled it.

The judge in *Maple City* was following *McIntosh v Leckie*,[26] an even earlier decision that was handed down in 1906. There again, the well was drilled by the lessee under a second lease that was taken in the mistaken belief that an earlier lease had terminated. (Those early Ontario wildcatters must have been a remarkably headstrong breed.) After finding the first lease was still valid, the court directed that if the lessee under that lease were to take the benefit of what had been done by the defendant or asked for an accounting of production, it was to be on terms of compensating the defendant company for what it had done.

These two early Ontario decisions (which appear to have been largely ignored in subsequent decisions) and *Weyburn*[27] are consistent in holding that where a party asks for an accounting of past production or takes the benefit of an improvement, the party who made the improvements under a mistaken view of its rights should be compensated.

---

24   (1912) 7 D.L.R. 345 (Ont. H.C.).
25   Ibid. at 352.
26   (1906) 13 O.L.R. 54.
27   *Supra*, n 1.

In *Republic Resources Limited v Ballem*[28] the issue was squarely raised because the lessee plaintiffs asked, in the alternative, that if the lease was held to have terminated, they be allowed to recover their costs of drilling and completing the well from future production. Their claim for compensation was based on unjust enrichment, and they placed considerable reliance on the *Weyburn* case. In the *Republic* decision the court agreed that *Weyburn* was authority for the proposition that a lessor may be required in equity to compensate a lessee for expenditures made in mistakenly drilling a well under an expired oil and gas lease. The court, however, distinguished *Weyburn* because there the lessors had, subsequent to the drilling date, knowledge of the lessee's drilling activity and had accepted royalty and other monetary benefits as well as requesting the lessee to drill an offset well, which request was complied with. In the *Republic* case the lessor had no knowledge that the well had been drilled until it was completed and had made no demands on the plaintiffs whatsoever. In *Weyburn* there was also production from which an accounting could be made, while in *Republic* there was none. The court also pointed out that neither the Saskatchewan Court of Appeal nor the Supreme Court discussed the principles on which they ordered restitutionary relief in *Weyburn*.

The plaintiffs' claim for restitution was denied primarily on the grounds that there had been neither an express nor an implied request by the lessor for the benefit in question (the drilling of the well), nor had there been subsequent acquiescence or adoption of the benefit on the part of the lessor. The plaintiffs argued that the court should accept the proposition that a restitutionary claim may lie, even in the absence of a request or free acceptance, if it could be shown that the defendant had incontrovertibly benefited from the services that had been rendered. The plaintiffs were asking the court to extend the rationale of *Greenwood v Bennet*,[29] in which Lord Denning's judgment suggested that where a plaintiff thinks he owns a chattel and improves it without the true owner having knowledge of the improvements, he should be compensated for the value of the improvements. In order for this approach to be of any assistance to the plaintiffs in the *Republic* case, the doctrine would have to be extended to apply not only to

---

28 [1982] 1 W.W.R. 692 (Alta. Q.B.). Professor Percy commented on this case in "The Law of Restitution and the Unexpected Termination of Petroleum and Natural Gas Leases" (1988) Alta. L. Rev. 105.

29 (1972) 3 All E.R. 586 (C.A.).

chattels, but also to interests in land. Characterizing *Greenwood v Bennett* as a controversial decision, the court refused to extend it.[30]

Holmes J also found that the plaintiffs had failed to establish that the defendant had received an incontrovertible benefit. The well was capped, as were other gas wells in the vicinity, for lack of a market, and there was no evidence as to when a market might develop. At best, the plaintiffs had established only that they had conferred an unascertained benefit on the defendant.

The trial judge, in passing, noted that it had not been suggested that the plaintiffs might have a lien or charge under section 60 of the *Law of Property Act*.[31] The relevant portions read:

Improvements made on wrong land through error	69(1)	When a person at any time has made lasting improvements on land under the belief that the land was the person's, the person or the person's own assigns

(a) are entitled to a lien on the land to the extent of the amount by which the value of the land is enhanced by the improvements, or

(b) are entitled to or may be required to retain the land if the Court is of the opinion or requires that this should be done having regard to what is just under all circumstances of the case.

(2) The person entitled or required to retain the land shall pay any compensation that the Court may direct.

The comment by the judge does not amount to a finding that the section does not apply to oil and gas situations, but rather that he did not have to decide the point. It is left to future cases to determine. The definition of "land" includes mines and minerals and expressly includes a *profit à prendre*, and it would seem there could be circumstances under which a productive well could be a "lasting improvement."

The Saskatchewan Court of Appeal weighed in on this vexed question in the *Williston* case. The trial judge had declined to deal with this matter because he was not apprised of all the facts. Both parties requested the

---

30 In doing so, Holmes J quoted Goff and Jones, *The Law of Restitution*, 2nd ed. (1978), which pointed out that, unlike chattels, land is unique and it might be unreasonable to require the owner to sell or mortgage it in order to pay for unsolicited improvements.

31 R.S.A. 2000 c L-7.

Court of Appeal to make a decision on the point, and agreed there was sufficient evidence before the court to enable it to decide the issue. In the normal course of events, the matter of who owns the well and, equally important, who is responsible for it, arranges itself satisfactorily. Production ceases, the lease comes to an end, and the lessee abandons the well in accordance with the regulations, and removes its equipment.

For years, oil and gas leases contained a provision virtually identical to clause 17 in the *Williston* lease:

> 17. REMOVAL OF EQUIPMENT: – The Lessee shall at all times during the currency of this Lease and for a period of Six (6) months from the termination thereof, have the right to remove all or any of his machinery, equipment, structures, pipe lines, casing and materials from the said lands.

Parenthetically, it should be noted the CAPL 99 form does not contain this clause. The reason for the omission is that the point is covered in the CAPL surface lease, where it probably belongs.

The court cited the widespread use of clause 17 in the industry as defining the standard practice regarding the ownership of the equipment and the right to remove it when production ceases. In the court's view, the clause indicates that the ownership of the equipment remains with the operator of the well, and not the owner of the mines and minerals. Following industry practice, the court concluded that the ownership of the downhole, wellbore, and surface equipment remains with the oil company operator.

The parties, however, still have to deal with the practicalities of the situation. While the physical well might belong to the lessee, conservation authorities would not look kindly upon the operator moving in on a producing well and removing the production casing, the wellhead, and other related physical facilities. Nor would it make economic sense. The sensible answer is that where there has been production, the lessee who drilled the well in good faith under an invalid lease should be compensated from the proceeds. This approach was followed in a number of decisions cited by the Appeal Court, particularly *Weyburn*. Where this has occurred either through restitution or the "mild rule," a strong case in equity could be advanced in favour of the well reverting to the mineral owner.

The present state of the law appears to be that, if there has been production and if the lessee has "clean hands," it will be entitled to be compensated from the proceeds for the costs it has incurred. What the result will be when there has been no production, and no demand to produce nor other intervention by the lessor, remains an open question.

18 Estoppel

On many occasions hard-pressed counsel for the lessee, realizing that the facts of the case and language of the lease will fall short of the tests applied by the courts, have fallen back on equitable defences outside the language of the document itself. Relief from forfeiture was summarily dismissed because the lessee had options, not obligations. The doctrine of estoppel, however, has always seemed to have potential if only the right fact pattern could be found.

The basic approach of estoppel is simply that the lessor by doing something, or neglecting to do something, may have placed himself in a position where he is prevented from denying the validity of the lease. The argument runs that because the lessor has accepted a delay rental payment, a shut-in well royalty, or production royalties, has allowed the lessee access to the well site, or has failed to treat the lease as cancelled, he can no longer deny the existence of an otherwise invalid lease. The underlying thrust of the doctrine of estoppel is simply that a party may be prevented from establishing the true state of the legal relationship where it would be unjust or inequitable to allow him to do so. The basic principle of estoppel may be stated as follows:

> Where one has either by words or conduct made to another a representation of fact, either with knowledge of its falsehood, or with the intention that it should be acted upon, or has so conducted himself that another would, as a reasonable man, understand that a certain representation of fact was intended to be acted on, and that the other has acted on the representation and thereby altered his position to his prejudice, an estoppel

arises against the party who made the representation, and he is not allowed to aver that the fact is otherwise than he represented it to be.[1]

The foregoing passage expresses the basic common law principle of estoppel. Estoppel takes a number of different forms, which may be subdivided into four main categories.

Estoppel by Representation

This is the fundamental form and has been defined in the leading textbook on the subject as follows:

> Where one person ("the representor") has made a representation to another person ("the representee") in words or by acts and conduct, or (being under a duty to the representee to speak or act) by silence or inaction, with the intention (actual or presumptive), and with the result, of inducing the representee on the faith of such representation to alter his position to his detriment, the representor, in any litigation which may afterwards take place between him and the representee, is estopped, as against the representee, from making or attempting to establish by evidence, any averment substantially at variance with his former representation, if the representee at the proper time, and in the proper manner, objects thereto.[2]

Estoppel by Acquiescence

This is really a refinement of estoppel by representation and deals with the situation where one party does nothing and thereby lulls the other party into a sense of security. It is the form that is most frequently relied on in cases involving the oil and gas lease. The difficult element here is that the acquiescing party may be required to have knowledge of the true position. Acquiescence combined with such knowledge gives rise to the implication of constructive or "equitable" fraud:

---

1 *Halsbury's Laws of England*, vol. 16, 4th ed. reissue (London: Butterworths, 1992) at para. 955.
2 Spencer, Bower and Turner, *Estoppel by Representation*, 3rd ed. (London: Butterworths, 1977) at 4.

It has been said that the acquiescence which will deprive a man of his legal rights must amount to fraud, and in my view that is an abbreviated statement of a very true proposition. A man is not to be deprived of his legal rights unless he has acted in such a way as would make it fraudulent for him to set up those rights. What, then, are the elements or requisites necessary to constitute fraud of that description? In the first place the plaintiff must have made a mistake as to his legal rights. Secondly, the plaintiff must have expended some money or must have done some act (not necessarily upon the defendant's land) on the faith of his mistaken belief. Thirdly, the defendant, the possessor of the legal right, must know of the existence of his own right which is inconsistent with the right claimed by the plaintiff. If he does not know of it he is in the same position as the plaintiff, and the doctrine of acquiescence is founded upon conduct with a knowledge of your legal rights. Fourthly, the defendant, the possessor of the legal right, must know of the plaintiff's mistaken belief of his rights. If he does not, there is nothing which calls upon him to assert his own rights. Lastly, the defendant, the possessor of the legal right, must have encouraged the plaintiff in his expenditure of money or in the other acts which he has done, either directly or by abstaining from asserting his legal right. Where all these elements exist, there is fraud of such a nature as will entitle the Court to restrain the possessor of the legal right from exercising it, but, in my judgement, nothing short of this will do.[3]

Promissory Estoppel

Equity is a constantly evolving process, and estoppel has been no exception. The limitation of estoppel by representation or by acquiescence lay in the fact that the representation must relate to an already existing fact. If the representation was made with respect to the future, the doctrine permitted no remedy. This hiatus was covered by the celebrated decision of Denning J in *Central London Property Trust Ltd. v High Trees House Ltd.*[4]

The *High Trees* case was a routine, unpretentious sort of dispute that involved the rent to be paid for a block of flats. The apartment block had been built in 1937, and at the outbreak of the war in 1939 few of the apartments had been let. The landlords agreed in writing in 1940 to

---

3 *Willmott v Barber* (1880), 15 Ch. D. 96, at 105.
4 [1956] 1 All E.R. 256, [1957] K.B. 130.

reduce the rent, but there was no consideration paid by the lessee. In an action by the landlords to recover the full rent the lessee attempted to set up estoppel by way of defence. Denning J noted that, under the current state of the law, estoppel could not have been maintained since the representation that the rent would be reduced was not a representation of existing fact but as to the future – a representation that the rent would not be enforced at the full rate but only at a reduced rate. The court observed that law could not afford to stand still and Denning J then struck off in a new direction:

> There has been a series of decisions over the last fifty years which, although said to be cases of estoppel, are not really such. They are cases of promises which were intended to create legal relations and which, in the knowledge of the person making the promise, were going to be acted on by the party to whom the promise was made, and have in fact been so acted on. In such cases the courts have said these promises must be honoured. There are certain cases to which I particularly refer: *Fenner v Blake* (3) ([1900] 1 Q.B. 426), *Re Wickham* (4) (1917) (34 T.L.R. 158), Re *William Porter & Co., Ltd.* (5) ([1937] 2 All E.R. 361) and *Butter v Pickard* (6) (1946) (174 L.T. 144). Although said by the learned judges who decided them to be cases of estoppel, all these cases are not estoppel in the strict sense. They are cases of promises which were intended to be binding, which the parties making them knew would be acted on and which the parties to whom they were made did act on. *Jorden v Money*, (2) can be distinguished because there the promisor made it clear that she did not intend to be legally bound, whereas in the cases to which I refer the promisor did intend to be bound. In each case the court held the promise to be binding on the party making it, even though under the old common law it might be said to be difficult to find any consideration for it. The courts have not gone so far as to give a cause of action in damages for breach of such promises, but they have refused to allow the party making them to act inconsistently with them. It is in that sense, and in that sense only, that such a promise gives rise to an estoppel. The cases are a natural result of the fusion of law and equity; for the cases of *Hughes v Metropolitan Ry. Co.* (7) (1877) (2 App. Cas. 439), *Birmingham & District Land Co. v London & North Western Ry. Co.* (8) (1888) (40 Ch. D. 268), and *Salisbury v Gilmore* (9) ([1942] 1 All E.R. 457), show that a party will not be allowed in equity to go back on such a promise. The time has now come for the validity of such a promise to be recognized. The logical consequence, no doubt, is that a promise to accept a smaller sum in discharge of a larger sum, if acted on, is

binding, notwithstanding the absence of consideration, and if the fusion of law and equity leads to that result, so much the better. At this time of day it is not helpful to try to draw a distinction between law and equity. They have been joined together now for over seventy years, and the problems have to be approached in a combined sense.[5]

The new promissory estoppel has been summarized in Halsbury:

When one party has by his words or conduct made to the other party a promise or assurance which was intended to affect the legal relations between them and to be acted upon accordingly then once the other party has taken him at his word, and acted upon it the one who gave the promise or assurance cannot afterwards be allowed to revert to their previous legal relations as if no such promise or assurance had been made by him, but he must accept their legal relations subject to the qualifications which he himself has so introduced.[6]

Estoppel by Deed

The fourth branch of estoppel, and one that has attracted a good deal of notice in cases involving oil and gas leases, has been that type of estoppel which arises when the parties have entered into some form of written agreement. This is close to, but not quite, a contract in that there is no binding undertaking between the parties on the express point, but rather the document itself leads to the inescapable conclusion that the parties have agreed to act upon an assumed state of affairs. Having done so, they cannot thereafter challenge the situation.

While the underlying principle remains constant, each category of estoppel requires a different mixture of ingredients and must pass different tests.

Estoppel in Oil and Gas Leases

From the very beginning estoppel seemed to have more chance of success than any of the other equitable principles. In an early Ontario case[7] the court estopped a wife from claiming a lease had not been validly

---

5 Ibid. at 258, 259.
6 *Supra* n 1 at 931, para. 1071.
7 *Maple City Oil and Gas Co. v Charlton* (1912), 7 D.L.R. 345 (Ont. H.C.).

executed by her. Her husband, who normally conducted her business affairs, executed the lease in her presence, she read the lease and expressed her approval, the husband later accepted rents under the lease, and she subsequently signed her name and affixed a seal to the instrument. The court treated the matter as one of estoppel, although her subsequent execution of the lease would seem to be sufficient by itself. The *Maple City* case has not been referred to in subsequent decisions bearing on the matter of estoppel and oil and gas leases.

In western Canada, while the courts found various reasons for not applying the doctrine under the facts of each case, they were careful to avoid rejecting its potential application. Then, in several trial decisions, estoppel was applied to revive an otherwise defunct lease. It looked as though estoppel might succeed where all others had failed.[8]

The first occasion on which estoppel managed to revive a terminated lease was in *Canadian Superior Oil Ltd. v Murdoch*,[9] where the circumstances were such that the lease had terminated because there was no production, constructive or otherwise, at the end of the primary term. The automatic termination was unknown to both parties at the time it occurred, but there were other disputes between the mineral owners and the lessee. After the expiration of the primary term the lessor's husband commenced an action claiming title to the hydrocarbon substances underlying both railway grounds and a right-of-way that adjoined the farm. The lessee contended that these minerals really belonged to the lessor and thus were included under the original lease. This dispute led to legal proceedings under which the lessor filed a statement of claim that, among other things, stated: "(b) that in the further alternative, that said lease has expired due to the fact that ten (10) years has [sic] elapsed from the date of commencement of the lease and that Canadian Superior Oil of California Ltd. is not engaged in drilling said land or working operations but has drilled on said land and has 'capped' wells on said land to the detriment of the plaintiff depriving her of oil royalties."

Eventually the various disputes were resolved and an agreement of settlement was entered into under which the lessor "does hereby ratify and confirm that the said Lease is in good standing and of full force and effect." Riley J defined the central issue of the case as that of estoppel.

---

8 On estoppel and leases generally, see Ballem, "The Continuing Adventures of the Oil and Gas Lease" (1972) 50 Can. Bar Rev. 423.

9 (1968), 65 W.W.R. (N.S.) 473 (Alta. S.C.TD.).

He found that the parties, although the lease had actually terminated, agreed to a different fact, namely, "the lease is in good standing and of full force and effect." There was nothing to prevent parties from agreeing that a certain fact is so and thereafter being bound by such agreement. This was equated by the trial judge to estoppel by contract, or estoppel by deed as above defined.

On appeal[10] the lease was maintained, but the fangs of estoppel were drawn. The Appellate Division, later affirmed by the Supreme Court, found that it was not necessary to resort to estoppel in order to give effect to the covenant contained in the settlement agreement. In fact, the parties had agreed by contract that the lease was still in effect and it was not necessary to go beyond the simple fact of an existing and binding contract.

The *Murdoch* case was followed in *Paramount Petroleum and Mineral Corporation Ltd. and Bison Petroleum and Minerals Ltd. v Imperial Oil Limited*,[11] although the point was not central to the decision. Those parties who were attacking the lease raised for the first time in final written argument the point that Imperial, because it had withheld the 15 per cent non-resident tax from the payment of delay rentals to a lessor living in the United States, had failed to comply with the requirements to pay the stipulated sum each year. The trial judge treated this argument as an afterthought on the part of the plaintiffs and pointed out that to give effect to it would be unjust, since the defendant had no opportunity to meet the contention with evidence. On this ground he refused to give effect to the submission.

He went on to state that even if he were wrong in that decision, he was of the view that the plaintiffs would also fail on the merits. The lessor had executed two partial assignments of the leases in favour of the plaintiffs and gave notice of such assignments to Imperial. In the assignments the lessor had covenanted that the leases "still subsist without variation." The assignments were executed after the withholding of the non-resident tax, and the court was of the view that the lessor, and the plaintiffs who claimed through him, would be estopped from raising the deduction of the non-resident tax in support of a contention that the lease had terminated.

---

10 (1969), 68 W.W.R. (N.S.) 390 (Alta. S.C., App.Div.); affirmed (1969), 70 W.W.R. (N.S.) 768, 6 D.L.R. (3d) 464 (S.C.C.).

11 (1970), 73 W.W.R. (N.S.) 417, [1970] S.J. No. 37; supplementary reasons [1970] S.J. No. 87 (Sask. Q.B.).

The Alberta Trial Division once again was prepared to use estoppel to revive an otherwise extinguished lease in *Canadian Superior Oil Ltd. v Cull*.[12] The fact pattern in this case was fully described in Chapter 7, and it will be recalled that the trial judge held the lease to have terminated because of the time gap that existed between "completion" of the well and the commencement of oil production. Having found that the lease had terminated on its own terms, Sinclair J went on to consider the effect of an agreement that had been entered into between the lessor and the lessee. There had been some dispute concerning that acreage underlying right-of-way lands; also the original lease was defective in that it did not contain a pooling clause. Negotiations took place and resulted in the execution of an agreement on 11 July 1958 (some months after the expiration of the primary term of the lease), but the agreement was made effective as of 21 November 1957 (prior to expiration of the primary term). The agreement amended the land description by including the right-of-way, added a pooling clause, and provided that "all other terms, covenants and conditions contained in the said lease remain in full force and effect."

It is noteworthy that at the time this amending agreement was entered into, there appeared to be no question in anyone's mind but that the lease was in full force and effect. Sinclair J applied the doctrine of estoppel by deed to the amending agreement and held that the fact that the lease was in effect was the conventional basis upon which the parties entered into the amending agreement.

As with the *Murdoch* decision, the higher courts upheld the lease but avoided the issue of estoppel[13] by holding that the requirements of the lease had been complied with. Thus, it was unnecessary to consider the question of estoppel.

Although the reasoning was neither accepted nor rejected by the higher courts, the Alberta Trial Division had twice utilized estoppel by contract or by deed to revive leases that it considered to have been extinguished, and the Saskatchewan Queen's Bench was prepared to use it if necessary. In short order, however, two other cases faced the higher courts with the doctrine of estoppel, and the result severely restricted the potential of the doctrine as a means of reviving an otherwise terminated lease.

---

12 (1970), 74 W.W.R. (N.S.) 324 (Alta. S.C.T.D.).
13 (1970), 75 W.W.R. (N.S.) 606, 16 D.L.R. (3d) 709 (Alta. C.A.); affirmed [1972] S.C.R. 89, [1971] 3 W.W.R. 28, 20 D.L.R. (3d) 360, [1971] S.C.J. No. 91 (S.C.C.).

The cases were *Canadian Superior Oil Ltd. v Paddon Hughes Development Co. Ltd. and Hambly*[14] and *Sohio Petroleum Co. v Weyburn Security Co. Ltd.*[15] They were heard back-to-back by the Supreme Court of Canada and, although the ingredients of estoppel were much less compelling in the *Paddon Hughes* case, that decision was delivered first and contains most of the reasoning of the court on the question of estoppel. It seems to have been used by the Supreme Court to make known its views on estoppel in oil and gas law. It must be borne in mind that in both cases there was no subsequent documentation that could have raised the issue of estoppel by deed or by contract. If estoppel existed, it did so only by reason of the conduct or acquiescence of the lessor. In both cases it was also conceded that the lease had terminated on its own terms so that estoppel was the only hope of the lessee.

The lease in the *Paddon Hughes* case had been – unknown to the parties at the time – terminated by a failure to make timely payment of the shut-in royalty. The acts and omissions that the lessee was able to muster were not very impressive from the point of view of establishing a representation on the part of the lessor that the lease remained in force. They were:

(a) The payment and receipt of shut-in royalties during the years 1958 to 1965. These payments went to a trust company by virtue of a royalty trust agreement that the lessor had entered into some years before. Under this agreement it was the duty of the trust company to receive all royalty income and distribute it among the royalty trust certificate holders. During the period there were only two distributions made by the trust company and the lessor returned his share of the second one.

(b) Rental payments were received and retained by the lessor pursuant to a surface lease.

---

14 [1970] S.C.R. 932, 74 W.W.R. (N.S.) 356, 12 D.L.R. (3d) 247, [1970] S.C.J. No. 48 (S.C.C.); affirming (1969), 67 W.W.R. (N.S.) 525, 3 D.L.R. (3d) 10 (Alta. C.A.); affirming 65 W.W.R. (N.S.) 461 (Alta. S.C.T.D.)

15 [1968] S.J. No. 114, 66 W.W.R. (N.S.) 155 (Sask. Q.B.); reversed 69 W.W.R. (N.S.) 680, 7 D.L.R. (3d) 277 (Sask. C.A.); affirmed [1971] S.C.R. 81, 74 W.W.R. 626, 13 D.L.R. (3d) 340, [1970] S.C.J. No. 65 (S.C.C.). The *Paddon-Hughes* and *Weyburn* cases are discussed in Currie, "Recent Cases and Developments in Oil and Gas Law" (1971) 9 Alta. L. Rev. 452, and also in Harrison, "Selected Cases, Legislation and Developments in Oil and Gas Law" (1972) 10 Alta. L. Rev. 391.

(c) When the lessee entered upon the lands to conduct operations such as to check or maintain the well, it sought and received consent from the lessor.
(d) In May 1960, the lessor happened to see a well pressure gauge that indicated the gas pressure was dangerously high and advised an employee of the lessee of this fact.
(e) The lessor had, as collateral security to a mortgage, executed an agreement that gave to the mortgage company "all bonuses, rentals, delay rentals, and other considerations and benefits" payable under certain leases and surface leases, and one of the described leases was the one under attack.

The Appellate Division held that these events and happenings did not constitute representation by word or conduct on which a defence of estoppel could be founded.

The Supreme Court of Canada agreed that the evidence did not support a plea of estoppel, but also made some observations as to the applicability of estoppel to oil and gas leases that raised the bar for any attempt to use the doctrine to revive a lease that had already terminated. The one possibility of reviving an expired lease that now appears to remain open is estoppel by acquiescence, which, as we shall see later, requires an element of fraud, although that fraud may be equitable or constructive.

Dealing with estoppel in general, Martland J said:

> Without attempting finally to determine the matter, I have serious doubt as to whether the issue of estoppel can properly be raised in the circumstances of this case. The appellants, as plaintiffs, seek a declaration that the lease is a good, valid and subsisting lease. For the reasons already given, it appears that the lease in question had terminated. It could not be revived thereafter except by agreement, for consideration, between the parties. To say that subsequent representations by Hambly could recreate the legal relations between the parties would be to say that such representations could create a new cause of action for Superior. But, subject to the equitable rule as to acquiescence, and to which I will refer later, a cause of action cannot be founded upon estoppel.[16]

---

16 *Supra* n 14, W.W.R. at 360.

Concerning estoppel by representation, Martland J said that the essential factors were: (1) a representation, or conduct amounting to a representation, intended to induce a course of conduct on the part of the person to whom the representation is made; (2) an act or omission resulting from the representation, whether actual or by conduct, by the person to whom the representation is made; (3) detriment to such person as a consequence of the act or omission. This branch of estoppel was disposed of because there was nothing that amounted to a representation by the lessor, Hambly.

The court's treatment of promissory estoppel is significant. Promissory estoppel was the branch of the doctrine that had been applied by Sinclair J in the earlier *Cull* decision to uphold the lease. It proceeds from the basis that, where the dealings between the parties lead one of them to suppose that the legal relations between them have a certain status, the other is estopped from denying that condition. Martland J, after quoting a well-known statement of the principle,[17] continued:

> This principle assumes the existence of a legal relationship between the parties when the representation is made. It applies where a party to a contract represents to the other party that the former will not enforce his strict legal rights under it. In the present case, however, the contractual relationship between the parties has come to an end before any representation is alleged to have been made. There is no allegation that Hambly, while the lease still subsisted, had ever represented that its provisions would not be enforced strictly.

It appears that promissory estoppel will be largely irrelevant to oil and gas lease cases. Usually the purpose of the plea of estoppel is to revive a terminated lease. The normal acts of promissory estoppel that would be relied upon must occur after the termination of the lease, which, in accordance with Martland J's reasoning, precludes the application of promissory estoppel.

Estoppel by acquiescence requires an additional ingredient: knowledge on the part of the representor that he has a right inconsistent with the right claimed by the other party. In other words, the acquiescing party is not bound unless he so acquiesces with knowledge of his own true legal position. Translated into oil and gas terms, it means that the

---

17 *Hughes v Metro Ry.* (1877), 2 App. Cas. 439, [1874–80] All E.R. Rep. 187 (H.L.).

lessor must know that the lease has terminated and, further, that the lessee must not have this knowledge. The principle appears to require such a degree of knowledge on the part of the lessor and innocence on the part of the lessee that the continued acquiescence by the lessor amounts to a fraud. To say the least, the area in which this principle could operate with respect to leases is very limited, as it usually takes several levels of judicial examination to determine whether or not a lease has terminated at any given point in time. Furthermore, the lessee is almost always in a better position to be aware of the termination than is the lessor.

The *Weyburn* case[18] was as powerful a vehicle to advance the plea of estoppel as any counsel could desire. The lessee was able to parade a number of positive acts by the lessor pursuant to a lease that (unknown to both parties) had terminated for lack of production at the expiration of the primary term. This was the pattern insofar as it related to estoppel:

1 The primary term expired on 27 October 1959, and production did not take place until some time in November of that year. This led to an automatic termination of the lease, although the parties did not then appreciate that fact. Production continued to be taken from the well over a period of years and the lessor received the appropriate royalty thereon.
2 The lessor, by a letter dated 5 April 1960, demanded that the lessee drill an offset well pursuant to the offset drilling clause in the lease.
3 The lessee complied with this demand and drilled the offset well.
4 The lessor as surface owner granted a surface lease for the drilling of the offset well.
5 The lessor demanded in each year (including a demand made during the very month of the trial) that the lessee reimburse the lessor for its seven-eighths share of the mineral taxes as required by the terms of the lease and the lessee did so.

The trial judge found that estoppel had been established; MacPherson J held the view that both estoppel by representation and promissory estoppel applied. He found that by demanding the drilling of the offset well and by granting the surface lease the plaintiff had conducted itself

---

18 *Supra* n 15.

so as to represent to the defendant that the lease was subsisting. The same reasoning applied to the demands by the lessor plaintiff for reimbursement of the mineral taxes. These were regarded as positive acts by which the lessor made a demand of the lessee under the terms of the lease after the alleged termination.

The Supreme Court of Canada, however, found that estoppel had not been established since the actions of Sohio as lessee did not result from representations or conduct of the lessor but were taken because Sohio, as well as the lessor, was unaware of the fact that the lease had come to an end. Since Sohio believed that the lease had not terminated, its actions could not have been induced by any representation on the part of the lessor.

The Supreme Court also quoted with approval the Saskatchewan Court of Appeal's findings on promissory estoppel and, by so doing, introduced the requirement of knowledge into promissory estoppel.

> In the instant case, if the conduct of the respondent could be said to amount to the type of promise, assurance or course of negotiation contemplated in the passages above set out, Sohio did not rely upon it to believe that the respondent would not contend that the lease had terminated.

> The acts of Sohio which were found by the learned trial judge to be alterations of its position to its detriment, – drilling of the off-set well, entering into the surface lease, and payment of one-eighth of the mineral tax, – were performed because Sohio considered it was obligated to perform them under the terms of the lease. The respondent, in requesting or demanding that Sohio carry out the terms of the lease, and in allowing Sohio to proceed as it did, simply accepted the mistaken position that the lease had not terminated. Because the respondent was not aware of the true legal position, it is not now precluded from exercising its rights.[19]

Even more significant was the reiteration by Martland J of his doubt as to whether a lease, once terminated, could be revived by estoppel unless there was fraud: "In *Can. Superior Oil Ltd. v Hambly* (1970) 74 WWR 356, affirming (1969) WWR 525, 3 DLR (3d) 10, I expressed doubt as to whether a lease, which had terminated, could be subsequently enforced

---

19 *Supra* n 15, W.W.R. at 631.

on the basis of representations or conduct occurring after its termination, unless, at least, they would amount to a fraud, of the kind defined by Fry J in *Willmott v Barber* (1880) 15 Ch D 96, at 105, 49 LJ Ch 792, ..."[20]

Martland J's reservation about using estoppel to resurrect a lease that had terminated was noted and acknowledged by the Alberta Court of Appeal in *Freyberg v Fletcher Challenge Oil and Gas Inc.*[21] At trial, where the lease was upheld on other grounds, Romaine J observed that while it was unnecessary for her to decide whether estoppel by election would apply, the defendant lessees "have made out a strong case for estoppel in these circumstances."[22]

On appeal, Ritter JA took this statement to mean that if the trial judge were to analyse the issue she would likely find that there was a potentially convincing case for estoppel. Because the trial judge's recitation of the evidence was brief and she cited no legal principles in support of estoppel, Ritter JA felt required to consider a matter of estoppel "afresh." In doing so, Ritter JA noted that the Supreme Court has expressed doubt as to whether estoppel could ever operate to revive a terminated lease and cited the *Hambly* case.[23] While noting the Supreme Court's doubt, the appeal court judge decided to examine the possible estoppel argument and concluded that it could not succeed.

The lessees submitted that Lady Freyberg was estopped due to her acceptance of the shut-in royalty payments. This argument was rejected because for her to be estopped by acceptance of the payments, Lady Freyberg must have made an unequivocal election with knowledge of not only her right to elect but also of the facts underlying the election. Furthermore, the respondent lessees must rely on the election to their detriment. The evidence indicated that while receiving the payments, the plaintiff was not aware that the well had been or was presently economical and profitable. She was not told that the well had been put on production. When she did become aware of the well being profitable, she commenced the litigation. This lack of knowledge resolved the matter of estoppel. The court pointed out that the requirement of knowledge is a common feature of estoppel and it was not present in the case.

---

20 Ibid. at 629.
21 323 A.R. 45, [2002] A.J. No. 1173 (Alta. Q.B.); reversed 42 Alta. L.R. (4th) 41, [2005] 10 W.W.R. 87, 363 A.R. 35, [2005] A.J. No. 108 (Alta. C.A.).
22 Ibid. 323 A.R. at para. 130.
23 *Supra*, A.R. at para. 133.

The plea of estoppel was also raised in *Republic Resources Ltd. v Ballem*.[24] The lease, which was found to have terminated because production had not been encountered before the expiry of the primary term, contained a provision that granted the lessee an option to renew the lease exercisable for a period of thirty days following the expiration of the primary term. The lease was dated 27 August 1973, which was after the effective date of the Alberta *Perpetuities Act*, so the option to renew was presumably enforceable, although it is doubtful if the condition precedent to the option, namely, that the leased substances were not being produced at the end of the primary term could be met in view of the plaintiff's assertion that there was deemed production through payment of a shut-in royalty.

In the event, however, that point was academic since the plaintiff did not attempt to exercise the option. At trial the plaintiff sought an order granting it the right to exercise the option on the grounds of estoppel. The basis of the alleged estoppel was that, shortly before the option period was due to expire, the defendant had formed an opinion that the lease had terminated but had not asserted that position until after the option period had expired. The court disposed of that contention on the ground that the defendant was under no duty or obligation to notify the plaintiff of the defendant's legal stance. The evidence also established that the plaintiff was acting solely on the advice of its legal counsel, and did not follow its course of conduct because of any inducements, representations, or conduct on the part of the defendant.

Voyager Petroleums Ltd. v Vanguard Petroleums Ltd.[25] is a case where estoppel actually preserved the lease. There are two important things to note about this case: the circumstances that gave rise to the estoppel occurred before the lease had terminated, and the estoppel operated to prevent the lessor from denying that a trust company acted as its agent in signing a unit agreement. In other words, what the lessor was estopped from denying was outside the four corners of the lease itself.

The case arose on the following fact pattern. A petroleum and natural gas lease was granted on 27 May 1966 for a ten-year primary term.

---

24 17 Alta. L.R. (2d) 235, [1982] 1 W.W.R. 692 , 33 A.R. 385, [1981] A.J. No. 559 (Alta. Q.B.).

25 (1982) Alta. L.R. (2d) 212, [1982] 2 W.W.R. 36, 47 A.R. 14, [1982] A.J. No. 629 (Alta. Q.B.); affirmed, 27 Alta. L.R. (2d) 1, [1983] 5 W.W.R. 622, 149 D.L.R. (3d) 417, [1983] A.J. No. 778 (Alta. C.A.); affirmed, [1984] 5 W.W.R. 1xiv. (Leave to appeal to Supreme Court denied.) This case is discussed in Booth and Desbarats, "Recent Developments in the Law of Interest to Oil and Gas Lawyers" (1983) 21 Alta. L. Rev. 114 at 130, 131.

The last payment of delay rentals was made by the lessee, Voyager, in April 1972, and that would maintain the lease in good standing up to 27 May 1973. The reason that the delay rentals were discontinued was that the lands were included in a unit agreement, which, if validly executed by the lessor, would continue the lease in force because of the allocation of production. The issue arose as to whether the unit agreement had been validly executed on behalf of the lessor.

The minerals were subject to a gross royalty trust agreement under which a 12½ per cent gross royalty was assigned to the trust company. The lessor was a corporation and the managing director and president was a lawyer experienced in oil and gas matters. He was examined for discovery and cross-examined on an affidavit prior to the trial, but passed away before the trial itself.

In the summer of 1972, and while the lease was still in force, Voyager formed a natural gas unit comprising twenty-eight tracts of land, including the land covered by the lease. Two copies of the unit agreement were sent by Western Land Services Co. Ltd., as agent for Voyager, to the lessor, Vanguard, for execution. The president of Vanguard forwarded both copies to the trust company appointed under the gross royalty trust agreement with a letter in which Vanguard confirmed "... our consent pursuant to Clause 16 of the Royalty Trust Agreement to the execution by your company of the Unit Agreement and its return to Western Land Services."

The trial judge found that this letter, because of its express reference to clause 16 of the gross royalty trust agreement, which clause dealt with the consent of the royalty owners, could not amount to an express authorization of the trust company to sign the unit agreement for Vanguard in any capacity other than as a holder of gross royalty. Therefore, if the execution by the trust company was to be binding upon Vanguard as lessor, it could not be by express authorization but only if Vanguard was estopped from denying that the trust company had acted as its agent in signing the document.

On 25 October 1972 the trust company returned two signed copies of the unit agreement to Voyager, which executed them and returned one copy to the trust company. The lessor, Vanguard, did not sign the unit agreement. The unit went on production and royalties were sent to the trust company, which, in turn, accounted for them to Vanguard.

There matters rested until August 1976, when Voyager drilled a successful natural gas well on lands just outside the quarter section covered by the lease, but within the same section. The well was completed for production in a different zone than the one that had been unitized and thus was not included in the unit. Voyager gave Vanguard a pooling notice under the lease, which pooled the quarter section covered by the lease with the remaining quarters in the section to form a spacing unit.

In his pre-trial examinations the president of Vanguard had testified that the first time he put his mind to the question of whether or not Vanguard ought to have been part of the unit agreement was upon receipt of the pooling notice in the autumn of 1976. The trial judge noted that this part of the agreed statement facts related only to the content of the deceased president's testimony and not to the truth of that testimony. He did not accept that testimony and instead found that the president must surely have considered his company's role when he received the two copies of the unit agreement.

On these facts the question comes down to whether or not Vanguard was bound by the unit agreement. If it were, the lease would be continued in force by the operation of that agreement, and if not, the lease would have terminated for failure to pay the delay rental in the year 1973.

Having found that Vanguard did not expressly authorize the trust company to sign the unit agreement on its behalf in any capacity other than as a holder of the gross royalty, the court then considered the question of estoppel. The plaintiff argued that Vanguard was estopped from denying that it was bound by the unit agreement, but the court narrowed the question down to whether Vanguard was estopped from denying that the trust company had acted as agent for it when it signed the unit agreement. Under the facts of the particular case the result would be the same under either approach insofar as the validity of the lease was concerned.

The trial judge discarded estoppel by representation on the ground that the actions of Vanguard did not constitute the type of positive or active representation of fact that was necessary for this type of estoppel. He then went on to consider estoppel by acquiescence, which can be created by mere silence and inaction rather than a positive act or representation. He commenced his analysis of the doctrine by citing the well-known five *probanda* that were set forth in *Willmott v Barber*.[26]

The five *probanda* have already been quoted in this chapter, but they may be summarized as follows:

---

26 *Supra* n 3.

1 The plaintiff must have made a mistake as to his legal rights.
2 The plaintiff must have expended some money or must have done some act (not necessarily upon the defendant's land) on the faith of his mistaken belief.
3 The defendant must know of the existence of his own right, which is inconsistent with the right claimed by the plaintiff.
4 The defendant must know of the plaintiff's mistaken belief.
5 The defendant must have encouraged the plaintiff in his expenditure of money or in the other acts that he has done, either directly or by abstaining from asserting his legal right.

When all of the above elements exist, estoppel by acquiescence finds there to be fraud of such a nature as will entitle the court to restrain the possessor of the legal right from exercising it. The trial judge in the *Voyager* case pointed out that "fraud" as used in the *Willmott v Barber* case was not used in the sense of wilful and deliberate dishonesty, but rather in the more limited sense accepted by the rules of equity and usually defined as "equitable or constructive fraud." This type of fraud arises when a person misconceives the extent of the obligation that a court of equity imposes.[27]

Having found that equitable or constructive fraud was sufficient to satisfy the meaning of fraud in *Willmott v Barber,* the trial judge examined the five *probanda* and found that all had been satisfied. The third *probanda*, which requires the defendant to know of the existence of his own right, was the most difficult one to hurdle. The court stated that if it found that Vanguard knew the material facts necessary to create that right, the right is presumed to have been known for the purposes of estoppel by acquiescence, citing *Holder v Holder*[28] for this proposition.

The *Holder* case relied on estoppel by acquiescence to prevent the plaintiff, who was a beneficiary of the estate, from having a sale of the estate farms to the defendant set aside. The defendant was an executor of the estate and had bought the farms at a public auction and had paid more than the reserve bid. The defendant had renounced his executorship prior to the sale, but his renunciation was invalid because he joined in some acts of administration of the estate. The plaintiff sought to have the sale set aside on the ground that the defendant was a

---

27 *Nocton v Ashburton*, [1914] A.C. 932 (H.L.).
28 [1968] 1 All E.R. 665 (C.A.).

trustee of the property he had purchased. The court found that, while the plaintiff did not know until later of the right to avoid the sale by reason of the defendant's renunciation of executorship being invalid, he had full knowledge of the sale, made no attempt to stop it, and had received money on account of the proceeds of the sale, and therefore must be taken to have acquiesced to it. Harmon LJ concluded: "There is, therefore, no hard and fast rule that ignorance of a legal right is a bar, but the whole of the circumstances must be looked at to see whether it is just that the complaining beneficiary should succeed against the trustee."[29]

Applying the *Holder* approach, the trial judge in *Voyager* had regard to the experience and knowledge of Vanguard's president, and even though he " ... may never have clearly and directly contemplated the possibility that his company could avoid the unit agreement because of Canada Permanent's signing in a limited capacity only, he nevertheless knew all material facts which would give rise to such an 'escape,' and that result was clearly inconsistent with Voyager's perception."

Having found that all the requirements of estoppel by acquiescence had been satisfied, the court went on to distinguish the *Hambly* and *Weyburn* cases. Stratton J found them to be distinguishable as, in both instances, the leases had already terminated, whereas in *Voyager* the facts giving rise to the estoppel had taken place prior to the "click date." This distinction was upheld by the Court of Appeal.

That basis for distinguishing *Hambly* and *Weyburn* could have the effect of severely restricting the scope of the *Voyager* decision because, in most instances, the lease will have expired or have been terminated before the circumstances giving rise to estoppel by acquiescence will have occurred. It was not really necessary to distinguish the Supreme Court decisions because, by finding that the five *probanda* of "fraud" had been satisfied, the court had brought the case within the exception mentioned by Martland J in *Weyburn*. If there is fraud in the *Willmott v Barber* sense, it appears that a terminated lease could be revived on the basis of representations or conduct occurring after its termination.

The trial judge in *Voyager* expressly took into account the knowledge and experience of the defendant's president in finding that he knew that his company should execute the unit agreement as registered owner. The trial judge did not go so far as to find that the defendant knew it might have been able to avoid the unit agreement because of

---

29 Ibid. at 673.

the trust company signing in a limited capacity only. He did find, however, that the president knew all material facts that would give rise to this conclusion and was, therefore, fixed with the knowledge.

This approach may be appropriate when, as was the case in *Voyager*, the legal issue is fairly straightforward and basic, such as what parties should execute a document. When it comes to matters of interpretation of the lease, however, the proper legal result is very difficult to ascertain and indeed may not be known until the courts have finally ruled on the point. Under these circumstances it would not appear to be "just" within the meaning of *Holder* to estop a mineral owner from asserting his right. It must, however, be conceded that the legal point in *Holder*, which the plaintiff was prevented from raising, was also a very sophisticated one.

The *Voyager* decision has undoubtedly made it easier for the lessee to meet the requirement of knowledge on the part of the lessor. It must, however, be remembered that the circumstances of that case were highly unusual, and it may not be "just" to fix an ordinary lessor with the kind of sophisticated knowledge that the defendant was deemed to have in *Voyager*. However, all five *probanda* must still be met, including reliance on the part of the lessee. The necessity for reliance was emphasized in both the *Weyburn* and *Republic* decisions, and it could prove to be a major stumbling block to estoppel, since most lessees are oil companies with their own legal staffs or access to legal advice and, in any event, will be proceeding on the basis of their own analysis and not because of some representation or silence on the part of the lessor.

It still appears as if the only instances in which estoppel can revive a terminated lease are: (a) when the parties have agreed in writing that the lease is subsisting – this is more a matter of contract than estoppel;[30] (b) possibly estoppel by deed where there is no written agreement between the parties but the lessor has represented in a written instrument that the lease is subsisting; and (c) when there is "fraud" within the meaning of *Willmott v Barber* on the part of the lessor.

Estoppel a Shield Not a Sword

In *Canadian Superior Oil Ltd. v Paddon Hughes Development Co. Ltd. and Hambly*,[31] Martland JA observed that "a cause of action cannot be

---

30 Ballem, "The Continuing Adventures of the Oil and Gas Lease," *supra* n 8 at 443.
31 *Supra* n 14.

founded upon estoppel."[32] In *Canadian Superior Oil Ltd. v Jacobson*[33] the Alberta Court of Appeal noted that the appellants were attempting to use the doctrine of estoppel as a sword rather than a shield when they sought to discharge a caveat. The court quoted with approval what was said by Denning LJ in *Combe v Combe*:[34]

> That principle does not create new causes of action where none existed before. It only prevents a party from insisting upon his strict legal rights, when it would be unjust to allow him to enforce them, having regard to the dealings which have taken place between the parties.

The validity of a lease was not the issue in *Jacobson*.[35] The action was an originating notice brought by Canadian Superior for a declaration that it was the beneficial owner of the lands. The defendants' predecessor in title had executed a transfer of the lands to Canadian Superior, but the transfer was never registered. Subsequently, Canadian Superior registered a caveat claiming an interest in the lands pursuant to the unregistered transfer. Some years later the parties entered into a royalty agreement in which Canadian Superior was described as "lessee" and the defendant appellants as "lessors." The court noted that the lawsuit arose as a result of the appellants seeking to discharge a caveat. In other words, estoppel was being used to assert a claim rather than defend against it. The court refused to apply estoppel, noting that there was no evidence that the appellants relied on the description of Canadian Superior as a "lessee" in the 1975 agreement to their detriment.

The type of estoppel that was at issue in *Jacobson* was estoppel by deed, and the appellate court adopted a statement in *Chitty on Contracts*[36] that estoppel by deed "only applies when an action is brought to enforce rights out of the deed and not collateral to it."

When it comes to the oil and gas lease, it is estoppel's role as a shield that is important. It is difficult to visualize a scenario in which estoppel would provide the basis for an action, particularly since estoppel by deed applies only to rights arising out of the document and not anything collateral to it.

---

32 *Supra* n 14 at 360.
33 (1989), 71 Alta. L.R. (2d) 229, 103 A.R. 161, [1989] A.J. No. 1164 (Q.B.); affirmed (1991), 81 Alta. L.R. (2d) 75, 81 D.L.R. (4th) 526, 115 A.R. 391, [1991] A.J. No. 496 (Alta. C.A.).
34 [1951] 2 K.B. 215.
35 *Supra* n 33.
36 25th ed., vol. 1 at p. 20.

The court also noted in *obiter* that even if the doctrine of estoppel were applicable, it would apply only during the term of the 1975 agreement, which was "surrendered" by the appellant in 1976. This statement, which is clearly *obiter*, would seem to suggest that estoppel created by a deed would survive only while the deed remained in force. This statement seems somewhat problematic since a reliance once created could still influence a party who originally relied on it.

Whither Estoppel?

Counsel for lessees will continue to plead estoppel in whatever form seems best to fit the facts in their case. Martland J's twice repeated view that he had serious doubts as to whether estoppel could be used to revive a lease that had terminated has not prevented the issue being raised and considered by courts in subsequent cases.

Two basic tenets of the doctrine, however, severely inhibit its application. For estoppel to succeed it must be established, at a minimum, that the lessor had knowledge of the problem, and the lessee relied in some fashion on either the lessor's failure to act or whatever assurances he may have given.

In the normal course of events, it will be the lessee, and not the lessor, who will be privy to problems with the lease and operations thereunder. This also holds true when it comes to the question of reliance. It is the lessee who will have the benefit of expert advice and knowledge of the operations, not the lessor. It may be different if the lessor gives assurances, particularly if written, such as gave rise to leave and licence in the *Montreal Trust v Williston Wildcatters Co.*[37] case, but, absent that, reliance by the lessee to its detriment will be hard to establish.

---

37 [2004] 3 W.W.R. 574, 239 Sask. R. 57, [2003] S.J. No. 523 (Sask. Q.B.); varied 254 Sask. R. 38, [2005] 4 W.W.R. 20, 243 D.L.R. (4th) 317, [2004] S.J. No. 541 (Sask. C.A.); leave to appeal refused [2004] S.C.C.A. 474 (S.C.C.).

19 Litigating the Oil and Gas Lease

Let us assume that the lessor, or more likely, his top lessee, has become aware of a potentially fatal flaw in the lessee's title. Frequently, a demand letter sent by the lessor to the lessee will mark the commencement of hostilities. The letter will describe the alleged defect and request the lessee to acknowledge that the lease has terminated and remove its caveat.

If the demand letter fails to achieve the desired result, the lessor is faced with a choice as to how to proceed. Should he give notice to lapse the lessee's caveat, or proceed immediately to commence a court action for a declaration that the lease is no longer in force, and for an accounting of production revenues from the date the lease is alleged to have ended?

Section 138 of the Alberta *Land Titles Act*[1] provides that a caveat shall be lapsed by the Registrar sixty (60) days after notice in the prescribed form to take proceedings in court has been served on the caveator, or sent by registered mail, unless the caveator takes proceedings in court by originating notice, or otherwise, to substantiate the title claimed by his caveat, and files a certificate of *lis pendens* in the prescribed form with the Registrar. Section 138(5) requires the person who serves the notice to prove to the satisfaction of the Registrar that he has an interest in the land. Both the mineral owner lessor and a top lessee would be in a position to satisfy this requirement.

---

1 R.S.A. 2000, c L-4.

The Saskatchewan procedure to lapse is set out in the *Land Titles Act* and *Regulations*.[2]

One advantage of proceeding by way of notice to lapse is that it may prompt the parties to enter into settlement negotiations. A satisfactory settlement, however initiated, is the preferred alternative to litigation. The negotiations leading up to a settlement can be a minefield for the unwary lessor if the negotiations do not result in settlement. The lessor and his advisers should ensure that everything is without prejudice so as not to fall into the leave and licence trap. This is also true of all interaction between lessor and lessee after the validity of the lease has been challenged. The lessor should be prepared to forgo royalties and refuse to accept them, and should avoid any request that the lessee do anything with the lease, the well, or other physical equipment.

One possible drawback to proceeding by way of notice to lapse is that it will have the result of making the lessee the plaintiff in the action. Being the plaintiff could give the lessee a measure of control over the timing and pace of the litigation. On the other hand, and for what it is worth, it will have the advantage of imposing whatever onus lies with a plaintiff on the lessee, although the cases make it quite clear that in any event the lessee has the onus of proving any defence raised in support of the lease.

Counsel for the lessor should ensure that the tort of conversion is before the court.

A lessor may prevail at trial, only to be disappointed by the amount of the award. If the court, as seems to be the trend, utilizes the damages approach, it may be persuaded to apply the "really mild rule" enunciated by the Saskatchewan courts in the *Williston* case. It will be recalled that in order to ascertain the damages suffered by the lessor, the court looked at what he might have expected to receive at the time the lease came to an end. The likely result is an award that reflects whatever bonus payments and royalty rates prevailed in the general area at that time. In *Freyberg* the damages approach was followed, but the amount of the court-approved settlement was much more substantial than would

---

2 *Land Titles Act*, S.S. 2000, c L-5.1 and *Regulations*, 2001, R.R.S. c L-5.1, Reg. 1. It should be noted that section 47 of the *Regulations* makes "an interest basesd on a lease" an exception to the lapsing process. However, an oil and gas lease is a *profit à prendre*, not a lease. Nor would the policy behind the exception apply to an oil and gas lease. In Manitoba the relevant Act is the *Real Property Act*, C.C.S.M. c. R30.

have been awarded by using the bonus and royalty rate prevailing at the time the lease came to an end. An award in the *Williston* mode, even when coupled with the court costs awarded to a successful litigant, may fall short of covering the legal costs incurred by the lessor.

The judicial reasoning behind the bonus and royalty approach to assessing damages is that the lessor, as a private individual, would have no other way of dealing with his mineral rights. To contradict this untoward result, the lessor should, to the extent possible, adduce evidence that he could have found a way to realize the benefits of production himself. This could be achieved by arrangements such as retaining an independent operator to produce the well, pooling, or farming out his minerals. Credibility is bound to be a problem; the court, properly, will need to be convinced that the lessor *can* make the arrangements to operate the property and obtain the benefits of production for himself.

Although it seems to have fallen out of favour, the alternative restitutionary approach reflects the fact that when a lease ceases to exist, the ownership of the minerals reverts to the lessor. Moreover, the reversion occurs on the date the lease expires. That date will be years before the courts finally determine the issue.

Combined with the right of the lessee to recover its drilling and operating costs, the result conforms to the *Weyburn* "equitable" solution.

Limitation of Actions

Insofar as a declaration that a lease has terminated is concerned, statutory limitation of actions will not be a factor in Alberta and Saskatchewan. The Alberta *Limitations Act* only applies to remedial orders, and not to declarations of legal relations.[3] Legislation in Saskatchewan[4] defines "claim" as a claim to remedy an injury, loss, or damage that occurred as a result of an act or omission, and so excludes declarations of title from its ambit.

The situation in Manitoba is less clear. The *Limitations of Actions Act*[5] includes actions for trespass to real property and imposes a six-year limitation period.[6] In the absence of any applicable case law, whether

---

3 *Limitations Act*, R.S.A. 2000, c L-12, ss 1 and 3(1).
4 *Limitations Act*, S.S. 2004, c L-16.1, s 2(a).
5 C.C.S.M. c L150.
6 Ibid., s 2(1) (f).

or not this could include an action seeking a declaration that a lease has terminated may be an open question. The Manitoba Act provides for an extension of the six-year limitation period where *inter alia*, the applicant satisfies the court that not more than twelve months have elapsed between the time the applicant first knew or ought to have known of the material facts on which the action is based, and making the application to extend the time. Although it requires an application, this section would apply in cases where there was a substantial delay before the lessor became aware of the circumstances that could have terminated the lease.[7] There is also an absolute bar to any action more than thirty years after the acts or omissions that gave rise to the course of action.[8]

While limitations legislation may not be a bar to declarations that a lease has terminated, at least in Alberta and Saskatchewan, it can operate to limit recovery of sums owing under a lease, such as royalties. The Alberta legislation has an ultimate limitation period of ten years. Section 3(3)(a), however, provides that "a claim or any number of claims based on any number of breaches of duty, resulting from a continuing course of conduct or a series of related acts or omissions, arises when the conduct terminates or the last act or commission occurs." This section would appear to have the effect of extending the ten-year limitation bar for the duration of the "continuing conduct." But not always.

In *Meek Trust v San Juan Resources Inc.* the plaintiff commenced proceedings in 2002 to enforce the non-payment of a royalty respecting certain producing oil and gas properties. The royalty arose under a 1952 agreement between Meek and a predecessor of the current operator. The agreement was an overriding royalty, not a lease. Two wells located on the royalty lands began commercial production in 1988, but no royalties were paid. The plaintiffs did not know about the non-payment until May 2002. They then brought a claim for unpaid royalties. The issues were separated into two hearings.

The first[9] held that the royalty was not an interest in land and the current lessee was obliged to pay the royalty without deductions for processing and transportation costs. The second hearing,[10] which was

---

7 Ibid., s 14(1).
8 Ibid., s 14(4).
9 [2003] A.J. No. 1599, 356 A.R. 72 (Alta. Q.B.).
10 (2005), 364 A.R. 309, 37 Alta. L.R. (4th) 23, [2005] A.J. No. 13 (Alta. Q.B.).

subsequently appealed, was to determine whether the action for roy-alty arrears was statute barred. The trial court found that the plaintiffs neither knew, nor ought to have known, of their claim prior to May 2002 and applied the rule contained in section 3(1)(a) of the Act to hold that their claim was not statute barred since it had been commenced within two years of their having knowledge of the breach.

This finding was appealed.[11] On appeal, Hunt JA, writing for the court, held that section 3(1)(b), which specified a limitation of ten years after the claim arose, was applicable and the plaintiffs' claim arose for the purposes of section 3(1)(b) when the first royalty payments were missed in 1988. The court expressly rejected the argument that the missed royalty payments were a series of individual breaches of duty resulting from a continuing course of conduct within the meaning of section 3(3)(a) of the Act. Instead, the court found that each non-payment thereafter gave rise to a separate claim; thus, their claim was barred for any payment due ten years prior to the commencement of their action. In reaching this decision, the court found that the purpose of the ultimate limitation period was to protect defendants from "ancient obligations" and to balance the rights of plaintiffs and defendants by providing "repose" at the end of the period.

In Saskatchewan, the legislation[12] does not have the provision for recurring acts or omissions, but does provide that the two-year period starts when the claimant first knew or ought to have known of the circumstances and also imposes a fifteen-year ultimate limitation on any claim for recovery. In Manitoba the basic limitation for trespass on real property is six years. As noted previously, it is possible to obtain an extension on application depending on the time the applicant first knew or ought to have known of his claim. The Manitoba Act also imposes an ultimate limitation of thirty years for any claims.[13]

Subsidiary claims, such as claims for unpaid royalties, not involving declarations that a lease has terminated, would fall within the "ultimate limitation period" of ten years in Alberta and fifteen in Saskatchewan. Ultimate limitation periods are not a purely academic consideration; breaches of obligations under the terms of a lease are known to have continued undetected for years, even decades.

---

11 (2006), 376 A.R. 202, 52 Alta. L.R. (4th) 1, [2005] A.J. No. 1754 (Alta. C.A.).
12 *Supra* n 4, ss 5, 6, and 7.
13 *Limitations of Actions Act*, C.C.S.M., c L150, s 14(4).

End Note

I would like to end as I began, with a fond salute to a remarkable legal document and the equally remarkable body of law it has spawned. Many questions have been answered, many issues resolved, but the stakes are high, and there are endless variables in the equation. It's not over!

Index of Legislation

Index of Cases

Index of Secondary Authorities

Bentley, McNair and Butkus, eds.,
*William and Rhodes, Canadian Law
of Landlord and Tenant*, 6th ed.
(Toronto: Carswell, 1988) 86

Bjornson, Boyd, Bredin, Brown and
MacWilliam, "Problems in Development of Leased Lands" (1965–
66) 4 *Alberta Law Review* 302   236,
250

Black's Law Dictionary, 8th ed.
(St. Paul, Minn.: West, 2004)
392

Booth and Desbarats, "Recent Devel-
opments in the Law of Interest to
Oil and Gas Lawyers" (1983) 21
Alberta Law Review 114   416

Bowker, "Reform on the Law of
Dower in Alberta" (1955–61) 1
Alberta Law Review 501   40, 46, 49

Breen, *Alberta's Petroleum Industry
and the Conservation Board* (Edmonton: University of Alberta Press,
1993) 10

Brown, *The Law of Oil and Gas Leases*,
2nd ed. (New York: Matthew
Bender & Co., 1997) 168, 292, 308

Brown, "Royalty Clauses in Oil and
Gas Leases," Sixteenth Annual
Institute of Oil and Gas Law and
Taxation 178

Brown, "Royalty Provisions of Oil
and Gas Leases" (September 1964)
The Landman, 6   192

Burn, ed., *Cheshire and Burn's Modern
Law of Real Property*, 16th ed.
(Markham, Ont.: Butterworths,
2000) 64

Byles, *Byles on Bills of Exchange*, 25th
ed. (London: Sweet & Maxwell,
1983) 39

C.E.D. (Western), 3rd ed., vol. 25   13

Chitty on Contracts, 25th ed. by Guest
(London: Sweet & Maxwell, 1983)
vol. 1   422

Chitty on Contracts, 29th ed. by Beale
(London: Sweet & Maxwell, 2004)
vol. 1   60, 83

Clerk & Lindsell on Torts, 19th ed.
(London: Sweet & Maxwell, 2006)
392

Côté, "The Introduction of English
Law into Alberta" (1962–64) 2–3
Alberta Law Review 262   61, 64

Côté, "The Reception of English
Law" (1977) 15 *Alberta Law Review*
29   61, 64

Crane, *Supreme Court of Canada Practice 2005* (Toronto: Thomson Carswell, 2004) 110

Curran, "Effect of Amendments to
Petroleum and Natural Gas
Leases" (1965–66) 4 *Alberta Law
Review* 267   331, 333

Currie, "Recent Cases and Developments in Oil and Gas Law" (1971)
9 *Alberta Law Review* 452   339, 410,
413

Davies, "The Legal Characterization
of Over-Riding Royalty Interests
in Oil and Gas" (1972) 10 *Alberta
Law Review* 232   181

Dea, "A Look at the Lease from the
Lessor's Point of View" (1965) 4
Alberta Law Review 208   299

Desbarat and Carson, "Recent
Developments in the Law of
Interest to Oil and Gas Lawyers"
(1985) 23 *Alberta Law Review* 183
217

General Index